Please return this book on or before the date shown above. To renew go to www.essex.gov.uk/libraries, ring 0845 603 7628 or go to any Essex library.

Essex County Council

Develop your legal skills with Longman

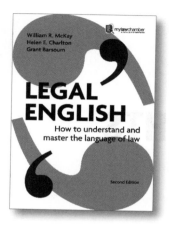

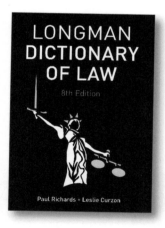

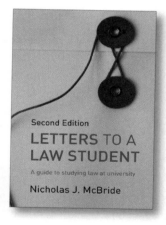

Question&Answer

HUMAN RIGHTS

Howard Davis
Bournemouth University

Longman
is an imprint of

Harlow, England • London • New York • Boston • San Francisco • Toronto • Sydney • Singapore • Hong Kong
Tokyo • Seoul • Taipei • New Delhi • Cape Town • Madrid • Mexico City • Amsterdam • Munich • Paris • Milan

Pearson Education Limited
Edinburgh Gate
Harlow
Essex CM20 2JE
England

and Associated Companies throughout the world

Visit us on the World Wide Web at:
www.pearson.com/uk

First published 2012

ISBN 978-1-4082-6679-3

British Library Cataloguing-in-Publication Data
A catalogue record for this book is available from the British Library

Library of Congress Cataloguing-in-Publication Data
A catalog record for this book is available from the Library of Congress

10 9 8 7 6 5 4 3 2 1
15 14 13 12 11

Typeset in 10/12pt Helvetica Neue LT Std by 3
Printed and bound by Ashford Colour Press Ltd., Gosport

Contents

Acknowledgements   vii

What you need to do for every question in Human Rights   viii

Guided tour   x

Guided tour of the companion website   xii

Table of cases and statutes   xiv

Chapter 1:   Human rights – general themes   1

Chapter 2:   The Human Rights Act 1998   27

Chapter 3:   Convention Rights: Ancillary Rights and Persuasive Principles   57

Chapter 4:   Articles 2 and 3 and the use of force by authorities   83

Chapter 5:   Articles 8 and 3: privacy and welfare   107

Chapter 6:   Article 5: the right to liberty and security   157

Chapter 7:   Article 6 and fair hearings   183

Chapter 8:   Political and religious expression and action   215

Chapter 9:   First Protocol Rights   241

Bibliography   259

Index   263

Supporting resources

Visit the **Law Express Question&Answer** series companion website at
www.pearsoned.co.uk/lawexpressqa to find valuable student learning material
including:

- Additional **essay and problem questions** arranged by topic for each chapter
  give you more opportunity to practise and hone your exam skills.
- **Diagram plans** for all additional questions assist you in structuring and writing
  your answers.
- **You be the marker** questions allow you to see through the eyes of the
  examiner by marking essay and problem questions on every topic covered in
  the book.
- Download and print all **Attack the question** diagrams and **Diagram plans**
  from the book.

Also: The companion website provides the following features:

- Search tool to help locate specific items of content.
- Online help and support to assist with website usage and troubleshooting.

For more information please contact your local Pearson sales representative or
visit www.pearsoned.co.uk/lawexpressqa

Acknowledgements

I wish to acknowledge the anonymous reviewers whose observations and advice have been very helpful (the normal disclaimers apply). I also wish to acknowledge the help and encouragement given by Zoë Botterill at Pearson, particularly in respect of the basic structure of this book.

Howard Davis

Publisher's acknowledgements

Our thanks go to all reviewers who contributed to the development of this text, including students who participated in research and focus groups which helped to shape the series format.

What you need to do for every question in Human Rights

Books in the *Question and Answer* series focus on the *why* of a good answer along side the *what,* thereby helping you to build your question answering skills and technique.

This guide should not be used as a substitute for learning the material thoroughly, your lecture notes or your textbook. It *will* help you to make the most out of what you have already learned when answering an exam or coursework question. Remember that the answers given here are not the *only* correct way of answering the question but serve to show you some good examples of how you *could* approach the question set.

Make sure that you refer regularly to your course syllabus, check which are covered (as well as to what extent they are covered) and whether they are usually examined with other topics. Remember that what is required in a good answer could change significantly with only a slight change in the wording of a question. Therefore, do not try to memorise the answers given here, instead use the answers and the other features to understand what goes into a good answer and why.

This book is focused on European human rights, found in the European Convention on Human Rights and on the reception of those rights into UK law under the terms of the Human Rights Act 1998. Human rights law can be taught at different levels. Courses may concentrate on the global level (concerned, in particular, with the treaty based obligations of states and the customary law) the regional level (studying, for example, the African Charter) and the domestic level (which looks at how human rights legal norms are integrated into national legal systems). It is very important always to be aware, in your answers, of the level involved and its implications in terms of, for example, the significance of a judgment by the UK Supreme Court compared with a judgment of the European Court of Human Rights.

This book also deals with 'law' (the rules and principles accepted by judges as the necessary and sufficient reasons for the remedies they grant). But human rights can also be explored in a moral way where the focus is on what freedoms people ought to have by virtue of their humanity. It is important, in answers, to keep the centre of your attention on the law.

Nevertheless, the 'moral' issue feeds into the 'legal' issue. Good answers will often be ones in which you demonstrate more than an ability to describe the rules and principles. You should be prepared for questions that invite a critical appreciation of the law. Human rights law sometimes discloses appalling offical wrongdoing which reasonable people can simply condemn. But part of the fascination of the subject is that it also deals with the state and its agents engaging with some genuinely difficult issues (such as how to preserve liberty whilst also protecting society). In this respect careful and nuanced criticism will gain most credit, because it will best reflect the issues in the law. Your answers may need to demonstrate how the particular content of human rights law often has to be related to the political and social context of the laws and actions being considered (the language of reasonable restrictions is commonly found). But also (again linking the moral and the legal) be prepared to communicate the sense of human rights law both developing with time as society changes and also how the ultimate aim is not fine words but, rather, effective protection.

Guided tour

What you need to do for every question in Human Rights

What to do for every question – Find out the key things you should do and look for in any question and answer on the subject in order to give every one of your answers a great chance from the start.

HOW TO USE THIS BOOK

Books in the *Question and Answer* series focus on the *why* of a good answer along side the *what*, thereby helping you to build your question answering skills and technique.

This guide should not be used as a substitute for learning the material thoroughly, your lecture notes or your textbook. It will help you to make the most out of what you have already learned when answering an exam or coursework question. Remember that the answers given here are not the *only* correct way of answering the question but serve to show you some good examples of how you *could* approach the question set.

Make sure that you refer regularly to your course syllabus, check which are covered (as well as to what extent they are covered) and whether they are usually examined with other topics. Remember that what is required in a good answer could change significantly with only a slight change in the wording of a question. Therefore, do not try to memorise the answers given here, instead use the answers and the other features to understand what goes into a good answer and why.

This book is focused on European human rights, found in the European Convention on Human Rights and on the reception of those rights into UK law under the terms of the Human Rights Act 1998. Human rights law can be taught at different levels. Courses may concentrate on the global level (concerned, in particular, with the treaty based obligations of states and the customary law), the regional level (studying, for example, the African Charter)

How this topic might come up in exams – Learn how to tackle any question on this topic by using the handy tips and advice relevant to both essay and problem questions. In-text symbols clearly identify each question type as it occurs.

 Essay Question

 Problem Question

Human rights – general themes

How this topic may come up in exams

A course on European human rights and the Human Rights Act 1998 is likely to involve background and contextual themes. Questions can relate to subjects such as the concept of human rights, the wider context of international law, the Council of Europe and the Convention system. Essay questions are more likely (though problems are possible). Answers need to show not only a good background of knowledge but, often, an ability to deal with theoretical and conceptual issues or to write about the historical development of institutions. Remember, that answers to questions on particular rights (as in Chapters 2–9) can be strengthened by references to these contextual matters.

Attack the question – Attack attack attack! Use these diagrams as a step by step guide to help you confidently identify the main points covered in any question asked.

Answer plans and Diagram plans – Clear and concise answer plans and diagram plans support the planning and structuring of your answers whatever your preferred learning style.

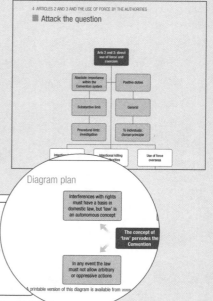

Answer plan

→ Introduce the idea of 'law' as a pervasive, autonomous, concept.

→ Discuss the meaning of 'law' and illustrate its application in UK law.

→ At the heart of your answer define and illustrate the requirement that there be in domestic law which is, also, accessible, foreseeable and non-arbitrary.

→ Explain the importance of process rights.

→ Discuss legality and the interpretation of statutes.

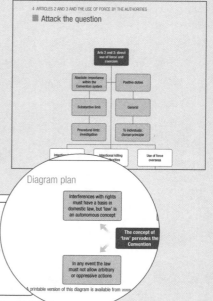

Diagram plan

Interferences with rights must have a basis in domestic law, but 'law' is an autonomous concept

The concept of 'law' pervades the Convention

In any event the law must not allow arbitrary or oppressive actions

A printable version of this diagram is available from www

Attack the question

4 ARTICLES 2 AND 3 AND THE USE OF FORCE BY THE AUTHORITIES

Arts 2 and 3: direct use of force and coercion

Absolute: importance within the Convention system

Positive duties

Substantive limb

General

Procedural limb: investigation

To individuals: Osman principle

Intentional killing by the authorities

Use of force overseas

x

Answer with accompanying guidance – Make the most out of every question by using the guidance to recognise what makes a good answer and why. Answers are the length you could realistically hope to produce in an exam to show you how to gain marks quickly when under pressure.

Case names clearly highlighted – Easy to spot bold text makes those all important case names stand out from the rest of the answer, ensuring they are much easier to remember in revision and in the exam.

Make your answer stand out – Really impress your examiners by including these additional points and further reading to illustrate your deeper knowledge of the subject, fully maximising your marks.

Don't be tempted to – Avoid common mistakes and losing easy marks by understanding where students most often trip up in exams.

Bibliography – Use this list of further reading to really explore areas in more depth, enabling you to excel in exams.

---

3 CONVENTION RIGHTS: ANCILLARY RIGHTS AND PERVASIVE PRINCIPLES

"You will get credit for this point – it both demonstrates knowledge of general themes about the way the Convention is interpreted and prevents you appearing to give an overly categorised view of how Convention rights are applied.

⁸Now move to this important theme, which is central to a good answer and shows subtlety in your understanding of all rights.

...this point – it will be...

'Absolute', 'limited' and 'qualified' are at best general classifications. The Convention is seen, by the European Court of Human Rights, as an evolving instrument of human rights and the aim is to make rights effective in their application and not merely notional or theoretical.⁷ The application of the Convention is not, therefore, based on strict adherence to formal categories.

The extent to which absolute rights are immune from a proportionality assessment can be debated.⁸ Rights which, on their face, are absolute, can be differentiated into those which can and those which cannot be derogated from⁹ (suspended) in time of 'war or other public emergency facing the nation' under the conditions in article 15. The ban on torture, slavery and retrospective crimes are examples of the former. Freedom of thought (article 9(1)), the right to marry (article 12) and fair hearings (article 6(1)) are examples of the latter. Whether the legal conditions for derogation exist includes a judgment, to be made by a court, about the need for measures interfering with rights considered in relation to the threat.

is independent of the executive and has the authority to call witnesses etc in order to get at the truth, allocate responsibility (including to officials) and learn lessons. Where possible it should be in public with a sufficient involvement of the family to secure their interests (**Jordan v UK** (2003) 37 EHRR 2).

¹⁰Move on to a general description of article 3.

Article 3¹⁵ prohibits 'torture' and 'inhuman or degrading treatment or punishment'. It is a fundamental, non-derogable right. The ban on torture expresses perhaps the most fundamental obligation on a state, based not just on its agreements but also on its status as a civilised state (*jus cogens*).¹⁶ In **Ireland v UK** (1978) 2 EHRR 25 the ECtHR defined 'torture' in terms of serious and deliberate inhuman treatment and inhuman treatment involving intense physical and

¹⁶It is important to show that the ban on torture is basic to international law. The term *jus cogens* is perfectly acceptable

---

✓ Make your answer stand out

■ Briefly discuss Lord Scott's observations in *A* on the application of article 15 and of s 14 HRA 1998. His point was that the impact of a derogation on domestic law was nil since the HRA 1998 allows Parliament to enact clear provisions which are incompatible with Convention rights. Section 14 HRA 1998 allows for the making of derogations but does not mention article 15; nor is article 15 a Convention right.

■ In discussing 'war or other public emergency facing the life of the nation' you could (briefly) mention Lord Hoffmann's famous dissent in *A*. A threat must be to the basic institutions, culture and way of life; not just of serious violence.

■ Discuss the issue at a more theoretical level by referring (regarding article 17) to the idea of 'militant democracy' (see, Harvey, 2004). More general references to the Convention concept of 'democracy' will also impress (see discussions in Gearty (2000) and Mowbray (1999)).

■ Be more critical and analytical of article 17 – is it possible that the article might allow states to suppress dissent merely because of its radicalism rather than it being a threat to democracy.

! Don't be tempted to ...

■ Use up a lot of space in showing the gradual removal of the executive from sentencing. It is a long and complex story which involves dealing with a lot of case law and explaining the differences between different types of sentence, such as mandatory and discretionary life sentences. Exam room discipline is necessary here.

■ Say too much on general matters (e.g. aspects of article 5 which are unlikely to apply to prisoners or in introducing other articles such as articles 7, 6 and 14 which are clearly relevant); keep focused on prisoners.

■ Go on too much about prisoners' rights based on matters other than those which bear on the right to liberty (e.g. prison conditions are normally dealt with under articles 2, 3 and 8; there are interesting discussions about prisoners' rights under article 10 (but see the point in 'Make your answer stand out', above)).

Bibliography

Allan, TRS (2001) *Constitutional Justice* Oxford: OUP.

Allan, TRS (2006) 'Human rights and judicial review: a critique of 'due deference' *Cambridge Law Journal* 65(3), 671–695.

Amos, Merris (2007) 'The Impact of the Human Rights Act on the United Kingdom's Performance before the European Court of Human Rights' *Public Law* 655.

Beattie, K. (2009) 'S and Marper v UK: Privacy, DNA and Crime Prevention' EHRLR 2,

Guided tour of the companion website

Book resources are available to download. Print your own **Attack the question** and **Diagram plans**

Additional **Essay and Problem questions** with **Diagram plans** arranged by topic for each chapter give you more opportunity to practice and hone your exam skills. Print and email your answers.

You be the marker gives you a chance to evaluate sample exam answers for different question types for each topic and understand how and why an examiner awards marks. Use the accompanying guidance to get the most out of every question and recognise what makes a good answer

All of this and more can be found when you visit
www.pearsoned.co.uk/lawexpressqa

Table of cases and statutes

■ Cases

A v B Plc [2002] EWCA Civ 337 127

A v Essex [2007] EWHC 1652 54

A v Essex CC [2008] EWCA Civ 364 249

A v Head Teacher and Governors of Lord Grey School
[2006] UKHL 14 249

A v Secretary of State for the Home Department [2004]
UKHL 56 50, 80, 172

A v Secretary of State for the Home Department [2005]
UKHL 71, [2006] 2 AC 221, HL, *Reversing* [2004]
EWCA Civ 1123, CA 88

A v UK (2003) 36 EHRR 51 201

A v UK (2009) 49 EHRR 18 79

A v UK (2009) 49 EHRR 29 36, 66, 171, 211, 212

A (Children) (Conjoined Twins Medical Treatment)
[2000] 4 All ER 961 116

AD v UK [2010] ECHR 28680/06 130

ADT v United Kingdom (2001) 31 EHRR 33 19

Abdulaziz v UK (1985) 7 EHRR 471 75, 130

Ahmed v Austria (1997) 24 EHRR 278 154

Aksoy v Turkey (1997) 23 EHRR 553 80

Al-Adsani v UK (2002) 34 EHRR 11 5, 6, 187

Ali v Birmingham CC [2010] UKSC 8 146, 192

Al-Khawaja v UK (2009) 49 EHRR 1 188, 207

Al-Saadoon v UK, application 61498/08, judgment of 2
March 2010 5, 106

American Cyanamid v Ethicon [1975] 2 WLR 316
226

Anufrijeva v Southwark LBC [2003] EWCA Civ
1406 145, 146

Application of JR17, *Re* [2010] UKSC 27 249, 250

Arrowsmith v UK (1981) 3 EHRR 218 238

Ashingdane v UK (1985) 7 EHRR 528 163, 176, 201

Ashley v Chief Constable of Sussex Police [2008] UKHL
25 91

Ashworth Security Hospital v MGN Ltd [2002] UKHL
29 221

Associated Provincial Picture House v Wednesbury
Corporation [1947] 2 All ER 680 20

Association Ekin v France (2002) 35 EHRR 35 219

Aston Cantlow and Wilmcote with BillesleyParochial
Church Council v Wallbank [2003] UKHL 37 43,
44, 148

Attorney General v Guardian Newspapers Ltd [1987] 3
All ER 316 223

Attorney-General v Johnathan Cape [1976] QB
752 223

Attorney General v Punch [2002] UKHL 50 223

Austin v Commissioner of Police of the Metropolis
[2009] UKHL 5 164, 167, 230

BM v Secretary of State for the Home Department
[2009] EWHC 1572 211

BX v Secretary of State for the Home Department
[2010] EWCA Civ 481 170

Bankovic v Belgium (2007) 44 EHRR SE5 84, 103–106

Barthold v Germany (1985) 7 EHRR 383 218

Begum v Tower Hamlets LBC [2003] UKHL 5 191–193,
197, 198

Belgian Linguistics Case (Case Relating to Certain
Aspects of the Laws on the Use of Languages In
Education In Belgium, No 6) (1979–1980) 1 EHRR
252 74, 249

Belilos v Switzerland (1988) 10 EHRR 466 252

Bellinger v Bellinger [2003] UKHL 21 40

Bensaid v UK (2001) 33 EHRR 10 155

Bibby v Chief Constable of Essex (2000) 164 JP
297 230

Botmeh v UK (2008) 46 EHRR 31 **210**

Brennan v UK (2002) 34 EHRR 18 **201**

Brogan v UK (1989) 11 EHRR 117 **162, 166, 167**

Broniowski v Poland (2006) 43 EHRR 1, (2005) 40 EHRR 21 **120, 245**

Brown v Stott [2003] 1 AC 681 **202**

Bryan v UK (1996) 21 EHRR 342 **192, 193, 195**

Buckley v UK (1997) 23 EHRR 101 **138**

Burden v UK (2008) 47 EHRR 38 **23, 31, 34, 128**

Burton v UK (1996) 22 EHRR CD135 **138**

Campbell v MGN [2004] UKHL 22 **123, 124, 126**

Campbell v MGN [2005] UKHL 61 **220**

Campbell & Cosans v UK (1982) 4 EHRR 293 **240, 250, 251**

Campbell & Fell v UK (1985) 7 EHRR 165 **196**

Chahal v UK (1997) 23 EHRR 413 **88, 153, 210**

Chassagnou v France (2000) 29 EHRR 615 **244, 246**

Chorherr v Austria (1994) 17 EHRR 289 **228**

Clift v UK, application 7205/07, judgment of 13 July 2010 **35, 75, 77, 180**

Condron v UK (2001) 31 EHRR 1 **201**

Conka v Belgium (2002) 34 EHRR 54 **61, 161**

D v UK (1997) 24 EHRR 423 **144, 154**

Danderyds Kommun v Sweden, application 52559/99, decision of 7 June 2001 **24**

De Freitas v Permanent Secretary of Ministry of Agriculture, Lands and Housing [1999] 1 AC 69 **67**

Dennis v Ministry of Defence [2003] EWHC 793 **121**

Derbyshire County Council v Times Newspapers [1993] AC 534 **20, 220**

Dobson v Thames Water [2009] EWCA Civ 28 **121**

Doherty v Birmingham City Council [2008] UKHL 57 **20, 21, 139, 141**

Dombo Beheer BV v Netherlands (1994) 18 EHRR 213 **187**

Doorson v The Netherlands (1996) 22 EHRR 330 **207**

Douglas v Hello! [2001] QB 967 **125, 126**

Dunn v Parole Board [2008] EWCA Civ 374 **54**

EM (Lebanon) v Secretary of State for the Home Department [2008] UKHL 64 **155**

Eckle v Germany (1983) 5 EHRR 1 **23, 53**

Editions Plon v France (2006) 42 EHRR 36 **124, 125**

Edwards v UK (2002) 35 EHRR 19 **100**

Engel v The Netherlands (1979-80) 1 EHRR 647 **172, 186, 204, 210**

Eren v Turkey (2006) 44 EHRR 619 **249**

Evans v Amicus Healthcare Ltd [2004] EWCA Civ 727 **129, 131**

Evans v UK (2008) 46 EHRR 34 **110, 129, 131**

Ezeh v UK (2004) 39 EHRR 1 **186, 205**

Ezelin v France (1992) 14 EHRR 362 **228**

F v Berkshire [1989] 2 All ER 545 **116**

F (a Child) (Northern Ireland), Re [2008] UKHL 66 **95**

Fadeyeva v Russia (2005), application 55723/00 **120**

Feldbrugge v The Netherlands (1986) 8 EHRR 425 **191**

Ferrazzini v Italy (2002) 34 EHRR 45 **186**

Findlay v UK (1997) 24 EHRR 221 **197, 205**

Folgero v Norway (2008) 46 EHRR 47 **250**

Fressoz v France (2001) 31 EHRR 2 **81, 218**

Friedl v Austria (1996) 21 EHRR 83 **149**

Gaskin v UK (1989) 12 EHRR 36 **134**

Ghaidan v Godin-Mendoza [2004] UKHL 30 **30, 39, 40, 138, 139**

Giacomelli v Italy (2007) 45 EHRR 38 **138**

Gillan v United Kingdom (2010) 50 EHRR 45 **61, 70, 161, 163, 165, 167, 231**

Gillow v United Kingdom (1989) 11 EHRR 335 **138**

Glass v United Kingdom (2004) 39 EHRR 15 **116**

Glimmerveen and Hagenbeek v the Netherlands (1982) 4 EHRR 260 **81**

Golder v United Kingdom (1979-80) 1 EHRR 524 **20, 179, 187, 200**

Goodwin v United Kingdom (1996) 22 EHRR 123 **217, 220**

Goodwin v United Kingdom (2002) 35 EHRR 18 **71, 129**

Gorgulu v Germany [2004] 1 FLR 894 **130**

Grainger v Nicholson [2010] ICR 360 **238, 239, 251**

Guzzardi v Italy (1981) 3 EHRR 333 **165, 170**

HL v UK (2005) 40 EHRR 32 **67, 130, 161, 175, 177**

Halford v United Kingdom (1997) 24 EHRR 523 **60**

Handyside v UK (1979-80) 1 EHRR 737 **65, 71, 72, 219**

Hashman and Harrup v United Kingdom, aApplication 25594/94 (1999) 30 EHRR 241, [2000] Crim LR 185 **62, 228**

Hatton v UK (2003) 37 EHRR 28 **121**

Hentrich v France (1994) 18 EHRR 440 **244, 245**

Helow v Advocate General for Scotland [2008] UKHL 62 **197**

HM Treasury v Ahmed & Others [2010] UKSC 2 **6, 106**

Herczegfalvy v Austria (1992) 15 EHRR 437 **97, 116**

Hirst v UK (2006) 42 EHRR 41 **254–257**

Hoekstra v HM Advocate [2001] 1 AC 216 **193, 197**

Huang v Secretary of State for the Home Department [2007] UKHL 11 **48, 49, 129, 130, 224**

Hutchison Reid v UK (2003) 37 EHRR 9 **163, 175, 177**

Ionescu v Romania (2010) 51 EHRR SE7 **25**

Ireland v UK (1978) 2 EHRR 25 **87, 95**

JE v DE [2006] EWHC 3459 **174**

Jameel v Wall Street Journal [2006] UKHL 44 **221**

James v UK (1986) 8 EHRR 123 **244, 246**

Jersild v Denmark (1995) 19 EHRR 1 **79**

Johnson v UK (1999) 27 EHRR 296 **176**

Jordan v UK (2003) 37 EHRR 2 **87, 93, 101**

Kadi v Council of European Union [2009] AC 1225 **6**

Kay v Lambeth [2006] UKHL 10 **139, 141**

Keenan v UK (2001) 33 EHRR 913 **88, 95, 97, 100**

Kennedy v United Kingdom, application 26839/05, judgment of 18 May 2010 **62**

Kiss v Hungary, application 38832/06, judgment of 20 May 2010 **255**

Kjeldsen v Denmark (1979-80) 1 EHRR 711 **75, 250**

Klass v Germany (1979-80) 2 EHRR 214 **24, 150**

Kroon v Netherlands (1995) 19 EHRR 263 **129**

LCB v UK (1999) 27 EHRR 212 **119**

Ladele v Islington LBC [2009] EWCA Civ 1357 **239**

Laskey, Jaggard and Brown v UK (1997) 24 EHRR 39 **72**

Lawless v Ireland No 3 (1979–80) 1 EHRR 15 **80**

Le Compte v Belgium (1982) 4 EHRR 1 **196**

Leander v Sweden (1987) 9 EHRR 433 **110, 134**

Lehideux v France (2000) 30 EHRR 665 **81**

Lithgow and others v United Kingdom (1986) 8 EHRR 329 **246**

Locabail v Bayfield [2000] QB 451 **193**

López Ostra v Spain (1995) 20 EHRR 277 **119**

Lorse v The Netherlands (2003) 37 EHRR 3 **98**

Ludi v Switzerland (1993) 15 EHRR 173 **205**

M v Secretary of State for Work and Pensions [2006] UKHL 11 **76**

MC v Germany, application 13079/87, admissibility decision of 6 March 1989 **228**

Maaouia v France (2001) 33 EHRR 42 **186**

McCann v UK (1995) 21 EHRR 97 **86, 89–92, 101**

McCann v UK (2008) 47 EHRR 40 **139**

McE, Re [2009] UKHL 15 **148, 151**

McGonnell v UK (2000) 30 EHRR 289 **197**

McMichael v UK (1995) 20 EHRR 205 **202**

McVeigh v UK (1993) 5 EHRR 71 **167**

Makaratzis v Greece (2005) 41 EHRR 49, [2004] ECHR 694 **92**

Malone v Commissioner of Police of the Metropolis [1979] 1 All ER 256 **63**

Malone v United Kingdom (1985) 7 EHRR 14 **18, 63, 112**

Manchester City Council v Pinnock [2010] UKSC 45 **140, 141**

Marcic v Thames Water [2003] UKHL 66 **121**

Marckx v Belgium (1979-80) 2 EHRR 330 **14, 244**

Marper v United Kingdom (2009) 48 EHRR 50 **61, 62, 132, 134–136, 150**

Mason v Ministry of Justice [2008] EWHC 1787 **180**

Mathieu-Mohin and Clerfayt v Belgium (1987) 10 EHRR 1 **253**

Matthews v UK (1999) 28 EHRR 361 **254**

Mayzit v Russia (2006) 43 EHRR 38 **98**

Mellacher v Austria (1990) 12 EHRR 391 **246**

Mersey Care NHS Trust v Ackroyd [2007] EWCA Civ 101 **221**

Metropolitan Church of Bessarabia v Moldova (2002) 35 EHRR 13 **238**

Ministry of Defence v Griffin [2008] EWHC 1542 **226**

Monnat v Switzerland (2010) 51 EHRR 34 **54**

Mosley v News Group Newspapers [2008] EWHC 1777 **149**

Murray v Express Newspapers [2008] EWCA Civ 446 **125**

Murray v UK (1995) 19 EHRR 193 **135**

Murray v UK (1996) 22 EHRR 29 **201**

N v United Kingdom (2008) 47 EHRR 39 **154**

NHS Trust v A [2001] 1 All ER 801 **116**

Napier v Scottish Ministers 2005 1 SC 229 **88, 96**

Neulinger v Switzerland, application 41615/07, Grand Chamber judgment, 6 July 2010 **5**

Nicol and Selvanayagam v DPP (1996) 160 JP 155 **230**

Niemietz v Germany (1993) 16 EHRR 97 **110, 138**

Norris v Ireland (1986) 8 EHRR CD 75 **54**

Norris v US [2010] UKSC 9 **155**

Norwood v UK (2005) 49 EHRR SE11 **81**

Nurettin v Turkey, application 32124/02, judgment of 18 December 2007 **230**

O'Halloran and Francis v UK (2008) 46 EHRR 21 **202, 206**

O'Reilly v Mackman [1983] 2 AC 237 **56**

Observer v UK (Spycatcher Case) (1992) 14 EHRR 153 **219, 222–224, 226**

Öcalan v Turkey (2005) 41 EHRR 45 **23**

Officer L, Re [2007] UKHL 36 **86, 100, 101**

Öneryildiz v Turkey (2005) 41 EHRR 20 **100, 119**

Open Door Counselling v Ireland (1993) 15 EHRR 244 **25**

Osman v UK (2000) 29 EHRR 245 **86, 99–102, 105, 119, 187, 201**

Othman v Secretary of State for the Home Department [2009] UKHL 10 **88, 154, 155**

Özgür Gündem v Turkey (2001) 31 EHRR 49 **218**

P v South Gloucestershire Council [2007] EWCA Civ 2 **131**

PG & JH v UK (2008) 46 EHRR 51 **150**

Partidul Comunistilor v Romania (2007) 44 EHRR 17 **234**

Peck v UK (2003) 36 EHRR 41 **96, 148, 149, 151, 186**

Percy v DPP [1995] 3 All ER 124, QBD **230**

Piersack v Belgium (1983) 5 EHRR 169 **196**

Plattform Ärzte für das Leben v Austria (1988) 13 EHRR 204 **229**

Poplar HRCA v Donoghue [2001] EWCA Civ 595 **44**

Porter v Magill [2001] UKHL 67 **192**

Pressos Compania Naviera SA v Belgium (1996) 4 EHRR 301 **244, 246**

Pretty v UK (2002) 35 EHRR 1 **87, 96, 109, 110, 113–115, 117, 144, 145**

Price v UK (2002) 34 EHRR 128 **97**

Purdy v Director of Public Prosecutions [2009] UKHL 45 **60, 61, 113, 114, 117**

Pye v UK (2008) 46 EHRR 45 **244**

Pyx Granite v Ministry of Housing and Local Government [1960] AC 260 **201**

Qazi v Harrow LBC [2003] UKHL 43 **139**

R v A [2001] UKHL 25 **30, 39, 41**

R v Bieber [2008] EWCA Civ 1602 **154**

R v Bow Street Magistrate, ex parte Pinochet 2 [2000] 1 AC 119 **197**

R v Davis [2008] UKHL 36 **207**

R v Director of Public Prosecutions, ex parte Kebeline [2000] 2 AC 326 **49**

R v H [2004] UKHL 3 **150, 151, 202, 205, 207, 210, 211**

R v Hammond [2005] UKHL 69 **40**

R v Horncastle [2009] UKSC 14 **36, 188, 207**

R v Looseley [2001] UKHL 53 **205**

R v Lord Chancellor, ex parte Witham [1998] 2 WLR 849 **19**

R v Lyons [2002] UKHL 44 **19, 29**

R v Mason [2002] EWCA Crim 385 **151**

R v Ministry of Defence, ex parte Smith [1996] QB 517 **48**

R v Remington [2005] UKHL 63 **138, 181**

R v Secretary of State for the Home Department, ex parte Daly [2001] UKHL 26 **67**

R v Secretary of State for the Home Department, ex parte Simms [2000] AC 115 **19, 62**

R v Shayler [2002] UKHL 11 **60, 62, 222, 225, 226**

R v Somerset County Council, ex parte Fewings [1995] 1 All ER 513 **46**

R v Spear [2002] UKHL 31 **36**

R (on the application of A) v Croydon LBC [2009] UKSC 8 **192**

R (on the application of A) v Bloody Sunday Inquiry [2001] EWCA Civ 2048 **102**

R (on the application of Alconbury) v Secretary of State Environment, Transport and the Regions [2001] UKHL 23 **191, 193, 197, 198, 245**

R (on the application of Al-Jedda) v Secretary of State for Defence [2007] UKHL 58 **5, 106**

R (on the application of Al-Saadoon) v Secretary of State for Defence [2009] EWCA Civ 7 **105**

R (on the application of Al-Skeini v Secretary of State for Defence [2007] UKHL 26 104

R (on the application of Amin) v Secretary of State for the Home Department [2003] UKHL 51 87, 92, 93, 101, 102

R (on the application of Anderson) v Secretary of State for the Home Department [2002] UKHL 46 30, 40, 180

R (on the application of Animal Defenders International) v Secretary of State for Culture Media and Sport [2008] UKHL 15 35, 49

R (on the application of B) v Ashworth Hospital Authority [2005] UKHL 20 176

R (on the application of Baiai) v Secretary of State for the Home Department [2008] UKHL 53 129

R (on the application of Barclay) v Lord Chancellor [2009] UKSC 9 254

R (on the application of Begum) v Denbigh High School Governors [2006] UKHL 15 239

R (on the application of Bloggs 61) v Secretary of State for the Home Department [2003] EWCA Civ 686 100, 101

R (on the application of Brehony) v Chief Constable of Greater Manchester Police [2005] EWHC 640 230

R (on the application of Brooke) v Secretary of State for Justice [2008] EWCA Civ 29 162, 181

R (on the application of Broughton) v Her Majesty's Treasury [2005] EWHC 1914 239

R (on the application of Burke) v General Medical Council [2005] EWCA Civ 1003 114, 117

R (on the application of Carson) v Secretary of State for Work and Pensions [2005] UKHL 37 76

R (on the application of Chester) v Secretary of State for Justice [2009] EWHC 2923 256

R (on the application of Clift) v Secretary of State for the Home Department [2006] UKHL 54 75, 77

R (on the application of Countryside Alliance v AG [2007] UKHL 52 110, 112

R (on the application of Daly) v Secretary of State for the Home Department [2001] UKHL 26 31, 48, 49, 224, 230

R (on the application of Dimmock) v Secretary of State for Education and Science [2007] EWHC 2288 251

R (on the application of Faizovas) v Secretary State for Justice [2009] EWCA Civ 373 96

R (on the application of Gentle v PM [2008] UKHL 20 87, 93, 101, 102, 105

R (on the application of Gillan) v Commissioner of Police of the Metropolis [2006] UKHL 12 61, 70, 161, 163–165, 167

R (on the application of Greenfield) v Secretary of State for the Home Office [2005] UKHL 14 55, 163, 177

R (on the application of H) v Secretary of State for Health [2005] UKHL 60 176, 177

R (on the application of Heather) v Leonard Cheshire Homes [2003] EWCA Civ 336 45

R (on the application of Hirst) v Secretary of State for the Home Department [2002] EWHC 602 256, 257

R (on the application of Howard League for Penal Reform) v Secretary of State for the Home Department [2002] EWHC 2497 53

R (on the application of Hurst) v London Northern District Coroner [2007] UKHL 13 20, 35

R (on the application of IH) v Secretary of State for Health [2003] UKHL 59 176

R (on the application of Jackson) v Attorney General [2005] UKHL 56 32

R (on the application of James) v Parole Board [2009] UKHL 22 180, 181

R (on the application of JF) v Secretary of State for the Home Department [2010] UKSC 17 41

R (on the application of JL) Secretary of State for the Home Department [2008] UKHL 68 92, 101, 102, 120

R (on the application of Johnson) v Havering LBC [2007] EWCA Civ 26 46

R (on the application of JS (Sri Lanka)) v Secretary of State for the Home Department [2010] UKSC 15 156

R (on the application of KB) v Mental Health Review Tribunal [2003] EWHC 193 55, 177

R (on the application of Kurdistan Workers Party) v Secretary of State for the Home Department [2002] EWHC 644 233

R (on the application of L) v Commissioner of Police for the Metropolis [2009] UKSC 3 132, 134, 136

R (on the application of Laporte) v Chief Constable of Gloucestershire [2006] UKHL 55 167, 229, 230

R (on the application of Limbuela) v Secretary of State for the Home Department [2005] UKHL 66 142, 143, 145, 146

R (on the application of M) v Secretary of State for the Home Department [2008] UKHL 63 **145, 146**

R (on the application of MB) v Secretary of State for the Home Department [2007] UKHL 46 **209–212**

R (on the application of McCann) v Manchester Crown Court [2002] UKHL 39 **186, 205**

R (on the application of Marper) v Chief Constable of South Yorkshire [2004] UKHL 39 **36, 132, 134, 136**

R (on the application of Middleton) v West Somerset Coroner [2004] UKHL 10 **87, 93**

R (on the application of N) v Secretary of State for the Home Department [2005] UKHL 31 **154**

R (on the application of Pearson) v Secretary of State for the Home Department [2001] EWHC Admin 239 **255, 257**

R (on the application of ProLife Alliance) v BBC [2003] UKHL 23 **31, 50, 218, 219**

R (on the application of Purdy) v DPP [2009] UKHL 45 **61, 113–115, 117**

R (on the application of Razgar) v Secretary of State for the Home Department [2004] UKHL 27 **65, 67, 110, 112, 155**

R (on the application of SB) v Governors of Denbigh High School [2006] UKHL 15 **44**

R (on the application of Smith) v Oxfordshire Coroner [2010] UKSC 29 **105**

R (on the application of Spinks) v Secretary of State for the Home Department [2005] EWCA Civ 275 **88, 97**

R (on the application of U) v Special Immigration Appeals Commission [2009] EWHC 3052 **212**

R (on the application of Ullah) v Special Adjudicator [2004] UKHL 26 **35, 39, 153–155**

R (on the application of Watkins-Singh) v Aberdare School [2008] EWHC 1865 **239**

R (on the application of Weaver) v LQHT [2009] EWCA Civ 587 **44–46, 140**

R (on the application of Wilkinson) v Broadmoor Hospital [2001] EWCA Civ 1545 **97, 116**

R (on the application of Williamson) v Secretary of State for Education and Employment [2005] UKHL 15 **238, 240, 250–252**

Ramsahai v The Netherlands, application 52391/99, (2007) 46 EHRR 983, [2007] ECHR 52391/99 **93**

Redmond-Bate v DPP [2000] HRLR 249 **229, 230**

Refah Partisi v Turkey (2003) 37 EHRR 1 **81, 235, 236**

Reinprecht v Austria (2007) 44 EHRR 390 **186**

Reynolds v Times Newspapers [1999] 4 All ER 609 **220**

Ringeisen v Austria (1979-80) 1 EHRR 455 **191**

Roberts v Parole Board [2005] UKHL 45 **181**

Rowe & Davis v UK (2000) 30 EHRR 1 **202, 210**

Ruiz Mateos v Spain (1993) 16 EHRR 505 **202, 210**

S, Re [2002] UKHL 10 **131**

SP v United Kingdom (1997) 23 EHRR CD 139 **252**

SRM Global Master Fund LP v Commissioners of Her Majesty's Treasury [2009] EWCA Civ 788 **246**

Saadi v Italy (2009) 49 EHRR 30 **154, 156**

Sahin (Leyla) v Turkey, application 44747/98, Grand Chamber judgment of 10 November 2005, (2007) 44 EHRR 5 **70, 234, 238, 239, 249**

Salesi v Italy (1998) 26 EHRR 187 **191**

Salim Sadak v Turkey (2003) 36 EHRR 23 **253**

Saunders v UK (1997) 23 EHRR 313 **202, 203, 206**

Schalk & Kopf v Austria, application 30141/04, judgment of 24 June 2010 **128**

Scordino v Italy (1) (2007) 45 EHRR 7 **25**

Seal v Chief Constable of South Wales [2007] UKHL 31 **187, 201**

Secretary of State for the Home Department v A [2007] UKHL 45 **165**

Secretary of State for the Home Department v AF [2009] UKHL 28 **36, 188, 211, 212**

Secretary of State for the Home Department v AP [2010] UKSC 24 **170, 171**

Secretary of State for the Home Department v AP (2) [2010] UKSC 26 **171**

Secretary of State for the Home Department v GG [2009] EWCA Civ 786 **170**

Secretary of State for the Home Department v JJ [2007] UKHL 45 **170**

Secretary of State for the Home Department v MB [2007] UKHL 46 **171, 207, 209, 211**

Secretary of State for the Home Department v Rehman [2001] UKHL 47 **49**

Selmouni v France (2000) 29 EHRR 403 **5, 87, 95, 96**

Sener v Turkey (2003) 37 EHRR 34 **219**

Sheldrake v DPP [2004] UKHL 43 **206**

Sidabras and Dziautas v Lithuania (2006) 42 EHRR 6 **76, 110**

Silih v Slovenia (2009) 49 EHRR 37 **86**

Smirnova v Russia (2003) 39 EHRR 450 **181**

Smith v UK (2000) 29 EHRR 493 **19, 20, 48**
Soering v UK (1989) 11 EHRR 439 **105, 153**
Somerville v Scottish Ministers [2007] UKHL 44 **21, 54**
Sporrong and Lonnroth v Sweden (1982) 5 EHRR
35 **48, 64, 71, 186, 245, 246**
Stafford v UK (2002) 35 EHRR 32 **179, 180**
Stankov v Bulgaria, application 29221/95, judgment of
2 October 2001 **235**
Starrs v Ruxton 2000 JC 208 **197**
Stec v UK (2006) 43 EHRR 47, (2005) 41 EHRR SE
18 **76, 145, 244**
Stedman v United Kingdom (1997) 23 EHRR CD
168 **239**
Steel and Morris v UK (2005) 41 EHRR 22 **221**
Steel v UK (1999) 28 EHRR 603 **61, 70, 164, 166, 168,
228, 229**
Sunday Times v UK (Spycatcher Case) (1979–80) 2
EHRR 245 **60, 62, 69, 117, 134, 222–224, 226**

TV v Finland (1994) 18 EHRR CD 179 **134**
Taylor v UK (1994) 18 EHRR CD 215 **102**
Teixeira de Castro v Portugal (1999) 28 EHRR 101
205
Tinnelly v UK (1999) 27 EHRR 249 **187**
Trafigura Private Ltd v Emirates General Petroleum
Corpn [2010] EWHC 87 (Comm), [2010] All ER (D)
39 (Feb), (2010) Guardian 25 January **126**
Tsfayo v UK (2009) 48 EHRR 18 **146, 191, 193**
Tsonev v Bulgaria (2008) 46 EHRR 8 **234**

Uner v Netherlands (2007) 45 EHRR 14 **155**
United Communist Party of Turkey v Turkey (1998) 26
EHRR 121 **233, 234**

V (a child) (care proceedings: human rights claims), Re
[2004] EWCA Civ 54 **131**
Valenzuela Contreras v Spain (1999) 28 ECHR 483
150
Van Colle v Chief Constable of Hertfordshire [2008]
UKHL 50 **101**
Van der Leer v The Netherlands (1990) 12 EHRR
567 **161**
Varbanov v Bulgaria, application 31365/96, judgment
of 5 October 2000 **175**
Von Hannover v Germany (2005) 40 EHRR 1 **124–126,
149, 150, 220, 221**

Webster v Norfolk County Council [2009] EWCA Civ
59 **131**
Weeks v UK (1988) 10 EHRR 293 **20**
Wemhoff v Germany (1979–80) 1 EHRR 1 **179**
Whiteside v UK (1994) 18 EHRR CD 126 **138**
Wieser v Austria (2007) 46 EHRR 54 **96**
Winder v Wandsworth LBC [1985] AC 461 **141**
Winterwerp v The Netherlands (1979) 2 EHRR
387 **160, 174, 175**
Wood v Commissioner of Police of the Metropolis
[2009] EWCA Civ 414 **149**
Worm v Austria (1998) 25 EHRR 454 **219**

X v United Kingdom (1982) 4 Crim LR 188 **176**
X & Y v Netherlands (1986) 8 EHRR 235 **111**

YL v Birmingham City Council [2007] UKHL 27 **44, 45**
Yasa v Turkey (1999) 28 EHRR 408 **23, 99**
Yumak v Turkey (2009) 48 EHRR 4 **23, 254**

Z v Finland (1998) 25 EHRR 371 **134**
Z v UK (2002) 34 EHRR 3 **130, 144, 187, 202**
Zdanoka v Latvia (2007) 45 EHRR 17 **81**
Zentralrat DSRR v Germany (1997) 23 EHRR 7 CD
209 **24**
Ziliberberg v Moldova, application 61821/00, judgment
of 1 February 2005 **229**

▮Statutes

Anti-terrorism, Crime and Security Act 2001
Pt IV **172**

Civil Procedure Rules 1998 (SI 1998/3132) **53**
Pt 54 **54, 56**
Contempt of Court Act 1981 **217**
s 10 **220**
Coroners and Justice Act 2009
s 5 **93**
Criminal Justice Act 1988
s 134 **95**
Criminal Justice Act 2003
s 116 **207**
Criminal Justice and Immigration Act 2008

s 76 91
Criminal Justice and Public Order Act 1994
  s 34 201
Criminal Law Act 1967
  s 3 91

Data Protection Act 1998 133

Employment Equality (Religion or Belief) Regulations
  2003 (SI 2003/1660) 238, 240
Employment Equality (Sexual Orientation) Regulations
  2003 (SI 2003/1661) 240
Equality Act 2010 77, 240
European Communities Act 1972 34
  s 3 35

Freedom of Information Act 2000 46, 137

Health and Social Care Act 2008
  s 145 45
Human Rights Act 1998 1, 16, 18–21, 23, 27–35,
  37–45, 47–49, 51–55, 57, 59–62, 64, 70, 76, 78,
  80, 82, 85, 88–90, 93, 98, 100, 103, 104, 106,
  118, 122–125, 131–133, 136, 137, 139, 140,
  142–144, 147, 150–152, 156, 157, 159, 170, 172,
  176, 178–180, 186, 189–191, 193, 194, 199–201,
  203, 204, 208, 210, 212, 215, 219–223, 225–227,
  236, 239, 241, 247–249, 251, 252, 257
  s 1 40
    (2) 251
  s 2 33–37, 39, 57, 60, 140, 191, 224, 249
  s 3 27–31, 33, 34, 37–43, 47, 53, 54, 62, 74, 85,
  90, 124, 136, 137, 140, 143, 153, 165, 171, 176,
  208, 209, 225, 227, 239, 249, 256
    (1) 34, 39
    (a) 30
    (b) 30
  s 4 11, 24, 27–31, 34, 37, 40–42, 172, 209
  s 6 27–29, 31, 33, 42, 43, 46, 47, 53, 62, 74, 85,
  90, 105, 143, 153, 165, 172, 194, 227, 249
    (1) 43, 44, 53, 133
    (2) 29, 31, 43, 151
    (3)(a) 124, 223
      (b) 43, 44
    (5) 42, 45, 133
    (6) 41

s 7 27, 28, 31, 42, 45, 47, 52–54, 99, 137
  (1)(a) 52–54
    (b) 52–54, 140
s 8 27, 28, 31, 47, 52, 55, 181
  (3) 55
s 9 27, 28
s 10 27, 28, 31, 37, 41
s 11 36
s 12 123, 125, 219, 223, 224, 226
s 14 80, 82
Sch 1 30, 33, 35, 39, 43, 57, 74, 221
Sch 2 31, 41

Immigration Act 1971
  s 3(5) 212
Interception of Communications Act 1987 18, 63
International Criminal Court Act 2001 106

Limitation Act 1980 54
  s 33(3) 54

Magna Carta 1215 160
Mental Health Act 1983 175–177
Mental Health Act 2007 177

Official Secrets Act 1989 221, 225, 226

Police and Criminal Evidence Act 1984 162, 165, 231
  Pt 1 165
  s 28 161
  s 78 148, 151, 206, 207
  s 117 88
Prevention of Terrorism Act 2005 168–171, 212
Prisons Act 1952 179
Public Order Act 1986 226, 227, 229, 231
  s 11 229

Race Relations Act 1976 239
Regulation of Investigatory Powers Act 2000 63,
  150–152
Representation of the People Act 1983
  s 3 255, 256
  s 8 256

Security Service Act 1989 19, 63
Senior Courts Act 1981

s 32 56
Sexual Offences Act 2000 19, 41

Terrorism Act 2000 165, 172, 231, 233, 236
  Pt 2 231

Youth Justice and Criminal Evidence Act 1995
  s 58 203
  Sch 3 203

EC and International Legislation

African Charter on Human and Peoples' Rights 1979 4, 6
American Convention 1969 4

EEC Treaty (Treaty of Rome) 6
EU Charter of Fundamental Rights 2, 3, 5, 77, 128, 131
  Art 9 128
European Convention on the Protection of Human Rights and Fundamental Freedoms 1950 1–6, 10, 12–21, 23–25, 27, 29, 31, 32, 34–36, 39, 42, 45, 46, 48–50, 54, 55, 57–74, 76–82, 85, 86, 88–91, 93, 94, 96–100, 102–106, 111–114, 116, 118–124, 127, 128, 131, 133–135, 138, 140, 144–146, 150–154, 156, 161, 164, 165, 168, 169, 171, 172, 174, 176, 179, 180, 185, 186, 200, 201, 204, 208, 215, 217, 220, 223, 227, 228, 230, 231, 233, 234, 238, 239, 245, 249–253, 255–257
  Pt 1 35, 37
  Art 1 13, 14, 17, 18, 29, 36, 41, 104, 130, 138, 144, 145
  Art 2 21, 23, 26, 65, 71, 80, 83–94, 98–103, 105, 106, 113, 114, 116–120, 122, 170, 182
    (1) 90, 92, 99
    (2) 65, 71, 86, 89, 90
      (a) 91
      (b) 91
      (c) 91
  Art 3 5, 23, 42, 52, 64–66, 76, 80, 83–85, 87–89, 94–98, 102, 103, 105–107, 111, 113, 114, 116,
117, 122, 130, 142–145, 147, 152–154, 156, 169, 171, 182, 227
  Art 4 81
  Art 5 5, 40, 52, 55, 59, 65, 67, 74–76, 80, 106, 130, 157–170, 172–176, 178–182, 184, 186, 227, 228, 230, 255
    (1) 65, 67, 75, 159–162, 166, 169, 175, 176, 178, 180
      (a) 160, 164, 166, 168, 169, 179
      (b) 160, 164–169
      (c) 160, 162, 164, 166, 168, 169, 179
      (d) 160, 166, 168
      (e) 160, 166, 168, 175, 176
      (f) 160, 166, 168
    (2) 158, 159, 161
    (3) 62, 158, 159, 161, 162, 179, 183–185, 188
    (4) 62, 158, 159, 161, 162, 171, 176–178, 180, 181, 183–186, 188, 189, 210, 211
    (5) 52, 55, 158, 159, 162, 163, 176, 178, 181
    (6) 55
  Art 6 33, 36, 37, 39–41, 62, 64, 66, 72, 79, 142, 143, 146, 151, 153, 155, 156, 168, 171, 177, 179, 180, 182–209, 211, 212, 225, 233, 241, 242, 246
    (1) 66, 169, 171, 184–186, 188, 191, 192, 199–206, 208, 210, 211, 246
    (2) 184, 185, 188, 191, 194, 200, 202–206, 208, 210
    (3) 179, 184, 185, 188, 191, 194, 200, 202–206, 208, 210
      (a) 200, 204, 206
      (b) 200, 204, 206
      (c) 200, 201, 204, 206
      (d) 188, 200, 204, 206, 207
      (e) 200, 204, 206
  Art 7 63, 81, 179–182
  Art 8 5, 6, 14, 19, 37, 39, 40, 46, 48, 49, 51, 60–62, 70, 73, 74, 76, 85, 86, 91, 97, 98, 107–116, 118–124, 127–134, 136–143, 145, 147–156, 161, 164, 165, 169, 170, 182, 219, 220, 234, 245
    (1) 108, 110, 113, 116, 120, 123. 125, 129, 133, 148–150
    (2) 63, 107, 109, 111–113, 115, 116, 118, 120, 121, 123, 125, 127–130, 132–139, 145, 147, 149, 150, 154, 155, 165, 166, 170, 171
  Art 9 48, 49, 60, 65, 70, 71, 82, 86, 91, 111, 115,

124, 149, 155, 215, 216, 234, 236–242, 245, 249, 252
  (1) 66
  (2) 63, 216, 237
Art 10 20, 21, 24–26, 48–50, 58, 60, 69–71, 81, 82, 86, 91, 111, 115, 122–124, 127, 149, 182, 215–225, 227, 231–235, 238, 245, 256
  (1) 125, 218, 219, 223, 233
  (2) 63, 72, 79, 123, 125, 216, 218, 219, 221, 222, 223, 225
Art 11 48, 49, 60, 70, 71, 82, 91, 111, 115, 124, 149, 215, 216, 227–236, 238, 245
  (1) 228, 233
  (2) 63, 216, 227–229, 233–235
Art 12 66, 127–129, 131
Art 13 13, 29, 35, 57, 126, 185, 186
Art 14 58, 73–77, 80, 111, 128, 139, 146, 147, 180, 182, 249
Art 15 58, 66, 78–82, 86, 154, 170, 237
Art 17 58, 78, 81, 82, 235, 237
Art 18 88
Art 28 22
Art 29 22
Art 33 13, 23
Art 34 13, 16, 22–25, 41–43, 52–54, 99
Art 35 14, 22, 26, 54
Art 41 52, 55, 181
Art 46 13, 18, 36
  (4) 13
  (5) 13
Arts 47–49 25
Art 57 252
European Convention on the Protection of Human Rights and Fundamental Freedoms 1950, Protocol 1 4, 241, 253
Art 1 24, 51, 58, 66, 74, 76, 122, 140, 142, 143, 145–147, 186, 241–247
Art 2 5, 238, 240–242, 247–252
Art 3 215, 233, 241, 242, 252–257

European Convention on the Protection of Human Rights and Fundamental Freedoms 1950, Protocol 4 170
Art 2 170
European Convention on the Protection of Human Rights and Fundamental Freedoms 1950, Protocol 7 4
European Convention on the Protection of Human Rights and Fundamental Freedoms 1950, Protocol 11 12–15, 18
European Convention on the Protection of Human Rights and Fundamental Freedoms 1950, Protocol 12 77
European Convention on the Protection of Human Rights and Fundamental Freedoms 1950, Protocol 13 154
European Convention on the Protection of Human Rights and Fundamental Freedoms 1950, Protocol 14 12, 14, 15, 25

Geneva Convention 3, 6
Art 13 5

International Covenant of Civil and Political Rights (ICCPR) 4, 5, 13, 16, 80, 106, 131
International Covenant of Socvial and Cultural Rights (ICESCR) 5

UN Convention against Torture 5, 87, 95, 96
UN Convention on the Elimination of all Forms of Discrimination Against Women 5
UN Convention Relating to the Status of Refugees 1954 156
Art 1F 156
UN Declaration of Human Rights 1948 (UNDHR) 3–5, 74
Arts 22–29 5

Vienna Convention on the Law of Treaties 1969 6

Human rights – general themes

1

How this topic may come up in exams

A course on European human rights and the Human Rights Act 1998 is likely to involve background and contextual themes. Questions can relate to subjects such as the concept of human rights, the wider context of international law, the Council of Europe and the Convention system. Essay questions are more likely (though problems are possible). Answers need to show not only a good background of knowledge but, often, an ability to deal with theoretical and conceptual issues or to write about the historical development of institutions. Remember, that answers to questions on particular rights (as in Chapters 2–9) can be strengthened by references to these contextual matters.

■ Attack the question

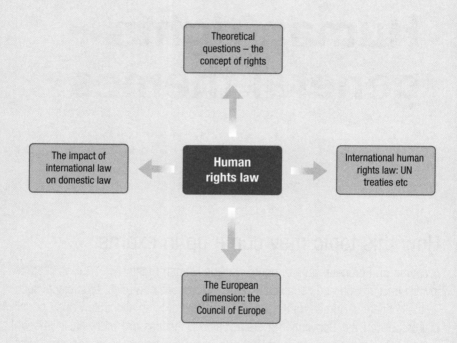

📰 Question 1

Discuss the influence of global international law on the way the European Convention on Human Rights (ECHR) is interpreted and applied.

Answer plan

→ Introduce the ECHR as part of and influenced by global international law.

→ Discuss UN-based treaty law (the UN 'bill of rights' and other UN treaties) and demonstrate influence on the application of the ECHR.

→ Note that the influence of international law can raise difficulties.

→ Discuss other sources of international law.

→ Consider the influence of customary international law.

→ Note the Vienna Convention and its general influence on the interpretation of the ECHR.

Diagram plan

Consider influences of UN treaties (Bill of Rights and others) on ECHR. ➡ Note examples of persuasive influence; but note also areas of tension ➡ Consider other sources of international law ➡ Discuss the importance of customary international law ➡ Note the Vienna Convention dealing with the interpretation of treaties

A printable version of this diagram is available from www.pearsoned.co.uk/lawexpressqa

Answer

[1]A brief historical introduction to early developments which prefigure the development of human rights law after the Second World War will improve your answer by providing context.

The European Convention on Human Rights (ECHR) is a regional development of what can be called the global human rights movement in international law. International human rights law has its origins in the codification of the laws of war of nations in the seventeenth and eighteenth centuries and in various formal treaties of the nineteenth and early twentieth century (e.g. Geneva Convention first signed in 1864).[1] But it is after the Second World War that, inspired by the United Nations, the human rights movement develops into its modern form.

[2]You will get credit for demonstrating your understanding of the nature of the authority of international law; later you will mention customary authority.

First, there are the treaty based obligations[2] based on the direct authority of the UN. The Charter of the UN refers to promoting and encouraging human rights as a UN purpose. The Declaration of

3

Human Rights 1948 (UNDHR) identified and expressed the main human rights. It does not have direct legal effect, though some international lawyers believe that it forms part of customary international law, thus it may have some authority in domestic law. The text of the Declaration influenced the drafting of the European Convention in 1950.[3]

[3]It will give a good structure to your answer if you proceed by identifying a provision or aspect of international law and then show its effect on the ECHR.

The ECHR is one of a number of initiatives that sought to give legal effect to the Declaration on a regional basis, where, given a degree of cultural homogeneity, success would be more likely. The American Convention dates from 1969; the African Charter has its beginnings in 1979.

Globally, it took until 1966 for the rights in the UNDHR to be agreed in legal form and a further decade to be brought into effect. The 'cold war' was the underlying explanation for the delay. Legal effect was through the International Covenant on Civil and Political Rights (ICCPR).[4] This is a treaty obligation accepted by a majority, though not all, of UN members.

[4]It is essential that you mention the ICCPR which is the major, general, human rights instrument of the UN.

The ECHR and the ICCPR include many of the same rights, and similar limits and qualifications.[5] The High Contracting Parties (HCPs) to the ECHR are also signatories of the ICCPR and the former has been amended to introduce rights in the Covenant, such as by Protocol 7. Some provisions, such as the prohibition of propaganda for war, are not expressly found in the ECHR (though implied).

[5]Now move on to discuss the similarities and differences between the ICCPR and the ECHR. Reference to Protocol 7 will impress.

The comparative strength of the ECHR lies in enforcement.[6] This is based on adjudication by the European Court of Human Rights (ECtHR). The HCPs must allow their citizens the right to apply to the court (until 1998 this was voluntary) and they agree to give effect to the ECtHR's judgments. The ICCPR, on the other hand, is enforced through a reporting process. Signatory states report on their fulfilment of their obligations to the Human Rights Committee (established by the ICCPR itself). This Committee can receive comments from NGOs. It makes observations back to the reporting state. It also can make general comments on specific ICCPR articles and makes a general report, ultimately, to the UN General Assembly. The Committee can receive individual complaints from persons from states which have adopted the First Optional Protocol. The Committee has three formal meetings a year. It clearly cannot have the extensive, direct, impact on individual cases and national laws enjoyed under the Convention

[6]You will get credit for being able to point up the relative strengths of the ECHR; all the more so if you can refer to the procedures under the ICCPR.

[7]You will get credit for your understanding that the successes of particular measures of international law are likely to depend on a range of non-legal factors which contribute to their authority and effectiveness.

[8]You need to show you understand the ICESCR as well as the ICCPR – the constituents of the 'UN Bill of Rights'.

[9]Showing your understanding of particular articles in the measures being discussed and, also, being able to relate UN international law to the ECHR, will get you credit. It demonstrates knowledge of detail which will impress an examiner.

[10]It is important to illustrate your knowledge of the many other measures of international law which directly or indirectly influence the ECHR.

[11]This is an interesting point (becoming quite important in the context of the 'war on terrorism' etc) for which you will get credit, especially if you can give some examples.

[12]Showing your understanding of the breadth of international law, including private international law, will impress the examiner, especially if you have examples of its influence on the ECHR.

and available under European political, social, cultural and economic conditions.[7]

As well as through the ICCPR, parts of the UNDHR were given treaty-based effect through the International Covenant of Economic, Social and Cultural Rights (ICESCR).[8] These refer to a range of social, cultural and economic rights found in articles 22–29 of the UNDHR. Legal obligations in relation to such rights are relatively 'soft'. The ICESCR has little direct influence on the ECHR (mainly a Convention of civil and political rights); though article 2 of the First Protocol is a less detailed right to education which echoes article 13 ICESCR.[9]

There are many other treaty-based instruments of international law that affect human rights and, though not directly binding on the ECtHR, are part of the general context within which the ECtHR interprets the ECHR.[10] Thus the UN Convention on the Elimination of all Forms of Discrimination Against Women was taken into account in determining the child's best interest test for the purposes of article 8 (**Neulinger v Switzerland**, app 41615/07, Grand Chamber judgment, 6 July 2010). The definition of torture in the UN Convention Against Torture was referred to in order to categorise police brutality under article 3 ECHR in **Selmouni v France** (2000) 29 EHRR 403.

The relationship of the ECHR to international law is not always comfortable.[11] Under the UN Charter resolutions of the UN Security Council have priority over other international law. In the context of the invasion of Iraq, detentions authorised by the UN have been incompatible with article 5 ECHR. In **R (Al-Jedda) v Secretary of State for Defence** [2007] UKHL 58 the House of Lords, held that there was no breach of article 5 to the extent necessary to fulfil the UN obligation (this case is pending before the ECtHR). General principles of international law can likewise create tension. The ECtHR, for instance, allowed state immunity to overreach a private law action alleging torture by foreign officials (**Al-Adsani v UK** (2002) 34 EHRR 11); though it held that the UK violated article 3 by handing over a prisoner to Iraqi authorities for possible execution even though the international authority of the UK to hold the prisoner had ceased (**Al-Saadoon v UK** app 61498/08, judgment of 2 March 2010).

Other international law, not UN based, also forms the context of ECtHR application of the ECHR.[12] **Neulinger**, for example, dealing with article 8 and family life, discussed the Convention dealing with child abduction produced under the auspices of The Hague Conference on Private International Law.

[13]Likewise it is essential to discuss customary international law, especially because of its current importance in the context of torture.

As well as treaty-based international law, the ECHR must also take into account customary international law, which is binding on states without their specific consent.[13] *Jus cogens* describes peremptory norms of this kind. Thus the ban on torture has this status so far as criminal law is concerned but the ECtHR interpreted the international and national case law and decided it did not have this status in respect of civil actions for damages (**Al-Adsani**).

[14]This is an interesting way of ending your answer which might easily be ignored. Apart from anything else it shows that you are aware of the importance of interpretative and procedural issues as well as just substantive rights.

Finally, as an instrument of international law, the ECHR is subject to other measures that apply to international law generally. In particular, the United Nations Vienna Convention on the Law of Treaties 1969 stipulates a range of principles dealing with general matters on how treaties, such as the Convention, should be interpreted.[14] The provision that treaties should be read in the light of their context, has often allowed the ECtHR to explain its decisions by reference to the ECHR's purpose: effective, practical, protection of human rights.

 ## Make your answer stand out

- A fuller discussion of developments prior to the formation of the United Nations could help with context as well as identifying instruments, such as the Geneva Conventions, which are still in issue. A general survey is in Smith (2010) (Chapter 2).

- Briefly describe and compare the features of some other regional developments with the ECHR. For instance, the African Charter on Human and Peoples' Rights gives greater prominence to the collective rights of 'peoples' rights compared with the possibly more individualistic approach of the ECHR.

- Make references to the Council of Europe as a source of principles bearing on human rights law and which the ECtHR takes into account. Thus other Conventions, recommendations, resolutions, declarations, etc, made by the various organs of the Council, can have a significant, persuasive, influence on the way the ECHR is interpreted.

- On the tensions between international law and human rights law you could also discuss the asset freezing cases (where the UN ordered individual's assets to be frozen without a fair hearing) – see *Kadi* v *Council of European Union* [2009] AC 1225 (an EU case) and *HM Treasury* v *Ahmed & Others* [2010] UKSC 2 (a UK case).

■ You could mention, as part of the context, more recent developments, such as the war crimes tribunals for Former Yugoslavia and Rwanda and, in particular, the Rome Statute which creates the International Criminal Court and gives a legal definition to war crimes and crimes against humanity.

! Don't be tempted to ...

■ Write too much in general terms on the various instruments of international law you mention. Remember, the focus of your answer should be the context within which the ECHR works and the influences of other aspects of international law on it.

■ Spend a lot of time on individual aspects of substantive rights. The question is looking for a general, thematic approach.

Question 2

The Council of Europe stands for both 'human rights' and 'democracy'. Discuss the view that, since human rights law can involve interferences with the will of the majority, these two concepts are contradictory.

Answer plan

→ Introduce the ideas of democracy and human rights in general terms, and note incompatibility in principle.

→ Discuss democracy as majority rule and show how aspects of human rights are necessary for coherence.

→ Introduce the complementary rather than contradictory relations of human rights and democracy.

→ Consider theoretical disagreements about the role of the courts.

→ Consider legal doctrines for ensuring mutual respect between courts, the executive and legislature.

Diagram plan

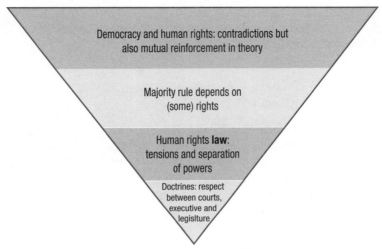

Democracy and human rights: contradictions but also mutual reinforcement in theory

Majority rule depends on (some) rights

Human rights **law**: tensions and separation of powers

Doctrines: respect between courts, executive and legislture

A printable version of this diagram is available from www.pearsoned.co.uk/lawexpressqa

Answer

¹Begin at a very abstract level by pointing out that neither term has a settled meaning.

Both democracy and human rights are contested concepts¹ with no agreed meaning and in respect of which a core idea or concept can be given expression in terms of different conceptions, many of which will not sit easily with each other.

The core idea of human rights (in its moral sense) is of some set of basic entitlements that ought to be enjoyed by all human beings, for the sufficient reason that they are human. These entitlements should be secured for all and respected notwithstanding benefits to other individuals or to the common good.²

²You will get credit for pointing out these conceptual points about human rights. They help to set you up for later arguments.

The basis of this moral account of human rights is disputed. Griffin (2001), for example, argues that it is simply personhood. Human rights are derived from the enlightenment conception of the person, the sense of autonomy: that human beings, in distinction from animals, are agents capable of reflecting on their own lives and, thereby, making choices which are appropriate for them. Others (e.g., in different ways, Finnis (1980) and Gearty (2005)) see human rights as connected with the conditions necessary for human flourishing.

³It is essential you make this point. The focus of the question is on human rights as law, not as a moral idea sounding in political theory (as significant as that may be).

But human rights also represent a 'movement' whose point is to ensure that these entitlements are protected as a matter of law.³ Since 1945 (inspired by the United Nations) many states have accepted the primary duty to secure human rights as part of their domestic law and also the supervisory jurisdiction of international courts and other institutions.

States have thus accepted limits to their sovereignty, not only in respect of other states but, crucially, over their own population. The question is whether, in a democratic state, this is necessarily a matter that can lead to a conflict of values, let alone political tensions.

⁴Continue by discussing the matter at a general level. Indeed a good structure for your answer is to move downwards from the general to discussion of issues of how human rights law is implemented.

⁵You should get credit for this because pointing out that human rights are inconsistent with violent dictatorship is hardly news; displaying a more subtle understanding of the kinds of regimes which, in principle, are hard to reconcile with human rights, will impress.

⁶But then develop the point to show how, even here, human rights can be, in theory, relevant.

At a general level there should not be a conflict.⁴ Humans are unavoidably dependent on others and live socially. Autonomy, in relation to processes for determining the common good, implies consent and rights of participation. Self-rule by the people is the underlying concept of democracy. It follows that it is not just fascist or Stalinist forms of government (based on theories of racial or class-based preference) which are excluded by human rights but also more gentle forms of autocracy, even enlightened ones. Thus a fully utilitarian government, based on the principle of maximising aggregate 'happiness' in society, would be one which, in principle, would subordinate human rights to that principle.⁵ Even here, though, human rights has a role since the calculation of aggregate happiness (certainly for Jeremy Bentham) relied on the principle that each person's interests are to be treated equally; a principle which invokes autonomy and is the ground of an enforceable right.⁶

⁷Having now moved on to discuss democracy it helps to show that even a simple majoritarian account of the concept is consistent, at a general level, with some individual entitlements.

There are many conceptions of democracy. If the term is taken to mean that the underlying principle of good government is the will of the majority, then there are obvious conflicts with human rights. One of the main benefits of human rights law is to protect unpopular individuals and minorities who might otherwise suffer from discrimination at the hands of the majority. However, even such a limited conception of democracy implies some important human rights,⁷ Majority rule implies political actions such as voting, communicating, assembly and protest, etc, through which the will of the majority can be identified and formulated. It is a contradiction of the principle of majority rule for a majority, at a particular time, to interfere with political freedom in order to secure its continuing dominance. Human rights are necessary in order to protect against this danger. Indeed for some writers, such as Gearty (2005), 'civil liberties' (defined in relation to political action) is one of the core values of human rights.

The same point can be raised in respect of other underlying principles which might be said to give a system its democratic character. A focus on political participation, for instance, must be one which necessarily protects individual human rights of association and assembly.

[8]Now move 'downwards' to discuss the tensions between democracy and human rights in terms of the practice of human rights law. It helps, and will gain credit, to situate the issues you discuss in terms of the European Convention on Human Rights as an example – about which you should be quite knowledgeable.

The reality is that, at least in European terms, the theoretical problems dissolve in practice.[8] There is no general tension between democracy and human rights since the one complements the other. The European Court of Human Rights, for instance, mandates no particular political system but asserts that democracy is the only system compatible with human rights. No particular conception of democracy is stipulated but it implies that the values of tolerance, broadmindedness and pluralism (and its correlating requirement that states be neutral on matters of belief) be part of the public reason of the state.

[9]Now move to the constitutional level (and then to the issues of deference, etc) at which the tension between democratic accountability and judicial interpretation of human rights is most closely felt.

Real tensions between the claims of democracy and human rights are most likely to be focused at the constitutional level.[9] Human rights, as law, is likely to mean a re-balancing of the constitution and the inherent separation of powers by a relative increase in the power of the judiciary. Through adherence to human rights, issues may no longer be dealt with in the way the majority of MPs wish, even though they are elected by, and accountable to, the people.

[10]You will get credit for giving an example of your point from academic writing. The Griffith article is, of course, famous; it helps to show, by citing Tomkins, that the tradition is still alive.

In Britain, for instance, supporters of a 'political constitution' (e.g. Griffith (1979), Tomkins (2005)) are sceptical about human rights.[10] Human rights, on this view, depend upon untestable metaphysical claims (that rights are 'natural') or assertions about matters on which there is disagreement (that rights are 'self-evident'). In fact, they suggest, human rights justify what are, in effect, political claims like any other (claims for powers, liberties or resources). It is wrong to remove them from the political realm to be resolved by judges.

[11]Now move on to consider some of the ways in which, through the structure of the law, the relations between courts and legislature and executive are structured in a democracy which also respects human rights in its law.

In practice this becomes a question of how human rights law can be applied compatibly with democracy; rather than a dispute between human rights and democracy (in which one must exclude the other).[11] Thus the power of the courts depends, for instance, on the structure of the domestic human rights law and the scope for interpretation that the law allows a court, or even whether courts are allowed to invalidate statutes. Likewise, the courts have developed concepts like (at the international level) the 'margin of appreciation' and (at the domestic level) 'deference'. In such terms the courts try to distinguish those issues which they are best suited to decide (bound by independence, impartiality, fair procedures, etc, and not subject to election) from those human rights issues which are best determined by legislature or executive,[12] with the courts taking merely a supervisory role to prevent decisions which undermine the absolute core or essence of the right in question.

[12]Noting these legal concepts helps you make your point effectively – but ensure you express the different 'levels' at which these concepts work.

Any theoretical tensions between human rights and democracy are not debilitating in practice. The practical focus is on the integration of the two concepts, as courts, legislature and executive seek to protect human rights in ways that respect the proper roles of each.

✓ Make your answer stand out

- Say more about the theory of rights. The idea that rights in some way 'trump' arguments about the common good is discussed in Ronald Dworkin's work, especially his early book (Dworkin, 1977).

- In the section dealing with the constitutional 'level' you could explore the different concepts and understandings of deference more explicitly. You could bring out the argument between, for example, those who believe that courts should defer on principle when this is necessary to respect the democratic authority of the decision in question and those for whom deference is just a reflection of the factual issue of whether courts, Parliament or the executive are best placed (in terms of knowledge of the issues, etc) to make the decision (compare Kavanagh (2009) and Hickman (2010)).

- Likewise you could introduce and discuss dialogue theory. This is the idea that the complementary relationship between human rights and democracy is expressed in that the courts engage in a dialogue on human rights with Parliament and the executive. Through measures such as s 4 HRA 1998 the courts can express a provisional view of what human rights law requires on a difficult issue; but then the issue is returned to Parliament and the executive for a final, statutory, determination of what is required (for discussion see, e.g., Hickman (2010) and Nicol (2006)).

! Don't be tempted to ...

■ Confine your answer to general philosophy and theory of rights. The question clearly relates to human rights law – general rights specified as rules of law.

■ Write about substantive rights, such as rights relating to political action. The question is clearly focused on democracy and human rights as general ideas and not on substantive law.

■ Explore the Council of Europe – it is mentioned in the question but should not be the focus of your answer.

🖎 Question 3

By reference to the provisions of the European Convention on Human Rights (ECHR), explain the success of the European Court of Human Rights (ECtHR) in attracting applications. Include in your answer discussion of attempts to deal with the Court's backlog of cases.

Answer plan

→ Introduce the enforcement mechanisms in Part Two of the Convention.

→ Discuss the right of individual application.

→ Discuss matters which contribute to success: broadly defined rights, rights for 'everyone'.

→ Discuss expansion after 1989 but note how political conflict also creates applications.

→ Discuss Protocol 11 and Protocol 14 as attempts to deal with the case load.

Diagram plan

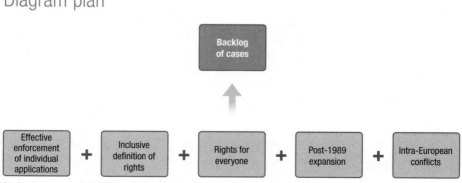

A printable version of this diagram is available from www.pearsoned.co.uk/lawexpressqa

Answer

Fundamental to the Convention's success is the enforcement mechanism in Section Two of the Convention which gives individuals a sense that applying to the ECtHR is worthwhile.[1] Section Two creates the ECtHR, which adjudicates claims brought to it which allege that a signatory state has violated one or more of the Convention rights. By signing the Convention, a state accepts primary responsibility for securing the rights and freedoms defined in Section One (article 1)[2] and that it will provide adequate procedures and remedies in domestic law for alleged breaches (article 13). The ECtHR, exercising what it often calls a supervisory power, is the final authority on whether this has been done successfully in particular cases. States agree to abide by the ECtHR's decisions, which may mean making necessary changes to their domestic law and practice (article 46). The execution of a judgment is supervised by the Council of Europe's (CE) Committee of Ministers which is able, under the procedure in article 46(4) and (5), to take 'measures' against the defaulting state.[3]

The right of individual application under article 34 perhaps best explains the ECtHR's attraction.[4] The right is in addition to inter-state applications under article 33. Since Protocol 11 (1998) signatory states agree not to hinder members of their population who seek to bring cases against them (originally the right could only be exercised if the states agreed, independently of signing the Convention).[5] The European system contrasts with, for example, the UN's International Covenant on Civil and Political Rights in which the right of individual application is still one that must be conceded by the state.[6] Individual application means that specific, individual, cases can be dealt with. This is in contrast to the cases of systematic and widespread abuse, which are likely to be the reason for inter-state actions (as well as generating many individual applications). Also states will only bring actions against other states if to do so is consistent with their overriding diplomatic interests.

Of course, article 34 is only a right of an individual to apply to the Strasbourg authorities. The case must be admissible,[7] and there are significant requirements, such as the need to have exhausted domestic remedies, or to be alleging a breach of a right which is found in the Convention and which the state concerned had agreed

---

[1] Get to the main point immediately, by referring to the enforcement mechanisms of the Court.

[2] This point is essential and will get you credit – it shows you understand the basic point of the Convention system.

[3] Giving this detail impresses – it shows the examiner you are not just familiar with the substantive rights in Section One but also can give chapter and verse on the procedural issues by which the Convention is made effective.

[4] This point is vital; you would lose credit drastically if you don't make it clearly and early on in your answer.

[5] Demonstrating a bit of historical knowledge of the Convention shows you are aware of developments which are crucial to its continuing success.

[6] By this point you get credit for showing your awareness of other international instruments to which the ECHR relates.

[7] Now move on to discuss admissibility – this is vital since it allows you, later, to mention the problems which have caused the backlog of cases.

to secure at the time the events in question took place (article 35). Major factors contributing to the ECtHR's workload and backlog of cases are the processing of a large number of inadmissible cases (over 90%) and dealing with continuing cases about an issue where the Court has already found a violation. Prior to 1998 and Protocol 11, admissibility was largely dealt with by the European Commission of Human Rights but now it is a matter for a single judge (Protocol 14), Committee or Chamber of the Court itself.

[8]Now move on to consider matters of substance as explaining the appeal of the Convention. In doing so you will get credit for widening the range of your discussion, which is not just focused on procedure.

A second important reason for the Convention's success, which reflects the issues brought to it because of individual petition, relates to the broad definition of some rights as reflected in admissible cases.[8] In an early case, **Marckx v Belgium** (1979–80) 2 EHRR 330, the ECtHR declared that Belgium's laws on illegitimacy breached article 8. Judge Fitzmaurice argued that such an issue was outside the proper scope of article 8 which, he thought, was confined to guarding against state practices which echo those of fascist or Stalinist dictatorship, and should not be applied to the ordinary laws. But he was dissenting. From such of its earliest decisions, the Court has admitted and adjudicated cases which relate to laws and policies chosen by democratic procedures in largely democratic states. These are laws and policies which do not in any way threaten the rise of totalitarianism, which do not involve widespread and systematic abuse and which, sometimes, do not involve direct state action at all but are to do with the legal regulation of private relations and personal status.

A third reason for the success of the Convention may also relate to the fact that article 1 requires states to secure Convention rights for 'everyone' within their territory. Thus the Court can receive applications from individuals who are, perhaps, marginalised in their society and disadvantaged in terms of domestic law. Prisoners, the mentally ill, homosexuals, gypsies, children, political protestors and radicals, etc, are examples of groups which may be the victims of prejudice or of official disfavour which is reflected in the domestic law and remedies available to them. They are able to claim fundamental rights before the Strasbourg court.

[9]This is an obvious but important point which helps to explain the huge leap in the number of cases during the 1990s.

The number of individual applications has expanded dramatically following the 'reunification' of Europe and the entry of 'Eastern-bloc' countries into the Council of Europe, including Russia and other one-time members of the USSR.[9] A strength of the system is some degree of a common heritage between members of the Council of Europe and, generally, good diplomatic relations between them. When conflict does occur, however, it can also generate not just inter-state actions but also a large number of individual applications. Examples are the Turkish invasion of Cyprus in 1974 and, more recently, the conflict between Russia and Georgia over South Ossetia in 2008.[10]

For reasons such as those given above, the Convention system has generated a large number of individual applications. Such 'success' has caused, and continues to cause, serious problems in terms of the ECtHR's workload.

Protocol 11 brought about major changes in 1998.[11] The original Court and Commission were both part-time and the assumption was that their caseload would be relatively light. This assumption was based on the primary responsibility of states to secure rights and give remedies in domestic law, mentioned above. Such states, being members of the Council of Europe, have to be pluralist and democratic states and must comply with the rule of law.[12] Under Protocol 11 the old Court and Commission were abolished and replaced by a full-time court with speeded-up procedures, especially regarding admissibility.

Nevertheless, the backlog continues. In 2009 about 120,000 pending applications were reported by the Council of Europe. Protocol 14 has been introduced.[13] It simplifies the admissibility process allowing, in some cases, a single judge to declare a clear case inadmissible. It has also introduced a new inadmissibility test: that the applicant has not suffered significant disadvantage and respect for human rights does not require the case be considered.[14] Whether it will succeed in reducing the backlog, in particular the unmeritorious cases, remains to be seen.

Though the ECtHR is clearly successful, its 'success' should be tempered to the extent that the number of applications suggests states are not always fulfilling their primary duty to secure rights adequately.[15]

[10]This point will gain credit because it shows you are not overly focused on the detail of individual applications from democratic societies but that you are aware of some of the big areas of conflict that erupt from time to time in Europe.

[11]Now move on to note some of the relevant changes made by Protocol 11. You will get credit for showing you are aware of major developments which relate to dealing with the number of applications received.

[12]This shows you understand the basic joining requirements of the Council of Europe and will get credit.

[13]The question clearly requires you to refer to Protocol 14.

[14]Make sure you mention this caveat regarding the significant disadvantage test. It shows you have read the full text and have not oversimplified.

[15]End with a conclusion that builds on some of the points you have made earlier.

✓ **Make your answer stand out**

■ Write more on the contrast with International Covenant on Civil and Political Rights and its system of enforcement. Although there is the optional protocol (allowing individual application) the main way is through the self-reporting mechanism to the Human Rights Committee. The Committee can make critical comments but does not, under the treaty, have similar authority to that enjoyed by the ECtHR under the European approach. For discussion see, on the Covenant generally, Nowak (2005) and Joseph et al., (2004).

■ Indeed, you could refer to other human rights instruments, both UN and regional, to draw contrasts with the success and practice of the European model.

■ Make more of the point that the Court has adopted an inclusive conception of rights and of the appropriate issues to which they refer. For further discussion of this in a historical context, see Nicol, (2005).

■ You could discuss more the role of the Council of Europe in helping to enforce the judgments of the Court and, in a sense more importantly, helping to create a Europe-wide political culture in which acknowledgement of and respect for human rights is paramount.

❗ **Don't be tempted to ...**

■ Go into too much detail on the facts and figures from Strasbourg on the number of cases etc. The question expressly asks you to discuss the popularity of the Convention primarily in relation to its terms, such as article 34, etc.

■ Spend too much time discussing individual cases. This is a very general question which will test your broad understanding of the Strasbourg processes rather than individual cases.

■ Spend too much time on the details of article 34 and who does or does not have standing to apply to the Court. The point is that there is a right of individual application. Discussion of broader questions, like the ban on applicants who are not the direct victim, will not improve your answer.

📝 Question 4

Discuss and evaluate the impact of the European Convention on Human Rights (ECHR) on the law of the United Kingdom prior to the coming into force of the Human Rights Act in October 2000.

Answer plan

→ Discuss international law in relation to domestic UK law.

→ Introduce UK obligations under article 1 ECHR; show how adverse Strasbourg judgments led to changes to law and practice.

→ Discuss the influence of the Convention on the interpretation of statutes.

→ Discuss the influence of the Convention on the development of judicial review.

→ Discuss the influence of the Convention on the development of private law.

Diagram plan

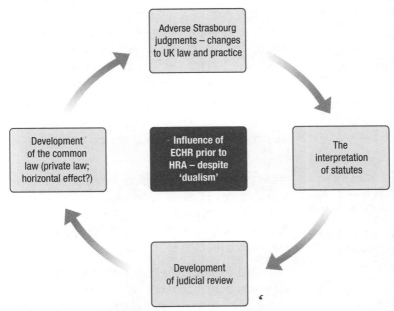

A printable version of this diagram is available from www.pearsoned.co.uk/lawexpressqa

Answer

¹Begin by discussing the ECHR as an obligation in international law on the UK.

The United Kingdom (UK) was one of the principal drafters and first signatory of the European Convention on Human Rights (ECHR) in 1950.¹ In 1966 it allowed anyone within its territory the right of individual petition to the European Court of Human Rights (ECtHR)

[2]Noting this point and, in particular, the 1998 changes, suggests a general understanding of the Convention and a historical perspective – it will gain credit.

[3]Move on to discuss the status of the ECHR in UK domestic law.

[4]Having established that the ECHR does not apply directly in the UK, now move on to reminding us of the general approach in England prior to the HRA 1998.

[5]Move on to discuss the impact of the responsibility of states, such as the UK, under the Convention. Your ability to cite Convention articles in Part Two of the Convention will impress.

[6]Using 'accessible and foreseeable' suggests to the examiner that you understand the principle of 'legality'.

– which, until the Protocol 11 reforms of 1998, was a voluntary obligation.[2]

Signing the ECHR creates obligations in international law which are accepted by the UK. However, under the 'dualist' conception of international law, it is not part of the domestic law of the UK. The ECtHR has no jurisdiction in the UK and its decisions do not directly affect the legal rights of claimants in ways which are enforced by UK courts.[3] Nor would a UK court grant a coercive order against a minister to compel adherence to an ECtHR decision and (unlike EU law) it is improbable that a declaratory remedy would be issued stating that UK law is incompatible with the Convention.

The traditional approach in the UK has been a focus on liberties rather than rights.[4] The general principle of the common law has been to presume in favour of individual subjective liberty and property. This can be interfered with by specific prohibitions found in statute or common law. Acts of Parliament which interfere with individual liberties are (normally) narrowly constructed.

Although treaty-based international law cannot be directly enforced in the UK it does, nevertheless, create obligations on the state which can include requiring changes to law and practice. This applies to the ECHR.

Article 1 requires states to secure for everyone the rights in the Convention and by article 46 to 'abide by' the judgments of the ECtHR in which they were parties.[5] This duty meant that, prior to HRA 1988, UK government and Parliament needed to change laws or administrative practices.

There were, for example, a number of areas in which state power was exercised on the basis of the Royal Prerogative or the underlying freedom of the common law. The absence or inadequacy of accessible and foreseeable regulation of powers which interfered with, for example, private life, was incompatible with Convention.[6] Thus authorisation for telephone tapping had to be put on an effective and sufficiently detailed statutory basis. This followed **Malone v UK** (1985) 7 EHRR 14 and resulted in the Interception of Communications Act 1987. Likewise at least one of the reasons for establishing the Security Service on a statutory basis, including a statutory process for obtaining warrants to permit otherwise unlawful

[7]A second example deals with the need to change the law. The point is that you will get credit for distinguishing different types of problem with UK law rather than mixing them altogether.

[8]Third, discuss changes to administrative practices; again you should get credit for differentiation.

surveillance, was this need to meet the 'legality' requirements of the Convention (Security Service Act 1989, etc).

In other instances it was necessary to change existing statutes.[7] In **A.D.T. v United Kingdom** (2001) 31 EHRR 33, for example, the ECtHR held that UK law discriminated against male homosexuals regarding consensual activity in private. This contributed to changes brought about by the Sexual Offences Act 2000. An example of a change to administrative practice[8] caused by an adverse Strasbourg judgment is the removal of the Ministry of Defence's ban on homosexuals in the armed forces. This followed the finding that the ban violated article 8 in **Smith v UK** (2000) 29 EHRR 493. Adverse judgments were not necessarily the sole cause of but rather reinforced or contributed to an already developing desire for change.

As state institutions, UK courts must accept appropriate responsibility for the UK's international obligations. So, subject to the ultimate supremacy of Parliament, they may be influenced by Convention principles in the way the law is developed. There is a general principle that, although international and domestic law are separate systems, they nevertheless complement each other. The former, including the Convention, is a 'persuasive and pervasive' influence on the latter[9] (**R v Lyons** [2002] UKHL 44).

[9]You will be expected to avoid giving the impression that 'dualism' means rigid separation.

[10]You will get credit for this point and it enables you to stress that the point in issue is the common law developing in line with the Convention and, emphatically, not a takeover of the common law by Convention rights.

Thus, prior to the HRA 1998, it was already a principle of statutory interpretation that ambiguous words in an Act should be interpreted for compatibility with Convention rights. At the same time English courts were emphasising the importance of 'fundamental' or 'constitutional' rights in the common law, not dependent on the Convention.[10] The principle of 'legality' means that general words in statutes cannot authorise secondary legislation (**R v Lord Chancellor ex p Witham** [1998] 2 WLR 849 or executive action (**R v Secretary of State for the Home Department ex p Simms** [2000] AC 115) which denies such rights. Of course, if the literal meaning is clear and not absurd then it must be given effect, fundamental or human rights notwithstanding (as in **Lyons**).[11]

[11]The examiner will be looking out for your understanding of the differences between UK law and Convention principles – that you can show why the HRA 1988 was felt necessary. You will get credit for reminders of the constitutional position of the courts in the UK system such as embodied in this sentence.

[12]Having discussed statutory interpretation you should now move on to judicial review.

Prior to the HRA 1998, the persuasive influence of the Convention could be observed in relation to judicial review.[12] Two lines of decisions, do not sit easily with each other. First, under ordinary principle of administrative law, decisions must be taken on relevant grounds. However, the courts did not impose a strict duty on officials

[13]Although you are not being examined on judicial review itself, you do need to show awareness of general principles.

[14]You will get credit for showing awareness of recent cases which have dealt with the issue of the relationship between ordinary judicial review and proportionality.

[15]Again, a crucial point that the examiner will be looking for concerning the essential difference between Convention law and ordinary judicial review.

[16]Be careful not to suggest wholesale adoption by the courts of Convention rights. Most of the time the autonomy of the common law is not challenged.

to take Convention rights into account as relevant when exercising statutory powers (recently confirmed, by a majority, in **R (Hurst) v London Northern District Coroner** [2007] UKHL 13, dealing with pre-HRA events). Secondly, though, where human rights are obviously relevant, the courts have developed a principle of more intensive scrutiny.[13] This requires a fuller, more closely reasoned, justification, than under ordinary judicial review, for an official decision which is at odds with Convention rights. This 'super-**Wednesbury'** level of judicial scrutiny of official reasoning has developed into something close to the Convention test of 'propor- tionality' (**Doherty v Birmingham City Council** [2008] UKHL 57).[14]

Despite this, it remained the case that, with ordinary judicial review, a properly taken and reasoned decision could not be set aside for failing to protect Convention rights (as in **Smith**).[15]

Where the common law was uncertain, the courts could be persuaded by the values in the Convention. This is not to suggest enforcement of the Convention by the back door but a recognition that, where appropriate, the common law should develop harmoniously with the Convention.[16] The Convention was, in fact, seldom the actual ground of the decision. Thus in **Derbyshire County Council v Times Newspapers** [1993] AC 534 it was held that a local authority could not protect its reputation through ordinary defamation. The reason was the 'chilling' effect this would have on freedom of expression. Though the Court of Appeal saw the decision as a reflection of Convention values in article 10, for the House of Lords the outcome was achieved by reliance on fundamental values in the common law.

Senior UK judges were among the main supporters of a Human Rights Act of some kind. It is clear that prior to the HRA 1998 they were already using it, at least as a source of legal principles, to develop UK law.

✓ Make your answer stand out

- You could widen the range of issues by referring to adverse Strasbourg decisions in prisoners' cases. Some of these led eventually to important changes in the UK on matters such as whether prisoners could pursue cases against the prison authorities in court (*Golder* v *UK* (1979–80) 1 EHRR 524) and the degree of executive involvement on controlling the length of time spent in prison of various types of serious offenders (e.g. *Weeks* v *UK* (1988) 10 EHRR 293).

- You can impress by referring to the fact that the extent to which principles of judicial review and scrutiny of administrative action under Convention rights are merging, is still a problem. The courts have not fully committed themselves, though, on whether proportionality is now a standard common to both 'ordinary' judicial review and the Convention (*Somerville* v *Scottish Ministers* [2007] UKHL 44; *Doherty* v *Birmingham City Council* [2008] UKHL 57.).

- Briefly discuss 'indirect horizontal effect' in the context of the influence of the Convention on private law (compare, for instance, Buxton (2000) with Hunt (1998) and Wade (2000).This will show you are aware of one of the tricky issues about the impact of the Convention, both before and after the enactment of the HRA 1998.

! Don't be tempted to ...

- Write too much about international law in general. You will use up too much space and you must focus on the impact of the Convention prior to the HRA 1988.

- Go overboard on the issues raised by the cases you are examining. In this question address the cases from the point of view of what they say, in general terms, about the pre-HRA impact of the Convention.

- Generally overplay the impact. In your approach do not underplay the general resilience of the common law prior to the HRA 1988. The Convention was influential but not adopted wholesale; Parliamentary supremacy was respected.

? Question 5

Able is shot dead by the police in controversial circumstances.

Advise the following on whether there are procedural obstacles to their taking a case to the European Court of Human Rights (ECtHR).

(a) Able's nephew who believes there was a violation of article 2, the right to life. His action in the High Court in England fails on the sole grounds that clear statutory authority prevents him from challenging the police evidence. He applies directly to the ECtHR.

(b) The National Victims Association (fictitious) which is a non-governmental organisation (NGO) and HM Commissioner for Victims (fictitious), a statutory body with powers and duties to assist victims.

(c) TV Corp, a large media corporation, is prevented by an injunction from access to relevant information. They think this is a breach of article 10. In fact they are not disadvantaged since the information is available to them through their US subsidiary and they have reported the matter freely.

Answer plan

→ Introduce the rules of individual applications and the admissibility criteria in article 34 and 35.

→ Discuss specific issues about 'victims' and whether the nephew is an indirect victim.

→ Discuss whether the nephew has exhausted domestic remedies.

→ Discuss the standing of NGOs and the circumstances in which they can be 'victims'; likewise consider whether a public body, such as the Commissioner, can apply to the ECtHR.

→ Note that corporations can apply under article 34 but consider the application of the 'significant disadvantage' criterion to TV Corp.

Diagram plan

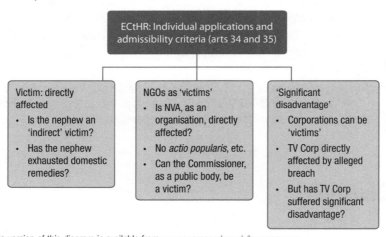

ECtHR: Individual applications and admissibility criteria (arts 34 and 35)

Victim: directly affected
- Is the nephew an 'indirect' victim?
- Has the nephew exhausted domestic remedies?

NGOs as 'victims'
- Is NVA, as an organisation, directly affected?
- No *actio popularis*, etc.
- Can the Commissioner, as a public body, be a victim?

'Significant disadvantage'
- Corporations can be 'victims'
- TV Corp directly affected by alleged breach
- But has TV Corp suffered significant disadvantage?

A printable version of this diagram is available from www.pearsoned.co.uk/lawexpressqa

Answer

[1]Begin by identifying the basic issue with which the question deals.

The European Court of Human Rights (ECtHR) will not accept an individual application unless the applicant has proper standing, as defined by article 34. Nor will it deal with such an application unless admissibility criteria in article 35 are satisfied.[1] Initially applications are made to the Registry. Admissibility decisions are made on the basis of articles 28 and 29, and in accordance with the Rules of Court.[2] Clearly inadmissible cases can be rejected by a single judge.

[2]You will show a broader understanding if you make this point.

Other applications can be declared inadmissible by a Committee. If not inadmissible at this threshold stage, the case goes to a Chamber which decides the merits but can also deal with issues of admissibility if these are not fully agreed. Single judge and Committee decisions that a case is inadmissible are final. A Grand Chamber, rehearing a decision by a Chamber, can also deal again with any admissibility issues which are in issue (e.g. **Yumak v Turkey** (2009) 48 EHRR 4).[3]

[4]Though not strictly relevant, making the point about inter-state cases shows your wider understanding.

[5]Make sure you learn this phrase in revision and use it. Any other term which is merely approximate is likely to make it harder to make your points.

[6]It strengthens your case if you explain not only what the Court accepts but also why it does so.

Individual applications are dealt with under article 34 ECHR (inter-state cases are dealt with differently under article 33).[4] The applicant must claim to be a 'victim' of a violation of a Convention right by one of the High Contracting Parties. In **Eckle v Germany** (1983) 5 EHRR 1 the ECtHR defined a victim as a person 'directly affected'[5] by the actions which caused the alleged breach. In one obvious sense, Able's nephew does not fit this category. However, the ECtHR interprets its rules in order to make the protection of the Convention effective and, to do so, will accept applications from indirect victims[6] in appropriate circumstances. In **Yasa v Turkey** (1999) 28 EHRR 408, the Court admitted a case alleging breaches of articles 2 and 3 brought by the direct victim's nephew.

[7]You will get credit for displaying a general understanding of the international law context within which the Convention operates.

The nephew applies under article 34 directly after losing in the High Court. Under article 34 an applicant should have exhausted domestic remedies. This reflects recognised rules of international law and embodies the point that the primary responsibility for securing human rights lies, under the Convention, with the High Contracting Parties.[7] Normally this requires an applicant to have pursued his or her case to the highest court in the land capable of giving a final and definitive ruling (usually the Supreme Court in the UK).

[8]It will impress if you don't just lay down the general rule but also show sensitivity to the exceptions and qualifications which apply in practice.

The Court, conscious of its need to be effective, interprets this rule flexibly. Non-exhaustion would not be a reason for an application to be inadmissible if the available remedies were clearly inadequate or available in theory but not in practice[8] (as was accepted as being the case in **Öcalan v Turkey** (2005) 41 EHRR 45). The question refers to clear statutory authority preventing the nephew from succeeding in his article 2 action against the police. Under the Human Rights Act 1998 (HRA 1998) the best the nephew can expect is a declaration of incompatibility – which does not alter the law or the applicant's legal situation. In **Burden & Burden v UK** (2008) 47 EHRR 38 the

[9]Making additional points such as this can strengthen your answer by showing you have read and attended to the material.

ECtHR held that the applicant did not need to take a case to the House of Lords in a similar situation since a s 4 HRA declaration was not an effective remedy for a violation of a Convention right. It noted, though, that if the UK was consistent in its practice of always responding to a declaration by putting right the defect in the law, such a declaration might become an effective remedy.[9]

The National Victims Association (NVA) is an NGO. Article 34 expressly says that NGOs can apply to the Court. But the NVA has not been directly affected. Applications from NGOs can be received in respect of laws or actions which affect the activities or status of the association itself. However, the ECtHR will not accept an *actio populationis* by which a case is brought on behalf of the public or a class of the public, such as victims generally.[10] Nor will it accept cases based upon a general disapproval in abstract terms of a law or practice (see, for example, **Klass v Germany** (1979–80) 2 EHRR 214). Likewise, an organisation cannot usually bring an action solely on behalf of its members. Representative actions are possible but the ECtHR requires express consent by the person represented and there is no evidence in the question of such consent[11] (e.g. **Zentralrat DSRR v Germany** (1997) 23 EHRR 7 CD 209).

[10]Having made the point that NGOs can apply under article 34, move on to point out why, in the case, the Association will not be a victim.

[11]You will get credit for considering representative actions – showing the width of your understanding.

For similar reasons as apply to the NVA, any application by HM Commissioner for Victims will be inadmissible. There is an additional point. Article 34 allows applications by any 'person, non-governmental organisation or group'. It follows that a 'governmental' organisation is excluded. This includes a body which 'participates' in government, like a local council (**Danderyds Kommun v Sweden,** App 52559/99, decision of 7 June 2001). It is likely to extend to a statutory, public body such as the Commissioner.

[12]You will get credit for showing you understand what the legal status of a corporation is …

There is no procedural barrier to a corporation having human rights and applying successfully to the ECtHR. A corporation is a 'person', albeit an artificial creation of the law, and is not excluded by article 34.[12] It has rights and liabilities in its own name independently of its owners, managers or employees. Corporations can enjoy all Convention rights bar those, like the prohibition on torture, that only make sense in relation to natural persons. The right to peaceful enjoyment of possessions (article 1 of the First Protocol, is the only article that makes express reference to 'legal persons'.)[13]

[13]… and for showing how it has 'human rights' under the Convention.

TV Corp claims to be a victim of a violation of article 10. It is clearly directly affected by the alleged breach. However, the question suggests that it has not been significantly disadvantaged by the alleged breach. Lack of significant disadvantage is a reason by which the Court can hold an application inadmissible. This is a new criterion of admissibility introduced by Protocol 14 to the Convention.[14] It is one of a number of measures aiming to deal with the backlog of unmeritorious cases pending before the court. In **Ionescu v Romania** (2010) 51 EHRR SE7, the applicant had lost a breach of contract case worth 90 Euros. Since this was, for him, a small sum the ECtHR found the application inadmissible.

[14]This point is clearly signalled in the question and you need to discuss it.

The new article 34 does, however, allow the ECtHR still to deal with a case where the applicant has not suffered significant disadvantage if required by the overriding need to protect human rights.[15] So, the Court's assessment of the importance of the issue under article 10 will be important. Also, such a case cannot be rejected if it has not been duly considered by a domestic tribunal. This does not apply here since a domestic court has ordered an injunction.

[15]You will get credit for this – as so often, you give the examiner confidence in your ability when you show you understand both the general legal point and the qualifications or exceptions that apply.

 Make your answer stand out

- When qualifying the idea of victims being directly affected, you could also note that a specific measure of implementation against the applicant is not always necessary. The fact that the applicant could, potentially, be directly affected can be sufficient. See, for example, *Open Door Counselling* v *Ireland* (1993) 15 EHRR 244.

- A fuller discussion of Protocol 14, perhaps with reference to its delayed introduction, could embellish your writing on the 'significant disadvantage' point. For analysis see Greer (2005). Few believe that Protocol 14 is enough to resolve the backlog of cases and mentioning this will impress the examiner. Mowbray (2006) explores some of the options for further reform.

- You will get credit if you note that, despite the general principle against *actio popularis* and its refusal to hear abstract cases, the Court can give advisory opinions on general issues under the provisions in articles 47–49. You will impress if you also note that where there is a law or state practice that has created a systemic breach of the Convention with a large number of actual and potential victims, the Court sometimes recognises this and makes a judgment that, in effect, requires a change in the general law on behalf of a large class of potential victims (see *Scordino* v *Italy* (1) (2007) 45 EHRR 7).

! Don't be tempted to ...

■ Discuss in any detail the substantive rights, specifically article 2 and article 10 which are referred to in the question. It is clear that the question is about admissibility rules before the Court of Human Rights.

■ Write extensively on other admissibility criteria, found in article 35, on issues such as the need to apply within six months, the rule against anonymous applications and the grounds, based on the lack of merits, on which an application can be refused. These are important matters but are not the focus of the question.

The Human Rights Act 1998

2

How this topic may come up in exams

There can be problem questions but essays are often more likely. Remember questions will be testing knowledge of the Act and not the Convention articles (so you will mainly refer to 'sections' not 'articles' – don't get confused). General themes to look out for include the extent to which it is a 'bill of rights' or merely gives effect to the ECHR and the effect it has on the separation of powers and the constitutional role of the judiciary. Specific questions are likely to test your understanding of the interpretative duty (ss 3, 4 and 10) and of public authorities (ss 6, 7, 8 and 9).

Attack the question

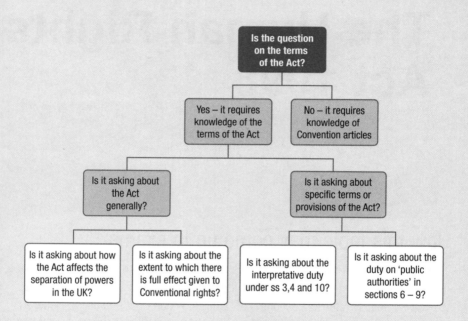

❓ Question 1

By reference to the reasons for its enactment and to its terms, discuss whether the Human Rights Act 1998 has radically changed the relationship of courts and Parliament under the United Kingdom's constitution.

Answer plan

→ Discuss the main reason why the HRA 1988 was enacted.

→ Introduce the idea of a constitutional balance between the courts and Parliament.

→ Discuss s 3 (statutory interpretation) and s 4 (declaration of incompatibility), including their constitutional effects.

→ Discuss s 6, including s 6(2) and consider the relationship between the courts and the executive.

→ Relate the terms of the Act to some general perspectives on the HRA 1998.

Diagram plan

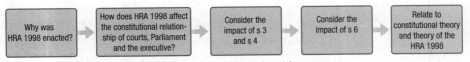

A printable version of this diagram is available from www.pearsoned.co.uk/lawexpressqa

Answer

A principal purpose of enactment was to give those with a well-grounded claim of a violation of the ECHR the ability to test that claim in a UK court and, if proved, to obtain an enforceable remedy. In this way the UK would give fuller effect to its duty under articles 1 and 13 of the Convention[1] to provide effective remedies to victims within the UK's jurisdiction. Until the Act the 'dualist' approach to international law meant that the Convention could not be directly applied in UK courts. It had an increasingly important influence but this was persuasive only and could not stand up to unambiguously incompatible statutes (**R v Lyons** [2002] UKHL 44). From its inception, therefore, there is space for tension with Parliamentary sovereignty.

[1] It impresses examiners if you show you understand broader aspects of the Convention and the relevance of different articles.

This tension is found in a degree of re-balancing of the 'checks and balances' of the UK constitution.

The Human Rights Act 1998 (HRA 1998) that emerged has brought about a gradual reconfiguration of the separation of powers in the UK. Unlike some Bills of Rights, the HRA 1998 does not give a court the power to invalidate an Act of Parliament. Section 3 says that primary and secondary legislation (whenever enacted) must be 'read and given effect' in a way that is compatible with the Convention rights in Schedule 1 'so far as it is possible to do so'. If such an interpretation is not 'possible' then the statute remains valid (s 3(1)(a) and (b)).[2] In this way (as the White Paper claimed) ultimate Parliamentary sovereignty is retained.[3]

The courts, not Parliament, interpret s 3.[4] Under the ordinary canons of statutory interpretation, ambiguities in a statute can be interpreted in a way that achieves compatibility with Convention rights. It has been held, therefore, that s 3, if it is to add to the law, authorises the courts to interpret statutes in ways which go beyond the clear meaning,[5] under the literal rule, of the texts (**Ghaidan v Godin-Mendoza** [2004] UKHL 30). Words may be read in or taken out, expressly wide discretions read down, etc, in order to achieve compatibility. There is possible tension here with the duty to give effect to the intention of Parliament (such as the controversial interpretion of Parliament's carefully chosen 'rape-shield' rules in **R v A** [2001] UKHL 25).

But s 3 preserves the supremacy of Parliament. The courts may interpret, not legislate.[6] Of course this is a hard distinction to make in practice. Where the will of Parliament is clear (especially if recent) or where achieving compatibility would mean going 'against the grain' of a statute (**Ghaidan**), the courts recognise that it would be constitutionally illegitimate for them to intervene (e.g. **R (Anderson) v Secretary of State for the Home Department** [2002] UKHL 46). In addition, achieving compatibility may require complex policy changes. In terms of legitimate decision taking, these decisions should be authorised by Parliament. But, also, they are likely to involve wide-ranging considerations which courts are procedurally and institutionally incompetent to undertake.

Where it is not possible to achieve compatibility under s 3, a court must give effect to the incompatible law. A senior court (e.g. High Court) may issue a 'declaration of incompatibility'[7] (s 4). This does

[2]Make sure that you show understanding of the actual terms of the HRA 1998. This is a clear requirement of the question and must be fulfilled.

[3]The question is about the constitutional effects of the Act so make sure, at least, that you refer to Parliamentary sovereignty.

[4]Gain credit by giving by showing your understanding of what is 'possible' for a court to do under s 3. Illustration from case law strengthens your answer.

[5]This point has been stressed by the courts. You will get credit by showing awareness of the presumptions about the meaning of words in statute that are already there, HRA 1998 notwithstanding.

[6]Move on to discuss what is not possible under the Act by exploring the 'interpret not legislate' distinction and the constitutional reasons for it.

[7]Introduce the declaration of incompatibility. Make sure you indicate that only the more senior courts (listed in s 4) have this power.

not affect the validity of the law nor the legal rights of the parties. Following a declaration, the government can do nothing, propose new legislation to Parliament or make fast track changes using the 'remedial order' procedure in s 10 and Sch 2. This has limited, though possibly effective, Parliamentary scrutiny.

[8]This is important if the idea is that s 4 reintroduced Parliament into the constitutional equation. The point about the effect of a declaration in practice is important but often not recognised, so mentioning it will gain credit.

A declaration of incompatibility, by returning the matter to the executive and legislature, goes some way to restoring the constitutional balance of the Act. In fact the UK as a matter of practice accepts an obligation to remedy the defects identified by declaration (see **Burden & Burden v UK** (2008) 47 EHRR 38).[8]

[9]Now move on to s 6, which is the other major strand of the Act. Peculiarly it is sometimes ignored by students who confine themselves to s 3. You will lose credit if you don't discuss it.

Section 6 HRA 1998 places a duty on 'public authorities'[9] to exercise their powers compatibly with Convention rights, failure to do so can lead to an action (s 7) and a remedy (s 8). If courts are putting an incompatible statute into effect they have a defence under s 6(2). This can lead to courts intervening in the discretionary choices of officials and public bodies[10] who are, directly or indirectly, accountable to Parliament or elected local councils. 'Proportionality' in human rights decisions means that a court must be satisfied that an act or decision does protect human rights; not just (under traditional judicial review) that the decision taker has taken human rights fully into account[11] in coming to the decision, whatever that is (**R (Daly) v Secretary of State for the Home Department** [2001] UKHL 26). In fact, recognising the mutual respect needed between judiciary and executive/Parliament, the courts may defer to the judgments of the authorities on whether some restriction on a Convention protected freedom is proportionate. Of course it is the judges who decide when such 'deference' needs to be shown. It will depend on the right and the issue involved. There will be less deference shown on issues like fair hearings, which courts consider their proper preserve; perhaps more on issues involving morality and taste (**R (ProLife Alliance) v BBC** [2003] UKHL 23).

[10]Keep to the focus of the question and now comment on the significance of s 6 for the constitutional relations of the courts and the executive.

[11]You will get credit if you try to state, briefly, the contrast between the judicial approach to what is a 'reasonable' exercise of discretion and what is 'proportionate'.

[12]Now move on to comment on your understanding of the terms of the Act in respect of underlying constitutional theory.

In constitutional theory[12] there is a tension between, as it were, the 'political constitution' (giving primacy to the political judgments of ministers, officials and legislators and to a concept of legitimacy based on accountability to Parliament) and a rights-based constitutionalism which acknowledges the primacy of the judiciary. In human rights law this rights-based approach can involve judicial assertions of what is 'necessary in a democratic society' and other judgments of public good. The Act seems to enhance the judicial role.

Some commentators (e.g. Nicol 2006) talk of the Act as providing the framework for a constitutional discourse between these different branches of the state on the issue of rights. The limited use of the declaration of incompatibility, and thus the limited opportunities of the executive and Parliament to consider and respond to the courts, is criticised from this perspective.

[13]Conclude by relating the Act to what Lord Steyn (in *Jackson*) called the constitutional hypothesis – the underlying theory of the constitution and the role of the courts.

An enhanced judicial role is not necessarily inconsistent with the political constitution.[13] The Act can be understood as Parliament delegating to the judges the job of ensuring UK law is in line with Convention rights, subject to Parliament expressly legislating otherwise. But the Act also gives ample evidence for those developing a rights-based account of the UK constitution. Under this account the HRA 1998 is an important theme in a 'new constitutional hypothesis' (**R (Jackson) *v* Attorney General** [2005] UKHL 56) where sovereignty is at least shared between Parliament and the judiciary; the latter able to constrain the former on the basis of their conception of human rights.

✓ Make your answer stand out

- There is a great deal of academic writing dealing with the constitutional implications of the HRA 1998 and you can cite this in your answer. For example, in general support of the 'political constitution' is Tomkins (2005). In general support of the rights-based (in some versions the 'common law') constitution, see Allan (2001) and Kavanagh (2009).

- Compare Nicol (2006) and Hickman (2005) on the idea of a discourse between the courts and Parliament and the extent to which the courts should be prepared to assert the fundamentals of the rule of law and lay down challenges to Parliament to think again or have more persuasive justifications for interferences with rights.

- Discuss more fully whether a declaration is an effective remedy which should be sought before taking a case to Strasbourg. It would be one if the UK, as a matter of policy, always remedies the defect identified in the declaration.

! Don't be tempted to ...

- Muddle the Convention and the Act. This is fundamental but not always grasped. The HRA 1998 is an Act of the UK Parliament. It is divided into sections. The Convention is an act of the Council of Europe and is divided into articles. The terms of the Convention are adopted into English law for the purposes of the Human Rights Act and are found in Schedule 1 to that Act. So 'section 6' is about public authorities, etc; do not, ever and in any event, muddle it with 'article 6' which is about the right to a fair trial. If you do this you will frustrate your examiners mightily.

- The case law is extensive (e.g. on s 3) so choose a few examples which make different, significant points; do not overwhelm your answer with lots of cases saying different things.

- Section 6 on public authorities must be mentioned. But there is no need to consider the issue of the definition of a public authority in your answer (it could easily come up in a different question).

Question 2

Can the Human Rights Act 1998, as enacted, be called a British bill of rights? Your answer should include a discussion of s 2 Human Rights Act 1998.

Answer plan

→ Give definitions of a 'British bill of rights'; reject alternatives that are inconsistent with the HRA 1998.

→ Introduce s 2 HRA 1998 and the way it has been interpreted.

→ Discuss s 2 and the 'mirror Strasbourg' principle.

→ Consider the effect of a more 'generous' interpretation of rights.

→ Compare with the effect of pro-state definitions.

→ Discuss 'dialogue' and the impact of disagreements between UK courts and Strasbourg.

Diagram plan

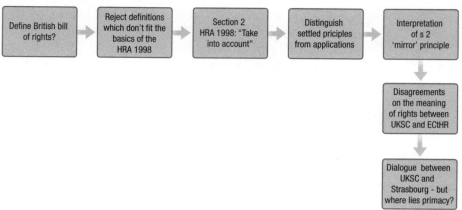

Define British bill of rights? → Reject definitions which don't fit the basics of the HRA 1998 → Section 2 HRA 1998: "Take into account" → Distinguish settled priciples from applications → Interpretation of s 2 'mirror' principle → Disagreements on the meaning of rights between UKSC and ECtHR → Dialogue between UKSC and Strasbourg - but where lies primacy?

A printable version of this diagram is available from www.pearsoned.co.uk/lawexpressqa

Answer

The status of the Human Rights Act 1998 (HRA 1998) is a matter of continuing debate. Many commentators (e.g. Kavanagh, 2009) believe the term 'bill of rights' is appropriate. The Act has special, superior, status in the sense that other statutes must be interpreted for conformity with Convention rights (s 3) and it is judges who decide this. If interpretation is not possible, it is true that the incompatible statute remains valid (section 3(1)) (there is no US-style power to strike down legislation). Nevertheless, the 'declaration of incompatibility' (s 4) seems, in practice, to give rise to a duty on government and Parliament to change the law (see government's argument in **Burden v UK** (2008) 47 EHRR 38). Finally, the Act is relatively entrenched in the sense that it is accepted as a constitutional statute which, like the European Communities Act 1972, can only be expressly repealed (by another human rights statute).[1]

[1]This is a good way to begin your answer because your understanding of what a bill of rights is in theory comes out in the way you discuss the effect of the particular terms of the Act.

However, even if the Act is, in effect, virtually a Bill of Rights, it is not one that meets particular British circumstances.[2] Its point is to give 'further effect' to the European Convention on Human Rights (ECHR) which was drafted in 1949/50 by the members of the Council of Europe. No attempt was made in 1998 to introduce, for example, social rights or rights to do with environmental protection, into the HRA.

[2]Now move on to discuss the second issue in the question – whether there is a distinctive 'Britishness' about the Act.

However, the HRA 1998 does not make the Convention itself directly part of UK law, which would give the European Court of Human Rights (ECtHR) jurisdiction in the UK. The Convention remains a separate obligation at international law[3] **(R(Hurst) v London Northern District Coroner** [2007] UKHL 13).The text of Part One of the Convention is in Schedule 1 to the Act. The right to a remedy (article 13) is the main exclusion. In the government's view it was unnecessary, since the Act itself provides adequate remedies.

[3]This point shows your basic understanding and so is worth making.

Section 2 HRA 1998 says that UK courts need only 'take into account'[4] the judgments etc of the ECtHR when applying scheduled Convention rights. This can be contrasted with s 3 of the European Communities Act 1972[5] which requires UK courts to follow the European Court of Justice on EU law. So HRA 1998 appears to provide room for distinctly British interpretations of Convention rights for the purposes of UK law.

[4]Move on to discuss s 2, which is clearly required by the question.

[5]The contrast with EU law helps to show you are aware of the differences, particularly at the constitutional level, of the law from the EU and from the Council of Europe.

However, s 2 has to be interpreted by UK courts. A judicial presumption has emerged against developing interpretations of Convention rights in Britain that stray far too far from what the ECtHR has said[6] (even when they think the Strasbourg position is unfair, as in **R (Clift) v Secretary of State for the Home Department** [2006] UKHL 54; though see now **Clift v UK**, app 7205/07, judgment of 13 July 2010). The UK courts have, therefore, rejected inferring from s 2 a power to develop the principles in Convention rights in a distinctly British way; UK law is to remain broadly in step with Strasbourg. In **R (Animal Defenders International) v Secretary of State for Culture, Media and Sport** [2008] UKHL 15 the suggestion by Lord Scott that some degree of divergence might have to be accepted, was rejected by other judges. The justification is that HRA 1998 aims to provide a remedy in the UK if, but only if, one would also be available in Strasbourg. Critics (e.g. Lewis, 2007) see this as a wasted opportunity. Section 2 could have been used to develop a higher standard of human rights in Britain which are more 'generous' to applicants.

[6]Now move on to discuss the way s 2 has been interpreted. Reference to the 'mirror Strasbourg' principle shows you are aware of how the UK courts have, by and large, addressed the problem and will get you credit.

It is the settled, constant rules and principles from the ECtHR that are to be followed[7] **(R (Ullah) v Special Adjudicator** [2004] UKHL 26). Where there are exceptional reasons relating less to principle and more to the application of rights in British circumstances, then previous case law from Strasbourg need not be followed (e.g. Strasbourg's rejection of the reformed Courts Martial system was not

[7]You will get credit for this point which shows you are aware of complexity – that UK courts do not follow Strasbourg in a slavish way.

followed by UK courts on the grounds that the ECtHR had not been properly informed (**R v Spear** [2002] UKHL 31)).

[8]This point is important since there is no reason in theory to assume that a British bill of rights would be more generous to applicants.

If 'Britishness' in terms of human rights was to result in rulings unfavourable to applicants,[8] those applicants retain their right to apply to the ECtHR (see s 11 HRA 1998). There have indeed been cases where UK courts have carefully considered Convention rights and found against applicants, who have then won at Strasbourg (e.g. **R (Marper) v Chief Constable of South Yorkshire** [2004] UKHL 39 (on storage of DNA)). In those situations UK law remains as stated by the House of Lords but the UK government is obliged at international law, under article 1 ECHR, to alter the law.

Thus if s 2 was used to develop more 'generous' interpretations of Convention rights, the 'mirroring Strasbourg' principle would be offended. UK courts do not think they have statutory authority for this. If it was used to develop interpretations more favourable to the public interest, as defined by Parliament and executive, the significance would be shortlived given the UK's duty to give effect to ECtHR judgments under article 46 ECHR.

[9]Reference to this dramatic and important case will impress the examiner by showing you are up to date. However, the consequences are not known (November 2010) – so keep an eye on it. Look out for the Grand Chamber decision in *Al-Khawaja* v *UK*.

In **R v Horncastle** [2009] UKSC 14[9] the UK Supreme Court (UKSC) has expressly challenged the settled principles of the ECtHR on the issue of whether article 6 is necessarily violated by a conviction based solely or decisively on hearsay evidence. It raises the possibility of the UKSC holding out for a distinctively British account of Convention rights on the issue. The alternative is to see this in dialogue terms[10] – the UKSC asking Strasbourg to think again on its principled jurisprudence. A similar issue arose in relation to fair hearings for terrorist suspects. After a Grand Chamber, in **A v UK** (2009) 49 EHRR 29, had reiterated the principle, a nine-judge House of Lords accepted and applied it on the sufficient ground (for the reluctant law lords) that it was the final, considered, authority of Strasbourg[11] (**Secretary of State for the Home Department v AF** [2009] UKHL 28).

[10]In mentioning dialogue theory you strengthen your answer by suggesting a principled basis in which the constitutional dispute can be approached – though the theory does not necessarily, in itself, imply Strasbourg primacy.

[11]Try the Latin, it might impress: '"Argentoratum locutum, iudicium finitum" – Strasbourg has spoken, the case is closed' (per Lord Rodger in *AF*).

[12]References to non-judicial statements by judges can be useful, particularly when made by a holder of high judicial office. They show wide reading and awareness of recent developments.

It is not certain that such an acknowledgement of the final primacy of the Strasbourg Grand Chamber will apply in a situation such as *Horncastle* where the British judges are all in agreement. The Lord Chief Justice has commented[12] on the desirability of upholding the independence of the common law which should not, in an automatic way, subordinate itself to Strasbourg (Judge, 2010). What may

[13]Try to make some concluding remarks which embody the basic ideas of the answer: that s 2 does not prevent the development of British solutions but doing so raises questions about the purpose of the HRA 1998 and also about the universality of human rights.

emerge is a more complex relationship between the UK courts and Strasbourg where,[13] within a general conformity, it is possible for distinctive British norms relating to traditional human rights to co-exist. Whether this could be both consistent with the idea of human rights as being universal (or at least reflecting a common European heritage) and with the institutional practices of the Council of Europe is uncertain.

✓ Make your answer stand out

- Academic commentary of s 2 includes Wright (2009).

- For relations between UK courts and the ECtHR, including discussion of dialogue approach: see Amos (2007).

- Make some reference to the wider debate, particularly from a Conservative Party perspective, about a British bill of rights which has a fuller focus on 'duties' (e.g. Fisher, 2007); and see also, embodying Labour Party concerns, Department of Constitutional Affairs (2006).

- Write more on what the specific content of a British bill of rights might be.

! Don't be tempted to ...

- Spend too much time exploring the reasons behind the HRA 1998. Your answer has to be succinct and the question points you towards s 2 HRA 1998.

- Discuss in too much detail the full range of debates about the different forms that a new bill of rights might take – an interesting topic but not in issue here. This question is about the extent the HRA 1998, as enacted, represents a bill of rights.

❓ Question 3

The Banking Act (fictitious) is enacted.

Section 1 authorises the police to 'to search the private dwellings of bank managers when they consider it appropriate'. A recent decision of the European Court of Human Rights rules that the power of random search in such circumstances, search without reasonable suspicion, violates the right to respect for private life guaranteed by article 8 of the Convention.

Section 2 authorises the Secretary of State to establish a procedure by which he is to decide certain financial disputes between banks. The Act contains no requirement for any system of review or appeal against the Secretary of State's decisions. The European Court of Human Rights has recently held that to decide such disputes without a system for appeal or review before an independent court or tribunal would violate article 6 of the Convention – the right to a fair hearing. The provisions establishing the procedure were brought into effect following a full debate and resolution by the House of Commons. The procedure is the government's solution to an urgent problem.

Advise Able, who advises banks, on the general principle which will govern how courts will interpret sections 1 and 2 of the Act in the light of the Human Rights Act 1998.

Answer plan

→ Introduce the 'interpretative' duty (s 3 HRA 1998); note that Strasbourg jurisprudence is normally followed (s 2 HRA 1998)

→ Can the search power be read compatibly with article 8 following the Strasbourg ruling? Consider what is 'possible' under s 3.

→ Application to part 1: read down police discretion to limit it to reasonable suspicion.

→ Can the absence of review provisions be made compatible with article 6? Consider a declaration of incompatibility (s 4 HRA 1998)?

→ Application to part 2: does the 'urgency' justify a remedial order (s 10 HRA 1998).

Diagram plan

```
┌─────────────────────────────────────┐
│  Introduction: the interpretative    │
│  duty – ss 3, 4 and 10 HRA 1998      │
└─────────────────────────────────────┘
```

Can the search power in the Banking Act be read down under s 3?	Can appeal or review provisions be read into the Banking Act?
• What is possible for a court to do under s 3? • Note the important case law • Apply to the broad subjective discretion in Banking Act - can it be read down to authorise only searches on reasonable suspicion?	• Consider the difference between interpretation and legislation (what is not possible under s 3?) • When can a declaration of incompatibility be issued? • Apply and consider whether, if a declaration, a remedial order would be appropriate

A printable version of this diagram is available from www.pearsoned.co.uk/lawexpressqa

Answer

[1]Begin by setting out the problem. The legality of the police search depends on the meaning of the statute under which they act.

[2]A wide subjective power (note it as you read through the question) in a problem question will usually be signalling a discussion of s 3.

[3]Make the point in this way to show your understanding that the HRA 1998 is domestic law. The rights in Sch 1 are legally distinct (though have the same text) from the rights in the European Convention.

[4]Mention s 2 in order to explain that the interpretation of article 8 by the ECtHR will be followed by UK courts.

[5]You will strengthen your answer if you demonstrate understanding of how the HRA 1998 adds to the ordinary common law principles of statutory interpretation.

[6]This is an important point which must not be omitted – s 3 undermines the dominance of the 'literal' rule.

Police searches purport to be authorised by s 1[1] of the Banking Act. This provision appears to give a wide subjective power[2] to the police to search on the grounds that they consider 'appropriate'. Section 3(1) of the Human Rights Act 1998 (HRA 1998) requires all legislation, whenever enacted, to be 'read and given effect' in a way that is compatible with the Convention rights in Schedule 1 to the Act.[3] Article 8 is one of those Convention rights. Section 2 HRA 1998 requires UK courts to 'take into account'[4] the judgments etc of the European Court of Human Rights (ECtHR). In **R (Ullah) v Special Adjudicator** [2004] UKHL 26 this was held to mean that the 'clear and constant' jurisprudence of the ECtHR should be followed unless there are special circumstances, such as if the ECtHR has applied a Convention in a way that reflects a mistaken understanding of UK law (e.g. **R v Spear** [2002] UKHL 31]). The ECtHR's understanding of article 8, as given in the question, is, therefore, likely to be followed, as a matter of law, by UK courts.

The general approach to what is 'possible' for a court in the UK to do under s 3 has been summarised in a number of cases, such as **Ghaidan v Godin-Mendoza** [2004] UKHL 30. The use of s 3 is not dependent on the statutory words being ambiguous. Ambiguity could already, without the HRA 1998, be resolved in favour of a compatible reading on the basis of the ordinary canons of statutory interpretation.[5] These presume an intention by the UK Parliament to legislate compatibly with its international obligations, including the Convention.

Likewise the words of a statute, as drafted and approved by Parliament, are no longer decisive[6] and may be modified by the court in order to achieve a compatible reading. So the will of Parliament in so far as it is expressed in the words of a statute can be amended by the courts, albeit under a power granted to them by Parliament. Quite radical things have been done. In **Ghaidan** the House of Lords held that the terms 'spouse … wife or husband'could include a same-sex partner. In **R v A** [2001] UKHL 25, s 3 was used to allow evidence about a rape-complainant's sexual history to be admitted in rape trials, if required by article 6, despite clear provisions to the contrary in deliberate and carefully crafted recent legislation.

[7]In a problem question which is in parts, it helps to draw a conclusion after your discussion of each part.

It is possible to use s 3[7] in order to read down the effect of the police discretion in s 1 of the Act so that it only authorises searches compatible with article 8, namely those based on reasonable suspicion.

[8]Now move on to discuss s 4. Show you understand its importance in the 'architecture' of the HRA 1998.

There are limits to what a court can do under s 3 HRA 1998.[8] If a compatible interpretation is not 'possible' a senior court (such as the High Court)[9] may issue a declaration of incompatibility (s 4 HRA 1998). There is no power to invalidate an incompatible statute and a declaration does not alter the law or the legal position of the parties.

[9]You get credit for pointing out that not all courts can use s 4.

In the context of rights to a fair trial (as are in issue here), radical amendments to legislation have been done under s 3. The courts may feel they are acting on their own constitutional terrain. Thus in **R v Hammond** [2005] UKHL 69 a right to an oral hearing was allowed, when needed for compatibility with article 6, for certain prisoners seeking a change in their status. The statute said prisoners' cases should be determined 'without an oral hearing'. A declaration of incompatibility is considered to be a last resort.

[10]Placing the HRA 1998 into its constitutional context helps to disclose your general understanding of the Act.

But there are limits to what is possible under s 3. Courts may interpret; they must not legislate. This is not an easy distinction to make. In **Ghaidan** Lord Nicholls referred to not interpreting a statute in a way that goes 'against the grain' of the statute or which is not compatible with the underlying thrust of the legislation. The courts should not act incompatibly with their constitutional role[10] and with the supremacy of Parliament (thus, in **R (Anderson) v Secretary of State for the Home Department** [2002] UKHL 46, the clear intention of Parliament that the Home Secretary should retain a role in sentencing some prisoners could not be read compatibly with article 5). Likewise the court is limited by its adjudicative function and should not use s 3 to bring about law changes that require considering a wide range of interests and issues that are not before the court (so they would not use s 3 to redefine marriage in **Bellinger v Bellinger** [2003] UKHL 21). In these circumstances a declaration of incompatibility is necessary (though not obligatory).

[11]Now draw a conclusion on the second part of the question.

Here it would be hard to see how the provisions authorising the minister to determine the disputes between banks could be read compatibly with article 6.[11] They represent the clear, recent and deliberate will of Parliament, an issue of significance in **Anderson**. The Banking Act contains no provisions requiring an appeal process.

[12]Note that the issue in the question is the absence of provisions in a statute – reading such provisions in is likely to seem like 'legislating'.

[13]Demonstrate in the next paragraph your understanding of the implications of a s 4 declaration.

[14]Get credit for noting this point; that the second part of the question involves a bank's claim to have human rights.

[15]Demonstrate understanding of the Act as a whole by discussing remedial orders.

[16]This point might well have been noticed in your original read through of the question – ask yourself why the point was in the question.

[17]Finish with a bit of a flourish – this point is seldom noticed!

Requiring them would require new provisions, not just interpreting provisions aleady present. In **R (JF) v Secretary of State for the Home Department** [2010] UKSC 17 the Supreme Court confirmed a declaration of incompatibility in respect of the absence of provisions[12] to review the otherwise lifelong requirement, in the Sexual Offences Act 2003, for convicted sex offenders to notify the police of their movements.

Therefore a declaration of incompatibility is most likely in respect of s 2 of the Banking Act. This then returns the matter to the executive and Parliament.[13] If no action is taken, aggrieved persons (which can include corporate bodies – see article 34)[14] may seek a ruling from the ECtHR. An adverse ruling means that, under Article 1 ECHR, the UK then has an obligation to change the law or administrative practice to make it compatible with the ruling. A second possibility is for the government to propose new legislation – usually this takes considerable time. Section 10 HRA 1998 allows a minister to make changes to legislation (such as introducing an appeals process) by order. These 'remedial orders' are subject to limited Parliamentary scrutiny under the procedure in Sch 2,[15] though there is no reason to think this scrutiny will not be effective. There must be 'compelling reasons' for the making of such orders. The reference in the question to 'urgency'[16] suggests introducing an appeals process to satisfy article 6 might be a suitable occasion for a remedial order, but the matter is for the minister. A court cannot order that one be made[17] since, although 'acts' of public authorities must be compatible with the Convention rights, failing to introduce a remedial order is not an 'act' (s 6(6) HRA 1998).

 Make your answer stand out

■ Show an understanding of the constitutional context of the HRA 1998: in particular, how s 3 and s 4 combined create, to some degree, a re-balancing of the constitutional relations of courts and Parliament/executive. Thus the willingness of the courts to 'amend' Acts of Parliament reflects the degree of 'deference' (respect for its constitutional role) shown to Parliament. This can depend on the right involved and the extent to which the issue is within the conventional domain of the judiciary or Parliament.

■ Look in more detail at some of the cases: R v A, for instance, was very controversial because it seemed to involve the courts using s 3 to undermine a carefully chosen and deliberate policy approved and enacted by Parliament. Critical commentary includes Nicol (2006), but compare Hickman (2008). The case may represent a high water mark in the use of s 3.

■ Make more of the issue of 'remedial orders' and whether they are undemocratic because they enable the executive to change primary legislation. There have been too few orders made for serious comment: though, again, this reflects the willingness of the courts to use s 3 rather than s 4 (the 'last resort').

! Don't be tempted to ...

■ Write about the substance of Convention rights. The question is about the Human Rights Act 1998.

■ Confuse sections of the HRA 1998 with Convention rights. It is not unknown for a question on s 3 HRA 1998 to be answered by a discussion of torture and inhuman treatment (article 3 ECHR). This tends to lead to zero marks – no complaints!

■ Spend too much time on issues which are ancillary to the main question: e.g. though a bank is involved, here is not the time for a full exploration of article 34 ECHR and s 7 HRA 1998.

📰 Question 4

'Public authority' and 'public function', in s 6 HRA 1998, have been interpreted in an over-restrictive way which leaves some vulnerable people without proper protection for their human rights.

Do you agree with this comment? Your answer should be illustrated from case law.

Answer plan

→ Introduce s 6 and the duty of public authorities.
→ Explore in some detail the legal definitions of both public authority and public function.
→ Relate 'hybrid' or 'functional' authorities to contracting and the modern administrative state.
→ Apply to examples of the vulnerable, such as care homes and the homeless.
→ Discuss s 6(5) and private acts.

Diagram plan

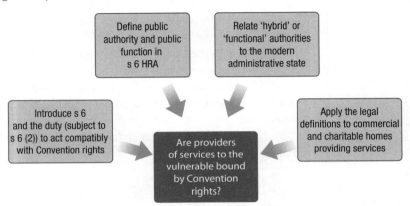

Define public authority and public function in s 6 HRA

Relate 'hybrid' or 'functional' authorities to the modern administrative state

Introduce s 6 and the duty (subject to s 6 (2)) to act compatibly with Convention rights

Apply the legal definitions to commercial and charitable homes providing services

Are providers of services to the vulnerable bound by Convention rights?

A printable version of this diagram is available from www.pearsoned.co.uk/lawexpressqa

[1]The question wants you to show your understanding of 'public authority' generally before considering the impact on welfare law (broadly defined) of the courts' approaches. So begin by describing s 6.

[2]Make sure from the beginning that you show you understand the two 'types' of public authority. Using the statutory language impresses but 'any person in so far as they are exercising public functions' will do for 'hybrid'.

[3]In your description do not forget s 6(2) HRA 1998 and relate it to s 3 HRA 1998; this will get credit since it is often forgotten.

[4]It strengthens your answer to show your overall understanding by linking the expressed inclusions and exclusions to the overall constitutional balance brought about by the HRA 1998.

Answer

Section 6(1)[1] requires a 'public authority' to act compatibly with the Convention rights in Sch 1 to the Human Rights Act 1998 (HRA 1998). Section 6(3)(b) extends the duty to 'any person certain of whose functions are functions of a public nature'.[2] Public authorities are not so bound if they are required so to act by provisions of primary legislation which cannot be read compatibly under s 3 (s 6(2)).[3] 'Public authority' is not defined except that courts and tribunals are expressly declared to be public authorities but the Houses of Parliament and proceedings in Parliament are excluded[4] (thus complementing s 3 in maintaining the supremacy of Parliament).

Public authorities identified by s 6(1) are described, in **Aston Cantlow ... PCC v Wallbank** [2003] UKHL 37 as 'core'. They are solely public bodies with no private side and are defined as 'governmental' in a broad sense of the word. This definition relates to the purpose of the Act (**Aston Cantlow**) – to allow a human rights claim before the UK courts but only where such a claim could be brought before the Court of Human Rights in Strasbourg – thus a public authority is any body for which the United Kingdom would have direct responsibility at Strasbourg. These (by implication of article 34 which refers to 'non-governmental organisations') are governmental bodies.

2 THE HUMAN RIGHTS ACT 1998

[5]Now discuss the general principles on the basis of which s 6(1) public authorities are recognised.

Core public bodies[5] are likely to have special powers, be democratically accountable, be publicly funded fully or partially, be created by statute and have an obligation to operate only in the public interest (Oliver, 2000; approved in **Aston Cantlow**). Ministers and departments, local authorities and the police, are amongst bodies which are 'intuitively' governmental. For other bodies, such as 'quangos',[6] there may be room for argument. Services providers like maintained schools, or NHS hospitals, are treated as public authorities, often without much argument and even though they may not be thought of as 'governmental' (e.g. **R (SB) v Governors of Denbigh High School** [2006] UKHL 15).

[6]You will get credit for context if you demonstrate your understanding of the modern administrative state and the central role of 'quangos' or 'non-departmental public bodies' in it.

[7]Now move on to describe 'hybrid' authorities – this is the definition most in issue regarding services to the vulnerable so must be given a proper treatment in answering the question.

Functional or 'hybrid' authorities[7] (identified under s 6(3)(b)) have private (e.g commercial) interests but also exercise some public functions. Such bodies must secure human rights but only if they are exercising public functions.

There is no single test for 'public' function. **Aston Cantlow** and **YL v Birmingham City Council** [2007] UKHL 27 (followed in **R (Weaver) v LQHT** [2009] EWCA Civ 587) suggest that pointers to a function being public (none are conclusive) include: general public funding (e.g. by block grants), the possession of special statutory powers conferred for public purposes, and providing a service to the public that otherwise central government would provide. Factors of little signficance include that the function would be subject to human rights if carried out by a core authority and the simple fact that the function is subject to regulation, or to judicial review. That a body is itself a creature of a 'core' public authority is not a relevant matter when determining public function (thus the approach in **Poplar HRCA v Donoghue** [2001] EWCA Civ 595 which emphasised institutional links, is not now followed).

[8]It helps to explain the structure of the Act in this way; the point is returned to later in the context of welfare provision.

[9]Having discussed the general definitions you should now apply them to the particular issue of welfare and vulnerable people.

The 'core' and 'hybrid' distinction in the HRA 1998 reflects the modern administrative state.[8] Many public functions are performed on the basis of contracts with commercial or charitable providers. This is particularly true of the provision of services to vulnerable people.[9] A local authority, for instance, may accept that it has statutory responsibility for care of an elderly person or to house a homeless person. Characteristically the service (the care or the home) is provided to the individual by a commercial or charitable organisation acting on the basis of a contract with the authority. Vulnerable people in this situation will only be able to secure their Convention rights directly if the provider is exercising public functions.

[10] Having discussed the law, you should now show your understanding of the theoretical issue about the concept of a function which is 'public'. You will get credit for this since it shows some familiarity with underlying theory, not just the 'black letter' law.

The definition of public function raises a controversial question of principle.[10] For some (e.g. Oliver, 2004) the distinctiveness of a public function is the possession and exercise of special, coercive, powers – the power to regulate and to determine 'who gets what, when and where'. For others (e.g. Craig (2002) and the Joint Committee (2003)) a function is public if it originates in the acceptance by the state of responsibility (e.g. for education, housing the homeless or care) and, on this view, the choices made about how the services should be delivered (directly or by contract) are irrelevant.

[11] Now move to the heart of the answer, which is the 'welfare gap' caused by the way public function has been applied to contracted service deliverers.

Applying the legal tests described above[11] it has often been the case that the commercial or service providers have been held not to be exercising public functions (e.g. **YL**) in respect of a commercial care home. The company fulfils a contract, it has no special powers, and is not an organisation created by statute. Responsibility for human rights remains with the LA (a core PA) and, it has been suggested (**R (Heather) v Leonard Cheshire Homes** [2003] EWCA Civ 336), this should be discharged through the contract terms.

The problem is that this leaves the residents and other vulnerable people without independent standing on human rights issues (they are not parties to the contract between the authority and the provider). Their only cause of action under s 7 HRA 1998 would be against the local authority, which is not directly responsible for their care.

The issue has been a matter of great controversy. Critical reports by the Joint Committee on Human Rights and other pressure led to a change in the law so that providers of nursing and personal care are now defined as exercising public functions (s 145 of the Health and Social Care Act 2008). But this statute does not apply to housing providers, for example.

[12] Do not miss this point – it demonstrates your overall knowledge of this part of the Act. *Weaver* shows how it could be important if eviction was to be a private act (not so on the facts in that case). Care home owners selling up is another likely example.

Private acts by 'hybrid' authorities are not subject to Convention rights (section 6(5)).[12] These can include, for example, entering into contracts or into leases. Core authorities, such as local authorities, on the other hand, are expected to ensure that all of their actions (including ones based on private law) are done compatibly with Convention rights.

This issue can raise difficulties in respect of the vulnerable. Is the eviction of a person who is then made homeless a private act (like the act of a landlord), which does not have to be compatible with article 8? In **Weaver** it was accepted that a Housing Trust providing low-cost housing was a 'hybrid' authority. Furthermore, actions done which were incidental to that function, such as terminating a tenancy, were so bound up with the exercise of the public function that they could not be differentiated as 'private'.

Thus the courts have interpreted s 6 in a way that leaves the effectiveness of Convention rights for vulnerable people dependent on the extent to which the position of the service provider is entirely contractual.[13]

[13]End with a brief conclusion which encompasses the points you have been making.

✓ Make your answer stand out

- Relate the idea that 'core' authorities are bound in all they do by Convention rights and have no 'private' side to similar developments in administrative law. E.g. local authority decisions as a landlord can be judicially considered on ordinary public law principles (*R* v *Somerset CC ex p Fewings* [1995] 1 All ER 513 (Laws J)). This helps with constitutional context.

- Constitutional context can also be enhanced by brief comparisons with 'emanation of the state' (EU law) and a 'public body' for judicial review purposes. Note, though, that these definitions are not considered helpful in the human rights context.

- Compare (briefly) other statutes, such as the Freedom of Information Act 2000, which simply list the public authorities to which the Act applies.

- Improve the subtlety of your answer by writing a little more on state responsibility at Strasbourg. States are responsible for their own actions in ways that can involve other organisations without it following that those other organisations would be 'governmental' and, therefore, public authorities (see *R (Johnson)* v *Havering LBC* [2007] EWCA Civ 26 paras 56–58 for examples).

! Don't be tempted to ...

- Explore 'indirect horizontal effect' (the courts, as public authorities, developing the common law in compatible ways); it is a complex matter and not really in issue here, though the courts are public authorities.

- Give many examples of cases in which it is taken for granted that a body is a public authority; only focus on those cases in which the question of this status is discussed.

■ Spend too much time, if any, on horror stories. There is plenty of evidence of abuse of people in care homes and of disadvantaged people being evicted (see Joint Committee, 2003). Their situation explains why human rights may matter but the question asks you to explore the law.

Question 5

Explain the concept of judicial deference as it applies to adjudication under the Human Rights Act.

Answer plan

→ Define deference and relate it to proportionality (properly defined).

→ Note briefly the acceptance of proportionality into UK law.

→ Relate proportionality and deference to the separation of powers and the constitutional position of the courts.

→ Discuss the factors influencing the question whether or not deference is appropriate.

→ Discuss the controversy on whether deference prevents courts properly securing human rights.

Diagram plan

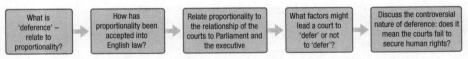

A printable version of this diagram plan is available from www.pearsoned.co.uk/lawexpressqa

Answer

¹It is always helpful to start with a definition or staking out of the ground which will be occupied in the rest of your answer. Also there is a point to putting 'deference' in quotation marks (at least for the first time of use) since the appropriateness of the term has been questioned, a matter you will mention later.

'Deference'¹ involves the relationship between the judiciary and the legislature and executive regarding the judgments that need to be made by courts applying the HRA 1998. The courts, when interpreting legislation under s 3 or judging the compatibility of the actions of a public authority under ss 6–8, may make rulings which interfere with previous judgments about the public interest

47

made by Parliament (and expressed in statute) or the administration. Deference raises the issue of the constitutional legitimacy of such interferences.

[2]Having introduced 'deference' you now need to introduce proportionality since the one relates to the other.

The issue is focused on the idea of 'proportionality'[2] which pervades the Convention. There is no definition in the Convention of proportionality but it is understood by the ECtHR as the judicial activity of ensuring decision makers have reached a 'fair balance' of an individual's interests against the interests of other individuals and, especially, against the public interest (**Sporrong and Lonnroth v Sweden** (1983) 5 EHRR 35).

[3]Although 'fair balance' is at the heart of the idea of proportionality you will get credit for demonstrating understanding of some of the issues taken, by the Strasbourg court, that contribute to this.

Proportionality is most prominent in respect of the 'qualified rights' (articles 8–11). These allow interferences with rights, such as freedom of expression, where these are 'necessary in a democratic society'. Proportionality requires consideration of issues[3] such as whether the interference is the least restrictive of rights amongst alternatives, whether the reasons for state action properly justify what was done, or whether the state has imposed, unnecessarily, a blanket ban preventing individual circumstances being taken into account.

[4]The question relates to UK law so you must now move your argument on the proportionality in domestic law.

Proportionality has been accepted by the English courts under the HRA 1998.[4] In **R (Daly) v Secretary of State for the Home Department** [2001] UKHL 26 the emphasis was on whether an interference with rights was the least onerous it could be. In **Huang v Secretary of State for the Home Department** [2007] UKHL 11[5] this was added to by reference to the overriding need to ensure a fair balance of the interests involved.

[5]You will get credit for noticing the important correction made in *Huang*.

[6]Now move on to discussing the separation of powers issue – it is necessary to do this in order to make sense of 'deference'.

Proportionality raises the issue of the proper separation of powers between judiciary, executive and legislature.[6] This is because it is the courts, with its assessment of fairness, rather than that of the legislature or executive, which must have the final word. In English law an important contrast can be made with 'ordinary' English judicial review.[7] This asks whether an official or body making a decision has taken statutorily relevant matters properly into account but, if so, the final weighing of those matters is left to the officials. Proportionality, on the other hand, requires the domestic courts to ensure that the resulting decision fully secures Convention rights (compare **R v Ministry of Defence ex p Smith** [1996] QB 517 to **Smith v UK** (2000) 29 EHRR 493). This point is accepted by UK courts at least

[7]Show your understanding of the point that 'proportionality' (and hence 'deference') alter, to some extent, the role of the court and this can be brought out by contrasting the two 'gays in the military' cases.

for the purposes of the HRA 1998 (see **Daly**), though, of course, under the HRA the courts may not be able to secure the rights but only issue a declaration of incompatibility.[8]

Deference arises when the courts in the UK accept that they must, over some issues, recognise a 'discretionary area of judgment' enjoyed by Parliament and the executive over where the fair balance of interests lies (**R v DPP ex parte Kebeline** [2000] 2 AC 326).[9] Here the courts accept that their job is to ensure that the decision taker has considered human rights issues but then accept the particular balance of interests that results. Thus deference means that there are some choices of the executive or Parliament which the courts will accept as within a range of proportionate outcomes – i.e. that on some issues a court cannot distinguish on proportionality grounds between a number of different options available to a public body to make.

[9]Now move on to define deference; you can do it because you have discussed proportionality and placed it in a constitutional context.

Deference can be seen as a constitutional doctrine which depends upon an underlying theory about the separation of powers and the appropriate roles of courts, executive and Parliament.[10] On this view the degree of deference depends on the nature of the article, the issue and constitutionally proper role of the institution involved.[11] Thus deference to the authorities will be appropriate when the Convention right expressly requires a balancing of interests (e.g. articles 8–11) rather than applying absolutely, or in respect of issues which are constitutionally within the domain of the executive, such as national security (**Secretary of State for the Home Department v Rehman** [2001] UKHL 47) or which reflect Parliament's view of issues of social policy; likewise there may be institutional deference where an issue has been clearly dealt with by an Act of Parliament (e.g. **R (Animal Defenders International) v Secretary of State for Culture, Media and Sport** [2008] UKHL 15). On the other hand, less deference will be shown to issues within the constitutional domain of the courts, such as fair hearings or the right to liberty;[12] and deference will be slight where a court has been especially established to determine an issue (such as an immigration tribunal in **Huang**).

[10]Now move on to consider, in this and the next paragraph, the theoretical disputes about proper deference. Discussion of this will impress the examiner.

[11]This is vital: you must show you understand that the degree of deference is a matter of judgment and can be controversial. It is not possible simply to identify issues on which the courts 'defer'.

[12]Make sure you communicate what some judges have said on when deference is and when it is not appropriate – but note also that it is a controversial doctrine and that, certainly, there is no straightforward 'tick box' way of identifying the relevant issues; as ever, it is a matter of interpretation.

But other writers (e.g. Hickman, 2010) reject this approach. They assert that under the Convention human rights are a matter of law and the courts must retain ultimate responsibility for determining whether there has been a violation by a state agency. The courts should accept the judgment of the authorities not on the grounds of a prior theory of the separation of powers but as a matter of effectiveness – because on the issue before the court the executive agency or Parliament is better informed or otherwise better able to come to the best judgment on what human rights require. Human rights law authorises the courts to protect individuals and groups from improper exercise of state power. Such power can be exercised by the executive or Parliament even when dealing with matters clearly within their constitutional role. It is wrong for the courts to defer on that basis.

[13]Make sure you show in your answer this underlying point – that deference should not be an abdication by the courts of their responsibilities to secure human rights.

[14]This is a good case to use to demonstrate your understanding of the controversial nature of deference.

The issue of deference has to be dealt with very carefully. Overall responsibility for securing the human rights of individuals lies with the courts, a responsibility they cannot surrender.[13] The judges may disagree when deference is appropriate. **ProLife Alliance v BBC** [2003] UKHL 23[14] a party election broadcast was banned by the BBC under (in effect) a statutory duty not to broadcast offensive material. For the Court of Appeal the ban was censorship violating article 10; the majority of the House of Lords upheld the ban by accepting that the BBC was best qualified to judge the matter of offence. Likewise the issues on which degrees of deference are based may conflict with each other. **A v Secretary of State for the Home Department** [2004] UKHL 56 involved imprisonment without trial of foreign terrorist suspects. This raises both national security (suggesting deference to the executive) and matters of liberty and fair hearings. In finding against the Secretary of State there was little deference to the Secretary of State's assessment of security.

✓ **Make your answer stand out**

- Demonstrate your understanding of the pervasive nature of proportionality: e.g. it applies to 'legality' which applies to all Convention rights. Laws which interfere with individuals' rights must be appropriately precise so that their likely application can be anticipated. What is appropriate depends on a judicial consideration on the degree of 'foreseeability' which is appropriate to the context, and this can be different from that of an elected legislature.

- Likewise: issues such as whether a deprivation of liberty is 'arbitrary' will clearly involve an issue of proportionality and could be mentioned if there is space.

- If you mention declaration of incompatibility as a human rights remedy you can gain credit by a brief discussion of the issue. In order for the Human Rights Act to provide adequate remedies the UK government will have to satisfy the Strasbourg Court that it always responds positively to a declaration.

- Develop more the tension between those who place greater emphasis on the sense of proper respect for each other's functions and those who are concerned to ensure that this is not taken too far so that the courts cease to be an effective guardian of human rights. See Steyn (2005) in which a disagreement on this issue between Lord Steyn and Lord Hoffmann is articulated.

- For contrasting views of academics refer to Allan (2006) and Kavanagh (2010).

! Don't be tempted to ...

- Write about 'margin of appreciation'. There are clear similarities, but margin of appreciation is a doctrine of international law; it applies to the judgments of the ECtHR but is not appropriate for domestic courts.

- Discuss deference without reference to proportionality – it would be hard to make sense of the idea.

- Treat the topic by itself without reference to the HRA 1998 and the constitutional relationship of courts to Parliament and the executive therein.

? Question 6

Advise the following:

(a) A is married and the father of two children. He is outraged at the practices of local authority social work departments in relation to the children of divorced couples. He wants to challenge these practices, using the HRA 1998, on the grounds that they violate the article 8 rights of fathers. However, he has been warned by a friend that he may be prevented from bringing such a case in the English courts because he is not divorced.

(b) B is the owner of some land which was compulsorily purchased by a local authority in 2008 and compensation was paid. In 2010 he is advised by a friend that the value of the compensation he received was so low it may violate his right to the peaceful enjoyment of possessions in article 1 of the First Protocol. He wants to test this in court under the HRA 1998. However, he is told by another friend that he may have waited too long before commencing his action.

(c) C is a prisoner. He is subjected to a range of conditions which are accepted by the prison service as being inhuman and degrading, in breach of article 3. In addition, he is held in prison for 14 days more than he should have been due to administrative oversight by the prison service. He intends to bring an action in the courts, using the HRA 1998, to challenge the Ministry of Justice's refusal to provide financial compensation in respect of both issues.

Answer plan

→ Introduce s 7 HRA 1998 and actions against public authorities.

→ Does A have standing? Discuss the victim rule (link to article 34).

→ Note that a victim can include a person at risk.

→ Has B delayed too long? Section 7 one-year test.

→ Discuss whether B can show it is 'equitable' to extend the limit.

→ Explain s 8 and principles relating to just satisfaction (link to article 41).

→ Discuss whether article 5(5) makes a difference for compensating breaches of article 5.

Diagram plan

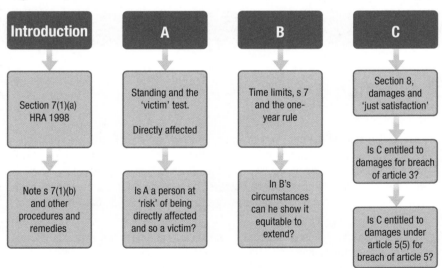

A printable version of this diagram is available from www.pearsoned.co.uk/lawexpressqa

[1]Begin by briefly outlining s 7(1)(a) and (b) and relate these provisions to s 6. By noticing that only s 7(1)(a) HRA 1998 is involved, in the question, you demonstrate, by implication, your understanding of how human rights claims can come up through other proceedings, such as 'ordinary' judicial review.

[2]Remember, briefly, to point out the two grounds of action under s 7 – this shows your overall knowledge of the Act.

[3]Make sure you show you understand that s 7 requires cases to be brought in the appropriate tribunal according to rules.

[4]Show you know that these exist, but you will not be expected to discuss them.

[5]Now move on to discuss standing. This is at the heart of A's issue and you need to show understanding of article 34 (referred to in s 7) and some of the case law.

[6]It will impress if you can put your points into a wider context – here of the general principles used by the courts to interpret the Act.

Answer

These will be actions before English courts under HRA 1988 and not on the basis of other procedures.[1] They will, therefore, need to meet the procedural requirements of that Act. Section 7(1)(a)[2] allows a person to bring proceedings directly against a public authority for allegedly failing to act compatibly with Convention rights as required by s 6(1). Section 7(1)(b) allows a person to rely on their Convention rights in 'any legal proceedings'.

A

A claim under s 7(1)(a) can be made in any appropriate court,[3] subject to rules and to the jurisdiction of the court. A is likely to be seeking a declaration and as such an application in the High Court is most likely to be appropriate (e.g. **R (Howard League for Penal Reform) v Secretary of State for the Home Department** [2002] EWHC 2497, though this was a s 3 case). He will need to follow the appropriate Civil Procedure Rules.[4]

A's problem is that he will have to show he has standing to bring the case.[5] Under s 7 any applicant bringing a case directly against a public authority, including by judicial review, must be in a position that they could bring a case before the ECtHR in Strasbourg. This illustrates the 'mirror' approach that runs through the Act[6] – that it provides a domestic remedy if but only if a remedy would be available from Strasbourg. Section 7 says that such a person must be the 'victim' of the alleged breach, and this is to be defined the same way as it is under article 34 of the Convention.

Article 34 says that any 'person, non-governmental organisation or group of individuals' who claims to be the 'victim' of a violation can bring a case. Strasbourg case law defines a 'victim' as a person 'directly affected' by the alleged violation: **Eckle v Germany** (1983) 5 EHRR 1. In particular, Strasbourg objects to *actio popularis*, a legal action brought to achieve a general or public interest. Such general political questions should be dealt with in Parliament.

It seems, therefore, that A, who has not been affected by local authority decisions, is not a victim. However, the ECtHR has said, from earliest cases, that a person who 'runs the risk' of being

[7]This point is very important. It gains credit because it shows you have understood some of the case law on article 34.

directly affected,[7] can be a victim (e.g. **Monnat v Switzerland** (2010) 51 EHRR 34). Thus in **Norris v Ireland** (1986) 8 EHRR CD 75, the claims of an association seeking reform of penal laws against homosexuals were not admissible but the similar claim of a homosexual man was because, as a homosexual, he was at risk from the laws. If A can show that he runs the risk of being directly affected by a breach of Convention rights, his case can be admissible under s 7 HRA 1998.

B

An applicant under s 7 HRA 1998 must bring the case within one year from the time of the act complained of. If some procedure is used with a shorter limitation period (such as the three-month maximum using judicial review under CPR Part 54), it is the shorter which applies. A court has discretion to extend the period if to do so is 'equitable having regard to all the circumstances'.[8]

[8]Try to remember the phrase if you can. If not, use 'equitable' since this links to the Limitation Act 1980; 'fair' is OK but misses that point.

[9]You will get credit for discussing the problematic aspects of the Act, and this is one.

This limitation period is controversial.[9] It does not mirror Strasbourg which, under article 35, requires cases to be brought within six months. There is not really a parallel since the Strasbourg limit starts from the end of domestic proeeedings. The justification for s 7, on the other hand, is to avoid prejudice to public authorities. Nor does the one-year limitation apply to actions not brought under section 7(1)(a). Human rights claims relied on in any other proceedings (s 7(1)(b)) depend on the limitation periods appropriate to those proceedings, as do claims based on the interpretation of statutes under s 3.[10] Nor is the moment from which time runs always clear, particularly respecting continuing or repeated breaches (see **Somerville v Scottish Ministers** [2007] UKHL 44: no clear conclusion reached).

[10]Whilst keeping to the point of the question, show your wider understanding of the Act.

[11]Give enough space to this issue since it is important for the answer. You are not given enough information to come to a final view. You get the marks by demonstrating your understanding of the issues that would be raised by a court deciding the matter.

The burden of proof is on B to explain the delay and show it would be equitable[11] to allow the case to proceed. There is no list of adequate reasons but courts can make reference to the reasons in s 33(3) of the Limitation Act 1980 (**Dunn v Parole Board** [2008] EWCA Civ 374): e.g. the effect on the evidence, the respondent's conduct and the nature of any legal advice obtained. Delays in obtaining legal aid or errors by legal advisers can be other reasons (**A v Essex** [2007] EWHC 1652). Without knowing the reasons for B's delay it is impossible to judge whether it would be equitable to allow the case. However, not only must B have appropriate reasons but those

[12]Make sure you communicate that the issue of equity is a matter of balance of factors – it shows awareness of the issue before the court.

reasons must be sufficient to outweigh contrary factors[12] such as the impact of the passage of time on the quality of evidence and the prejudicial effects, if any, on the public authority.

C

Section 8 HRA 1998 authorises a court to award remedies which it considers 'just and appropriate' against public authorities and which are within its jurisdiction.[13] Remedies are discretionary.

[13]You will impress by making this point, which is easily forgotten.

C will need to bring his case before a UK court that can award damages. The court will need to accept that damages are needed to provide 'just satisfaction'[14] (s 8(3)). This term comes from article 41 ECHR. The Act requires a UK court to take into account the principles for applying article 41 developed by the ECtHR. These principles, adopted into the UK in **R (Greenfield) v Secretary of State for the Home Office** [2005] UKHL 14, include that the aim of just satisfaction is restorative and that compensation will only be paid to losses caused by the breach. C is seeking 'non-pecuniary' losses and these can include, for instance, compensating psychological distress, which may well apply to C. However, another principle is that the finding of a violation is often sufficient and Strasbourg's application of the principles can reflect a moral judgment against persons such as convicted prisoners. C may fail on this point, depending on the circumstances.

[14]Try to remember this term – it shows you understand the mirroring link to the Convention.

English courts, awarding just satisfaction, accept that human rights claims are different from claims in tort and have suggested that awards should often be lower (**Greenfield**).

Being detained too long is likely to be a breach of article 5 and under article 5(5) C has an 'enforceable right to compensation'.[15] This should be awarded in the UK on the basis of s 8. However, article 5(5) does not create an absolute right. Following article 41, it does not require compensation in cases where there has been no substantial loss (**R (KB) v Mental Health Review Tribunal** [2003] EWHC 193).

[15]Having discussed the just satisfaction generally, make sure you move on to article 5(6) – the only express reference to compensation in the Convention.

Make your answer stand out

- Discuss issues caused by the different rules on standing, depending on procedure, that exist. In particular, human rights claims (based on the ECHR's persuasive force and fundamental rights in the common law) can be brought under 'ordinary' judicial review). Under judicial review the standing test is 'sufficient interest' (s 32 Senior Courts Act 1982), which the UK courts have interpreted more broadly than the ECtHR has interpreted the 'victim' test. In particular, UK courts are, apparently, more accommodating of cases brought by interest groups where there is a well-founded claim of unlawful action by a public body and if the group is well placed to bring it (not an *actio popularis*, but getting there).

- Likewise (regarding B's case), if the case is brought using CPR 54 (judicial review) then the three-month maximum time limit applies. Note, though, that it is subject to a general exceptional power in a court to extend time limits. This is at the court's discretion but allows the applicant to present compelling arguments.

- Discuss the reasons why claims against public authorities are subject to strict procedural rules such as in A's and B's cases. In *O'Reilly* v *Mackman* [1983] 2 AC 237, 237–285 Lord Diplock gives a good survey of the reasons; but you might consider whether they are rather executive friendly.

! **Don't be tempted to . . .**

- Discuss the issues of substance (e.g. whether fathers' rights really are ignored by child welfare departments of local authorities).

- Spend much time discussing complex procedural questions in English law such as the grounds in which a declaration might be an issue. The question assumes the availability of an appropriate remedy and procedure and is questioning you on possible barriers to access to these procedures or remedies. Procedure comes up more in the Legal Practice Course or Bar Vocational Course.

Convention rights: ancillary rights and pervasive principles

How this topic may come up in exams

Examiners may well want to test your knowledge of these general issues. They pervade the Convention and influence the way particular rights are applied (so these points are also useful for questions on substantive rights). Recall s 2 HRA 1998 – UK courts must normally follow Strasbourg interpretations, so these principles and rights apply in the UK under the HRA 1998 (even when not in Sch 1). All the themes mentioned here can be the subject of either essay or problem questions, though perhaps the former may be more expected. Article 13, the right to a remedy, is not the subject of a question here, but could come up.

■ Attack the question

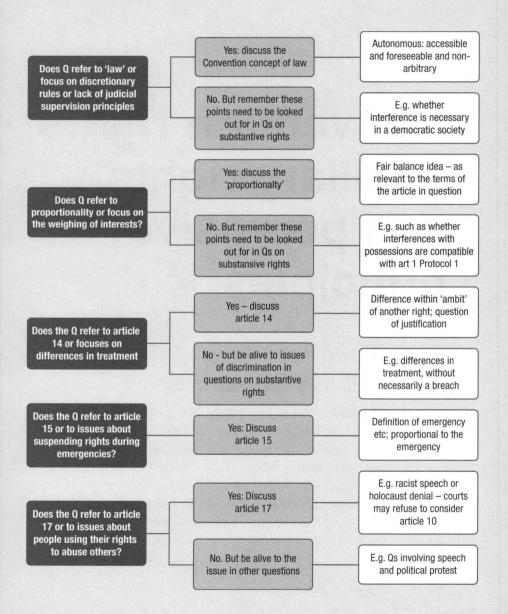

A printable version of this diagram is available from www.pearsoned.co.uk/lawexpressqa

🔍 Question 1

Describe and analyse the concept of 'law' in the European Convention on Human Rights (ECHR) and illustrate its significance for UK law both before and after the enactment of the Human Rights Act 1998 (HRA 1998).

Answer plan

→ Introduce the idea of 'law' as a pervasive, autonomous, concept.

→ Discuss the meaning of 'law' and illustrate its application in UK law.

→ At the heart of your answer define and illustrate the requirement that there be a basis in domestic law which is, also, accessible, foreseeable and non-arbitrary.

→ Explain the importance of process rights.

→ Discuss legality and the interpretation of statutes.

Diagram plan

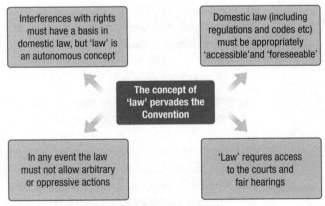

A printable version of this diagram is available from www.pearsoned.co.uk/lawexpressqa

Answer

[1]Begin by discussing and illustrating the way the rule of 'law' pervades the Convention.

The idea of 'law' pervades the Convention.[1] It is expressly referred to in some articles. Thus a deprivation of liberty must be in accordance with a procedure 'prescribed by law' if it is to be compatible with article 5. In particular interferences with the freedoms protected by articles 8–11 can only be justified if they meet the second paragraph conditions and these include being 'in accordance with' or 'prescribed by'[2] 'law'.

From the earliest cases (e.g. **Sunday Times v United Kingdom**[3] (1979–80) 3 EHRR 245) the European Court of Human Rights (ECtHR) has insisted that 'law' is an autonomous concept[4] and is not dependent on how an issue is regarded in domestic law. Domestic law must meet the standard of law as defined by the ECtHR.

The Convention concept of 'law' has been received into English law (following s 2 HRA 1998),[5] in, for example, **R v Shayler** [2001] UKHL 11. It must be said, though, that the Convention concept builds on the existing commitment of the common law to the rule of law,[6] which is one of the foundations of UK constitutional law. Nevertheless, the Strasbourg principles can reach those parts the common law cannot get to[7] and it has a significant impact on English law.

First, there must be a legal basis in domestic law for state interferences with rights. An interference by a state in breach of its own laws or without domestic legal authority would be a violation. Likewise, failure to regulate by law, in appropriate ways, can be a breach. In **Halford v United Kingdom** (1997) 24 EHRR 523 the tapping of internal communications systems was not expressly dealt with by legal rules and the ECtHR held there was a breach of article 8.[8]

The courts are looking for effective, legally enforceable, rules. 'Law' does not have to be statute or delegated legislation.[9] Codes of Practice, for example, are widely used in the United Kingdom. They are not directly binding but have to be taken into account. As such they can contribute to the overall legality of the way in which some matter is regulated. Thus in **Purdy v Director of Public Prosecutions** [2009] UKHL 45 the House of Lords accepted that the Prosecutors Code was a form of 'law'.

Secondly, the domestic 'laws' must be accessible and foreseeable.[10] Accessible means that a person, him or herself or through legal advice, must be able to identify the laws that apply to them. Foreseeable means that a person can predict with reasonable certainty the circumstances in which the law will be applied and so determine their conduct accordingly. These are not mechanical

[2] If you can remember these two different phrases – the first in article 8, the second in articles 9–11 – you impress by demonstrating your knowledge of the Convention text.

[3] An important case but you don't need to explore it if you are explaining 'law' through English cases.

[4] You will gain credit if you use the term 'autonomous' and show you understand its meaning.

[5] Now give 'law' its Convention meaning as adopted into English law under the HRA 1988. You will get credit for just mentioning s 2, but you don't need a full discussion.

[6] It is important you make this point, otherwise it will seem as if you think the Strasbourg principles are dramatically new.

[7] This demonstrates the complementary nature of Convention and common law (it is from Hickman, 2010).

[8] This is a difficult point to make concisely in an exam but you will get credit for showing you understand the need for sufficient certainty in the law.

[9] This point can easily be missed and you will gain credit for making it.

[10] Make sure you both use these terms (they show you have read the case law) and spend some time discussing what they mean. They are at the heart of the answer and will be looked for by the examiner.

[11]You gain credit for this.

tests.[11] They require judgment based on circumstances and context. In particular, the article involved, the accumulated effect of the laws and regulations involved and the degree and seriousness of interference are matters to be taken into account. An element of flexibility, allowing official discretion, is to be expected in laws that are not over-formal and rigid. Thus the need for clear and detailed rules and appropriate protections for those affected are likely to apply more emphatically in respect of, for example, secret surveillance than the policing of public demonstrations. Both, though, require what the court considers appropriate regulation (**Marper v United Kingdom** (2009) 48 EHRR 50; **cf Steel v United Kingdom** (1999) 28 EHRR 603).

[12]Having made the point in general terms, now illustrate it from two important post-HRA decisions.

Thus in **R (Gillan) v Commissioner of the Metropolitan Police** [2006] UKHL 12[12] the House of Lords found that the exercise of statutory powers of random stop and search were in accordance with the law even though the authority necessary for police to be able to use the powers had not been publicised. In **Purdy**, by contrast, it was held that the Code of Practice, used by the Crown Prosecution Service, was not appropriately specific in relation to assisted suicide. A person could not predict with sufficient certainty whether a prosecution was likely or not.

[13]Don't forget this third principle (it is often forgotten). Furthermore, make sure you show you understand it is fundamental and show you know that these principles are not to be applied in a mechanistic way.

Underlying this is the third, overriding, principle: domestic laws, even if accessible and foreseeable, must be sufficient to prevent the arbitrary use of power. In fact this relates to the way accessibility and foreseeability are understood.[13] Thus when Gillan went to Strasbourg, the ECtHR found a breach of article 8 on the grounds that there was insufficient legal control and proper safeguards over the way in which the power was exercised; it gave the police excessive and disproportionate discretion (**Gillan v United Kingdom** (2010) 50 EHRR 45). Likewise, exercises of power in bad faith will violate the Convention commitment to the rule of law, e.g. the 'administrative ruse' used in order to detain and then deport the applicants in **Conka v Belgium** (2002) 34 EHRR 54.

The Convention is not applied in a 'tick-box' fashion and points such as the above are also relevant in considering whether an exercise of power is proportionate and reflects a fair balance of interests. Thus in **Marper v United Kingdom** the ECtHR held that the legal control over the DNA Database was too vague and non-discriminating

[14]You get credit for not being hung-up on categories; in *Marper* the court declines to consider the quality of law issue because the issues are closely related to matters relevant to the fair balance.

[15]You will get credit for showing your understanding of the importance of judicial supervision of rights under the Convention.

[16]Conclude by showing how these principles come into English (and UK) law and linking to common law 'legality' shows your awareness of the human rights/common law relationship.

between different classes. These matters were discussed in terms of proportionality.[14]

Another important aspect of the 'law' and Convention rights relates to legal procedures and access to court. Article 6 provides a general right to a fair hearing regarding civil and criminal trials whilst article 5(3) and (4) require proper judicial supervision of deprivations of liberty. Likewise under other articles, such as article 8, proper legal procedures for the scrutiny of exercises of power that interfere with Convention rights such as private life etc may be necessary in order that legal regulation be effective, even though this is not expressly stated by the article. Effective supervision, using an adversarial process, in a tribunal independent of the executive with procedures based on equality of arms, will be required.[15] Such bodies need not be courts in the strict sense of the term. They may have closed procedures but these can be acceptable if joined with appropriate safeguards. What is required depends upon the context. In **Kennedy v United Kingdom** app 26839/05 judgment of 18 May 2010, the ECtHR held that the Investigatory Powers Tribunal, though not a court, had powers, procedures and safeguards that were appropriate in the context of secret surveillance.

The rule of law is an autonomous Convention principle with the characteristics outlined above. This principle is received into English law though the HRA 1998[16] as a standard against which to scrutinise public authorities (s 6 HRA 1988). It is also a principle governing the interpretation of legislation under s 3 HRA 1998. 'Law' means that wide discretion granted to officials in Acts of Parliament must be read down and cannot be used to authorise interferences with human rights. The 'legality' principle in **R v Secretary of State for the Home Department ex p Simms** [2000] 2 AC 115, by which express and specific statutory words are otherwise necessary, is thus adopted under the HRA 1998.

 Make your answer stand out

- *Sunday Times* v *United Kingdom* is the seminal Convention case on the autonomous concept of law and could be discussed in more detail (though its main terms are repeated in *Shayler*). Other cases in which the requirements are summarised and the requirements of non-arbitrariness made more explicit include **Hashmann & Harrup** (2000) 30 EHRR 241.

■ Discuss the impact of 'law' on the regulation and control of official activities taking place under the Royal Prerogative or the negative freedoms of the common law (e.g. the activities of the Security Service until 1989 or police phone tapping until 1985). Such activities, if they involve interferences with human rights (like unauthorised entry of property), need appropriate regulation in order to be compatible with the Convention. This goes some way towards explaining various enactments such as the Security Services Act 1989 and the Regulation of Investigatory Powers Act 2000. You could compare the domestic position in *Malone* v *Commissioner of Police of the Metropolis [1979] Ch 344* with *Malone* v *United Kingdom (1991) 13 EHRR 448* which led to the (now replaced) Interception of Communications Act 1987.

■ A brief reference to article 7 and the rule against retrospective application of laws will also impress on account of your overall knowledge of the Convention.

! Don't be tempted to ...

■ Write on 'rule of law' matters that are not directly relevant, such as equality under the law or whether a separate system of administrative law exists, is a good thing or leads to officials enjoying privilege.

■ Write material about the other matters that relate to justification under, for instance, article 8(2), 9(2), 10(2) and 11(2), such as legitimate purpose and necessary in a democratic society. Although you must be non-mechanistic in your approach, keep your focus on the issue of law.

■ Give too much detail on the various articles to which 'law' relates, though they need brief mention at the beginning.

📝 Question 2

Explain the differences betweeen Convention rights which are absolute, limited and qualified. How significant are the differences between these three types of rights in terms of the application of Convention rights?

Answer plan

→ Identify and explain 'absolute', 'limited' and 'qualified' rights.

→ Discuss the idea of 'proportionality'.

→ Show how proportionality can apply even to absolute rights.

→ Show how limited rights are subject to an overriding non-arbitrariness requirement.

→ Conclude by stressing the need for judgment in the effective application of rights.

Diagram plan

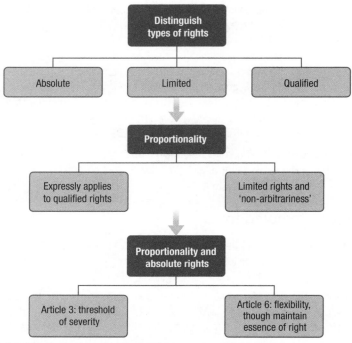

A printable version of this diagram is available from www.pearsoned.co.uk/lawexpressqa

Answer

The Convention rights, given further effect in UK law through the Human Rights Act 1998 (HRA 1998) are different not only in content but can be distinguished in terms of the kinds of judgment required from the domestic courts when giving effect to these rights. Specifically, the question is whether or not a court is required, under the terms of the article, to balance the applicant's claim to an entitlement against the rights of others or the common good.[1]

¹Begin by identifying the issue.

²You will get credit for using the correct term and showing understanding of how it has been defined under the Convention.

Proportionality is the name given to this kind of judgment.[2] It has been defined in various ways by ECtHR, but the common theme is for a court to assess whether, in the end, a fair balance of interests has been achieved between the impact on the individual whose right is in question and the interests of others and the common interests of society (e.g. **Sporrong and Lonnroth v Sweden** (1983) 5 EHRR

35). This view has been fully adopted into UK law in **R (Razgar) v Secretary of State for the Home Department** [2004] UKHL 27.

On their face, textually, Convention rights can be grouped into three general types: absolute, limited and qualified. These will be exemplified in what follows. It is not necessarily the case that an article is confined to one category.[3] Article 9, for example, has both absolute rights (e.g. the right to change religion) and a qualified right (the right to manifest religion or belief).

Absolute rights guarantee an entitlement without qualification or limit. Specifically, restrictions on the freedom they protect cannot be justified by reference to contrary interests such as the rights of others or the general social good. In that sense they are not subject to a proportionality judgment. Prominent examples are article 3, the right not to be tortured or suffer inhuman or degrading treatment or punishment, and the right to freedom of thought, conscience or religion (article 9).[4]

A second group of rights are limited in the sense that they guarantee a fundamental right in an apparently unrestricted way. These rights, however, do not apply in certain situations.[5] Thus article 2 requires states to prohibit intentional killing but then accepts that it can be legitimate to take life in certain situations defined in article 2(2). Article 5 creates a general right to liberty which the state must guarantee but then lists, in article 5(1), the sole circumstances under which the right to liberty does not apply.

A third group of rights are 'qualified'. In terms of the Convention text they have a similar structure. States must guarantee particular rights or freedoms, namely: respect for private life, manifestation of belief, freedom of expression, association and assembly.[6] But these rights can be justifiably restricted on the basis of law and for specific purposes. Most significantly, a third requirement for any effective justification is that any such restrictions must be 'necessary in a democratic society'. This means that the restriction must be a proportionate way of meeting a pressing social need (a phrase that goes back to **Handyside v United Kingdom** (1979–80) 1 EHRR 737). The application of these rights involves, therefore, some kind of judicial assessment of the balance of individual and collective interests and whether this can justify the restriction on the claimant's rights.

[3] It helps to point out you understand that Convention rights are not applied in a mechanical fashion.

[4] This is an unusual example which you will get credit for noticing – it needs to be distinguished from 'manifestation of belief', which you should refer to later.

[5] Now move on to introduce the second group of rights.

[6] Identify the rights you are referring to as 'qualified rights'; it shows greater relevant knowledge on your part if you can refer to the freedom that is protected rather than just the article number.

[7]You will get credit for this point – it both demonstrates knowledge of general themes about the way the Convention is interpreted and prevents you appearing to give an overly categorised view of how Convention rights are applied.

[8]Now move to this important theme, which is central to a good answer and shows subtlety in your understanding of all rights.

[9]Make this point – it will be anticipated by the examiner and you would lose credit if you did not make it.

[10]This point is confined to article 3, but since this is seen as the most absolute of all the rights, it helps to make the point in a sense of 'even article 3 ...'.

[11]The counter-terrorism example is a good one, but be careful to show the limit to the 'flexibility' of article 6 – it does have some iron in its backbone.

'Absolute', 'limited' and 'qualified' are at best general classifications. The Convention is seen, by the European Court of Human Rights, as an evolving instrument of human rights and the aim is to make rights effective in their application and not merely notional or theoretical.[7] The application of the Convention is not, therefore, based on strict adherence to formal categories.

The extent to which absolute rights are immune from a proportionality assessment can be debated.[8] Rights which, on their face, are absolute, can be differentiated into those which can and those which cannot be derogated from[9] (suspended) in time of 'war or other public emergency facing the nation' under the conditions in article 15. The ban on torture, slavery and retrospective crimes are examples of the former. Freedom of thought (article 9(1)), the right to marry (article 12) and fair hearings (article 6(1)) are examples of the latter. Whether the legal conditions for derogation exist includes a judgment, to be made by a court, about the need for measures interfering with rights considered in relation to the threat.

Similarly, a remedy for breach of an absolute right requires the existence of a state of affairs which, itself, can involve a proportionality-type judgment by the courts. Thus there will be a breach of article 3 only if the treatment in issue overreaches a threshold of severity.[10] Where that threshold should be placed (albeit in cases that are not obvious) can involve judgments about the need for various actions.

Article 6 is considered an absolute right. But what counts as a fair hearing is very flexible and dependent on context. In the context of counter-terrorism measures, for instance, principles relating to equality of arms between the parties in an adversarial system can be limited, subject to alternative, proportionate ways of safeguarding defendants' interests which preserve the core entitlement[11] (e.g. **A v United Kingdom** (2009) 49 EHRR 29). This flexibility reflects a further distinction. General expressions such as 'fair hearing' (article 6) or 'peaceful enjoyment of possessions' (article 1 of the First Protocol) are given effect in terms of more concrete rights which are implied or inherent in the general expression. Such implied or inherent rights, since they have no express textual basis, are more easily made subject to limits and restrictions which the court, on the basis of a fair balance, thinks is reasonable.

Secondly, limited rights are not immune from the need for judges to consider a balance of interests. The basic rule in article 5 is not whether the authorities have, in a mechanistic way, met the express criteria in article 5(1). Even if that is the case the overriding concern is that any deprivation of liberty should not be 'arbitrary'[12] (e.g. **H.L. v UK** (2005) 40 EHRR 32).

Applying Convention rights is likely to involve judges in assessing,[13] to some degree, whether an interference with rights is justified in terms of a balancing of interests including the interests of others and collective interests. This applies whatever the express form of the right: even rights which are apparently absolute have aspects of their application which require judgments of this kind. Such judgments are not necessarily made directly. They involve a prior consideration on when it is appropriate for a court, in the light of its proper judicial function of weighing relevant factors, to accept the judgment of the executive or legislature over the need for an interference with rights.

✓ Make your answer stand out

- Discuss the way the European Court of Human Rights has unpacked the idea of 'proportionality'. The application of the doctrine depends on the facts and context of the issue: matters such as whether a less restrictive alternative was available, whether domestic law was too rigid, laying down a rigid rule automatically applied rather than one more responsive to individual circumstances and the extent to which a restrictive legal provision provides compensating safeguards thus maintaining the essence of the right (see Rivers (2006) for a broad examination of European cases and of their application in the UK).

- Discuss the way proportionality has been received into UK law by the UK courts. In the context of administrative law the leading cases are *De Freitas* v *Permanent Secretary of Ministry of Agriculture, Lands and Housing* [1999] 1 AC 69, a Privy Council case adopted into UK law in *R* v *Secretary of State for the Home Department ex p Daly* [2001] UKHL 26, with crucial development (to make the need for a fair balance clear) in *R (Razgar)* v *Secretary of State for the Home Department* [2004] UKHL 27. Again, Rivers (2006) provides academic analysis.

! Don't be tempted to ...

- Expend too much energy in writing in detail about each of the Convention rights you identify and discuss. The question clearly requires a wide-ranging answer, dealing with examples from throughout the Convention, but there will not be enough time to explore the structure and case law of each article in any detail.

■ Over-categorise and make it seem as if rights are applied in an automatic way; this is clearly a danger in a question that is addressing types or categories of rights. Both expressly, and in the way you discuss cases and principles, try to communicate the flexible way the Convention is interpreted as an instrument dealing with the effective protection of human rights in the real world.

❓ Question 3

Jones has a contract with a foreign publisher to import and distribute in the UK a book on sado-masochistic practices. UK customs officials confiscate the book at Dover. They are exercising wide discretionary, statutory powers to confiscate any 'indecent material' which is being imported. A confidential Code of Practice indicates factors that officers should take into account when deciding whether a matter is indecent. There is no right of appeal from the exercise of these powers.

Having lost his legal challenges in the UK, Jones applies to the European Court of Human Rights in Strasbourg. Jones and the UK government both accept that there has been an interference with Jones's right to freedom of expression and that the interference served a legitimate purpose (the protection of morals). They disagree on whether the customs officials' actions were prescribed by law and proportionate (necessary in a democratic society).

Advise Jones on the general principles developed by the European Court of Human Rights for dealing with the two areas of disagreement.

Answer plan

→ Has the interference with Jones's freedom of expression been prescribed by law?

→ Consider 'law' as an autonomous concept: accessibility, foreseeability and adequate judicial supervision of discretion.

→ Was the interference with Jones's freedom of expression proportionate?

→ Define proportionality.

→ Consider 'margin of appreciation'.

→ Apply the law to the facts of the case: noting, especially, wide discretion, Codes of Practice, unpublished rules, no right of appeal, and that the issue is about protection of 'morals'.

Diagram plan

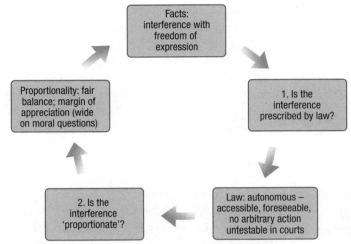

A printable version of this diagram is available from www.pearsoned.co.uk/lawexpressqa

Answer

The requirement that any interference with freedom of expression must be prescribed by law is both an express provision in article 10 and is pervasive of the Convention. Actions taken by state authorities which interfere with Convention rights and which are unlawful will violate the Convention for that reason alone.

The Convention concept of 'law' is autonomous – it is defined by the Strasbourg institutions and so compatibility with domestic law is not sufficient.

First, the interference must be in accordance with domestic law.[1] This is true in Jones's case since the lawfulness of Customs' actions is confirmed by the UK court and the European Court of Human Rights (ECtHR) has no jurisdiction to determine UK law.[2] Secondly, though, under the autonomous concept, a rule of 'law' must be 'accessible' and 'foreseeable'[3] (**Sunday Times v UK** (1979–80) 2 EHRR 245). Accessible means that the rules of law relied on by the authorities must be capable of being identified by the applicant or his or her advisers. Secret laws, not publicly promulgated, are not 'law' in the autonomous Convention sense. In the question the powers of

[1]Having identified the idea of autonomous concepts, now go on to consider the terms of the autonomous concept of 'law'.

[2]Briefly noting this point illustrates your understanding of the Convention as a matter of international law.

[3]It is important to discuss and apply these two concepts; it is clear from the question that they should form an important section of the answer (the sort of point you should note down as you read through the question).

the Customs officers are derived from ordinary statute, which is accessible. 'Foreseeable' means that the application of the laws, where, when and how they may authorise interferences with rights, needs to be foreseeable and predictable. The degree of foreseeability depends on the article and the circumstances. The implication here is that the statute, of itself, could authorise arbitrary, because unpredictable, actions. This need not be so where the uses of wide discretionary powers have been structured and limited by case law (such as in **Steel v UK** (1999) 28 EHRR 603). To similar effect the government will rely on the Codes of Practice. Under English law, breach of a Code is not normally unlawful. But if the courts take a Code of Practice into account when interpreting a statutory provision, it, the Code, can form part of the law and indicate its foreseeability[4] (**Sahin v Turkey** [2007] 44 EHRR 5). If so, in the question, the confidentiality of the Code may mean that it is not accessible. In **R (Gillan) v Commissioner of the Metropolitan Police** [2006] UKHL 12, the House of Lords accepted that a statutory power of random stop and search, whose application was glossed in a Code of Practice, met the 'law' test[5] even though it needed to be brought into effect by an undisclosed police authorisation. What is required for sufficient foreseeability depends upon the context. In a prevention of terrorism context the standard may be relatively low. It was enough that a person could know that the powers were available and could be used. This particular matter was not considered by the ECtHR in **Gillan v UK** (2010) 50 EHRR 45 (which found a violation of article 8). In Jones's case the context is different and, it is submitted, the 'protection of morals' (see article 10) may be too indeterminate and lacking in serious impact on individuals' lives to justify the use of non-disclosed legal regulations.

'Law' also means that the relevant laws and other rules must not permit arbitrary actions,[6] over which there is insufficient control. The wide discretion and the absence of any effective judicial control[7] either at the time confiscation is decided upon or through a post hoc appeal is striking, and in itself likely to be the basis of a violation.

'Necessary in a democratic society' (which is a term qualifying legitimate interferences with freedoms protected by articles 9–11) has been interpreted, by ECtHR, as requiring the Court to be satisfied that the restriction is a proportionate way of meeting a 'pressing social need'.[8]

[4]Again, spotting this point and showing how it contributes to the overall concept of 'law' will gain credit.

[5]There is no harm in using a UK, HRA 1998 case, in an answer that is mainly focused on Strasbourg case law; though you need to make it clear you know the origin of the case.

[6]This point is sometimes missed, so the examiner will be looking out for it and will award credit for it.

[7]The need for judicial-type supervision (i.e. by an independent and impartial body acting on the basis of a fair procedure) is another central aspect of the rule of law in the Convention sense and should not be ignored.

[8]Try to remember key phrases as part of your revision – it can impress.

[9]Having introduced the term, now give a general definition of proportionality.

Proportionality[9] has been discussed in various terms but the overriding point, which pervades the Convention, is to ensure that there has been a 'fair balance' between the various interests involved (**Sporrong and Lonnroth v Sweden** (1983) 5 EHRR 35).

[10]It increases credibility to show your understanding of this point and, also, that domestic courts have primary responsibility (first, not ultimate) for human rights protection.

Proportionality is a rule of law and so these are matters for judicial determination ultimately by the ECtHR but, primarily, by domestic courts.[10] It follows that a court may disagree with the assessment of fair balance made by a legislature (if the basic balancing of the interests involved is found in legislation) or the executive (where a balance of interests is made by a politician or official exercising discretionary authority).[11]

[11]You get credit for showing you understand the potential political tensions which the Convention can give rise to.

The balance must be 'fair' in relation to the burden of the particular article involved and the type and scope of considerations it gives rise to.[12] For instance, once it is determined that treatment meets the 'threshold of severity', it must be prohibited. In article 2 the balance will be tested against whether the use of force was 'no more than absolutely necessary', which gives a state little scope over the use of force and is a test a court can quite easily apply without making policy choices. Regarding articles 9–11 the test is whether an interference with rights is 'necessary in a democratic society',[13] which means whether it is a proportionate way of meeting a pressing social need. This is less demanding on states than the strict necessity appropriate to article 2(2) (**Handyside v UK** (1979–80) 1 EHRR 737). Different problems have different significance in different societies and need different solutions.[14] In this situation the ECtHR, as an international court,[15] recognises that states enjoy a 'margin of appreciation'. This means that the national authorities, because of their connection with the 'vital forces of their countries'[16] (**Handyside**) are better able to judge the need (in this less demanding sense) for restrictions. There is no clear Europe-wide standard for the Court to insist upon. But the Court retains its ultimate reviewing power and will examine the policies and decisions made in the case to ensure they are within the range which is compatible with the Convention.

[12]This point is important and it is useful because it allows you to get to margin of appreciation, which is clearly a focus of the question.

[13]You will get credit for examples taken from the Convention; doing this shows you are alive to the Convention as a whole and the different standards it requires.

[14]You should not normally use the same word four times in one sentence, but here it helps with emphasis.

[15]You must show you understand that 'margin of appreciation' is only applicable to an international court.

[16]Again a good phrase to try to remember – it will impress examiners if you can.

Where evidence of a common European standard emerges, the margin can be narrowed to exclude some options which were previously acceptable. Thus medical, social and ethical changes led the ECtHR to restrict the margin of appreciation as regards the law on transsexuals in **Goodwin v UK** (2002) 35 EHRR 18.

[17]The last paragraph should try to draw a conclusion based on case law. Of course other cases could be used where these seem to have links with the subject matter of the question.

In **Handyside** the Court accepted there was a margin of appreciation in relation to the necessity in a democracy for restrictions on publishing which threatened morals (under article 10(2) the 'protection of morals' is a purpose that can be served by restraints on freedom of expression). In **Laskey, Jaggard and Brown v UK** (1997) 24 EHRR 39, criminal penalties imposed upon consenting sado-masochists were upheld as within the margin of appreciation. This is likely to be the approach in Jones's case.[17]

✓ Make your answer stand out

- Discuss further the significance of the absence of a right of appeal. Article 6 requires access to court where a matter involves 'civil rights' (like Jones's rights to his property). Likewise a right of access to a court to have the legality of official action tested is a fundamental principle of common law. One possible response by the UK government might be that judicial review by the High Court of the action by HM Customs & Excise is available. But if you raise this point you need also to point out that, from the Convention perspective, judicial review may be inadequate. This is because it may not be possible to raise all the relevant questions dealing with the proportionality of the Customs' action using judicial review. This could be true, in particular, if testing foreseeability, accessibility and proportionality require judges to consider contested factual claims.

- Mention some of the academic discussion on the standards of review (e.g. Hickman, 2010, pp. 116–125).

! Don't be tempted to ...

- Write much on 'deference'. The question is focused on Convention rights and margin of appreciation, which is a principle relevant to an international court. 'Deference' applies only in domestic law and should not be merely equated with margin of appreciation. A wide margin of appreciation may offer a domestic court a degree of flexibility in terms of the meaning of a Convention right, but it does not require (though may permit) domestic courts to accept the proportionality judgement of legislature or executive.

- Write at length about too many other articles: they merely need to be mentioned in order to exemplify the variable standards of review.

- To discuss the Convention idea of lawfulness as if it just meant lawful under domestic law. This mistake is quite common and it is clear that the question needs you to discuss the autonomous Convention concept

❓ Question 4

Fletcher was convicted of murder and sentenced to life imprisonment (a 'lifer'). He was a low-risk prisoner unlikely to offend again. Under a statutory scheme he was allowed to live in the community after serving a number of years in prison. This is part of his sentence and occurs before the question of eligibility for release on licence arises. It is allowed only under certain conditions. The scheme applies to all low-risk prisoners convicted of serious violent offences whether serving life sentences or not.

First, like all prisoners released under this scheme, he was required to stay in his accommodation between 4.00 pm and 10 am (18 hours) and it is agreed by all parties that he is being deprived of his liberty.

Secondly, no matter what his behaviour was like, as a lifer the conditions were to apply for five years. In comparison, prisoners convicted of other serious offences could apply for the conditions to be removed after one year.

Thirdly, under the conditions, lifers are not allowed to seek employment. Other prisoners, however, are allowed to work up to 20 hours per week.

Fourthly, lifers are allowed only limited state benefits whilst other prisoners, released under the same scheme, have rights to the full range of benefits.

Fletcher is aggrieved at the difference in his treatment from other prisoners and believes he may be discriminated against in a way that is incompatible with his human rights. Advise him on the general principles of law, derived from the European Convention on Human Rights (ECHR), which will apply in this case.

Answer plan

→ Introduce article 14 and its main provisions, in particular that article 14 is not a free-standing right.

→ Fletcher is subject to the conditions for longer than others: discuss article 14 issues, especially whether being a certain category of prisoner is 'other status'.

→ Fletcher is not allowed to work: focus your discussion on whether this is within the 'ambit' of another Convention right, such as article 8.

→ Fletcher has lower benefits: focus your discussion on the need for justification for differences in treatment.

Diagram plan

Article 14 – general introduction	Fletcher – longer under 'conditions'	Fletcher – unable to work	Fletcher – lower benefits
• Not free-standing ('ambit' of another right) • Who are victims – 'other status' • Need for objective and reasonable justification	• Deprivation of liberty so article 5 engaged • Prisoners and 'other status' • Justification?	• Article 14 and ambit of another right • Article 8 and right to work? • No need to show a breach	• Ambit of article 1 of the First Protocol • Justification – core issues or social policy

A printable version of this diagram is available from www.pearsoned.co.uk/lawexpressqa

Answer

[1] Introduce article 14 early on.

[2] Although the question focuses on the principles coming from the ECtHR, you will get credit by pointing out that article 14 is a scheduled Convention right; this also enables you to use UK cases later on.

[3] This is the first general point that you should introduce now and then apply to the question later.

[4] This provision (which is found in the UN Universal Declaration on Human Rights) is very important and, again, is developed later.

[5] Again, it makes it easier to apply this vital point if you introduce it early. It shows you have understood the basic issues that article 14 raises for a court to determine.

Fletcher is complaining about differences in treatment between himself and other prisoners allowed to live in the community under the same statutory scheme. He will need to invoke article 14 ECHR.[1] This applies in the UK as a Convention right in Sch 1 Human Rights Act 1998 (HRA 1998)[2] and so the statutory scheme must be read and given effect to, if possible, with article 14 (s 3 HRA 1998) and the Prison Service as a public authority must act compatibly with article 14 unless the statute compels them otherwise (s 6 HRA 1998).

Article 14 prohibits discrimination. This is not a free-standing anti-discrimination provision. It applies only where there have been differences in treatment in respect of how the other, substantive, Convention rights are given effect. Therefore, there always has to be a link with another right; article 14 is not a ground of action by itself.[3] In terms of grounds of discrimination, article 14 lists specific grounds, such as sex, race and colour, which would be expected in an anti-discrimination provision, but then includes a residual provision: 'or other status'. This gives space for the categories of unlawful discrimination to be developed by case law.[4] Article 14 only prohibits differences in the way Convention rights are applied which cannot be justified. If a court accepts that there is an objective and reasonable justification[5] for the difference there will be no breach (**Belgian Linguistics Case** (1979–1980) 1 EHRR 252).

Fletcher is kept under 'the conditions' longer than other prisoners. The question makes it clear that he has been deprived of his liberty and therefore article 5 is engaged. It is unlikely that there is a breach of article 5(1) since there is no suggestion that his deprivation of liberty did not follow a lawful conviction for an offence. But it is possible to have a breach of article 14 without a breach of the substantive right[6] to which the discrimination claim is linked (e.g. **Abdulaziz v UK** (1985) 7 EHRR 471). Thus Fletcher can put article 14 in issue.

[6]This is the point this bit of the question is getting at, so make it clearly.

Fletcher then has to show that the difference in treatment between himself, as a lifer, and other categories of prisoners engages article 14 because it involves distinguishing on grounds of 'other status'. In **Kjeldsen v Denmark** (1979–80) 1 EHRR 711 the ECtHR held that 'status' needed to refer to a personal characteristic, suggesting something innate or inherent. Following this the House of Lords reluctantly denied the protection of article 14 to a long-term prisoner treated differently from long-term prisoners of a different category **(R(Clift) v SSHD** [2006] UKHL 54). However, the ECtHR has now made it clear that 'personal characteristic' is broadly drawn,[7] not confined to innate or inherent matters nor is it confined to matters *ejusdem generis* the express list[8] (**Clift v UK,** app 7205/07, judgment of 13 July 2010); and in **Clift** the ECtHR applied article 14 to differences in the treatment of different categories of prisoner.

[7]You will get credit for being up to date; also for recognising that the facts of the question suggest references to the *Clift* case.

[8]Use of Latin legal terms can be controversial but this is a well-known one (see your English Legal System notes on statutory interpretation) and, anyway it is the term used by the ECtHR.

Fletcher must show he is in a similar position, as regards relevant criteria, to the other more favourably treated prisoners.[9] A court must identify the relevant criteria that explain the applicant's position. In **Clift** the relevant criterion was a general concern with levels of risk. It is then necessary to decide whether the applicant's situation can be compared with that of the other prisoners. The ECtHR refers to the situations being broadly analogous, not identical. Following **Clift** it is likely that Fletcher's position can be compared with the other prisoners – they are all low risk.

[9]You will get credit for this and for distinguishing two issues: (a) whether groups of people are in the same situation; and (b) whether, being in the same situation, their position is broadly analogous and can be compared.

The final issue is whether there is an objective and reasonable justification for the difference in treatment. The difference must be a proportionate way of pursuing a legitimate aim. The ECtHR allows a margin of appreciation.[10] Here the issue is whether the state can establish an objective basis for the distinction between lifers and others. It may well be that a broad distinction based on the gravity of offences is such a justification. In that case Fletcher's argument

[10]Having introduced 'justification' earlier on, you will get credit for defining the idea more specifically in order to apply it to Fletcher's situation.

that the comparatively long time he is subject to the conditions is a breach of article 14 linked to article 5, will fail.

The comparatively more onerous conditions imposed on lifers as regards the opportunity to work could raise an article 14 issue but only if the conditions engage one of the substantive rights. There need not be a breach but, in the ECtHR's term, the discrimination must relate to a matter which is within the 'ambit' of a Convention right; it has to relate to a matter which is also the concern of the substantive right. UK courts, under the HRA 1998, have required there to be something more than a tenuous link with a substantive right; rather the alleged discrimination must affect the core interest that the substantive right[11] guarantees (**M v Secretary of State for Work and Pensions** [2006] UKHL 11). There is no express right to work in the Convention. The best Fletcher can hope for is that the Court accepts a link based on article 8. In **Sidabras and Dziautas v Lithuania** (2006) 42 EHRR 6 restrictions on employment opportunities for ex-KGB[12] officers were said to violate article 14 linked to article 8. Alternatively, if the rules leave Fletcher destitute then his treatment might be within the ambit of article 3.[13] If it is accepted that article 14 with article 8 is in issue, the other issues, referred to above, of comparison and justification will need to be dealt with.

The lower benefits available for lifers such as Fletcher may engage article 14. Although there is no positive duty on states to provide welfare benefits (so long as article 3 is not violated), if they choose to do so, the benefits may be 'possessions' protected by article 1 of the First Protocol.[14] This now applies even to non-contributory benefits (**Stec v UK** (2006) 43 EHRR 47). Fletcher's case is likely to focus on justification. Where a difference in treatment seems to challenge core values of the Convention and represents a failure to respect the autonomy and dignity of the individual (particularly when based on traditional categories of prejudice such as race or gender) the Court will undertake close scrutiny and require convincing justification. Differences of treatment in terms of social policy, including the distribution of welfare benefits, are more likely to enjoy a wide margin of appreciation[15] (**Stec**). If there is a rational basis for the difference in treatment of lifers and others, the policy is unlikely to be successfully challengeable under article 14 (e.g. under HRA 1998, **R (Carson) v Secretary of State for Work and Pensions** [2005] UKHL 37).

[11]You will get credit for awareness of both UK and ECtHR on the issue of 'ambit'.

[12]One of the difficulties of a question dealing with an ancillary right is that you need to demonstrate awareness of relevant substantive rights. You will get credit for spotting this possibility.

[13]This point will also gain you credit by showing you have broad knowledge of the Convention.

[14]Again, you need to ask yourself what right is engaged and, if you can show your understanding of the welfare points you will demonstrate a good general understanding and gain credit.

[15]Don't miss this important point. You will show, amongst other things, your understanding that the Convention aims to secure fundamental civil and political rights. Social rights (and, indeed, third generation rights to a clean environment,etc) are not its focus.

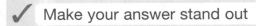

✓ Make your answer stand out

■ Show awareness of other forms of anti-discrimination law in which article 14 has a somewhat limited place. Thus the most effective and widely used provisions flow from EU law and are embodied in UK legislation such as the Equality Act 2010. These provisions mainly relate to discrimination in employment, the provision of services to the public and the activities of public authorities.

■ Discuss Protocol 12 to the ECHR. This does purport to be a free-standing anti-discrimination provision and prohibits discrimination in respect of 'any right set forth in law'. The UK has neither signed nor ratified this Protocol. You could also mention the EU Charter of Fundamental Rights. It, too, has a free-standing provision. The Charter is not directly binding in the UK but it will influence the development of UK law, at least on EU matters.

■ Discuss *Clift* more fully. It involved differences of treatment between prisoners seeking early release. Those serving a determinant sentence of less than 15 years or those serving life were more favourably treated than someone such as the applicant who was serving an 18-year determinant sentence. The UKHL and ECtHR disagreed on whether article 14 applied (the 'other status' point). This was not, though, a case involving tension with Strasbourg since UKHL only reluctantly followed their understanding of what was meant by personal characteristic. The ECtHR found there was no justification for the difference in treatment.

❗ Don't be tempted to …

■ Discuss irrelevant issues such as whether Fletcher was deprived of his liberty. The point is clearly given in the question – remember always to read questions carefully, asking yourself why certain matters have been included.

■ Write a great deal on UK or English prison law. The question is clearly asking you to discuss general principles of Convention law which will apply to the English law.

📰 Question 5

How do rights in the European Convention on Human Rights apply in respect of extremism, intolerance and actions aimed at undermining democracy?

Answer plan

→ Introduce the problem as one recognised in the Convention.

→ Discuss the preferred way – using the restrictive clauses and the context-flexibility of many rights.

→ Discuss article 15, the conditions under which it applies and the approach of the Strasbourg Court to it.

→ Note applications under the Human Rights Act (HRA 1998).

→ Discuss article 17 and give some measure of its impact.

Diagram plan

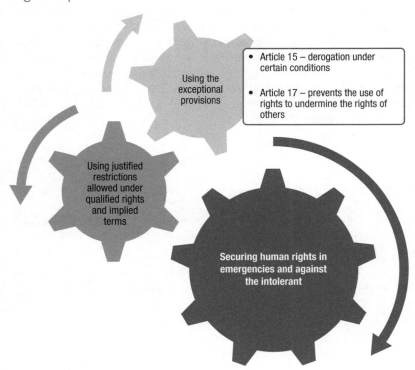

Using the exceptional provisions

- Article 15 – derogation under certain conditions

- Article 17 – prevents the use of rights to undermine the rights of others

Using justified restrictions allowed under qualified rights and implied terms

Securing human rights in emergencies and against the intolerant

A printable version of this diagram is available from www.pearsoned.co.uk/lawexpressqa

Answer

A significant dilemma is how to deal with political emergencies and with illiberal and intolerant political individuals and movements in ways that are consistent with human rights.[1] The European Convention on Human Rights (ECHR) was drafted with the fear of dictatorship and totalitarianism very much in mind. Likewise the Convention, as an instrument of the Council of Europe, stands four square for the values of democracy, pluralism and the rule of law. The drafters recognised that actions which might be needed to protect these values might require actions hard to reconcile with the values they are aimed to protect.[2]

[2]You will get credit for pointing out that the dilemma, and how to deal with it, was much in the drafters' minds at the end of the Second World War – demonstrate a historical sense about the development of the Convention.

Under the terms of the Convention there are two ways in which these matters are approached.

[3]It would be easy to miss this point since the focus is on the exceptional measures, but it is vital you don't.

First, through the contextual flexibility that is inherent in most Convention rights either from the express terms or from implied rights.[3] Thus article 10(2) allows free expression to be restricted on the basis of lawful and proportionate measures that protect the 'reputation or rights of others'. Racist speech can be restricted on these grounds (**Jersild v Denmark** (1995) 19 EHRR 1). Likewise it is accepted that rights inherent in the concept of a fair hearing (article 6) in trials can be limited in relation to anti-terrorism measures, so long as there are countervailing measures which are enough to uphold at least the core of the right in issue (e.g. **A v UK** [2009] 49 EHRR 18).

[4]You will get credit for not just making the point about preference but also for explaining why this is so.

This approach is preferred. It enables the courts to insist on the core, the essence, of the rights involved and so the protection of democratic values is maintained by applying Convention rights rather than setting them aside.[4]

The second approach uses the exceptional provisions in the Convention. These involve a court's inability or refusal to apply the right in question and for that reason are less desirable.

Article 15 allows a signatory state to 'derogate' (suspend) some of their Convention obligations. This power is available only in respect of a 'war or other public emergency facing the life of the nation' and any measures taken must be no more than what is 'strictly required' by the situation and not incompatible with international

[5]Having introduced exceptional powers and article 15, show that you have read and understood the latter's terms by discussing the conditions necessary for its exercise.

law.[5] In the UK, s 14 HRA 1998[6] allows existing derogations to be continued and new derogations to be made. Article 15 is not a scheduled Convention right, nevertheless it was accepted in **A (FC) v Secretary of State for the Home Department** [2004] UKHL 56, that the power to make and amend derogations must be exercised in accordance with article 15.

[6]A brief discussion of s 14 HRA 1998 gets you credit because it shows you are aware of derogation under UK law and are aware of issues discussed in **A**, the leading case.

The existence of a war or national emergency is a matter of law. However, in **Lawless v Ireland No 3** (1979–80) 1 EHRR 15 the European Court of Human Rights allowed a wide margin of appreciation on this point. The majority in **A** treated this as a signal that they, as a national court, should defer to the executive's assessment[7] of the seriousness of the situation.

[7]You will get credit for showing your understanding that 'margin of appreciation' is a term of international law significance only. It leaves the domestic courts free to take a more demanding legal approach if they want.

The need for the particular measures to be strictly required by the emergency is subject to closer scrutiny.[8] Measures which are disproportionate are likely not to be strictly necessary. Thus in **Aksoy v Turkey** (1997) 23 EHRR 553 the applicant was held for a long period of time by the authorities without proper judicial supervision and adequate safeguards. The ECtHR held that Turkey's derogation from article 5 (the right to liberty and security) did not allow such measures.

[8]You need to make this distinction; it shows, again, your familiarity with **A**.

[9]This case is clearly very important in this context and you will get credit from a very brief summary of the issue.

Likewise in **A**, under the HRA 1998, the executive could not demonstrate the strict requirements for the particular measures in issue. The case involved the detention without trial or conviction of foreign terrorist suspects who could not, for legal reasons, be deported. There was a purported derogation from article 5.[9] The House of Lords held that the strict requirement for these measures was not shown because of the difference in treatment between foreigners and equally dangerous citizens (who were not detained). There was also a breach of article 14 (the right not to be discriminated against in the application of rights)[10] in respect of which there was no derogation.

[10]You will get credit for showing you know the limited effect of article 14.

[11]Being able to give an example of these international obligations demonstrates an understanding of the international commitment to human rights of which the ECHR is part, and will impress the examiner.

Article 15 requires that the measures taken must not be incompatible with other obligations at international law. Since a measure such as the International Covenant on Civil and Political Rights[11] includes similar rights to those found in the Convention, this must be taken to refer to obligations other than those that mirror the ones derogated from.

[12]This point must not be missed if article 15 is properly understood.

Article 15 does not allow derogation from certain rights:[12] in particular, article 3 (torture etc), article 2 (respect for life, except lawful acts of war), article 4 (slavery and forced labour) and article 7 (retrospective crimes and punishments). Thus even in times of war, etc, states must guarantee a minimum protection for rights. The terrorist suspect must not be entirely beyond the human rights pale.

[13]Having discussed exceptional provision relating to national emergencies, now move on to discuss how the Convention deals with intolerance.

Article 17 stipulates that no one (including a state) has any right based on the Convention to engage in activities aimed at destroying the rights and freedoms protected by the Convention.[13] Its effect is to make a case inadmissible or to provide grounds for rejecting a claim that rights have been violated. It is recognised by the ECtHR that states must be able to defend their democratic system by taking exceptional measures which may limit individual freedom.[14]

[14]Try to stress the point that exceptional measures are allowed only if necessary for protecting democracy.

Such measures will need careful scrutiny by the judicial authorities (**Zdanoka v Latvia** (2007) 45 EHRR 17).

Article 17 has been used against those who espouse values or policies which are inconsistent with the democratic values inherent in the Convention. These include, for instance, 'pluralism, tolerance and broadmindedness' (e.g. **Fressoz v France** (2001) 31 EHRR 2.[15] They do not enjoy the protection of article 10. Expressions of racial hatred (**Glimmerveen and Hagenbeek v The Netherlands** (1982) 4 EHRR 260) or religious hatred (**Norwood v UK** (2005) 49 EHRR SE11) are examples, as is holocaust denial which is considered to be outside the pale of reasonable discourse because it denies established facts (see **Lehideux v France** (2000) 30 EHRR 665). Most controversially, states have been able to use article 17 to pre-empt the introduction of laws[16] and policies which, if implemented, would seriously undermine human rights and democracy. In 2003, for example, it was used against a party with major electoral support which would, if in power, have introduced Sharia law (**Refah Partisi v Turkey** (2003) 37 EHRR 1).

[15]You will get credit for referring to the conception of democracy espoused by the ECtHR, especially if you can give a typical quotation.

[16]By giving prominence to this principle, and to the *Refah Partisi* case which follows, you show your understanding of how great the tension between supporting human rights and giving effect to the will of the people for the time being can sometimes be!

The Convention gives scope to allow states to restrict political activity which would otherwise undermine democracy and pluralism. Such measures can clearly create tension with human rights and so, first, should be considered in respect of the powers of interference and restriction allowed for in the Convention text. Articles 15 and 17 go further and prevent the application of Convention rights, so most careful judicial scrutiny is required.

✓ **Make your answer stand out**

■ Briefly discuss Lord Scott's observations in *A* on the application of article 15 and of s 14 HRA 1998. His point was that the impact of a derogation on domestic law was nil since the HRA 1998 allows Parliament to enact clear provisions which are incompatible with Convention rights. Section 14 HRA 1998 allows for the making of derogations but does not mention article 15; nor is article 15 a Convention right.

■ In discussing 'war or other public emergency facing the life of the nation' you could (briefly) mention Lord Hoffmann's famous dissent in *A*. A threat must be to the basic institutions, culture and way of life; not just of serious violence.

■ Discuss the issue at a more theoretical level by referring (regarding article 17) to the idea of 'militant democracy' (see, Harvey, 2004). More general references to the Convention concept of 'democracy' will also impress (see discussions in Gearty (2000) and Mowbray (1999)).

■ Be more critical and analytical of article 17 – is it possible that the article might allow states to suppress dissent merely because of its radicalism rather than it being a threat to democracy.

❗ **Don't be tempted to ...**

■ Overextend yourself on the philosophical issue of tolerance of the intolerant, etc. It is a major issue about which philosophers and theorists have written and disagreed. In a law answer you cannot allow yourself to get too bogged down in this. You have to focus on articles 15 and 17, as demanded by the question.

■ Write too much on the qualified rights. They are clearly relevant and all (or at least articles 9, 10 and 11) have public and political action as a focus of their application. It would be easy to use up too much space on broad, general, descriptive writing on them.

Articles 2 and 3 and the use of force by the authorities

How this topic may come up in exams

Questions can be general or ask more specifically about particular themes. The main focus is on the application of these articles to the deliberate use of lethal force by the state and to the treatment of detained persons. There will be both problem and essay questions (for the former, examiners may have some recent event, like a police shooting, in mind). Questions will test not only knowledge of the negative but also the positive obligations that can arise. A common theme is the 'procedural' obligation of investigation. Articles 2 and 3 can also come up in other contexts such as are considered in the next chapter.

■ Attack the question

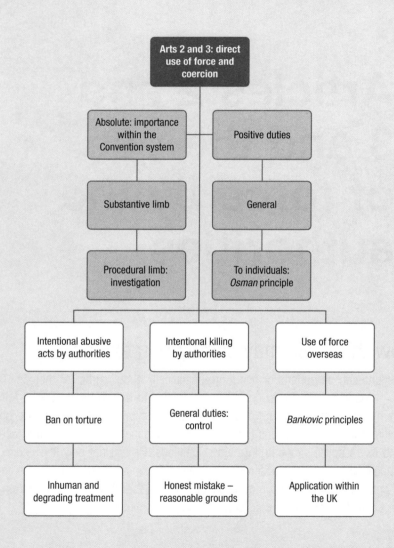

A printable version of this diagram is available from www.pearsoned.co.uk/lawexpressqa

 Question 1

Identify and evaluate the general standards concerning the state's use of force required by articles 2 and 3. Refer in your answer to both the Convention and to its reception into English law. Illustrate your answer with appropriate cases.

Answer plan

→ Introduce article 2 and 3 and their role under HRA 1998.

→ Discuss the 'absolute', non-derogable status of both articles (compare with article 8).

→ Outline the principal state obligations under article 2 (substantive and procedural limb).

→ Outline the principal state obligations under article 3.

→ Exemplify the impact of both articles on the use of force in England.

Diagram plan

State agents and Human Rights Act	Article 2: Substantive limb	Article 2: Procedural limb	Article 3: Prohibition of torture etc	Impact in UK
• Police etc are public authorities (s 6 HRA) • Police etc claim statutory authority (s 3 HRA)	• General duty to respect life • Possible specific duties to individuals • Ban on intentional killing • Possible justifications for intentional killing	• Duty of full investigation of death involving state responsibility • The nature of a full investigation	• Definitions of torture, inhuman and degrading treatment etc • Absolute nature of the ban	• Eg: prison conditions, investigations of prison deaths, police methods • Deportations

A printable version of this diagram is available from www.pearsoned.co.uk/lawexpressqa

[1]Start by showing why police etc, on the basis of domestic law, are required, given the terms of the HRA 1998, to respect Convention rights.

[2]It is reasonable to use the titles in the Convention – though note that article 3 includes inhuman and degrading treatment and punishment.

Answer

The United Kingdom (UK) exercises its 'monopoly of legitimate force' through agencies such as the police and prison service which, as 'public authorities' much of whose authority flows from statute, must act compatibly with Convention rights[1] unless compelled otherwise by statute.

Article 2 is the right to respect for life and article 3 the prohibition on torture[2] and inhuman and degrading treatment. The Court of

[3]Now discuss the 'absolute' nature of both rights; a point of comparison with other rights.

[4]This is the first case in which the Court explored article 2 and should be referred to.

[5]You will get credit for signalling your understanding that some degree of proportionality is found in all articles, even those that are fundamental.

[6]Move on to discuss article 2 in general terms.

[7]Show that article 2(2) defines the only circumstances in which intentional killing can be excused; this strengthens your answer.

[8]A summary of the text is preferable here – there are no marks for copying from a statute book.

[9]Knowledge of recent cases will impress.

[10]Make sure you discuss the positive duties, both general and particular.

[11]Show you understand that the Convention aims at effective, not just formal, human rights protection.

[12]Move on to consider the exceptions – how intentional killing may be lawfully excused or justified.

[13]Point out the pervasiveness of (albeit limited) proportionality.

[14]The procedural limb must be discussed – it has had a considerable impact on the law in the UK.

Human Rights (ECtHR) has frequently described these articles as being fundamental[3] and particularly important within the Convention scheme (e.g. **McCann v UK**[4] (1995) 21 EHRR 97). Under article 15 neither article can be derogated from in times of emergency (apart from, in respect of article 2, deaths from 'lawful acts of war'). Nor is there scope for a proportionate balancing of rights against common interests, as is allowed under article 8, for instance, in respect of restrictions on private life (though judgements of proportionality cannot be completely avoided[5] – see below).

Article 2[6] places a general duty on states to protect life and, secondly, it requires states to prohibit intentional killing. States may have laws which excuse intentional killing but only[7] if death results from a use of force which is a strictly proportionate ('no more than absolutely necessary') means of defending a person from unlawful violence, giving effect to a lawful arrest or quelling a public disturbance.[8]

The ECtHR has distinguished 'substantive' and 'procedural' limbs to article 2 (e.g. **Silih v Slovenia**[9] (2009) 49 EHRR 37). The substantive limb refers to the general duty in the first sentence to protect the right to life in the way in which lethal force or coercion is used. Positive duties[10] are implied. These ensure that there are proper systems and institutions in place (such as police, prosecutors, courts and prisons) to give practical effect[11] to the article through punishment, deterrence and compensation (**Osman v UK** (2000) 29 EHRR 245). Where there is a known 'real and immediate' risk to an individual's life there may be a particular duty to take reasonable protective steps (**Osman**; adopted into domestic law in **Re Officer L** [2007] UKHL 36).

The exceptions to the prohibition[12] on intentional killing, in article 2(2), must be strictly applied. States must show that their use of potentially lethal force (there does not need to be a death) was for one of the three purposes in article 2(2) and that the decision to use it was 'absolutely necessary'. Although this introduces a measure of proportionality[13] there is greater judicial scrutiny and less balancing of interests than is allowed for the question of what is 'necessary in a democratic society' in articles 8–10.

The procedural limb[14] includes a duty on states to hold an effective investigation into deaths for which it has responsibility, especially where state agents were the direct cause. An effective investigation is independent of the executive and has the authority to call witnesses etc in order to get at the truth, allocate responsibility (including to officials) and learn lessons. Where possible it should be in public with a sufficient involvement of the family to secure their interests (**Jordan v UK** (2003) 37 EHRR 2).

[15]Move on to a general description of article 3.

Article 3[15] prohibits 'torture' and 'inhuman or degrading treatment or punishment'. It is a fundamental, non-derogable right. The ban on torture expresses perhaps the most fundamental obligation on a state, based not just on its agreements but also on its status as a civilised state (*jus cogens*.)[16] In **Ireland v UK** (1978) 2 EHRR 25 the ECtHR defined 'torture' in terms of serious and deliberate inhuman treatment and inhuman treatment involving intense physical and mental suffering. In later cases, such as **Selmouni v France** (2000) 29 EHRR 403 it also referred to the UN Convention Against Torture whose definition is more particular in terms of purpose and the involvement of officials. Degrading treatment was defined in **Pretty v UK** (2002) 35 EHRR 1 and includes causing humiliation, fear, anguish or inferiority so as to break an individual's resistance.

[16]It is important to show that the ban on torture is basic to international law. The term *jus cogens* is perfectly acceptable in this context.

Article 3 is absolute in the sense that it is not possible to justify torture etc in terms of the collective benefits, the rights of others or the wickedness of the victim. Nevertheless, article 3 is only engaged in respect of sufficiently serious treatment[17] and whether this threshold is passed will depend upon the context, which itself can be a measure of the importance of the purpose being served, etc. Likewise there is a threshold between 'torture' and 'inhuman treatment' which may change as European standards develop (**Selmouni**).

[17]Show how the application of article 3 can depend upon context.

[18]Move on to discuss reception in domestic law.

[19]Remember the focus of the question is on the coercive side to state power (police, prisons, etc).

The impact[18] of articles 2 and 3 in respect of the coercive power[19] of the state in England has been significant. The approach to the investigation of deaths in prison, including murders by other inmates and suicides, has been transformed in terms of independence, thoroughness and family involvement (**R (Amin) v Secretary of State for the Home Department** [2003] UKHL 51. Coroners may now explore not just the immediate cause of a death but also, where necessary for article 2, the surrounding circumstances (**R (Middleton) v West Somerset Coroner** [2004] UKHL 10), although[20] this does not apply to examining the wider policy choices which are the context of the death (**R (Gentle) v PM** [2008] UKHL 20).

[20]Although you are recognising the positive impact, 'critically evaluate' requires you to be sensitive to limits.

The ban on torture etc, in article 3, was used in **A v Secretary of State for the Home Department** [2005] UKHL 71, to reinforce the ban on the use in courts of evidence obtained by torture; though the majority accepted that evidence could be admitted unless the court was satisfied that the evidence had been obtained by torture (as distinct from being satisfied that there had not been torture).

Both articles 2 and 3 have had an impact on prison conditions. In **Napier v Scottish Ministers** 2005 1 SC 229 'slopping out' violated article 3. Article 2 imposes duties on prison authorities to have proper regard to ill or disabled prisoners (**Keenan v UK** (2001) 33 EHRR 38); the duty is to take reasonable steps (**R (Spinks) v Secretary of State for the Home Department** [2005] EWCA Civ 275).

The most controversial impact of the articles relates to deportation. A state violates the Convention if it deports a person to a country where they might be killed or suffer a violation of article 3. This applies no matter how great is the threat to the UK if the person is allowed to stay (**Chahal v UK** (1997) 23 EHRR 413). The UK government seeks to avoid this matter on the basis of diplomatic assurances and these are consistent with article 3 in principle (**Othman v Secretary of State for the Home Department** [2009] UKHL 10).

 Make your answer stand out

- Introduce specific detail – e.g. s 117 Police and Criminal Evidence Act 1984 authorises the use of force by the police which could reinforce the opening.

- When referring to allowable exceptions and restrictions (e.g. excusable intentional killing), refer to article 18 – restrictions on rights are allowable only if applied for the purposes given in the Convention.

- Quote certain phrases like 'war or other public emergency threatening the life of the nation'; but avoid copying large chunks of text if you are allowed to bring a statute book into the exam.

- Show clear understanding of the 'level' of law you are describing – the deportation issue, for example, relates to the Convention and is not a consequence of the HRA 1998.

? Question 2

The Allchester police receive a call from a member of the public that there is an armed man in the local car park. Trained, armed officers attend the scene. They spot Bloggs, 50 yards away, who has blond hair, is wearing an overcoat and is holding a package. They receive a clear message from the officer in command in the police station that Bloggs fits the description given by the member of the public and that he is armed. The officers shout 'Stop! Armed police'. Bloggs turns and seems to wave the package. PC Irons believes that Bloggs is about to fire at him. He shoots and kills Bloggs. Bloggs turns out to be unarmed and the package to contain a small table lamp.

Identify and discuss the general Convention principles with which the domestic law governing these matters needs to be compatible and which should guide the government in its responses.

Answer plan

→ Show how article 2 is engaged and applies to English law through the HRA 1998.

→ Briefly introduce the main themes of article 2. Note *McCann* v *United Kingdom* (1995) 21 EHRR 97.

→ Consider the ban on intentional killing and the exceptions in article 2(2).

→ Discuss the issue of an honest mistake as to the need for the use of force; is English law fully compatible with the Convention?

→ Refer to the issue of control and organisation of the use of force.

→ Discuss the duty on the state to hold an independent investigation.

Diagram plan

A printable version of this diagram is available from www.pearsoned.co.uk/lawexpressqa

[1] Since there are no particular difficulties about the relevance of article 2, don't allocate much time to the point.

[2] A brief title to each section can assist the examiner.

[3] You will get credit for this; it shows you are aware of the full text of article 2.

[4] You will get credit for showing your understanding of the importance of remedies.

[5] Move on to the ban on intentional killing, which is the focus of the question.

[6] 'Excuse' is probably the right word here rather than 'justify'. Excuse implies that intentional killing remains wrong but can be accepted in some circumstances; justify implies that the killing was the right thing to do..

Answer

The use of potentially lethal force by the police and other state agents engages article 2 ECHR under HRA 1998[1] because police etc are public authorities (s 6 HRA 1998) and the use of force engages statutes that must be interpreted compatibly, if possible (s 3 HRA 1998). Article 2 is fundamental in the sense that it does not allow the protection of life to be compromised in terms of the needs of a democratic society and there can be no derogation, in times of war or public emergency, except in 'respect of deaths resulting from lawful acts of war'.

The shooting of Bloggs[2]

Article 2 involves a general duty to protect life.[3] Fulfilling this duty requires an effective system of criminal law aimed at the punishment of offenders and the deterring of others; and perhaps also compensation through civil law.[4] There is also an obligation on states to prohibit intentional killing though this is subject to three exceptions[5] found in article 2(2). States may have laws which excuse[6] an intentional use of lethal force which causes death if, first, the use of

[7]Try to remember the phrase. If not, make sure you get across the crucial points: that the use of force should be no more than is 'absolutely necessary' and that it can be used to defend a person from 'unlawful violence'.

[8]It is not necessary to quote article 2 (2)(b) and (2)(c).

[9]The question makes English law relevant and so at least a reference to 'reasonable force' is necessary.

[10]This is the leading Convention case on article 2 and should be referred to.

[11]Though the different meanings of 'necessary' need to be noted, avoid a discussion of articles 8–11 except on the 'trade-off' point.

[12]Do not indulge in pointless speculation about what the facts might be.

[13]*McCann* is a factually complex case. Avoid spending too much time on the facts and address the relevant legal points.

force was 'no more than absolutely necessary'[7] and, secondly, the use of force was for one or more of three listed purposes and not for any other purpose. Relevant to this question[8] is article 2(2)(a) 'in defence of any person from unlawful violence' (including, of course, self-defence). In English law,[9] section 3 of the Criminal Law Act 1967 allows the use of 'force as is reasonable in the circumstances' in order to prevent crime or effect a lawful arrest. Both provisions permit self-defence which is the defence PC Irons is likely to use.

Mistake

In **McCann v United Kingdom** (1995) 21 EHRR 97,[10] it was accepted that the difference between the necessity and reasonableness tests was not significant enough in practice to be the basis of a violation of article 2. A court must be satisfied that the actions of the police were 'strictly proportionate in the circumstances'. This is a more demanding justification than is required by 'necessary in a democratic society' and means that the kind of 'trade-off' between individual and collective interests, allowed in respect of articles 8–11,[11] is not permitted under article 2.

The issue of reasonableness and necessity is largely a matter of detailed fact.[12] However, the question raises the legal issue whether PC Irons can rely on his mistake of fact as to the danger he was in. Here there is a possible incompatibility between English law and the Convention. In **McCann**[13] the Court of Human Rights (ECtHR) accepted there is no violation if the use of lethal force is based on an honest but mistaken belief itself as to the facts which was 'perceived, for good reasons, to be valid at the time'. However, under English law the honesty of the belief, whatever its grounds, is sufficient. The reasonableness of the belief may, as a matter of fact, affect the assessment of honesty; it is also decisive in respect of a civil action (**Ashley v Chief Constable of Sussex Police** [2008] UKHL 25). The position is reinforced by s 76 Criminal Justice and Immigration Act 2008). So if it is accepted that PC Irons had an honest belief that he was about to be shot, the fact that Bloggs turned out to be unarmed will not affect the success of his defence.

Organisation

[14]The issue of planning and organisation (based on *McCann*) is clearly important and needs to be addressed.

Article 2 imposes a duty on state agencies to ensure that the use of lethal force is properly regulated, planned and controlled[14] (**Makaratzis v Greece** (2005) 41 EHRR 4). In **Bubbins v UK** (2005) 41 EHRR 24 the shooting of a man carrying a replica gun did not involve a violation of article 2. As well as an honest and reasonable fear that the officer's life was in danger, there was no evidence that the operation had been planned other than in a way that sought to minimise the risk to life. The killing in 2005 of Jean Charles de Menezes, who was shot dead by police who believed he was a terrorist, led not to prosecutions of individual officers but to the conviction of the Metropolitan Police Service under Health and Safety legislation[15] based on general failures of organisation. Thus the accuracy and basis of the message about Bloggs that was communicated to PC Irons is a highly relevant matter in assessing the compatibility of the police's actions with article 2.

[15]This issue has had such a major impact that it is worth introducing into your answer.

Investigation

[16]Now move on to the issue of the procedural 'limb' of article 2(1).

The general duty in article 2(1) has a procedural 'limb'[16] which imposes a duty to provide an adequate investigation into a death (**McCann**). This duty has been fully accepted as a matter of English law in **R (Amin) v Secretary of State for the Home Department** [2003] UKHL 51. It applies to any death for which the state has responsibility[17] and this will clearly apply to deaths caused by the use of lethal force by state agents.

[17]There is no need to explore the complexities of the scope of state responsibility, which is a big topic.

[18]You will impress the examiner if you can indicate the main aspects of an effective investigation.

The requirements of an adequate investigation[18] depend upon the particular circumstances of the case. The investigator needs to be independent of the authorities and the parties but other requirements will relate to context. However, where the circumstances (either obviously or after an initial enquiry) indicate direct state responsibility, a full inquiry will be necessary (e.g. **R (JL) Secretary of State for the Home Department** [2008] UKHL 68 which involved attempted suicide by a prisoner).[19] Where, as here, the deceased was killed by the intentional actions of state agents, a full investigation is necessary. Its purpose is to discover what happened, allocate responsibility (including the grounds of possible criminal prosecution) and to learn lessons for the future (**Amin** and **JL**). The investigation must be initiated by the state, independent, able

[19]Show you understand that the nature of an effective investigation can depend on the context.

to exercise sufficient authority to be able to compel witnesses and get at all the relevant issues. It must be conducted with reasonable promptness, with an appropriate element of public scrutiny and with sufficient family involvement to protect their interests (**Amin** following **Jordan *v* UK** (2003) 37 EHRR 2).

In England such investigations may be conducted by coroners. Where there is state responsibility, article 2 requires a coroner to be able to explore the circumstances in which the deceased met his death (though not the broad policy background, **R (Gentle) *v* PM** [2008] UKHL 20) and not be confined to the simple cause of death (**R (Middleton) *v* West Somerset Coroner** [2004] UKHL 10 and s 5 Coroners and Justice Act 2009). The article 2 duty may also be discharged by other investigative bodies such as the Independent Police Complaints Authority or, if necessary, ad hoc or statutory investigations.

The government, therefore, must ensure that there is an adequate investigation into Blogg's death.

✓ Make your answer stand out

- Add more detail and references to cases if you can. An important decision of a Grand Chamber on the duty to provide an adequate investigation, *Ramsahai* v *The Netherlands*, (2008) 46 EHRR 43 could be mentioned.

- Show awareness of the controversial nature of these cases which involve the use of force by the state. Very often there are disputes over the facts which don't necessarily affect the law.

- The Convention has made a considerable impact on UK law in this area (especially the procedural limb), so make sure you are aware of the 'level' of the piece of law you are discussing – is it a decision by the Court of Human Rights on the Convention or an English court dealing with the Human Rights Act?

! Don't be tempted to …

- This is a problem question so you must concentrate on the specific issues raised in the question. Although you need to introduce the subject matter (article 2) make sure you do this briefly and do not get swept away with demonstrating your knowledge of the background to the question.

■ Avoid spending too much time on article 2 issues that do not relate to the use of lethal force by the state. The application of article 2 to hospitals or to deaths caused by environmental hazards is interesting but not relevant.

🗨 Question 3

A Discuss the impact of article 3 on the treatment of persons detained by the state in the United Kingdom.

Answer plan

→ Article 3 in general: negative and positive duties.

→ The prohibition on torture: definitions and application.

→ Inhuman treatment: definition.

→ Application of the ban on inhuman treatment to detained persons in both Convention and UK law.

→ Application of the ban on inhuman treatment in various circumstances such as control methods, prison conditions, ill or disabled prisoners, compulsory treatment.

Diagram plan

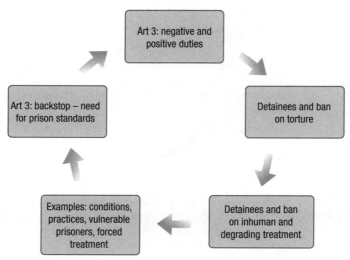

A printable version of this diagram is available from www.pearsoned.co.uk/lawexpressqa

Answer

[1]Begin by introducing article 3; but do so briefly.

[2]It is worth quoting the article in full since it is short.

[3]Show you understand the point that there are also positive duties.

[4]Defining 'detained persons' makes it clear to the examiner how you understand the question.

[5]Show the difference, in relation to the absolute nature of article 3, between negative and positive duties.

[6]Show you understand this important point.

[7]Now move on to discuss the specific provisions of article 3.

[8]It is important to make the point that the illegality of torture is not just found in article 3.

[9]Note that the international duty includes the creation of domestic offences.

[10]A leading early case ('five techniques') on the definition of torture which needs to be cited.

[11]Define torture – if you can, briefly quote the definitions given.

[12]This is an important case dealing with the threshold between torture and inhuman treatment.

Article 3[1] ('No one shall be subjected to torture or to inhuman or degrading treatment or punishment')[2] imposes a combination of negative and positive duties[3] on the state in relation to detained persons (e.g. arrested persons, convicted prisoners or those detained under mental health laws).[4] Negative duties require officials to refrain from certain practices, like torture. Positive duties require officials to exercise appropriate care to avoid placing detainees in situations in which article 3 might be violated. The Strasbourg Court has recognised the special vulnerability of detainees (who are under the complete control of the state) as imposing positive duties to ensure that treatment does not violate article 3 (e.g. **Keenan v UK** (2001) 33 EHRR 913). There is an important difference.[5] Negative duties apply 'absolutely' in the sense that treatment violating the article 3 standard cannot be justified in terms of a fair balance with the social good or the rights of others. A positive duty, on the other hand, is only to take proportionate steps to deal with a threat, coming from others, which could breach the article 3 standard (this point was affirmed in domestic law in **Re F (a Child)(Northern Ireland)** [2008] UKHL 66). Article 3 only applies to treatment that reaches a necessary degree, or threshold, of severity.[6] This threshold, however, is not constant but depends on a range of circumstances such as the age of the people involved.

The torture of detainees[7] is absolutely prohibited by article 3. This reinforces at the European level the illegality of torture[8] found in treaty-based international law (in particular the UN Convention against Torture, UNCAT) and in *jus cogens*, the compulsory part of customary international law. International law requires that torture by officials be made a domestic offence[9] (see, for the UK, s 134 Criminal Justice Act 1988).

In **Ireland v UK**[10] (1978) 2 EHRR 25 the Court of Human Rights (ECtHR) defined torture[11] as 'deliberate inhuman treatment causing very serious and cruel suffering' which extends to both physical and mental effects. In later cases (e.g. **Selmouni v France**[12] (2000) 29 EHRR 403) the UNCAT definition has been used which includes an express reference to official acquiescence. Special opprobrium is reserved for torture and (as **Ireland** demonstrates) distinguishing it from inhuman treatment is important. In **Selmouni**, the ECtHR accepted that this threshold could develop over time.

Much ill-treatment of detainees will not involve torture but will still be sufficiently severe to be prohibited by article 3. Inhuman treatment has been defined in terms of treatment which deliberately causes intense physical or mental suffering, or which humiliates and debases the victim or which arouses fear likely to break physical or moral resistance[13] (see **Pretty v UK**[14] (2002) 35 EHRR 1).

Article 3 has been applied to prison conditions in, for example, **Peers v Greece** (2001) 33 EHRR 51. There are now numerous cases dealing with issues like overcrowding and purposeless humiliation. The application of article 3 links with other international and European initiatives,[15] such as the visiting procedure based upon the European Convention for the Prevention of Torture. It must be stressed that article 3 is only engaged by treatment that goes beyond the normal consequences of lawful imprisonment.

The threshold of severity to engage article 3 is determined contextually and domestic courts will consider the matter in terms of national expectations[16] which may be more demanding than the minimum standards of the Convention. In **Napier v Scottish Ministers** 2005 1 SC 229, for example, Scottish courts held that article 3 was violated by the continued (at one time common) practice of slopping out.

There are a number of practices that are used on detained persons which can be acceptable if used for proper purposes,[17] such as preventing escape, maintaining the security of a prison or proper punishment, but which, if used to humiliate and degrade or subordinate, may violate article 3. The use of handcuffs, strip and intimate searches and seclusion are examples. In **Wieser v Austria** (2007) 46 EHRR 54, for example, handcuffing out of public view did not violate article 3 but an unnecessary strip search did. In **R (Faizovas) v Secretary State for Justice** [2009] EWCA Civ 373 English courts held that handcuffing a prisoner, on the basis of a risk assessment, whilst he was undergoing chemotherapy did not in itself violate article 3, but that the local guidelines needed to be reviewed to enable individual circumstances to be taken into account.

Inherent in the general positive duty are more specific duties owed to especially vulnerable prisoners[18] such as those who are ill or

[13]Attempt a general summary of the definition of inhuman treatment; this is taken from *Pretty*.

[14]Like *Ireland, Pretty* (though not a case about detainees) is one of the important cases dealing with basic definitions of the terms of article 3.

[15]You will get credit for pointing out that there are other Conventions etc that apply to prison conditions.

[16]The question requires you to make reference to the impact of article 3 in the UK.

[17]Now move on to discuss practices commonly used against prisoners. Note the point that, in this context at least, the application of article 3 depends not on what is done but on the purpose.

[18]Note the particular care that is required for ill or disabled prisoners.

disabled. There is an enhanced positive duty to deal with known, real and immediate risks (see, for example, **Price v UK** (2002) 34 EHRR 128 where the failure to give proper care to a detained person with severe disabilities was a breach). However, if the authorities have taken steps which are reasonable in the context, there will be no violation (see **Keenan v UK** (2001) 33 EHRR 913). Thus, in **R (Spinks) v Secretary of State for the Home Department** [2005] EWCA Civ 275, the Court of Appeal refused to set aside the Secretary of State's decision not to release a mortally ill prisoner on compassionate grounds. In the particular circumstances, retaining S in prison would not breach the threshold of severity.

Another area[19] where article 3 applies to detained prisoners relates to forced medical treatment. Whilst compulsory treatment of a fully competent prisoner[20] would be unlawful (and a breach of article 8), the problem arises in respect of those detained on mental health grounds who cannot make choices for themselves. The general principle is that treatment that is a 'therapeutic necessity' to preserve the patient's life or health and is properly administered under the national law, albeit without consent, is unlikely to violate article 3 (**Herczegfalvy v Austria** (1992) 15 EHRR 437.[21]) However, such highly vulnerable patients do not lose the protection of article 3 and particular vigilance is necessary. This was demonstrated in English law in **R (Wilkinson) v Broadmoor Hospital** [2001] EWCA Civ 1545 where the Court of Appeal held that the therapeutic need for the treatment had to be proved in an adversarial process.

Article 3, therefore, remains as a basic backstop to protect the interests of detained persons and to ensure they are treated with basic humanity. It does not, however, lay down or require states to set out basic prison standards[22] covering all aspects of the way prisoners and detained persons are treated.

[19]There is a whole range of topics that you could mention. But be selective – a few topics is enough. What is important is that you demonstrate your understanding of the general principles.

[20]Use this expression to describe a person able to make decisions for him or herself.

[21]Not all ECHR cases are easy to spell – do your best; this case is often quoted.

[22]A good way to conclude is to make the point that article 3 is a backstop provision and not a substitute for the articulation and imposition of a set of basic standards for prisoners.

✓ **Make your answer stand out**

■ Mention the general position of prisoners, both under the Convention and in Common Law, that they retain their rights subject to restrictions necessarily following from imprisonment; though note that under domestic law prisoners lose rights which have been taken away expressly (like the right to vote – itself subject to adverse Strasbourg judgment).

- There are plenty of examples of abusive treatment of prisoners from the European case law which could be mentioned, such as *Lorse* v *The Netherlands* (2003) 37 EHRR 3 or *Mayzit* v *Russia* (2006) 43 EHRR 38.
- Refer to academic writings such as Foster (2005b) which considers European case law and the relevance of the Human Rights Act.
- Make fuller reference to the work of the European Committee for the Prevention of Torture and Inhuman or Degrading Treatment or Punishment whose visiting/reporting activities and standard setting is a useful background to the judgments of the Court of Human Rights on prison conditions (http://www.cpt.coe.int/en/about.htm).

! Don't be tempted to ...

- The question refers specifically to article 3 so do not spend time and energy on discussing other Convention rights, such as article 2, article 8 or article 3 of the First Protocol which can also be relevant to the treatment of detained persons; at most, a brief reference can be helpful. (A more wide-ranging question on prisoners' rights is possible, depending on your syllabus; the issues in this question would clearly be relevant but you would need to add more.)
- Though (highly) selective use of cases can be helpful, avoid the grisly details (the facts of some European cases are shocking).

? Question 4

Paul is a convicted child molester who is serving his time in HM Prison Slade. He believes that child mostesters are badly treated by fellow prisoners and so he asks for extra protection. The prison authorities refuse because there are no prisoners with a known record for violence in the prison and because they have not heard of any specific threat to Paul. Paul is murdered by a fellow inmate. There is an internal prison service investigation held behind closed doors.

Paul's mother does not accept the outcome of the investigation and seeks your advice on whether her rights under article 2 have been violated.

Answer plan

→ Note the issue that Paul's mother has standing to bring a case in respect of her son's death.

→ Introduce the 'positive duties' under the substantive limb of article 2(1).

→ Describe the positive duty owed to individuals known to be at risk based on *Osman*.

→ Consider the adoption of the *Osman* duty into English law and apply it to the facts in Paul's case.

→ Discuss the state's duty under the procedural limb to hold an adequate investigation, including family involvement, and apply it to Paul's case.

Diagram plan

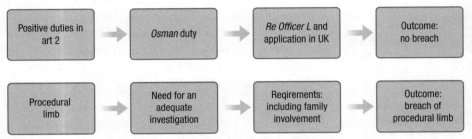

A printable version of this diagram is available from www.pearsoned.co.uk/lawexpressqa

Answer

[1]Begin by noticing and dealing with the question of whether Paul's mother has standing to bring a case based on Convention rights.

As the most immediate relative of the victim, Paul's mother could bring a case[1] based on an alleged violation of article 2 (the right to life) to the European Court of Human Rights (ECtHR). She is treated as the directly affected 'victim' for the purposes of article 34 (e.g. **Yasa v Turkey** (1999) 28 EHRR 408). Section 7 of the Human Rights Act 1998 (HRA 1998) allows actions alleging breaches of Convention rights by public authorities to be brought in the UK courts but only if they could, also, be taken to Strasbourg.

[2]Move on to introduce the general idea of 'positive' duties under article 2(1) as an aspect of the substantive 'limb' of article 2(1). Remember that, later, you will be dealing with the procedural 'limb' of article 2.

Paul's mother will allege a breach of the state's duty under article 2 even though Paul was not intentionally killed by state agents. The first sentence of article 2(1) has been interpreted by ECtHR as imposing on states general positive duties[2] to take appropriate steps to protect the right to life (e.g. in **Osman v UK** (2000) 29 EHRR 245). These include establishing appropriate laws, etc, for dealing with those responsible for threats and deaths and they have also been extended to impose duties on states to secure safety in respect

[3]Get to the main issue in the question, the *Osman* duty.

[4]This point is important as regards the *Osman* duty; explore the scope and nature of the duty a bit.

[5]Give a very brief outline of the main facts of the case. *Osman* is one of the big cases and needs to be known.

[6]Now move on to apply the *Osman* duty to prisoners, such as Paul.

[7]Since Paul's mother wants to allege a breach of the Convention before the UK courts, this is important.

[8]This is the leading case in which the House of Lords adopted these Strasbourg principles and you will get credit for referring to it.

[9]Showing the often complementary relationship of common law and Convention rights will impress. It shows you have a good understanding of the relationship of human rights and domestic law.

[10]Try to keep to the factual context of the question. Some of the important cases of general application involve prisoners.

[11]This is a relevant case because of its facts (though slightly modified by *Re Officer L*).

[12]You will get credit for exploring this case. You can then apply the general principles, about the *Osman* duty, that it lays down as binding in English law.

of dangerous environments (e.g. **Öneryildiz v Turkey** (2005) 41 EHRR 20). Emphatically, these duties extend to places such as prisons, for which the state has direct responsibility. The duty to protect the right to life of prisoners is particularly acute because of their vulnerability and dependency on the state (**Edwards v UK** (2002) 35 EHRR 19).

Where officials, such as police officers, know or ought to know of a 'real and immediate risk' to the life of an individual they have a positive duty to take steps to protect that person[3] (**Osman v UK** (2000) 29 EHRR 245). The duty is not absolute.[4] Its extent must depend on the circumstances and it should not be interpreted so as to impose an unreasonable burden on the authorities. Nevertheless, the authorities are required to do what they reasonably can; a breach does not require gross negligence. In **Osman**[5] the police had responded to concerns about a teacher's behaviour in ways which reflected their understanding of the degree of risk, and so there was no breach.

The **Osman** duty has been applied to prisoners.[6] In **Keenan v UK** (2001) 33 EHRR 913, ECtHR found no breach of article 2 in respect of the way the authorities dealt with a known suicide risk; in **Edwards**, however, there was a violation in respect of a prisoner killed by a cell mate with a known history of violence.

This specific **Osman** duty has been fully adopted into UK law under the Human Rights Act[7] (**Re Officer L**[8] [2007] UKHL 36), and reinforces existing common law principles.[9] It has been applied in the Prison context[10] such as in **R (Bloggs 61) v Secretary of State for the Home Department** [2003] EWCA Civ 686. Here the Court of Appeal held[11] that there was no breach of the duty when prison authorities proposed removing Bloggs from a protected witness programme.

Re Officer L clarifies a number of issues[12] regarding the application of the **Osman** duty on the basis of the Human Rights Act and, although not a prisons case, it is relevant to Paul's situation.

First, the Law Lords rejected the idea, canvassed in earlier cases, that the duty on an authority is greater where, as in Paul's case, the alleged risk is caused directly by the authority's own decisions. There is a single test ('real and immediate risk') which must be applied in the particular context. Secondly, the risk must be 'real' in the sense of being based on objective evidence and not just the subjective fears of the person. It must also be 'immediate' in the sense of ongoing. The authority's own risk assessment is likely to be important here. In particular, they stressed that there must be some additional risk created by the authority's action or inaction that is complained about. The evidence for proving the risk must be strong and compelling; it is not a simple thing to do. Thirdly, the duty is to take proportionate steps as measured by the degree of real risk. In **Van Colle v Chief Constable of Hertfordshire** [2008] UKHL 50 the House of Lords stressed a further point: that the extent of the duty must be measured by the state of real or constructed knowledge[13] of the authorities at the time. If the facts as, reasonably, they were understood at the time did not point to a real and immediate risk to life, then there is no breach of the **Osman** duty.

Neither **Re Officer L** nor **Van Colle** are prisons cases. Nevertheless, when considered in the light of **Bloggs 61**, they suggest a lack of objective evidence of risk that, at the time of denying Paul protection,[14] should otherwise have triggered the **Osman** duty. This would be enforced on the evidence that the authorities had undertaken a specific risk assessment.

Paul's mother objects to the investigation. The 'procedural limb' of article 2[15] requires an adequate investigation (**McCann v UK** (1995) 21 EHRR 97). It applies[16] when there is an 'arguable breach' of the substantive duty (**R (Gentle v PM** [2008] UKHL 20) but is not confined to that and so it can apply in other circumstances such as where there has been a failure in the protection owed to prisoners. The procedural duty was adopted into UK law, regarding the investigation of prison deaths, in **R (Amin) v Secretary of State for the Home Department** [2003] UKHL 51. Following **Jordan v UK** (2003) 37 EHRR 2, **Amin** identifies the main characteristics of such an investigation:[17] in particular, it must be instigated by the state, independent of the authorities and have sufficient authority to compel witnesses and evidence in order to make effective findings about what happened and who was responsible (including, if necessary, making recommendations for criminal prosecution) and learn lessons for the future[18] (**R (JL) v Secretary of State for the Home Department** [2008] UKHL 68). The full extent of the investigation will depend on the circumstances which may be only fully understood after a preliminary, independent inquiry (**JL**).

[13]Remember to point out the importance of this point about the state of knowledge of the authorities; it shows you have a full understanding of the issue.

[14]Apply some of these principles to the facts of the question.

[15]Now move on to discuss the procedural, investigative, limb of article 2. This is important for the overall coherence of your answer.

[16]The authorities are not clear on this and you will get credit for raising the point.

[17]Remember to be able to summarise the main characteristics of an adequate investigation. If nothing else remember independence and, given the question, family involvement.

[18]By adding this point you will get credit for showing you are up to date with developments in English law.

Family involvement, to the extent necessary for them to protect their interests, is vital. In **Amin** it was one of the main reasons for finding that article 2 had not been complied with. However, family rights are not absolute and, for example, a family's desire to have a public inquiry will not necessarily outweigh serious considerations to the contrary (**Taylor v UK** (1994) 18 EHRR CD 215).

Clearly there has been a breach of the procedural limb of article 2.

✓ Make your answer stand out

- Make reference to the duty to protect life in administrative law, such as *R (A)* v *Bloody Sunday Inquiry* [2001] EWCA Civ 2048, which complements Convention law.
- Refer to academic analysis of the *Osman* duty such as is discussed in numerous articles, e.g. McIvor (2010).
- Refer to relevant articles on prisoners' rights in the context of article 2, in particular Foster (2005a).
- Show awareness of the limits to the positive obligations in article 2 based, in particular, in *Gentle*. This is an interesting case which indicates the limits, in terms of background policy, to the state's duties.

! Don't be tempted to ...

- Spend too much time on the full scope of positive obligations but get on to the focus on prisoners.
- Spend too much space in exploring all the requirements of a fair procedure – the focus in the question is on family involvement.
- Go too far out in your discussion of article 2, especially in respect of other contexts such as the duties owed by hospital authorities to patients including vulnerable mental patients. These are very interesting but not sufficiently focused on the prisons context of the question.

📝 Question 5

Discuss the extent to which Convention rights, especially articles 2 and 3, have an impact on the legality of the activities of British forces when acting overseas outside Europe.

Answer plan

→ The Human Rights Act 1998 mirrors the Convention in terms of its jurisdiction.

→ Note definition of 'jurisdiction' in *Bankovic*.

→ Consider the protection given by articles 2 and 3 to alleged victims of the action of UK forces.

→ Consider, the protection given by articles 2 and 3 to British military personnel.

→ Discuss the situation of UK forces acting as agents of another power or the UN.

Diagram plan

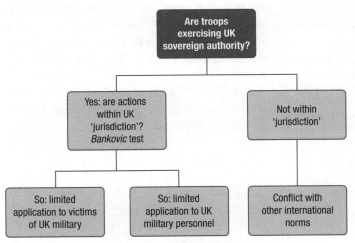

A printable version of this diagram is available from www.pearsoned.co.uk/lawexpressqa

Answer

In places such as Afghanistan and Iraq British forces are exercising force outside the United Kingdom and outside Europe.¹ Difficult questions of law have arisen relating to whether not only the armed forces but also the local population enjoy the protection of Convention law, in particular articles 2 and 3.²

The issue is whether servicemen and local people have, because of the Human Rights Act 1998 (HRA 1998), rights under English and

[3]Strengthen your answer by showing you understand the difference between Convention rights as part of the international obligations of the UK and as part of UK domestic law.

[4]Discussion of this important case will be expected; it provides the basic principles for the jurisdictional scope of the Act in UK law.

[5]This is how you should refer to states when it is the fact of their having obligations under the Convention which is important.

[6]You will get credit for noting that *Bankovic* is a Grand Chamber decision. It is an authoritative decision which has been broadly followed by the UK courts.

[7]As UK courts have noticed, the extent of the exceptions is not altogether clear; try to summarise them.

[8]Now move on to discuss how these principles have been applied in the UK under HRA 1998.

[9]You will show your understanding of the case if you note the fate of the majority of applicants even if Baha Mousa, the one successful applicant, is the one we remember.

UK law actionable before UK courts. This is a different question[3] from concerns about the UK's international obligations under the European Convention (ECHR) dealt with by an action before the Court of Human Rights (ECtHR).

In **R (Al-Skeini v Secretary of State for Defence** [2007] UKHL 26[4] the House of Lords held that the area of application of a UK statute was, subject to express exceptions, the United Kingdom. However, a principle of statutory interpretation is that Parliament intends to legislate compatibly with UK's international obligations. These obligations included article 1 ECHR: the duty of a High Contracting Party (HCP)[5] to secure Convention rights to everyone within its 'jurisdiction'. The aim of the HRA 1998 is to provide remedies in UK courts only where they could also be available before the Strasbourg court. The term 'jurisdiction', therefore, should be understood the same way as under the ECHR. In **Bankovic v Belgium** (2007) 44 EHRR SE5 a Grand Chamber[6] of the ECtHR held that, normally, the Convention applied only within a state's geographical territory or where the state had taken over effective control of a part of the territory of another HCP (the Convention laid down standards not for the world but for the European 'espace juridique'). Based on case law, however, it acknowledged exceptions.[7] Thus the Convention could apply to non-European territory which was under the exclusive control of an HCP or in respect of places such as the HCP's consular buildings. What is not accepted is that Convention obligations are attached, as it were, to HCP's officials, such as its soldiers, and so applies to all their actions wherever they are.

These principles are applied by UK courts.[8] There have been allegations by non-British nationals that they were victims of violations by British troops in Iraq. The Convention is, however, of only limited assistance. In **Al-Skeini** it was accepted that procedural rights under article 2 applied to an Iraqi beaten to death by British troops inside a British army prison established in Iraq after the invasion. Following **Bankovic** the prison could be seen as a place of exclusive British control or, by analogy, comparable to a diplomatic building. However, the UK Supreme Court agreed that a number of other allegations[9] which related to actions by troops outside their bases did not engage Convention rights. Britain was not in legal and political control of this part of Basra and Convention rights do not attach to

[11]You strengthen your answer by showing understanding of the basic principles to be applied. There is no need to explain 'substantive' or 'procedural' limb in such a question so long as you use the terms correctly.

[12]Again, you need to demonstrate knowledge of some major aspects of article 2.

[13]You indicate your understanding of article 2 with this phrase and, so long as you use it in an appropriate way, you don't need to explain it further and you will get credit.

[14]This is a complex matter, involving some difficult case law which you need to summarise. In your revision keep an eye on latest developments from the Strasbourg Court.

officials wherever they are. This point is now before the Strasbourg Court.[10]

A different issue is whether article 2 and other rights must be secured by the UK government for British military personnel operating in Iraq. The issue in **R (Smith) v Oxfordshire Coroner** [2010] UKSC 29 was whether a coroner was required to investigate the death, in Iraq, of a soldier from heatstroke in a way that met the procedural limb of article 2. The Supreme Court (UKSC) reversed the Court of Appeal and held that soldiers did not benefit from article 2 just because they were on active service abroad. Convention rights would only apply, following **Bankovic**, to deaths on an exclusively controlled British base. The UKSC also held that, even where Convention rights applied, the mere fact of a death whilst on active service would not amount to an arguable breach of the substantive limb of article 2,[11] thus triggering a full investigation.

If soldiers do not, subject to **Bankovic** exceptions, enjoy Convention rights directly relating to actions outside Europe, what rights do they have in respect of decisions taken by public officials (bound by s 6 HRA 1998 to act compatibly with Convention rights) in the UK? In **R (Gentle) v PM** [2008] UKHL 20, the UKSC accepted that UK officials in the UK had to act compatibly with Convention rights. But the impact will be limited. Putting troops in danger is not, in itself, an arguable breach of the substantive limb of article 2 and the **Osman** duty,[12] to take appropriate protective steps, requires a real and immediate risk to a known individual and so is not likely to be relevant to general policy decisions. Nor does article 2 impose a duty to obtain proper legal advice and not send troops to an illegal war. Finally, the procedural limb of article 2[13] does not require a broad-ranging investigation into underlying policy issues.

Troops abroad must act with proper legal authority and difficulties can arise when British troops act in the name of a non-Convention country or organisation.[14] Thus, in **R (Al-Saadoon) v Secretary of State for Defence** [2009] EWCA Civ 7, the applicant prisoner had been transferred from a British base in Iraq to the Iraqi authorities. There was a real risk that he would suffer the death penalty. Removing someone from the protection of the Convention where there is such a risk violates article 3 (**Soering v UK** (1989) 11 EHRR 439). British courts, however, held that British troops, at the time, were agents of the Iraqi government without independent legal authority. **Bankovic** exceptions regarding 'jurisdiction' do not apply unless such authority existed. The ECtHR, however, has held that article 3 was violated in **Al-Saadoon v UK** 08, judgment of 2 March 2010. The UK should not have entered into an agreement with a state where capital punishment was a risk and it had not taken effective steps to seek to negate that risk.

In **R (Al-Jedda) v Secretary of State for Defence** [2007] UKHL 58, a prisoner was detained by British troops acting on UN authority. His detention violated article 5 ECHR but was authorised under the UN Security Council (UNSC). UNSC Resolutions have priority over incompatible rules of international law. UKHL allowed this violation of article 5 but only to the extent necessary for detention. **Al-Jedda** is pending before the ECtHR.

[15]You will impress the examiner and get credit if you can refer to ongoing (November 2010) issues like this inquiry which are a direct consequence of the HRA 1998.

The **Bankovic** approach limits the application of articles 2 and 3 in respect of British troops and to those affected by their actions. Some serious wrongs may not be adequately dealt with. On the other hand, as the public inquiry into the death of Baha Mousa[15] indicates, where they apply, Convention rights can bring about important results.

✓ Make your answer stand out

- The *Bankovic* decision has been subject to critical discussion which can be referred to, such as Loucaides (2006).
- You could briefly compare the concept of jurisdiction under the Convention with jurisdiction under the ICCPR (see King (2009).
- Refer to the changed context brought about, in the UK, by the International Criminal Court Act 2001 (see, for example, Rasiah (2009)).
- Briefly refer to other areas of tension involving the relationship of the UN and human rights law. A good example is the controversy over the freezing of assets (see, for instance, *HM Treasury* v *Ahmed & Others* [2010] UKSC 2).

! Don't be tempted to …

- Explore the impact on other Convention rights, unless necessary to make a point about article 2 or 3.
- Overstress any political objections you may have – these are controversial decisions. Remember to focus on the law – it is quite complicated enough!

Articles 8 and 3: privacy and welfare

How this topic may come up in exams

You may get questions looking at article 8 generally (see Q1 below). Given the wide and indeterminate range of applications, article 8 lends itself to problem questions. Given the reach of the topic, though, questions may focus on particular aspects or particular applications of the article. Usually these will be related together (e.g. respect for 'home' and its application to evictions). Always remember and be prepared to discuss justification – make sure you understand the issues raised by the terms of article 8(2). Questions can invoke the overlap between article 8 and article 3 (e.g. on welfare or deportation). Be sensitive to this, especially in problem questions, and be able to contrast article 3 and article 8, especially on the issue of justification.

Attack the question

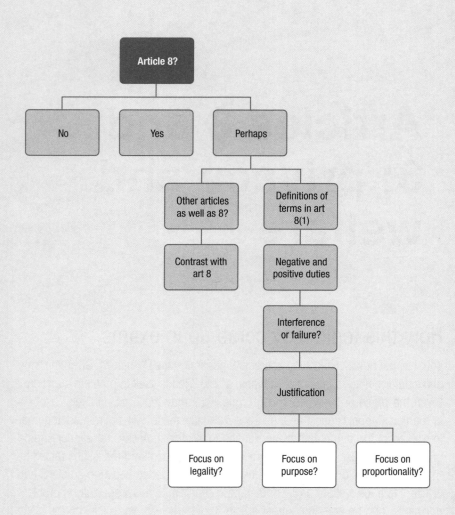

A printable version of this diagram is available from www.pearsoned.co.uk/lawexpressqa

📰 Question 1

Discuss the general standards article 8 requires of domestic law in light of the way the concept of 'private life' has been interpreted by the European Court of Human Rights.

Answer plan

→ Discuss the interpretation of 'private life' by the European Court of Human Rights.

→ Give examples of the policy areas in which this wide interpretation is likely to have an impact.

→ Note that states have positive duties as well as negative ones.

→ Discuss the issue of justification under article 8(2).

→ Note the importance of 'proportionality'; discuss 'margin of appreciation' and (for domestic courts) 'deference'.

Diagram plan

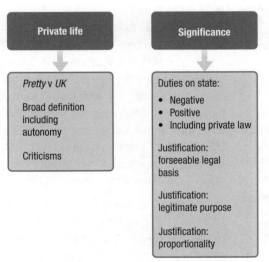

A printable version of this diagram is available from www.pearsoned.co.uk/lawexpressqa

Answer

¹Begin by discussing and illustrating the wide definition of private life given by the Court.

Article 8 guarantees a right to 'respect' for 'private life' (as well as family life, home and correspondence). The European Court of Human Rights (ECtHR) has drawn a broad conception of private life[1] and has refused to give an exhaustive definition of the term and has given it a meaning going beyond simply being left alone. Respecting 'private life' involves upholding a range of factors necessary for the adequate development of personality and individual well-being.

²*Pretty* is one of the leading cases which needs to be discussed.

Factors that constitute private life have been summarised in **Pretty v UK** (2002) 35 EHRR 1.[2] Thus laws, practices, etc., which interfere significantly with physical or psychological integrity (such as conditions of imprisonment or laws governing sexual offences), or which restrict a person's ability to express their sexuality, sexual life or affect other features of identity, such as gender and name, can be covered by the term 'private life'. Of great importance to private life

³You will get credit if you can give references for some of the examples you give – *Leander* is one of the important early cases.

is personal information and so article 8 can be engaged when it is taken, stored, used or distributed (**Leander v Sweden** (1987) 9 EHRR 433).[3] **Pretty** also makes it clear that restrictions on personal development and the ability to form relationships with others can also come within the protection of article 8(1) (**Niemetz v Germany** (1993) 16 EHRR 97). In **Pretty**, the ECtHR also extended 'private life' to include 'autonomy'. This is the idea that people should be free to live their lives as they wish and, in particular, should be free to make life-determining decisions, such as choices about the ending of life (**Pretty**) or if and when to procreate (**Evans v UK** (2008) 46 EHRR 34). Later cases have even brought restrictions on economic life, such as on access to the labour market, within the scope of article 8 (**Sidabras and Dziautas v Lithuania** (2006) 42 EHRR 6).

⁴Points like this show your understanding of difficult and controversial areas of the law, that it is not just automatic rule following. This goes well with examiners.

The concept of private life is, therefore, broadly defined and the structure and boundaries of the concept not determined. In the UK this has caused some criticism[4] on the grounds of a lack of certainty of the law (**R (Razgar) v Secretary of State for the Home Department** [2004] UKHL 27) and also on whether the Convention ought to embody a general right to do as one pleases (**R (Countryside Alliance v AG** [2007] UKHL 52).

⁵Move on to briefly illustrate policy areas on which article 8 has an impact.

State institutions must respect this broad and somewhat indeterminate conception of private life in the policies they pursue.[5] Even

6This term, which is a bit odd, is used quite a lot. By addressing it directly you can also make the point about article 14. There is not space to discuss article 14 in detail but show, at least, your understanding that it deals with differences in treatment which are unjustified and confined to the way Convention rights are secured. You impress examiners by thinking of the Convention generally, not just the specific article in issue.

7Discuss the role of positive duties in respect of article 8; this will be expected and should not be forgotten since they are of particular significance respecting article 8 (especially the possible requirement to regulate the private sector).

8You gain credit for distinguishing article 8 from other articles such as article 3. Again, this shows awareness of the ECHR as a whole (it also enables you to move to the issue of justification under article 8(2)).

9A proper discussion of justification which, in respect of a qualified right, is vital and will be expected.

10Try to use the phrase in the text of article 8 – it will impress the examiner more than 'prescribed by law' (used in Articles 9–11) or some general descriptive phrase. It is worth learning these little phrases from the Convention text in your revision.

in ostensibly public situations – situations that are not private in the narrow sense of the word – public bodies have to be aware of how their policies impact on individuals. Thus decisions taken about prison conditions, immigration policy and deportation, media regulation, secret surveillance and welfare entitlement are based on policies, the impact of which on individuals can engage article 8. Environmental law is a good example: although there is no express right to a clean environment, in so far as private (and family life) is affected by pollution, etc, article 8 may be engaged.

The term 'engaged'[6] refers to, first, the state having consequential duties to ensure that private life is respected in the circumstances. Secondly, it can mean that a matter is within the 'ambit' of article 8 and so the state must ensure that its policies and practices do not involve unjustified 'discrimination', in terms of article 14, regarding the ways policies have an impact upon the 'private life' of different categories of the population.

The authorities must refrain from actions which interfere in an unjustifiable way with a person's private life, as defined. From its earliest cases (e.g. **X & Y v Netherlands** (1986) 8 EHRR 235), however, the ECtHR has also imposed on states positive duties,[7] requiring 'positive' measures, involving the expenditure of resources, to create the conditions in which private life can be properly secured. This can include a duty to regulate the private sector (e.g. the media) and private law. It is the overall position which is to be considered; there is no neat distinction between positive and negative duties. Furthermore, the law must not place unreasonable burdens on the authorities.

There is a breach of article 8 if public authorities interfere with private life (and family life, etc) without justification. The issue of justification distinguishes article 8 from other rights, especially article 3,[8] which can involve private life. Article 8 is likely to be engaged at a lower threshold of severity and there will be no breach of article 8 if the interference with private life can be justified. This allows interferences with private life to be measured against the rights of others or social benefits, a 'trade-off' that is not permitted under article 3.

Justification for actions taken by the state must be in terms of article 8(2).[9] First, the interference must be 'in accordance with the law'[10] and properly authorised by laws which are accessible and foreseeable in the sense that their application is reasonably foreseeable in the circumstances. That interferences with private life are properly regulated, in sufficient detail, and on a legal basis, is very important (e.g. **Malone v UK** (1985) 7 EHRR 14).

Secondly, any interference must serve one of the purposes listed in article 8(2). These include, for example, prevention of crime, protecting the rights of others or protecting 'health' and 'morals'. Private life can also be restricted in the 'interests of the economic well-being of the country',[11] which is unusual in that it appears to allow a trade-off between rights and wealth.

[11]It is worth noting this because it is unique in the ECHR; it will show you have read article 8(2) carefully and this will impress the examiner.

Finally, any interference must be 'necessary in a democratic society' in the sense of being a proportionate way of meeting a pressing social goal;[12] this is often expressed as a court accepting that there has been a fair balance reached between the different interests involved. Where the state's failure to fulfil its positive obligations is in question, justification is normally couched in terms of the proportionality and balance of interests inherent in the state's non-action.

[12]Have ready a brief way of describing the point; also a brief definition of proportionality – this helps to make your answer effective.

Many, if not most, article 8 cases are decided on the proportionality issue. This means that domestic courts (and, if it comes to it, the Strasbourg Court) must be satisfied that the impugned interference with private life involves a fair balance of interests. Though a matter for the court, at least some private life issues can be ones in which a wide 'margin of appreciation'[13] is allowed state institutions on the grounds of their closer involvement in society and culture. This applies to matters such as protecting morals where there is no clear European consensus. The same idea can be reflected in domestic law where, depending on the issue, UK courts may think it appropriate to 'defer' to the judgements of executive or legislature.

[13]It is important to introduce this term; make sure you understand it. Remember that it is relevant only to international law so you need to go on to refer to 'deference' in domestic law.

✓ Make your answer stand out

■ Show a fuller awareness of the more critical approach referred to above; quote Lord Walker in *Razgar*. Some indication of your own view might be helpful – it clearly relates to the separation of powers issue and the role of law and the courts discussed in earlier questions.

■ Refer to the categorisation of 'private life' in the UK courts; Lord Bingham's summary in *R (Countryside Alliance* v *AG* [2007] UKHL 52 was described by Lord Brown in that case as 'masterly'.

■ Refer to the academic writings on the scope of article 8 – note the way Moreham (2008) categorises article 8.

! Don't be tempted to ...

■ Spend too much time on individual issues; this question is seeking your understanding of general issues about article 8 and 'private life'.

■ Although comparison with other rights, especially article 3, is important in order to stress the point that article 8 is 'qualified', do not spend too much time on exploration of the other right. Keep focused on the question, which is about article 8 and private life.

? Question 2

What are the human rights, if any, which should be recognised by courts determining the law in the following cases?

(a) Margaret suffers from a serious, terminal illness which, in its final stages, will leave her dependent upon others. She is fully aware of her condition. She wishes to be able to choose the time of her death but understands that anyone assisting her suicide will commit a serious criminal offence.

(b) Nancy suffers from a serious mental illness which makes her apparently unaware of the consequences of her actions. She has just begun a relationship with a man. Her doctors believe she should be sterilised in her best interests but her mother disagrees.

(c) Olivia is an old lady. She believes she is suffering from a debilitating disease but insists that she should be kept alive as long as possible.

Answer plan

➔ Margaret
  – Consider the position (following *Pretty*) under articles 2 and 3.
  – Consider the position under the qualified right, article 8(1) and (2).
  – Discuss justification under article 8(2) with particular reference to 'in accordance with the law' and refer to *Purdy*.

➔ Nancy
  – Note that Nancy is incompetent. Refer to the best interests test in domestic law and the need to apply this compatibly with Convention rights.
  – Consider the issue of non-life-saving treatments, such as sterilisation.

➡ Olive
 – Apply the general principle in *Burke*.

Diagram plan

Margaret
• Application of arts 2 and 3
• Application of art 8 and issue of justification
• Prosecution policy and *Purdy*

Nancy
• Incompetence and best interests test
• Apply to the issue of sterilisation

Olive
• Discussion of the principles on *Burke*

A printable version of this diagram is available from www.pearsoned.co.uk/lawexpressqa

Answer

Margaret

[1]It is not uncommon to find questions which relate to a particular case; but look out for additional points of difference.

[2]Show your understanding of *Pretty* by identifying article 3 as the relevant article in this context.

[3]You will demonstrate an appropriately subtle understanding of article 8 by pointing out that the duty on states is to 'respect' (not secure or protect) private life, etc. This shows a thoughtful reading of the Convention and increases the examiner's confidence in your answer.

There are obvious factual parallels with **Pretty v UK**[1] (2002) 35 EHRR 1. Here the European Court of Human Rights (ECtHR) ruled, first, that the duty on states to protect the right to life (article 2) did not imply an opposite right to die. There was no positive duty on states to allow assisted suicide. Issues of the quality of life were addressed under article 3.[2] Leaving a patient to die in degrading and distressing circumstances could, in principle, engage article 3. However, this had to be as a consequence of a relevant action by the state (such as deportation). There was no such action in Mrs Pretty's case. Article 3 could not be read as imposing a positive duty on states to allow assisted suicide.

Most importantly, Margaret, like Mrs Pretty, is asserting a right to autonomy, to be able to decide for oneself the important incidents of life, given one's circumstances. In *Pretty*, autonomy was recognised as an incident of private life, needing 'respect' under article 8[3] (though it should be noticed that the House of Lords had denied that

[4]It is vital that you make this point and it then assists you to move on to discuss justification more specifically and in relation to the question.

[5]You demonstrate care and detail in your reading of article 8 by referring to interference by 'public authorities'.

[6]The point expresses the idea that states must have a well-reasoned justification, based on a rational relationship of means and ends, in order to interfere with a right; making it will gain credit.

[7]There is no point in listing all the purposes given in article 8(2); this would not gain credit, especially if you are allowed the text in the exam with you.

[8]Again, try to remember the correct term. In article 8 it is 'in accordance with the law'; in articles 9, 10 and 11 it is 'prescribed by law'. Although little seems to turn on this, the examiner will be pleased that you are correct.

[9]There is much to be said on the topic but keep to what is relevant. The words 'accessible' and 'foreseeable' come from the case law and use of them suggests you know this.

[10]You will gain credit by showing your understanding that the DPP does not make 'law' in the strict sense; he is producing guidelines on the basis of authority delegated to him.

article 8 was engaged at all). Article 8 is a 'qualified' right[4] and public authorities may interfere with private life, etc,[5] under the conditions of article 8(2). The interference must be instrumentally related to one of the legitimate purposes listed in article 8(2) (it is unlikely that it could be based on an asserted religious belief or prejudice.)[6] The 'rights of others'[7] is likely to cover the principal reasons states have for keeping assisted suicide as a crime (such as the right to be protected from unprincipled relatives). The interference must also be 'necessary in a democratic society' and, again, in *Pretty*, the interference was necessary to protect vulnerable people.

Interferences with autonomy must, under article 8(2), be 'in accordance with the law'.[8] This has been held to embody the principle of the certainty of law: that a person needs to know with an appropriate degree of precision what the legal rules are that apply to their situation and how they will be applied (in the language of the ECtHR the applicable laws must be accessible and foreseeable)[9]. In **R (Purdy) v DPP** [2009] UKHL 45 the House of Lords held that there had been a breach of article 8 and the certainty principle. The Director of Public Prosecutions did not have or publicise guidelines of sufficient precision detailing the way in which he would exercise his discretion, under English law, on whether or not a prosecution for assisting someone's suicide was in the public interest. Following that case, in order to fulfil obligations under article 8, the DPP's guidelines made it clear that prosecution would depend less upon the act of assistance and more on the intentions of the assister.

For Margaret, therefore, the most determinant article is article 8, which protects her autonomy. The ECtHR does not assert a positive duty on states to develop a law allowing euthanasia. However, any criminal offences that interfere with a person's autonomy must be justified under article 8(2) and, from a European perspective (following **Pretty**), a blanket ban on assisted suicide can be proportionate. However, not all assisted suicides are then prosecuted and, under UK law, the DPP must publish guidelines indicating the way his discretion is exercised. Though not directly enforceable as law,[10] Margaret ought to be able to depend on these to determine whether or not a person assisting her would be prosecuted.

Nancy

Nancy is, apparently, incompetent[11] in the sense that she does not understand the consequences of her actions. Her rights under article 8(1) and the concept of autonomy are likely to be limited. In such circumstances, under UK law, treatment is determined on the basis of the patient's best interests as these are determined by medical practitioners in conjunction with family members and other interested parties. Such an approach is not inconsistent with the patient's Convention rights under article 2 (life) nor, where best interests are agreed, under article 3 (**NHS Trust v A** [2001] 1 All ER 801).[12]

Conversely, incompetent patients still enjoy a right not to be left in degrading or humiliating conditions in violation of article 3 (though that might be so in respect of a person in a persistent vegetative state (PSV): see **A**). Life-saving treatment or the withdrawal of treatment from a person in PSV can be authorised by a court on the basis of the best interests test. This can be done even against the wishes of parents (as in the conjoined twins case, **A (Children)** (**Conjoined Twins Medical Treatment** [2000] 4 All ER 961, where the separation operation would preserve the life of one twin at the cost of the other). Parental rights under article 8, or even, as in **Glass v UK** (2004) 39 EHRR 15, as a parental surrogate for a child, do not 'trump' the balancing approach of the best interests test. Where there are significant disputes, however, a full adversarial court hearing will be required (**Glass**).

Sterilisation is not a life-saving procedure.[13] Nor is it a simple 'therapeutic necessity' to do with treating a disease. Such ordinary treatments, properly administered, are unlikely to violate article 3, which, rather than article 8, seems to be treated as the decisive article in cases where it cannot be proved that the patient was competent (**Herczegfalvy v Austria** (1992) 15 EHRR 437, discussed in **R (Wilkinson) v Broadmoor Hospital** [2001] EWCA Civ 1545). In **F v Berkshire** [1989] 2 All ER 545, a sterilisation of an incompetent woman was permitted under English law by reference to the best interest principle. Neither hospital nor Nancy's mother have a trump card under the Convention; any decision must be consistent with article 3. To the extent that Nancy, despite her incompetence, retains article 8 rights, such a decision will need to be fully justified under the provisions of article 8(2).

Olive

You need to refer to this important case in which much of the law is summarised.

Olive's position mirrors that of Mr Burke[14] (**R (Burke) v General Medical Council** [2005] EWCA Civ 1003). He argued that guidelines on the withdrawal of treatment were not sufficiently clear to ensure that he would receive nutrition and hydration until his death. Where a competent patient consents, doctors are allowed to withdraw life-preserving treatment and, indeed, may be required to do so to prevent a violation of article 3. The Court of Appeal made it clear that, for English law, there would be a violation of article 2 if doctors withdrew treatment from a competent patient without consent even if this meant leaving the patient in a state that violated article 3.

✓ Make your answer stand out

- Refer, if you have time, in more detail to the cases of Mrs Pretty and Mrs Purdy.
- There has been lots of academic discussion of the legal issue of euthanasia and the other issues raised in the question. For instance: Greasley (2010) and Pedain (2003).
- Likewise there is further discussion of the other issues raised in the question in Dupre (2006).
- When discussing the autonomous concept of 'law', you might also refer to, for example, *Sunday Times* v *United Kingdom* (1979–80) 2 EHRR 245, one of the great early cases (the Thalidomide case) in which the principle was first elucidated.
- In discussing *Purdy* you could refer to the law on guidelines and codes of practice etc. Broadly speaking they must be taken into account by the public authorities to which they relate, normally followed but also, sometimes, there may be valid reasons for not following them. ECtHR recognises such (relatively) 'soft' measures as 'law' for the purposes of there being accessible and foreseeable rules on which a person can rely.

! Don't be tempted to ...

- Remember that the question is asking you about human rights law; you are not asked to explore in any detail the statute and common law that applies to these issues. Of course, it may be difficult to avoid at least minimal references to the basic principles, but these will normally have been part of your course anyway.
- Write too much on the underlying moral and ethical issues that surround these topics. There is, no doubt, much of interest to say but the question is focused on the law.

📝 Question 3

Although there is no express right in the European Convention to a clean and safe environment, such rights have been inferred from the terms of express rights. Discuss.

Answer plan

➡ Note the absence of express rights dealing with the environment.

➡ Consider article 2 and state's positive duties.

➡ Note the non-absolute nature of positive duties.

➡ Discuss the investigative, procedural limb of article 2.

➡ Consider article 8 and positive duties.

➡ Consider justification under article 8(2) in this context.

➡ Evaluate the application of environmental rights in domestic law.

Diagram plan

Absence of express rights
- Implied rights in the Convention
- General limits to implied rights
- Positive duties and the extent of state responsibilities

Article 2
- Positive duties to take adequate steps to protect life
- Procedural limb of art 2
- Need for adequate remedies including against officials

Environmental rights

Application under HRA 1998
- Need to integrate human rights into domestic environmental law
- Statutory interpretation and deference to Parliament
- Human rights and common law remedies

Article 8
- Environmental laws and procedures must repect private and family life
- Positive duties and issue of justification (relevance of art 8(2))

A printable version of this diagram is available from www.pearsoned.co.uk/lawexpressqa

Answer

[1]Though this is an important
point with which to start,
you don't need to know
the content of these other
instruments and measures.

[2]It will suggest a close reading
of the text, and get credit, if
you refer to the relevant part
of the article.

[3]Discuss the duty owed
to individuals. You will
strengthen your answer by
naming the case, though
remember *Osman* concerned
intentional criminal threats.

[4]Give the examiner confidence
in your ability by showing you
understand the application of
article 2 even in the absence
of the intentional use of force
by state agents.

[5]By showing your
understanding of the
importance of remedies and
making the ECHR effective,
you will get credit.

[6]Demonstrate your
understanding that article 2
has both a substantive and a
procedural limb. Turn to the
latter in the next paragraph.

Environmental rights are increasingly derived from general or specific instruments dealing with environmental matters and enacted at the international, European (regional) or national level.[1] Classic human rights instruments, such as ECHR, deal with civil and political rights and not the 'third generation' concerns that are reflected in direct environmental law.

But the Convention is not silent on the matter. Environmental laws must be compatible with Convention rights. A failure of a state to enforce its own environmental laws in a way that interferes with Convention rights may cause a violation, as in **López Ostra v Spain** (1995) 20 EHRR 277 (breach of article 8).

State responsibility for a clean environment can be based on the general duty in the first sentence of Article 2:[2] that 'everyone's life shall be protected by law'. Clearly a state which took intentional steps that poisoned the environment, threatening death, could be liable under article 2. But the case law tends to deal with a failure by states satisfactorily to exercise 'positive duties', under the article, to secure a safe environment. These positive duties can, first, relate to the need to keep an individual safe in circumstances where officials knew or ought to have known of a real risk to his or her life (a form of the **Osman duty**).[3] In **LCB v UK** (1999) 27 EHRR 212 a daughter claimed that her parents should have been told of risks of causing cancer in children conceived after the father's participation in Britain's nuclear testing programme. The Court of Human Rights (ECtHR) held that the dangers, as known and understood at the time, did not give rise to a duty of disclosure.

Öneryildiz v Turkey (2004) 41 EHRR 20 suggests that such positive duties can be owed to the population more generally.[4] In **Öneryildiz** officials failed to guard against known safety risks in a rubbish tip, thus failing to prevent an explosion causing the death of the applicant's family. The ECtHR held that a life-threatening environment required proper regulation and an effective system of enforcement. A failure to act in the face of known dangers should be treated, under domestic law, as if state agents had deliberately used force. Criminal penalties[5] against responsible officials must be available in order to discharge the substantive limb of article 2[6] (depending on the degree of fault, civil action for damages may be sufficient).

[7]Frankly, it can sometimes be difficult to remember names and spellings of cases – a factual specification can sometimes do (check with your lecturer). Of course giving the proper name is best (see above).

[8]This will impress the examiner by showing your awareness of the debate about when the investigative duty is triggered.

[9]Although the case mentioned relates to an attempted suicide, the learning lessons point could be of general application.

[10]You will get credit for making this point, it demonstrates your resistance to an over schematic, simplified, approach.

[11]This strengthens your answer – it shows you have noticed that a failure to exercise a positive duty is not a purposive interference which can be measured against article 8(2) but is still open to justification by the state.

[12]Such a summary may not be necessary if it is implicit in what you say – nevertheless, on a belt and braces principle it can be useful, but do not elaborate unless on matters relevant to the answer.

[13]Use this phrase – it permeates the Convention.

However, positive duties, which require expenditure, etc, tend not to be absolute. Though the duty can be to take appropriate (not just reasonable) steps, the ECtHR has frequently said that unreasonable burdens should not be imposed upon the authorities. The Court is not sympathetic, however, when officials, as in the rubbish tip case,[7] fail to exercise the powers they have.

Where there is an arguable breach of the substantive limb of article 2,[8] the procedural limb of article 2 applies. There is then a need for an independent investigation with sufficient authority and powers to get at the truth of what happened and recommend criminal prosecutions if necessary, including of officials. The investigation will not only have a deterrent effect but, as UK courts have added (**R (JL) Secretary of State for the Home Department** [2008] UKHL 68), will enable lessons for the future to be learned.[9]

Environmental rights have also been implied from Article 8 and the need for states to respect private and family life and a person's 'home'. Failures by the authorities to protect people living near plants giving off noxious fumes, including by giving them adequate information about the dangers, will engage article 8(1). In **Fadeyeva v Russia** (2005) App 55723/00 (pollution from an iron smelter) the ECtHR held that to engage article 8 the pollution needed to pass a threshold of severity. Most of these cases do not involve polluting acts by the state but a failure of a positive duty to regulate polluting commercial companies. Positive duties tend not to be absolute but to require states to take appropriate measures, without bearing unreasonable burdens, to secure respect for private life, etc. Given the facts of individual situations, the Court notes that making a hard and fast distinction between negative and positive duties can be arbitrary (**Broniowski v Poland** (2006) 43 EHRR 1).[10]

Where article 8 is engaged there will not be a breach of article 8 if the combination of action and inaction can be justified by the state.[11] Even in the case of pure positive duties (if such exist) this matter will be considered in the light of article 8(2) (interferences may be justified if they are lawful, for a listed purpose and proportionate – necessary in a democratic society).[12] Proportionality characteristically focuses on whether a fair balance[13] of interests has been obtained. Of particular significance is that the protection of environmental rights may be somewhat weakened under the Convention

[14]It is important to identify this purpose, amongst the others in article 8(2), as not only found nowhere else but also of particular, perhaps negative, significance in the environmental context.

because article 8(2) allows lawful interferences with private life, etc, for the purpose of the 'economic well being of the country'.[14] In a challenge to night flying regulations at Heathrow Airport, for instance, this purpose contributed to the proportionality assessment leading the Grand Chamber to find that there was no violation of article 8 (**Hatton v United Kingdom** (2003) 37 EHRR 28).

[15]Putting 'defer' in inverted commas signifies your understanding that the term, though used, is not to be taken to be subordination of courts to Parliament; rather a recognition of the appropriate constitutional relationship between courts and democratic legislature.

The absence of express environmental provisions in the Convention and, conversely, their existence in other instruments, can make them hard to apply in domestic law. Where there is a statutory scheme which allocates rights and duties for environmental protection a domestic court is likely to 'defer'[15] to Parliament's assessment of how the fair balance of interests is achieved (e.g. **Marcic v Thames Water** [2003] UKHL 66). In the absence of a statutory scheme, article 8 can contribute to the way the common law deals with cases. In **Dennis v Ministry of Defence** [2003] EWHC 793, noise nuisance interfered with the claimant's article 8 rights and it was held that a 'fair balance' required financial compensation. Likewise article 8 has potential to increase the range of persons entitled to a remedy for environmental harm where it is otherwise restricted under domestic law (e.g. to children of the occupiers of premises – **Dobson v Thames Water** [2009] EWCA Civ 28).

Focused instruments of international, European and domestic law make the major contribution to environmental law. Nevertheless, under the ECHR, states have duties to protect the environment, not for its own sake but to protect the fundamental human rights of its citizens, specifically their rights to life and to respect for private and family life. Environmental law, and the way it is put into effect by official action, must be consistent with these rights.

✓ **Make your answer stand out**

■ Make reference to wider debates about the scope of the rights in the ECHR and whether they are adequate to the political agenda of the twenty-first century.

■ Likewise refer to the jurisprudential question whether it is better to approach issues such as the environment through general human rights instruments or those which are specifically focused on the environment.

■ There is a wide literature on the broad, global perspectives on human rights and the environment (e.g. Postiglione, 2010) which could be referred to briefly for contextual purposes.

- Make reference to the role of article 1 of the First Protocol, which deals with the right to peaceful enjoyment of possessions (see, for instance, Morrow (2005)).
- Academic writing on environmental rights includes Cook (2002) and Postiglione (2010).

! Don't be tempted to …

- Write too much in general terms of article 2, 3 or 8. Keep to the question. You can, however, imply a more general knowledge through the issues you raise and the terminology you use.
- Write too much about the general principles of environmental law and the various instruments in which it is found – the point is that these must be compatible with the other human rights in the Convention.
- Write about the controversies of environmental science, such as whether man-made global warming exists, etc. Though interesting, they are not relevant.

? Question 4

The *Daily Keyhole* (a tabloid newspaper) wants to know if it might be prevented, by an injunction based on legal principles derived from the Human Rights Act, from publishing a 'kiss and tell' story. The story is based on claims made by Miss X that she had a torrid sexual relationship with Bill Bloggs MP. Bill Bloggs is a campaigner for family values and faithfulness in marriage. The paper wishes to support the story (which it believes to be true) with a photograph of Bill Bloggs playing in a public park with his wife and children under the heading 'Hypocrite'.

Advise the newspaper.

Answer plan

→ Consider why articles 8 and 10 are relevant and how they can be effective given the terms of the Human Rights Act 1998 and the absence, in the question, of a statute or a public authority which is part of the executive.

→ Show knowledge of how the common law remedy based on breach of confidentiality has developed into one based on a reasonable expectation of privacy; show understanding of the application of 'indirect horizontal effect' in this context.

→ Note and discuss the issue of an injunction in this context and the problem of 'prior restraint'; consider s 12 HRA 1998.

→ Assume the application of article 8(1) to Bloggs's case and so consider the issue of justification for interference in terms of article 8(2) and, from the media point of view, article 10(2).

→ Identify and discuss a range of factors which relate to the 'proportionality' of the interference with Bloggs's article 8 rights.

Diagram plan

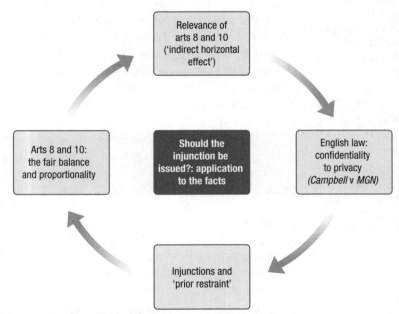

A printable version of this diagram is available from www.pearsoned.co.uk/lawexpressqa

Answer

[1]Get the answer going by identifying, in very general terms, the rights which will be in issue. You will get credit for remembering that article 8(1) is a right to 'respect' for private life, etc.

Bill Bloggs MP (Bloggs) could pursue a remedy based on a right to respect for his private life in article 8. He will be resisted by the *Daily Keyhole* asserting its right to freedom of expression under article 10.[1] However, Bloggs cannot, directly, have such a Convention right against the *Daily Keyhole* because, as part of the commercial press,

[2]You need to show that you understand why the rights are relevant under the terms of the HRA 1998; you will strengthen your answer by showing, from the beginning, an understanding of the interrelationship of human rights and the common law.

[3]The question is clearly about remedies available from English courts, not the Strasbourg Court – so you need to show an understanding, derived from the relevant cases, of the basic issues of English law on this topic.

[4]Campbell is the leading case for the purposes of UK law and needs to be referred to.

[5]The qualified nature of both rights is important and so for a question such as this (or indeed for other questions involving articles 8–11) have prepared a brief summary of what this means.

[6]The US term 'prior restraint' is also used by the ECtHR and you strengthen your answer by using legal terms.

it is not a 'public authority'.[2] Likewise there is no statute, apart from the Human Rights Act 1998 (HRA 1998) itself, to be interpreted for compatibility with Convention rights as required by s 3 HRA 1998. Convention rights are relevant, however, because the UK courts, which have the power to grant an injunction, are 'public authorities' (s 6(3)(a) HRA 1998). This means that, in some areas of law, they will develop the domestic law in a way which secures Convention rights ('indirect horizontal effect'). They are prompted in this by the duties imposed by the Convention on states to take, through their institutions, positive steps to secure respect for private life (e.g. **Von Hannover v Germany** (2005) 40 EHRR 1).

Prior to the HRA 1998, English law[3] would require Bloggs to show that he was seeking to protect information which was 'confidential' rather than simply private. Following the Act, and influenced by the need to align English law with the Convention, a legal claim can now be based upon a 'reasonable expectation of privacy' which does not require demonstrating a pre-existing relationship of confidentiality (**Campbell v MGN** [2004] UKHL 22). In **Campbell**[4] the House of Lords indicated that the proper approach to cases involving the media and privacy was to structure legal reasoning around articles 8 and 10 in relationship with each other but with neither having priority in principle. Both are qualified rights[5] in the sense that a claim to private life or a claim to freedom of the press are both subject to restrictions which are 'prescribed by' or 'in accordance with the' law, which serve one or more of the purposes listed in the second paragraph (which include the 'rights of others') and are 'necessary in a democratic society' in the sense of being a proportionate means to a pressing social need and a 'fair balance' between the different interests at stake.

Bloggs is seeking an injunction to prevent publication. This involves 'prior restraint'[6] of the press. Both at common law and under the Convention it is recognised that preventing information getting into the public domain (as distinct from leaving a person seeking damages) can seriously undermine the public interest in freedom of expression. Nevertheless, prior restraint may be necessary in order to protect matter which is genuinely confidential. Therefore prior restraint is allowed under the Convention but domestic courts are required to give 'anxious scrutiny' to the matter when seeking the fair balance between the two rights (e.g. **Editions Plon v France**

(2006) 42 EHRR 36). Section 12 HRA 1998[7] requires UK courts to take into account matters such as whether information is likely to be available to the public, the public interest but also the relevance of privacy codes, such as that of the Press Complaints Commission.[8] Injunctions can be 'interim' (preventing publication in the short term until the matter is properly decided at trial) and s 12 also requires courts to refuse such injunctions unless satisfied that the applicant is likely to prove the need for restraint at the full trial. Reasons for refusing an injunction in **Douglas v Hello!** [2001] QB 967 included the commercial motive behind the applicant's privacy claim. In **Murray v Express Newspapers** [2008] EWCA Civ 446[9] an injunction was arguable by reference to the particular weight given to the protection of children.

Sexual life is accommodated by the idea of 'private life' and so Bloggs is likely to have, in English law terms, a reasonable expectation of privacy, based on article 8(1). But the question is whether this is outweighed by the right to freedom of expression in article 10(1) enjoyed by the *Daily Keyhole*. Both rights can be interfered with under the terms of articles 8(2) and 10(2) respectively.

First, it is likely that the legal basis of an injunction, given the post-HRA case law in particular, is likely to meet the criteria of 'accessibility' and 'foreseeability'[10] that human rights law demands.

Second, it will be easy to show that the interference serves a legitimate purpose: to protect the 'rights of others', either as the media's right to free expression or Bloggs's right to respect for his private life.

The case will turn on 'proportionality',[11] specifically, whether the injunction would represent a 'fair balance' ('necessary in a democratic society') between the interests involved. Given that he is seeking prior restraint Bloggs will need compelling reasons. Proportionality is factually sensitive. Ultimate responsibility lies with a court, which will seek the balance by reference to the terms of the articles involved but, mainly, by taking into account a range of factors.

For example, Bloggs is an active politician. Though public figures retain rights to privacy (**Von Hannover**), active politicians (in contrast to figures, like Princess Caroline, who merely interest the public) may need to accept greater intrusion into their private life. Likewise, possible hypocrisy on the part of the public figure (such as was alleged in **Campbell**) and also alleged wrongdoing can also weigh, regarding proportionality, in favour of refusing an injunction.

If the matter is also confidential (within the accepted categories recognised by law), then, again, an injunction may be a proportionate interference with freedom of expression. Thus in **Campbell**, albeit a damages case, it was the disclosure of the claimant's access of medical treatment, normally a matter of confidentiality, which was crucial to her success. Likewise a photograph is treated differently. By conveying a mood, for instance, photographs may involve a more significant, more weighty, interference with privacy than simple text (e.g. **Douglas**).

[12]This is a helpful way of bringing to focus your discussion of factors likely to influence a court in its judgment of proportionality.

Underlying the issue of proportionality is whether, all in all, publication would be in the public interest.[12] Following **Von Hannover** the English courts should consider the role of the press. In so far as it is informing the people of serious matters dealing with public life, broadly defined, it is the 'watchdog' and must receive the highest protection and an injunction will be hard to obtain. The commercial interest of the media in purveying trivia or gossip receives lesser protection weighed against privacy claims even though the public may be interested in the gossip. It is this point which is most controversial in that it appears to be a court-created right to privacy.

Given that Bloggs is a politician and there is evidence of hypocrisy, there is unlikely to be an injunction.

✓ Make your answer stand out

- Fuller references to injunctions could include 'super injunctions' in which even the existence of the injunction cannot be reported (see the *Trafigura* case, Zuckerman (2010) and Geddis (2010)).

- Note (briefly) the controversial nature of this development of the law. Elements in the media are fearful of the development of a law of privacy by the courts. This raises two questions: the content of a law of privacy, if any; and the proper role of Parliament in deciding what it should be.

- Say more on the Press Complaints Commission. This is a non-statutory voluntary regulator of the press. It cannot prevent publications or award damages and so, in this context, its effect may be slight. Other questions might be more focused on the control of the press and the need under article 13 ECHR to have effective remedies, which the PCC may not provide.

- Academic commentary on the issues raised in the question includes: Moreham (2006), (2008) and O'Beirne (2009).
- References to other English cases could be helpful (e.g. *A* v *B* plc [2002] EWCA Civ 337) but remember there is not a lot of point in discussing cases which have been somewhat superceded or which do not enable you to make a new point of substance.

! Don't be tempted to ...

- Simply assume the relevance of articles 8 and 10 without discussing the why and how of their relevance to a question like this (i.e. the issue of 'indirect horizontal effect').
- Spend too much time simply exploring the general character of articles 8 and 10.
- Speculate on the factual detail. In the end you can only make a provisional judgment of where the 'fair balance' is likely to come out; it is the way you reason on the matter and your knowledge of relevant cases that counts.

Question 5

Discuss the impact of Convention rights on a person's ability to marry the partner of their choice, found a family and keep it together in the face of actions by public authorities.

Answer plan

→ Identify article 12 and define marriage and family in that context.

→ Discuss the recognition of same-sex relationships under the Convention.

→ Explore the 'national laws' qualification to article 12.

→ Consider founding a family both in respect of article 12 and article 8.

→ Discuss justification under article 8(2) for interferences with family life by the authorities for purposes such as immigration control.

Diagram plan

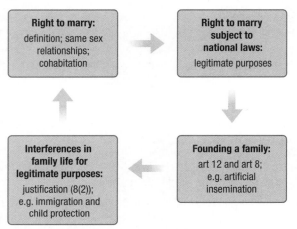

Right to marry: definition; same sex relationships; cohabitation

Right to marry subject to national laws: legitimate purposes

Interferences in family life for legitimate purposes: justification (8(2)); e.g. immigration and child protection

Founding a family: art 12 and art 8; e.g. artificial insemination

A printable version of this diagram is available from www.pearsoned.co.uk/lawexpressqa

Answer

[1]This case is not specifically about article 12 but does involve the concept of marriage in the Convention and so you will get credit for mentioning it.

[2]Move on to discuss these controversial matters.

[3]In this way you strengthen your answer by indicating your understanding of the difference between a state discretion and state obligation.

[4]Reference to the EU Charter of Fundamental Rights shows you are aware of recent developments.

Article 12 provides for a right 'to marry and to found a family'. The essence of marriage is, under the Convention, the acquiring of a particular legal status rather than recognising a close relationship. The Court does not, therefore, give full protection under article 12 to unmarried cohabiting couples (see **Burden *v*UK** (2008) 47 EHRR 38).[1]

Marriage is still understood, under the Convention, in terms of a relationship of men and women.[2] However, change is occurring. Where states allow civil partnerships or homosexual marriage these may be treated, depending on their terms, as equivalent with or comparable to heterosexual marriage (e.g. for the purposes of discrimination and article 14) (though there is not a duty to ensure that if same-sex relationships are given legal status it should be equivalent to marriage). However, the European Court of Human Rights remains unwilling to impose a positive duty on states requiring them[3] to give legal status to same-sex relationships, even though taking into account that the right to marry under article 9 EU Charter does not refer to men and women.[4] The matter remains within the margin of appreciation of the states (see **Schalk & Kopf *v* Austria** app 30141/04, judgment of 24 June 2010). Positive duties are, however, imposed on states to ensure that transgendered people can marry on the basis of their acquired, not birth, gender. Changes in scientific understanding and social attitudes and expectations mean that this matter is no longer within states' margins of appreciation (**Goodwin v UK** (2002) 35 EHRR 18). Likewise, article 12 does not require states to allow divorce

[5] It is essential you make this point – it comes from the text of article 12 and will be expected.

The right to marry is subject to the 'national laws'.[5] Thus marriage may be subject to procedural requirements (like matters of ceremony) or substantive requirements (such as those limiting marriage between relatives) which relate to marriage. Restrictions cannot be imposed in order to achieve other political or social purposes, such as immigration control, though they can be aimed at preventing fraudulent marriages designed to avoid immigration controls (see the UK case **R (Baiai) v Secretary of State for the Home Department** [2008] UKHL 53).

[6] So long as you stay focused on the issue it will gain credit to show your understanding of the Convention as a whole and how different articles link with each other; try to avoid an over-rigid approach which puts each article into its own sealed capsule.

The right to found a family, under article 12, links with the duty on states to respect 'family life' under article 8.[6] It is not seen in absolute terms. Under article 8 the issue is, first, whether a matter involves 'family life' and then, if it does, whether any interference by the authorities is justified under the terms of article 8(2).[7]

[7] You need a brief introduction to the issues that are raised by article 8.

Restrictions on the availability of artificial insemination, which prevent founding a family, need, therefore, to be justified by reference to the language of proportionality and the fair balance of interests. In **Evans v UK** (2008) 46 EHRR 34 and **Evans v Amicus Healthcare Ltd** [2004] EWCA Civ 727, for example, the legislative requirement for the husband's consent for the use of stored sperm represented a fair balance of interests for both the British and European courts.

[8] Move on to discuss article 8 in the context of social policy. One or two examples of different areas of concern are enough and can be signalled early on.

Public authorities can interfere with family relationships for a number of legitimate purposes. Examples are immigration and child protection, both purposes likely to be accommodated by the list of legitimate purposes in article 8(2).[8]

[9] Note this point – it is an area of difference from article 12.

The concept of 'family' that authorities must 'respect' under article 8(1) is given a broad definition. It includes informal relationships, not confined to marriage[9] (**Kroon v Netherlands** (1995) 19 EHRR 263). Thus state policies on, for instance, adoption or immigration control which are based simply on legal status (marriage or civil partnership) rather than a broader recognition of 'biological and social reality' might be too narrowly defined for compatibility. In

[10]Show you understand that 'in accordance with the law' involves the accessibility and foreseeability requirement. Though not the focus of this question, remember that this pervasive issue can come up whenever a question, problem or essay, involves officials acting on the basis of broad powers; so it is worth preparing for.

[11]You gain credit for pointing out that the jurisdiction point (courts, not executive, have the last word) is the important issue here.

[12]Note the importance of article 3 and the duty to protect children even though the stress here is on the issue of family life.

[13]Demonstrate your understanding of the qualified nature of article 8 by the terms you use and how you apply them; this will impress the examiner more than if you merely copy out the text (if you are allowed it in the exam room).

[14]The legality point is important and well illustrated by *HL*, even though it is an article 5 case.

[15]Proportionality can be illustrated in many ways. Focusing on a particular issue, such as procedure (e.g. delay or whether there had been a risk assessment) is the best way of making your points in the space and time available.

Huang *v* Secretary of State for the Home Department [2007] UKHL 11, Lord Bingham, articulating English law, referred to the 'core value' of article 8 as the need for family contact in order to lead 'full and fulfilling lives'.

Immigration decisions on admission or removal may interfere with personal or family life (**Abdulaziz *v* UK** (1985) 7 EHRR 471) and must be justified in terms of article 8(2). In particular, as well as being for a legitimate purpose, immigration decisions must not be based on too wide executive discretion, otherwise the need for interferences to be based on 'law' which is accessible and foreseeable may not be met.[10] Furthermore, interferences must be proportionate (necessary in a democratic society). This requires a 'fair balance' between the interests involved. On the one hand, there is a clear right of states to refuse entry, remove or deport foreigners. On the other hand, significant individual circumstances may outweigh this right given the need to respect the family life of 'all people' (article 1 ECHR). Since proportionality is a matter of law such judgments, which are fact sensitive, are, in the last resort, for the judicial bodies, not the executive, to make (see, for the UK, **Huang**).[11]

Public authorities may take steps to protect children which can involve family separations. Indeed, a failure to protect children in distressed conditions can violate article 3[12] (**Z *v* UK** (2002) 34 EHRR 3). Article 8 is engaged in child care disputes (e.g. **Gorgulu *v* Germany** [2004] 1 FLR 894) and so such interferences need justification under article 8(2).[13] In particular, there needs to be a legal basis which is accessible and foreseeable. A broad, discretionary right to act on the basis of necessity might (depending on the circumstances) be a violation (see **H.L. *v* UK** (2005) 40 EHRR 32,[14] a case involving the lawfulness of a deprivation of liberty under article 5). Proportionality involves a fair balance. Major failures in procedures[15] followed (not just initial diagnostic errors) can be unjustifiable (e.g. **AD *v* UK** [2010] ECHR 28680/06).

There can be a problem if the domestic law gives an unchallengeable priority to the interests of a child. Parents and others have rights under article 8 which cannot just be ignored. Where removal is permanent and parental rights extinguished, it may be harder to show proportionality than where, for instance, a care order is made in good faith which restricts but does not extinguish the parental connection. Broad compatibility of English care orders was accepted by the House of Lords in **Re S** [2002] UKHL 10. But English law on adoption involves a severance of parental rights and there is concern that this may not be easily compatible, especially where a mistaken diagnosis cannot be rectified (**Webster v Norfolk County Council** [2009] EWCA Civ 59).

States, therefore, have legitimate concerns which can lead them to restrict marriage and interfere with family life. Compatibility with the Convention, particularly article 8, requires state actions to have a proper legal basis and to be justifiable before an independent and impartial tribunal.

✓ Make your answer stand out

■ Refer to other instruments – not only the EU Charter but also, for instance, International Covenant on Civil and Political Rights. In doing so you might note that the position under the Convention appears to be comparatively conservative.

■ Show knowledge of UK cases on this issue – though most of your answer is to do with the general standards required by the Convention; (e.g. *Re V (a child) (care proceedings: human rights claims)* [2004] EWCA Civ 54; *P* v *South Gloucestershire Council* [2007] EWCA Civ 2).

■ Consider some of the academic writing on the subject such as Johnson (2010) (on same-sex relationships under the Convention); Young and Leech (2001) (on article 12 and post-HRA impact in the UK); Morris and Nott (2009) (on *Evans* and assisted reproduction services).

! Don't be tempted to ...

■ Spend too much time exploring the difficult moral and policy issues that relate to this topic; the question wants you to focus on the law. It is clear, though, that moral issues can relate to legal ones.

■ Simply quote the terms of article 8 – it doesn't help (especially if your examiner knows you have access to a statute book in the exam). Unless the question is directly on article 8 it is better to imply your basic knowledge of the article by the issues you raise.

🛈 Question 6

Legislation (fictitious) allows the Bank of England to obtain and store personal information about senior managers in the banking industry, including all criminal convictions. The purpose is to provide the banking and finance industry with full information about potential managers at a time of financial crisis.

John Self understands that the Bank of England told a potential employer about his conviction for a minor assault which took place ten years ago. As a result he failed to get a job. He seeks your advice on whether the legislation is compatible with his right to respect for private life under article 8 ECHR.

Answer plan

→ Note the relevance of article 8 given the terms of the HRA 1998.

→ 'Private life' (article 8) includes personal information and so states are duty bound to ensure it is properly respected.

→ A disclosure of personal information is, therefore, an interference with private life.

→ Discuss the question whether the interference is justified under the terms of article 8(2).

→ Is the Bank's action 'in accordance with the law'? Explore the foreseeability of the way the Bank exercises its powers under the statute.

→ Does the disclosure serve a purpose listed in article 8(2)? Discuss the issue of 'economic well-being'.

→ Is the interference necessary in a democratic society – a proportionate action? Consider issues raised by *Marper* and *L* (cited below).

Diagram plan

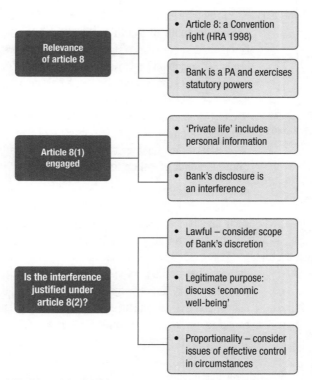

Relevance of article 8
- Article 8: a Convention right (HRA 1998)
- Bank is a PA and exercises statutory powers

Article 8(1) engaged
- 'Private life' includes personal information
- Bank's disclosure is an interference

Is the interference justified under article 8(2)?
- Lawful – consider scope of Bank's discretion
- Legitimate purpose: discuss 'economic well-being'
- Proportionality – consider issues of effective control in circumstances

A printable version of this diagram is available from www.pearsoned.co.uk/lawexpressqa

Answer

[1]Begin by showing why article 8 is relevant to a discussion of English law.

[2]Although not in issue, given the advice the question is seeking, the existence of this otherwise important statute is worth a sentence.

Article 8 is a scheduled Convention right to the Human Rights Act 1998 (HRA 1998).[1] Therefore the legislation referred to must be interpreted so far as possible for compatibility. Furthermore, the Bank of England is likely to be a public authority required to act compatibly by s 6(1) HRA 1998 (for instance, it has regulatory, statutory powers which make it 'governmental' in a broad sense); it has no 'private' side and so its status does not depend on s 6(5) HRA. The main rights enjoyed in respect of protecting personal information are in the Data Protection Act 1998, which is not in issue in this question.[2]

Securing respect for a person's 'private life' (under article 8) requires states to ensure that personal information held by the

133

[3]You have to show that personal information is covered by the term 'private life' in article 8.

[4]The *Marper* litigation (though about DNA rather than criminal convictions) is relevant on the issue of keeping and using personal information. The disagreement between the House of Lords and Strasbourg makes it all the more interesting.

[5]Since this is a problem question, remember to relate your general observations to the question scenario.

[6]The question is clearly expecting you to note this point (it came up in *L*, discussed later.

[7]The *Leander* case is one of the important early cases which needs to be referred to and supports the view that dealing in personal information is an 'interference'.

[8]Throughout, make it clear to the examiner that you understand that article 8 is a qualified right and (most importantly) that you understand the three considerations (law, purpose, proportionality) that structure a court's approach to the issue of justification. This also gives your answer a clear structure.

authorities is properly dealt with.[3] At the heart of the Convention definition of the term is information about an individual from which he or she can be identified. The House of Lords, **R (Marper) v Chief Constable of South Yorkshire** [2004] UKHL 39, and the European Court of Human Rights (ECtHR), **Marper v UK** (2009) 48 EHRR 50 disagreed,[4] for example, on whether DNA samples had that character. The information must be personal. In John Self's case[5] the information is in principle 'public', in so far as it relates to criminal offences.[6] Under English law, however, such information can become private through the passage of time and on the basis of legislative provisions that allow offences to be 'spent' (**R (L) v Commissioner of Police for the Metropolis** [2009] UKSC 3).

Article 8 is in issue when there has been an 'interference' with personal information by the authorities. For example, failing to make such information available, where it is necessary for a person's 'private life' can be an interference; as in **Gaskin v UK** (1989) 12 EHRR 36 where confidential social work records contained the principal account of his early life and were central to his personal identity. Likewise the taking, retaining and using of personal information by the authorities is likely to be an interference, thus engaging article 8 (e.g. **Leander v Sweden** (1987) 9 EHRR 433).[7] The disclosure of private information without a person's consent, or for a different purpose than that for which it was obtained, is a clear interference and one that requires rigorous justification (**Z v Finland** (1998) 25 EHRR 371 and **TV v Finland** (1994) 18 EHRR CD179).

Thus, by disclosing personal information, the Bank of England has apparently interfered with John Self's right to respect for private life under article 8.

The issue then becomes one of justification under the terms of article 8(2).[8]

First, interferences, such as these, must be 'in accordance with the law'. The basic requirement (from **Sunday Times v UK** (1979–1980) 2 EHRR 245) is that not only must there be authority under domestic law for the interference but the domestic law must be 'accessible' and 'foreseeable' and compatible with the rule of law. What this means is context dependent but where a public body is retaining, using and passing on personal information it is likely that a detailed set of rules will be necessary in order to meet Convention rights. **Marper v UK** dealt with the National DNA Database. The ECtHR held that where public authorities were, in various contexts, handling large amounts of personal information there needed to be proper control on the basis of 'clear, detailed rules',[9] and these should cover relevant issues such as the use of the information by others. The extent to which the legislation in issue meets this standard will have to be assessed, though, as in **Marper**, some of the salient issues are more relevant in respect of proportionality.[10]

Secondly, interferences must be for at least one of the purposes listed in article 8(2) and not for any other purposes (see article 18). The abstract nature of the terms means that this is often not in issue. One of the purposes in article 8(2) is that the interference is in the interests of the 'economic well-being of the country'.[11] This, along with the 'prevention of crime', is likely to be sufficient in the case being discussed. However, a simple trade-off between individual rights and national wealth is hard to square with most conceptions of human rights, whose point is to protect the vital interests of individuals and minorities in the face of the collective interest. This may be reflected in the weight given to the pursuit of economic well-being when measuring the proportionality of the interference with John Self's rights. The ECtHR accepts that the taking and retention of personal information in the context of fighting crime or anti-terrorism may, subject to proportionality, be justified and states may enjoy a wide margin of appreciation (e.g. **Murray v UK** (1995) 19 EHRR 193). Stress on this rather than economic well-being may be a better strategy for the authorities seeking to justify their actions.

Thirdly, the interference must be 'necessary in a democratic society',[12] which means a proportionate means of meeting a pressing social need, often expressed in terms of a court accepting that the legislation or the authorities have achieved a 'fair balance' between the individual and collective interests involved. In Marper,[13] for example, the criteria for entry and retention for the DNA database failed to differentiate between different categories of people who ought to have been considered for different treatment. Ignoring issues such as age, the gravity of the relevant offence and whether there had been a conviction meant that a fair balance, taking into account relevant differences between individuals, could not be achieved.

[9]Use this quotation, if you can – it suggests you have read the case and noted the crucial point. Remember to show you understand that 'foreseeability' is context dependent.

[10]Show your understanding by pointing out this overlap between legality and proportionality; you will get credit if you avoid being too mechanistic in your approach.

[11]It is pretty obvious from the nature of this question that a reference to 'economic well-being' is necessary. It is a unique aspect of the Convention and so a discussion is expected.

[12]Now move on to discuss proportionality. A short definition, such as is given here, can be useful in this and other contexts, so prepare one during revision.

[13]Refer again to this important case and get credit by showing you understand the grounds on which it was decided.

[14]This case, though about a playground assistant rather than a banker, raises many of the important points for the answer.

In **R (L) *v* Commissioner of Police for the Metropolis** [2009] UKSC 3,[14] the police had disclosed to an employer that an employee's child was on the child protection register. They had done so in the purported exercise of a statutory duty of disclosure of the results of a criminal records check in respect of people working with children. The question was whether the interference was proportionate. The question, for the Supreme Court, was whether the reasons for disclosure outweighed the effect on the individual. This had to be a fact-dependent decision. There was no axiomatic priority for the protection of children over individual rights nor could the police act on the basis of a presumption in favour of disclosure.[15] Under the HRA 1998, the legislation under which the police had acted could be read down, under s 3, to require a properly proportionate decision and hence there was no need for a declaration of incompatibility. It is likely that the same approach can be relevant in respect of the power of disclosure given to the Bank of England in John Self's case.

[15]Thus make it clear that, as so often, the issue turns on proportionality. This is fact dependent rather than rule or principle based. Drawing a conclusion can be difficult on the information given (the examiner is mainly interested in your approach).

✓ Make your answer stand out

■ Build a little on the peculiar point that, by reference to economic well-being in article 8(2), article 8 appears to allow a trade-off between rights and national wealth. Such trade-offs are not normally permitted in rights-based political theory. A brief consideration of the 'deontological' account of rights (e.g. rights as side-constraints) in contrast with a 'utilitarian' position (which evaluates 'the good' in terms of the consequences that best maximise happiness, or at least preferences), might help. But be careful, in a law essay, not to get too involved in philosophical discourse about which, perhaps, you have not been taught.

■ Say a bit more on the *Marper* case, both as decided by the House of Lords and then, in contrast, by the ECtHR. Academic writing on the case includes Beattie (2009).

■ Discuss in more general terms the tension between private life and freedom of information (e.g. Pitt-Payne (2003)).

! Don't be tempted to ...

■ Explore 'private life' as a general issue – it relates to so many issues and many of them have little to do, directly, with the protection of personal information.

■ Discuss freedom of information in general – the issue in the question relates to personal information which may engage with the right to respect for private life; freedom of information (e.g. relating to the Freedom of Information Act 2000) usually involves public affairs which the authorities wish to keep confidential.

Question 7

Does article 8 give a right to a home and does it deny a landlord an unqualified right to evict? How has the issue of eviction been addressed in English law under the Human Rights Act 1998?

Answer plan

→ Explain 'respect' and define 'home' in article 8.

→ Note that article 8 is a qualified right.

→ Discuss whether there is a right to a home.

→ Discuss interference and justification (article 8(2)).

→ Address the issue of eviction and proportionality.

→ Discuss the proportionality 'gateways'.

→ Discuss whether private landlord evictions are subject to the same restraints.

Diagram plan

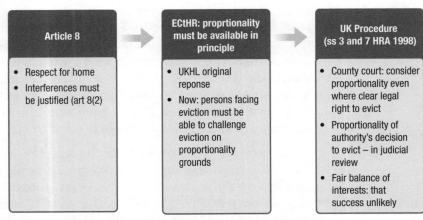

A printable version of this diagram is available from www.pearsoned.co.uk/lawexpressqa

Answer

[1]Begin by making clear you understand the basic limit to article 8 – that it is not a 'social right' to a home.

[2]It is worth making this point – a legally enforceable human right of the homeless to a home, particularly when applied in concrete situations, could lead to these issues of law versus policy which are faced by social rights generally.

Human rights protect the fundamental interests of human beings. There are few things more fundamental to these interests than having a home.[1] Article 8 ECHR requires states to 'respect' a person's 'home'. But the right is not only qualified (in the sense that it is subject to proportional restrictions under article 8(2)) but also limited to requiring respect for the home a person has. It is not a right of the homeless to be housed (**Ghaidan v Godin Mendoza** [2004] UKHL 30). Generally the European Convention does not guarantee social rights. An enforceable human right to be housed would require resolving the conflicts[2] (faced by policy makers) between the claims of individuals and the availability of resources and the competing demands from other policy areas. Characteristically these are conflicts properly resolved through political procedures.

Nevertheless article 8 does give some degree of protection to those faced with being made homeless.

[3]Move on to define the concept of 'home'.

[4]Then discuss the idea of 'respect'. It is most important in an answer such as this that you show you understand that article 8 is limited to this term.

Home is defined as the physical space where 'private and family life develops'[3] (**Giacomelli v Italy** (2007) 45 EHRR 38) and relates to where a person lives or intends to live on a settled basis (though it can include professional premises – **Niemietz v Germany** (1993) 16 EHRR 97). Given that, under article 1, human rights are available to all, respect for home[4] is not dependent on the place being lawfully occupied (**Buckley v UK** (1997) 23 EHRR 101) but, as discussed below, this is of quite limited effect. Normally, just as there is no right to be housed, there is no right under article 8 to a particular home (**Burton v UK** (1996) 22 EHRR CD135). In exceptional circumstances 'respect' may mean allowing a person to remain in the particular home of their choice. In **R v N & E Devon HA ex p Coughlan** [2001] QB 213 the Court of Appeal accepted that a woman with serious disabilities had a right to continue living in a facility which had been described as her 'home for life'. The case was decided on administrative law principles influenced by article 8.

Whether there has been sufficient 'respect' for a person's home is a question raised when there are interferences with home and associated rights by public authorities. Thus restricting occupation rights (**Gillow v UK** (1989) 11 EHRR 335) or failing to protect from harassment (**Whiteside v UK** (1994) 18 EHRR CD126) could engage article 8. Likewise there must not be discrimination in such matters, which could breach article 14 linked to article 8 (**Godin**).

There is only a breach if the interference by a public body cannot be justified under the terms of article 8(2):[5] there must be a proper, foreseeable, legal basis, the interference must be for a purpose listed in article 8(2) and the breach must be proportionate. Public landlords will normally be acting on the basis of statutory powers. The ECtHR accepts a significant margin of appreciation on this matter[6] (though it reduces given the seriousness of the consequences) and so domestic courts are able to give considerable weight to the way Parliament has balanced the various interests. Thus a breach, in circumstances such as the above, may only arise in the most extreme circumstances (repair), or in the absence of effective remedies at the time (harassment).

[6]Use the term 'margin of appreciation' – if you use it correctly you will not need to expend space on defining it. It is important regarding the issue of eviction (which follows) since the ECtHR restricts the margin when the consequences are severe.

[7]Now move to the rather complex issue of local authority evictions under UK law, to which you are steered by the question.

A major issue under the Human Rights Act 1998[7] is whether a person whose tenancy agreement with a public authority (specifically a local authority) has been lawfully determined (ended) can challenge the possession order, needed by the authority if it is to proceed to eviction, on article 8 grounds.

Initially, in **Qazi v Harrow LBC** [2003] UKHL 43, the House of Lords held that, where a person no longer has a legal right of occupation, article 8 will not help them. However, the ECtHR subsequently made it explicit that it must, in principle, always be possible for the person at risk of losing his or her home to challenge the eviction on proportionality grounds, even where they no longer have a legal right of occupation (**McCann v UK** (2008) 47 EHRR 40).

In response the UKHL felt able only to moderate the principle in **Qazi** by, in particular, recognising possible challenges to an authority's decision to evict based on ordinary principles of judicial review (see **Kay v Lambeth** [2006] UKHL 10 and **Doherty v Birmingham** [2008] UKHL 57). But, ordinary judicial review (conducted by the High Court) has not developed into full proportionality assessment. It is an inappropriate procedure for dealing with the kinds of factual assessments likely to arise when assessing proportionality. Also this approach did not allow a county court to test proportionality, particularly where the statute authorising the eviction did not require the reasonableness of issuing a possession order to be judicially considered.[8]

[8]This is a complicated issue and you will get credit for showing you understand the difficulties and issues.

[9]This is now the main UK authority and you will be expected to discuss it.

[10]Using the terms 'clear and consistent' demonstrates your awareness of s 2 HRA 1998 and how the duty on UK courts to take the ECtHR into account has been understood.

[11]It is particularly important, and will earn you credit, if you show you understand that there are two issues: does proportionality apply and, if so, how; through what procedures, can it be brought to bear on the eviction issue? This involves considering the terms of the HRA 1998.

[12]Show you understand that the case law above is confined to local councils and, presumably, other public landlords. Private landlords are not involved and give rise to other issues. But a final reference to the position of Housing Authorities is very important since they are often the immediate landlord.

So in **Manchester City Council v Pinnock** [2010] UKSC 45,[9] the Supreme Court accepted that UK law should follow the clear and consistent Strasbourg approach[10] and ensure that, in principle, it must be possible for the proportionality of an eviction to be raised by a person at risk of losing their home.

Where the statutory requirement was that a county court should only grant a possession order if it was 'reasonable', it was easy to use s 3 to read in a proportionality test. But even in cases, such as **Pinnock**, where the county court was solely concerned with procedure, the UKSC held that s 3 HRA 1998 and s 7(1)(b) (which allows Convention rights to be raised in any proceedings) meant that the lawfulness of the procedure should be tested by proportionality. In all cases the right to seek judicial review of the authority's decision to seek eviction should be extended to include an assessment of proportionality.[11]

Importantly, UKSC noted, as does the ECtHR, that proportionality requires a court to seek a fair balance. Given a good faith decision by an authority based on its legal position as landlord, its concern for others (such as neighbours) and the social policy arguments underlying the decision to evict, a successful proportionality challenge is likely to be rare.

Private landlords are not bound by these cases.[12] There is little possibility of positive duties being imposed on states in respect of them since this would involve disturbing property rights under article 1 of Protocol 1. Housing Associations, however, may be different, depending on the circumstances. In **R (Weaver) v LQHT** [2009] EWCA Civ 587 it was held that the decision by a housing association to move to eviction was a public act of a body performing public functions and, therefore, bound to act compatibly with article 8.

Significant private circumstances can, albeit with rare success, be argued in possession proceedings. English law on the matter is now compatible with article 8.

Make your answer stand out

- Refer to some of the academic writings, especially Loveland (2009). Though to some extent these have been overtaken by the decision in *Pinnock*.

- Show you have a full understanding of the judicial review point by reference to, in particular, *Winder* v *Wandsworth* LBC [1985] AC 461, where the House of Lords allowed a challenge on public law grounds to a local authority decision to evict.

- You can also put the judicial review point into the wider context of the debate, in administrative law, on the extent to which, if at all, a public body, such as a local authority, has private law powers which it can exercise as if it was a private right holder (e.g. when it enters into contracts or acts as a landlord). This is worth mentioning even though the details take us outside the confines of a human rights law course.

- Although you should not spend much time exploring *Kay* and *Doherty* (since these have been overtaken by *Pinnock*), you could note the importance in the development of the law of the dissents by Lords Bingham and Mance in the two former cases. These dissents are more in line with the law as now pronounced in *Pinnock*.

! Don't be tempted to ...

- Although the question clearly engages with the idea of social rights in general, there is not enough time to explore the arguments too far (though for an interesting recent discussion, see Fredman (2010)).

- As with all questions which are focused on a general aspect of article 8, do not spend too much time on a general description, but get to the point of the question.

- The question expressly seeks knowledge of recent English cases (especially decisions of the House of Lords and Supreme Court), so don't over-focus on European or international law issues.

❓ Question 8

Billy is an asylum seeker. He failed to apply for welfare benefits immediately on landing in Britain and is living rough. He applies for housing and welfare benefits from the authorities but is turned down. No reason is given and there is no right of appeal.

Billy believes that the rules on welfare benefits for asylum seekers, which were followed by the officials making the decisions affecting him, have not secured his Convention rights under English law.

Advise Billy.

Answer plan

→ Explain why, under the HRA 1998, Convention rights would be relevant.

→ Explore article 3 and its application in respect of the unintended consequences of administrative decisions.

→ Note the absence of an express duty to provide welfare and note separation of powers issues that might arise if there were.

→ Relate these points to UK law, especially in respect of *Limbuela*; suggest a likely conclusion in Billy's case.

→ Consider the possible relevance of article 8 and of article 1 of the First Protocol.

→ Discuss whether there could be procedural issues under article 6.

Diagram plan

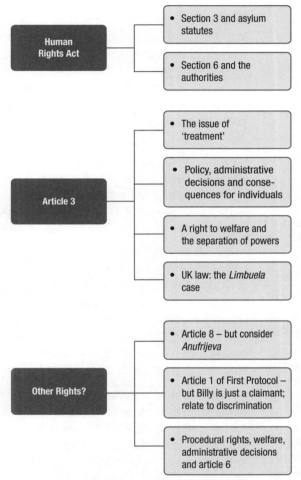

- **Human Rights Act**
  - Section 3 and asylum statutes
  - Section 6 and the authorities

- **Article 3**
  - The issue of 'treatment'
  - Policy, administrative decisions and conse-quences for individuals
  - A right to welfare and the separation of powers
  - UK law: the *Limbuela* case

- **Other Rights?**
  - Article 8 – but consider *Anufrijeva*
  - Article 1 of First Protocol – but Billy is just a claimant; relate to discrimination
  - Procedural rights, welfare, administrative decisions and article 6

A printable version of this diagram is available from www.pearsoned.co.uk/lawexpressqa

Answer

[1] The question is clearly about Convention rights under English law, so begin by outlining the general position under the HRA 1998 in respect of statutory interpretation and the duties of officials. For problem questions it is always a good idea to have a general summary prepared.

[2] Remember, you are not being tested on the substance and detail of UK law on asylum (thank goodness – it is very complicated); but rather on the Convention rights with which that law, whatever it is, should be compatible.

[3] You will get credit for observing the central point that human rights do not depend on some prior civic or legal status; strengthen the point by reference to article 1.

[4] Now move on to consider article 3. You will strengthen your arguments by observing the range of its application.

[5] Note this point – it explains why there was no breach of article 3 in *Pretty*. You will impress the examiner if you can give examples from other areas of administrative activity which potentially engage article 3.

Under the Human Rights Act[1] the issue will be, first, whether the legislation followed by the officials[2] can be given effect, by them, in a way which is compatible with Billy's Convention rights; if it cannot be, the High Court will have to consider a declaration of incompatibility (this would not directly affect Billy's legal position under English law). If the legislation can thus be given effect, officials must give effect to Billy's human rights.

But what are Billy's human rights? Under article 1 ECHR, human rights are available to all in the country, irrespective of status (e.g. whether a citizen or not).[3] Although article 1 is not a scheduled Convention right, British courts accept the point both in principle and because the principal aim of the HRA 1998 is to give a remedy in the United Kingdom where one would be available in Strasbourg.

Article 3 bans not just torture but also inhuman and degrading treatment and is not confined to the deliberate infliction of harm by state agents in the context of punishment, interrogation or the protection of others.[4] In **Pretty *v* UK** (2002) 35 EHRR 1, the ECtHR defined ill-treatment by reference to bodily injury or intense physical or mental suffering; degrading treatment involves, amongst other things, treatment which humiliates, debases or arouses feelings of fear or inferiority capable of breaking a person's moral or physical resistance.

For article 3 to be breached there must be 'treatment' by state agents. In **Pretty** the government had not in any way contributed to the applicant's situation but where administrative decisions are taken that, consequently, leave people ill-treated or degraded, article 3 may be breached (e.g. **D *v* UK** (1997) 24 EHRR 423 – deportation; **Z *v* UK** (2002) 34 EHRR 3 – child protection).[5]

In principle, therefore, article 3 can be relevant to issues involving the denial of welfare. States may have (the Strasbourg case law is not clear) a positive duty not to apply policies in ways which cause a person to be left in an inhuman or degrading situation. However, there is no express right to welfare and the Strasbourg case law does not assert such a positive duty in general terms.

A positive duty to provide welfare would raise problems about whether the judiciary, by requiring a particular distribution of

6You will gain credit
by demonstrating an
understanding of how
underlying constitutional
issues about human rights
can arise in particular
contexts.

7Now move on to discuss
the *Limbuela* case. This is
an important decision in this
area of the law and one which
is clearly hinted at by the
question and which you would
be expected to discuss.

8In terms of the structure of a
problem answer, make sure
you make such references
with reasonable frequency to
the facts of the question so
that you provide an answer to
the question asked.

9You will get credit for
considering other rights
which might be relevant. This
shows you are aware of the
Convention as a whole, not
just a grouping of discrete
rights with little to do with
each other.

10Remember to note that
article 8, unlike article 3, is a
'qualified right'.

11This shows you know the
text of article 8 on what is a
legitimate purpose and that
the economic well-being point
is unusual and important.

12The article 1 point, though
limited given the facts, is
worth making to show your
awareness of the different
articles in issue in respect of
welfare.

resources, would be interfering in matters normally the responsibility of executive and legislature.[6]

The justification is that article 3 is involved only when the consequences of the treatment reach a high threshold of severity. Where that threshold is placed is a matter for the judiciary. Issues relevant to this question came up for UK law in **R (Limbuela) v Secretary of State for the Home Department** [2005] UKHL 66.[7] Asylum seekers were not allowed to work and the relevant statute allowed the government to refuse welfare provision to any who had not claimed asylum immediately on entry into the country. There was a statutory proviso that welfare payments could be made if, otherwise, there would be a breach of article 3.

The House of Lords adopted the **Pretty** definitions into UK law. It also held that, under the Strasbourg case law, article 3 did not impose a general duty to provide welfare. But administrative decisions about individuals involved 'treatment'. Where such treatment results in the denial of the basic necessities of life, article 3 may be violated. On the facts there had been violations where the asylum seekers were left sleeping rough and begging, etc. Depending on his circumstances, Billy may have a right to welfare,[8] but only to bring him below the article 3 threshold.

It is unlikely that article 8 could be an independent basis for a positive duty to provide welfare rights[9] for someone in Billy's position. It could be invoked if treatment led to a loss of autonomy (such as leaving a person in a situation which is dominated by the need to obtain food and shelter). But such a situation is likely to invoke article 3 anyway. In **Anufrijeva v Southwark LBC** [2003] EWCA Civ 1406 the Court of Appeal held that it was unlikely that there would be a positive duty to provide welfare unless needed to prevent breaching article 3 (though there might be such a duty where family life and children are involved). Anyway, even if failing to provide welfare engages article 8, this might be justified under article 8(2)[10] – as (referring to cost and resources) a proportionate way of protecting the economic development of the country.[11]

Existing welfare rights are likely to be 'possessions'[12] in respect of article 1 of the First Protocol, including non-contributory benefits (**Stec v UK** (2006) 43 EHRR 47 followed, for example, in **R (M) v Secretary of State for Work and Pensions** [2008] UKHL 63).

But Article 1 does not give a right to claim property to which there is no entitlement (so it may not apply directly to Billy). However, the denial of a non-contributory benefit can, perhaps, be said to be within the 'ambit' of article 1. If so, an asylum seeker might argue that his or her less favourable treatment, compared to non-asylum seekers in the same situation, is discrimination in breach of article 14. In **M**, homeless people in receipt of disability benefit were treated less favourably than others, also in receipt of the benefit, with homes. Even so, there is no discrimination if the difference in treatment can be justified, which is likely in this case given the distinct status of asylum seekers.

[13]Procedural rights are very important in the Convention scheme generally. You will get credit for mentioning them.

Finally, applicants for welfare have procedural rights.[13] Decisions on welfare can be 'determinations of civil rights and obligations'. If so, Billy could have a right to an independent and impartial hearing under article 6, which he has not had. But there are two important qualifications. First, though in **Tsfayo v UK** (2009) 48 EHRR 18 the ECtHR held that some welfare disputes engage article 6, the extent of this is not clear. The UK Supreme Court has held that article 6 is not engaged when an applicant for welfare is relying not on a clear right but on discretionary decisions made by officials (**Ali v Birmingham CC** [2010] UKSC 8) – this is likely to be the case here. Secondly, even if a civil right is being determined by officials, there may be no breach of article 6 if the issues can be considered judicially (on appeal or review) by a court with full competence. It could be (following **Tsfayo**) that if Billy (assuming article 6 applies) is only able to challenge the refusal of benefits by judicial review, this would not be adequate.

✓ Make your answer stand out

- Discuss socio-economic rights, such as the right to welfare, in more detail (see, for instance, Palmer (2007)). Don't go too far since they are implied rather than expressed in the ECHR – that is a point you could make.

- Spend more time exploring the separation of powers issue – that a positive right to welfare could involve courts in political judgments about resources (note, for instance, Fredman (2010) for a recent critical approach to this objection).

- For a full analysis of *Limbuela* see O'Cinneide (2008).

- For a full analysis of *Anufrijeva* (and other cases) see Billings and Edwards (2004).

- Note that, like so much of human rights law, when considered in terms of its actual application in concrete situations (i.e in the detail of the cases), a very great deal depends on the specific facts.

! Don't be tempted to …

- Use up a lot of time and space with general introductions to articles 3 and 8.
- Over-egg article 1 of the First Protocol. It is worth mentioning, but remember that this is a bit of a long shot; also it will work only as a form of discrimination in relation to article 14.
- Explore in detail UK law on immigration and asylum – you are not being tested on that. The point is to show you understand the human rights framework to and limits of the law.

? Question 9

Bloggs is chairman of Snodbury Football Club. He is married but is having an affair with Amelia. They are photographed late at night by CCTV operating lawfully in the town centre. The pictures show them in a compromising position. Officers of the local council, which operates the CCTV, make the footage available to local media who publish and broadcast it. Next day the council's chief executive is badly beaten up. Bloggs is lawfully arrested and lawfully detained in a police station cell. He is allowed to meet with his lawyer, to whom he confesses to organising the beating up of the chief executive. Unbeknown to Bloggs, the cell has been bugged.

Discuss whether Bloggs's right to private life has been violated, first, in relation to the CCTV filming and its usage, and, secondly, in relation to the bugging in the police station.

Answer plan

→ Introduce article 8 and show its relevance to domestic law under HRA 1998.

→ Show how article 8 applies and discuss the idea of 'private life' in respect of CCTV in public places.

→ Given an interference, discuss whether it can be justified in terms of article 8(2); focus in particular on 'law' and proportionality.

→ Show how secret surveillance engages article 8.

➡ Discuss justification for the surveillance in the police cell, noting in particular the issue of professional legal privilege (be able to distinguish directed and intrusive surveillance, based on *Re McE*).

➡ Conclude by references to remedies and admissibility under s 78 PACE.

Diagram plan

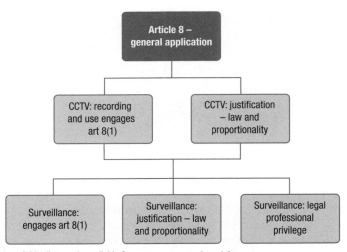

A printable version of this diagram is available from www.pearsoned.co.uk/lawexpressqa

Answer

[1]Begin by showing why, as a matter of domestic law, article 8 is relevant to the answer.

[2]Show you understand the basic structure (the two paragraphs) of article 8: this is essential and expected.

Bloggs will argue in terms of article 8 and his right to respect for his private life. The local authority and the police, whose actions are in question, are both core public authorities[1] (obviously 'governmental' – **Aston Cantlow v Wallbank** [2003] UKHL 37). Their actions are unlawful if incompatible with Convention rights such as article 8 (unless required by statute to act otherwise). Under article 8[2] the question is, first, whether there has been an interference with private life and, second, whether the interference is justified.

The mere fact that a person is monitored by CCTV in a public place will not engage article 8. Article 8 is significant once some kind of record is made and distributed (**Peck v UK** (2003) 36 EHRR 41). The recording and holding of information is likely to interfere with a person's sense of autonomy and, therefore, with their 'private life'. Likewise, the concept of private life includes the possibility of enjoying social relationships. Thus article 8 can apply to an individual even where the alleged interference relates to actions in public places. Indeed police use of film of people attending public events, including political protests, can engage article 8(1) – though this must depend on the circumstances such as the reason for the interference and the use to be made of the film (compare **Friedl v Austria** (1996) 21 EHRR 83 (no breach) with the UK case **Wood v Commissioner of Police of the Metropolis** [2009] EWCA Civ 414 (breach)).

[3]Now move on to justification. This is often the focus of questions involving articles 9–11, so it needs to be prepared for and properly discussed.

Bloggs's situation has similarities with **Peck v UK**. Here CCTV images of a young man attempting suicide in a town centre were distributed to local media with insufficient anonymity. The ECtHR held that there had been an interference with the applicant's private life. Though a prominent local citizen, Bloggs is entitled to a private life (**Von Hannover v Germany** (2005) 40 EHRR 1). The issue then becomes one of justification.[3]

[4]Like the courts, you can go through the issues raised by article 8(2). But focus on the particular points regarding justification that are raised by the question.

The first issue is whether there is a legal basis,[4] which is accessible and foreseeable in its application, for the interference. This may be statutory but, if not, 'softer' forms of regulation, such as Codes of Practice, are accepted as forms of 'law'.[5] These are widely used in this context in the UK. The issue is whether the relevant Code regulates the recording and use of the images. Likewise, compatibility with article 8 requires appropriate regulation of the media regarding the broadcasting.

[5]You will get credit for showing you understand the way 'law' has been understood by the ECtHR. The identity of what counts as a 'legal' rule is often missed.

[6]By noting that sometimes 'foreseeability' and proportionality relate to similar matters you will impress the examiner. It helps you avoid an over mechanistic, tick-box, approach to justification.

The interference must serve a legitimate purpose (listed in article 8(2)). On the facts as given, it is the right to freedom of expression of the media ('rights and freedoms of others') that is in issue. Purpose may well link to the third issue, which is proportionality.[6] In particular, a court will be concerned with the fair balance of interests.[7] Bloggs's private interest might seem weaker than the applicant in **Peck**. However, in English law terms, people have a reasonable expectation of privacy in respect of sexual life and the issue of adultery, or other moral condemnation is likely to be irrelevant (see **Mosley v News Group Newspapers** [2008] EWHC 1777). Likewise, it is doubtful that the public interest in the media disclosures is particularly strong, though, perhaps, stronger than in **Von Hannover** where the

[7]Move on to discuss the kinds of issues that will be balanced in a judgment of proportionality. These will be hinted at in the question and you should try to pick them up.

applicant had no public role. **Von Hannover** suggests that the public interest must be something more than mere sensationalism.

Bloggs's treatment in the police cell raises different issues.

[8]Move to the second part of the question and consider the general approach to surveillance.

Secret surveillance must be compatible with article 8. States may legitimately interfere with private life by engaging in secret surveillance[8] in order to prevent crime, amongst other purposes (**Valenzuela Contreras v Spain** (1999) 28 ECHR 483). Likewise, the House of Lords accepted the overall legality in English law of covert practices of crime prevention, if properly regulated (in **R v H** [2004] UKHL 3).

Such rights apply to prisoners and detainees, who retain all rights other than those necessarily lost by detention or imprisonment itself. Thus the use of surveillance devices in police stations is likely to interfere with the private life of the detainee and so engage article 8(1).

[9]You will gain credit for demonstrating awareness of the particularly important issue of legality in this context – the secrecy of the interference requires adequate safeguards.

The issue, then, is justification under article 8(2). Interferences must be properly regulated on the basis of an accessible set of legal rules[9] whose application is sufficiently foreseeable in the circumstances (**Klass v Germany** (1979–80) 2 EHRR 214). These rules need to deal with matters such as authorisation, purpose and subsequent use (e.g. **Marper v UK** (2009) 48 EHRR 50). In **PG & JH v UK** (2008) 46 EHRR 51, there was a violation of article 8 in respect of police cell surveillance because, at the time (1995), there was an absence of statutory regulations dealing with secret surveillance in a police station.

[10]It is helpful to show that you understand the basic pattern of domestic law. Though the detail of this would come from a civil liberties course, you should demonstrate at least the knowledge that comes from the HRA cases (i.e. the two types of covert surveillance).

In England, secret surveillance in a police station is now lawful if carried out in accordance with the Regulation of Investigatory Powers Act 2000 (RIPA) 2000.[10] Covert surveillance which is 'directed surveillance' is subject to a relatively soft statutory regulation, though supplemented by Codes of Practice. 'Intrusive surveillance', which involves, for example, covert surveillance of residential premises, is subject to stricter control as to purpose and a narrower, more senior list of authorising officials. Under the Act, glossed by accompanying Codes,[11] covert surveillance within a police station can be authorised as 'directed surveillance'.

[11]As above, show you understand that the legislation is reinforced by Codes and these can meet the Convention's conception of 'law'.

The legal rules must be sufficiently precise and protective to allow the balance of factors inherent in a judgment of proportionality (required under article 8(2)) to be made. Bloggs is consulting with

<table>
<tr><td>[12]Move on to discuss the professional legal privilege point. This is clearly signalled in the question – it is the sort of point worth noting in your read through of the question.</td></tr>
</table>

his lawyer[12] and so, it would seem, his conversation should be protected from disclosure by legal professional privilege. In **Re McE** [2009] UKHL 15 the House of Lords held that RIPA 2000 allowed 'directed surveillance' for all purposes, including interfering with legal privilege, but that this was incompatible with article 8. Compatibility required that the more demanding and precise requirements relating to 'intrusive' surveillance should be made to apply in these circumstances. Declarations that the directed surveillance was unlawful were upheld.

[13]In discussing consequences, you gain credit by reminding the examiner you know the terms of the Human Rights Act 1998.

Following **Re McE**, therefore, any evidence against Bloggs is likely to be unlawfully obtained unless the police have a defence under s 6(2) HRA 1998[13] that they were giving effect to an incompatible statute. If unlawfully obtained, though, it is not necessarily inadmissible. English law does not have, nor does the Convention (respecting article 6) require, an absolute bar to the admissibility of unlawfully obtained evidence (**R v H**).

[14]Section 78 PACE is very important as a means in domestic law for giving effect to fair hearings (article 6). It is a good point to conclude with.

Based on the breach of legal privilege, Bloggs may be able to persuade the trial judge to exclude the evidence by exercising his discretion under s 78 PACE 1984[14] (though in the absence of bad faith or deliberate flouting of the rules this may be difficult: **R v Mason** [2002] EWCA Crim 385).

✓ Make your answer stand out

- In discussion of s 78 PACE 1984 you can raise the issue of whether the lack of a clear rule against the admissibility of illegally obtained evidence diminishes the effectiveness of article 8.
- A brief reference to article 6 on the issue of the admissibility of unlawfully obtained evidence shows awareness of the Convention as a whole.
- In respect of both CCTV and surveillance a brief discussion of the effectiveness of remedies and compatibility with article 13, could be had. A very brief reference to remedies in RIPA 2000 (the Tribunal) could be useful. In respect of the CCTV issue, the effectiveness of remedies against the media (especially under statutory regulation of broadcasting and self-regulation of the press) could be mentioned – these were relevant in *Peck*, though have improved somewhat since then.
- References to further academic discussion can be helpful, such as, on *Re McE*, Requa (2009) and, on police covert surveillance, Loftus *et al.* (2010).

> ! **Don't be tempted to ...**
>
> ■ Although you need to show understanding of some basic points about the Regulation of Investigatory Powers Act 2000, understanding which comes from reading relevant Human Rights Act cases, do not spend too much time in exploring the general terms of this long Act.
>
> ■ Treat the question as requiring a general, descriptive answer going through all the features of article 8. Your understanding in general terms should be inferred from the way you treat the specific issues that come up in the question.

🖎 Question 10

To what extent do Convention rights restrain the Home Secretary in the way she exercises her legal powers to deport foreigners from the UK?

Answer plan

➜ Outline the basic grounds of removal in the UK; explain why these need to be exercised compatibly with Convention rights.

➜ Discuss the Convention ban on removals where there is a real risk of an article 3 violation in the receiving country.

➜ Note governments' attempts at change.

➜ Consider the impact of a risk of violations of other rights.

➜ Focus on article 8; distinguish domestic and foreign cases.

Diagram plan

Application of Convention rights	Article 3	Other rights, esp art 8
• Statute law on extradition, deportation and removal (s 3 HRA 1998) • Acts of public authorities, e.g. Home Secretary (s 6 HRA 1998)	• General rule: if 'real risk' in receiving state (e.g. *Soering*, *Chahal*) • Wider application (e.g. health)? • Seeking change • Threshold of severity: distinguish extradition from deportation	• *Ullah* and 'flagrant breach' test • Article 8 and 'domestic' and 'foreign' cases • Balance of private and family life against justification for removal • Article 6 – torture and flagrant breach

A printable version of this diagram is available from www.pearsoned.co.uk/lawexpressqa

[1]Indicate your understanding, from the beginning, that the ECHR (international law) has an important role to play in this topic.

[2]It is a good idea to start with this basic principle. Students are known to giggle at 'aliens' but it is a proper term to use, though 'foreigner' can also be used. It refers to those who are liable to removal.

[3]Try to give a brief outline of the main grounds on which removal can take place; this is a highly complex area of law and so you are not expected to be too detailed.

[4]Make sure you explain why Convention rights are relevant under UK law.

[5]It is important to use this phrase since it indicates the standard of judicial review.

Answer

It is accepted at international law, including under the Convention,[1] that states have power to control the entry into and require the removal of aliens from their territory.[2] In the United Kingdom, broadly speaking,[3] ordinary overstayers can be removed and deportation can be ordered to follow criminal conviction and punishment. Individuals can also be deported if, according to the Home Secretary, 'conducive to the public good' (e.g. on national security grounds). These are mainly statutory powers which must be interpreted, so far as possible, for compatibility with Convention rights (s 3 HRA 1998). They also involve the executive and the courts – both public authorities bound to act compatibly (s 6 HRA 1998). UK law expressly provides for incompatibility with Convention rights to be a ground of appeal.[4]

The ECtHR has long held that article 3, the prohibition on torture, etc, prevents removal from a signatory state if there is a 'real risk'[5] of torture, etc, in the receiving country. In **Soering *v* UK** (1989) 11 EHRR 439 a proposed extradition to the US of a wanted murderer violated article 3 because, if convicted, he might be placed on death row; and in **Chahal *v* United Kingdom** (1997) 23 EHRR 413 the

[6]You will get credit for mentioning Protocol 13 – it shows awareness of post-1998 developments.

principle was applied in a public interest deportation case. Protocol 13 (which bans the death penalty in all circumstances)[6] means that removal to face a real risk of capital punishment is also prohibited.

[7]Move on to make the point that this Convention barrier to deportation remains politically controversial.

The principle is controversial because article 3 applies absolutely:[7] there can be no justification (in terms of the rights of others or the public interest) for treatment above the article 3 threshold; nor can article 3 be derogated from in time of 'war or other public emergency threatening the life of the nation'[8] (article 15). Thus major criminals (such as in **Ahmed v Austria** (1997) 24 EHRR 278), and those whom the government believes are a threat to national security, cannot be deported if the real risk is established.

[8]Again, one of the phrases from the Convention that are worth remembering for questions on this and other topics.

[9]This will strengthen your answer by showing awareness of how the controversial nature of the principle showed itself in government activity.

Governments are faced with considerable difficulties over what should then be done. In the context of anti-terrorism, the UK and other governments sought, but failed, to persuade a Grand Chamber to introduce a proportionality test[9] which would allow removal where the risk of torture, etc, was relatively low and the threat to the security relatively high (**Saadi v Italy** (2009) 49 EHRR 30). An alternative pursued is to seek, through diplomacy, assurances from the receiving state as to the treatment of the deportee. Sceptics argue that such assurances are in principle not reliable but the House of Lords held that reliability was a matter of fact to be dealt with at first instance (**Othman v Secretary of State for the Home Department** [2009] UKHL 10).

[10]Although 'absolute', you get credit for demonstrating your understanding, when dealing with article 3, that the treatment involved must be sufficiently serious, and what is sufficient depends on the context. The point will come up again by reference to justifications under article 8(2).

Removal is only prohibited when the threshold of severity under article 3 is passed. Context and purpose are important.[10] Thus UK courts have not stopped extraditions to the USA where the defendant can expect a disproportionately longer prison sentence than in the UK (**R v Bieber** [2008] EWCA Civ 1602). Part of the reasoning relates to distinguishing extradition from deportation, with the former being seen as part of the judicial process.

[11]Move on to discuss removals of those who are sick, etc, and start by showing your understanding of the scope of article 3. This section also provides a useful bridge to the discussion of article 8 which follows.

Article 3 can apply more widely than just to wilful acts of public officials.[11] There have been cases in which the deportation of a dying person violated article 3 (**D v UK** (1997) 24 EHRR 423) but, normally, lack of equal medical care will not cause a violation of article 3 (**R (N) v Secretary of State for the Home Department** [2005] UKHL 31, confirmed in **N v UK** (2008) 47 EHRR 39).

[12]Now build on your answer by discussing whether removals can be stopped on the grounds of a violation of other rights.

What about other rights?[12] In **R (Ullah) v Special Adjudicator** [2004] UKHL 26 the House of Lords ruled (following ECtHR case law) that any alleged breach in the receiving country needed to be 'flagrant' (involving a complete denial or destruction of the very essence of the right) in order to stop the removal. This applies particularly to qualified rights (in **Ullah** it was freedom of religion in article 9).

The main focus is on article 8, the need for a state to respect private and family life subject to justification in terms of article 8(2). In **R (Razgar) v Secretary of State for the Home Department** [2004] UKHL 27, the House of Lords distinguished between domestic cases (where the person has established strong ties in the UK) and foreign cases (relating to the conditions in the receiving country).[13]

[13]It is helpful to make this distinction; you can show the different types of concern that arise and that you are aware of the terminology in the case law.

Domestically, not all aliens will enjoy article 8 rights. But a well-settled migrant is likely to face an interference with family life or private life (given that this term is applied, for instance, to the right to build social relationships).[14] Since article 8 is a qualified right, the validity of the removal depends on the degree of interference balanced with the justification for the removal. The reliance of dependent children on the deportee is likely to be a factor, for instance. There is, however, full recognition of the importance to states of their right to deport aliens (**Uner v Netherlands** (2007) 45 EHRR 14).

[14]It is important to demonstrate your understanding of the wide definition of 'private life'.

Foreign cases involve proving a flagrant denial of rights in the receiving state. Having a less good health service (**Bensaid v UK** (2001) 33 EHRR 10) or a legal system that denies some important rights (**EM (Lebanon) v Secretary of State for the Home Department** [2008] UKHL 64) will not be enough. However, individual factors might convince the courts of a real risk that a complete denial of the right is possible (as in **EM**).

The fair balance under article 8 is determined by context. Extradition, for instance, is distinguished from deportation. As part of the criminal justice system, refusing extradition on family life grounds would require weighty reasons, the sort that (highly unusually) might be sufficient to prevent a person going to prison where it would otherwise be justified (**Norris v US** [2010] UKSC 9).

[15]Finish your answer by reference to article 6 and the issue of torture evidence. This will impress the examiner by showing your awareness of developments.

A deportation to a country where there is a real risk of an unfair trial, otherwise in breach of article 6,[15] will be subject to the **Ullah** test of flagrant breach. In **Othman**, the House of Lords held that the UK court deciding the issue of fact had to be satisfied that the fundamental fairness of the trial would be destroyed and that there was no rule (as the Court of Appeal had suggested) that a risk that evidence from torture would be admissible in the receiving country was itself evidence of a flagrant breach.

[16]Now try to draw together your main points into a conclusion.

It is clear that Convention rights are a significant restraint on the way states may exercise their power to remove aliens.[16] People must not be sent to face a real risk of torture and states must take into account a person's rights to private and family life.

 Make your answer stand out

- Make references to the extensive discussion on this highly controversial matter, e.g. (on *Saadi*) Gentili (2010); (on diplomatic assurances) Tooze (2010).
- A brief reference to alternatives (such as control orders) and the problems they give rise to might help: see Ewing and Tham (2008).
- A brief comparison with the UN Convention Relating to the Status of Refugees 1954 (Cm 9171) could be useful – article 1F allows the Home Secretary to refuse to grant asylum to a person responsible for war crimes, etc (for a recent discussion see *R (JS (Sri Lanka) v SSHD* [2010] UKSC 15).
- In the context of article 6, point out that the procedure for dealing with deportation in the removing (as distinct from receiving) country is not covered by the right to a fair hearing. It does not involve the determinations of 'civil rights and obligations', nor of a 'criminal charge'.

! Don't be tempted to ...

- Though this is legally controversial, and the controversy can be properly referred to, avoid at all costs a 'tabloid' approach about how the HRA is a prisoners' charter that leaves us unsafe in our beds, etc, etc.
- Don't spend too much time on the detail of the UK's laws on deportation, extradition and removal. They are important in establishing the context of the application of Convention principles but are too complicated for anything more than a general introduction in a question such as this.
- Just concentrate on article 3 in terms of deportations; other rights, especially article 8, are just as important.

Article 5: the right to liberty and security

6

How this topic may come up in exams

Questions could focus on an important issue, like defining 'deprivation of liberty'. Alternatively, they might explore the impact of the article generally or an essay or problem question could look at a theme like police powers, mental health or prisoners. Remember, in any event, the general themes (like legality and non-arbitrariness) as well as the express requirements (and don't forget judicial supervision). Be aware that a theme focused question might also expect knowledge of other relevant rights. You may need to have a certain amount of knowledge of UK or English law in order to show the impact of article 5 under HRA 1998.

■ Attack the question

```
┌─────────────────────┐     ┌─────────────────────┐     ┌─────────────────────┐
│   Is the question   │     │  Consider the basic │     │  Discuss or apply   │
│ concerned with whether│ ──▶ │ principle against   │ ──▶ │   the principle of  │
│   art 5 is in issue?│     │  arbitrary          │     │   legality          │
│   If so define      │     │  detention – this   │     │ ('procedure prescribed│
│ 'deprivation of liberty'│  │  supports the way   │     │  by law') (note art 5(2)│
│                     │     │  express terms in   │     │  and information)   │
│                     │     │  art 5 are interpreted│   │                     │
└─────────────────────┘     └─────────────────────┘     └─────────────────────┘
                                                                    │
                                                                    ▼
                                                        ┌─────────────────────┐
                                                        │  Discuss or apply   │
                                                        │  the requirement    │
                                                        │  for judicial       │
                                                        │  supervision (art 5(3) and│
                                                        │  (4)) – including   │
                                                        │  authority to       │
                                                        │  release and fair procedures│
                                                        └─────────────────────┘
                                                                    │
                                                                    ▼
                                                        ┌─────────────────────┐
                                                        │  Note  art 5(5) and │
                                                        │  compensation       │
                                                        │                     │
                                                        └─────────────────────┘
```

A printable version of this diagram is available from www.pearsoned.co.uk/lawexpressqa

📝 Question 1

Does article 5 add anything to the protection of liberty already guaranteed under common law principles in England?

Answer plan

→ Consider the idea that article 5 provides specific principles reinforcing the common law.

→ Discuss the relation of common law principles to Parliamentary supremacy and whether this is altered by HRA 1998.

→ Discuss article 5:
  – non-arbitrariness;
  – the exclusive purposes for which a person can be deprived of their liberty (art 5(1));
  – the legality principle;
  – the requirement for notice (art 5(2));
  – the requirement for proper judicial supervision (art 5(3) and (4));
  – the compensation principle.

→ Conclude.

Diagram plan

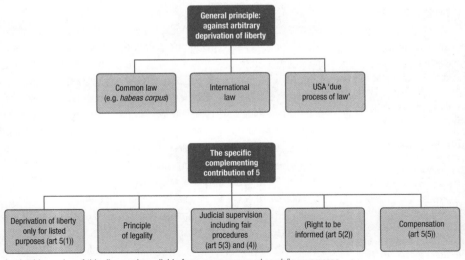

A printable version of this diagram is available from www.pearsoned.co.uk/lawexpressqa

Answer

[1]The question is clearly exploring your knowledge about article 5 in general, so start with this observation. Other, more existential, conceptions of freedom are not in issue.

Article 5 deals with physical liberty[1] – a person's right and ability to be free from control over their movements by others. The basic dignity of the individual means that a person should not be arbitrarily deprived of their liberty. This principle, found in Magna Carta (originally 1215), is embodied in the writ of *habeas corpus* and reinforced by landmark decisions of the common law.

Such laws simply require that liberty should not be taken away other than on the basis of law. The problem is that by its legal and constitutional supremacy Parliament can authorise, through legislation, inroads into liberty on any grounds. Thus foreign terrorist suspects who could not be deported were imprisoned without trial, between 2001 and 2004. Though inconsistent with article 5 (discussed below), nothing in the general principles of English law made this unlawful. If Parliament legislates with sufficient clarity of purpose and intention, the UK courts must follow, no matter how fundamental a contrary principle may be. The best they can do is issue a declaration of incompatibility.

[2]The principle of non-arbitrariness is fundamental and should form a continual reference in your answer. It prevents article 5 being applied in a mechanical, tick-box way.

Article 5 is, perhaps, more specific in its demands than the common law. First, article 5 lays down the general right to liberty and security.[2] This is the basis of the underlying principle that deprivations of liberty should never be arbitrary.

[3]Article 5(1) must now be discussed. Spend some time on this because it specifies purposes of detention, which is unlike other liberty-protecting instruments.

Secondly, article 5 then identifies the only purposes for which lawful deprivations of liberty are permitted.[3] It is this which distinguishes the protection of liberty in article 5 from the more ancient constitutional instruments. Thus, under article 5(1) (in outline)[4] a person can only be deprived of his liberty for the purposes of: punishment following conviction for a crime; securing the fulfilment of an 'obligation prescribed by law'; arresting on suspicion of an offence; securing the education of minors; and in the contexts of mental health and immigration control. The text of article 5(1)(a)–(f) contains more detailed qualifications. Thus arrest under article 5(1)(c) requires 'reasonable' suspicion. Similarly, the text of article 5 has been interpreted in ways that make it more precise and demanding.[5] **Winterwerp v The Netherlands** (1979) 2 EHRR 387, for example, deals with detentions in the mental health context. Unsoundness of mind must be professionally confirmed and detention must be

[4]The question needs you to summarise as well as you can the grounds of non-arbitrary deprivation of liberty in article 5(1); try to do this. Even if you are allowed a statute book, there is far too much to copy.

[5]By using an example you show you are familiar with the way in which some of the terms in article 5(1)(a)–(f) have been interpreted; try to convey this sense of being thoroughly knowledgeable, as if this is one of many examples you could have chosen.

'warranted' (changed to 'necessary' in later cases). This focus on purpose is very important and distinctive. It must be said that, unsurprisingly, this list of purposes covers most of the purposes for which states, in normal times, may deprive people of their liberty.

[6]The question is asking you to explore the general principles in article 5; the compatibility of a deprivation of liberty with the rule of law is fundamental and so you need to give it full consideration.

Article 5 also imposes formal and procedural requirements.

A deprivation of liberty for one of the purposes in article 5(1) must be 'in accordance with a procedure prescribed by law'.[6] This is found in the common law but under article 5 may be more exacting. Deprivations of liberty must be based on national law. An unlawful deprivation of liberty or one based on administrative dishonesty (as in **Conka v Belgium** (2002) 34 EHRR 54) will breach article 5. Also, national law must be accessible (not secret, for example) and foreseeable (couched in terms which, to a degree appropriate to the context, allow a person to foresee the likely legal consequences of his or her actions); above all they must provide sufficient control, in context, over the actions of the authorities and, so, protection against arbitrary action. In **HL v UK** (2005) 40 EHRR 32, for instance, the applicant had been 'informally' but lawfully admitted to a mental hospital. Informal admission did not have any of the substantive and procedural protections attached to admission under statutory powers and the ECtHR held there had been a violation of article 5. Of course these requirements may lose some force in the way they are interpreted and applied in particular circumstances.

[7]This case is relevant even though it mainly involved article 8; the interrelationship of the Convention articles is unavoidable and you will get credit for discussing it.

In **R (Gillan) v Commissioner of Police for the Metropolis** [2006] UKHL 12 (a case that is mainly concerned with article 8)[7] the House of Lords allowed that a stop and search had been on the basis of law even though the applicant could not know that the relevant police powers had been brought into effect (the ECtHR later held that article 8 had been breached (**Gillan v UK** (2010) 50 EHRR 45).

[8]Now move on to discuss article 5(3) and (4). These are very important and discussing them shows you understand the importance of the rule of law in the Convention. Note that article 5(3) has a narrower focus to that of 5(4) which applies to all grounds of detention.

Article 5(2) requires all arrested or detained persons to be informed, in clear language that they can understand, of the reason for their loss of liberty (**Van der Leer v The Netherlands** (1990) 12 EHRR 567). In English law this is found expressly in respect of police arrests (s 28 PACE 1984) but is a more discretionary requirement in respect of other types of detention.

There must be proper judicial supervision[8] over deprivations of liberty.

Article 5(3) requires there to be a system by which anyone arrested on reasonable suspicion of an offence (article 5(1)(c)) must be brought promptly before a judge or other judicial officer who has the authority, if necessary, to order the person's release. The detained person is entitled either to be released on bail or, if remanded in custody, to be tried within a 'reasonable time'. English law, under the Police and Criminal Evidence Act 1984 normally requires a person detained to be released within 36 hours; any further detention must be authorised by a magistrate. In **Brogan v UK** (1989) 11 EHRR 117 it was held that there had been a violation of article 5(3) when a suspected terrorist could be held for seven days without judicial supervision.

Article 5(4) requires anyone arrested or detained for any of the article 5(1) purposes to have access to a court or tribunal in order to test the legality of their detention before an independent body capable of ordering their release. Mental patients, for example, must have access to a First Tier Tribunal (Mental Health) for this purpose.

[9]Stress the importance of proper judicial supervision based on an independent tribunal following a fair procedure. To repeat, the idea of the rule of law is absolutely central to the way the Convention acts as a restraint on arbitrariness by the authorities and must come out in your answer.

The court or tribunal respecting both article 5(3) and 5(4) must be judicial[9] in the sense of being independent of the executive and operating with a procedure that is adversarial and based on principles of fairness such as equality of arms. In **R (Brooke) v Secretary of State for Justice** [2008] EWCA Civ 29, it was held that the Parole Board (which decides whether it is safe to release certain categories of prisoner after they have served the punitive part of their sentence) was too closely linked to the executive to satisfy article 5(4).

[10]Don't forget article 5(5) – it is the only express requirement for compensation in the Convention.

Finally, article 5(5)[10] requires there to be a system for compensating a person detained in breach of article 5.

Although the principle of non-arbitrary detention is firmly rooted in the common law, article 5 adds to this by being the basis of additional particular rights and being more specific in the demands it makes of the courts and executive.

✓ ## Make your answer stand out

- A more critical approach could be taken. If so you would emphasise the open texture, even vagueness, of the language of article 5 and point out how, in the context of, for example, anti-terrorism, or police powers, it has been relatively easy for the authorities to establish compatibility (see, for example, Ewing and Tham (2008) or *Gillan* (above)). You might also discuss how the article 5 standard is not particularly high in some areas, such as (in mental health law) whether detention must be confined to patients with treatable conditions or whether the hospital must be appropriate to the severity of the condition (see *Hutchison Reid* v *UK* (2003) 37 EHRR 9 and *Ashingdane* v *UK* (1987) 7 EHRR 528).

■ Discuss more fully the 'formal approach' such as in the US and 'due process of law' test. But be careful to state that this does not reduce to a simple contrast between formal and substantive concepts; 'substantive' due process links 'law' to non-arbitrary purposes.

■ In your discussion of article 5(5) you could note that a breach of article 5 is not necessarily the same thing as a wrong conviction; that the courts in the UK are turning away from basing the *quantum* on tort principles (*R (Greenfield)* v *Secretary of State for the Home Office* [2005] UKHL 14); and that article 5(5) complements the general power to require 'just satisfaction'.

! Don't be tempted to ...

■ Unbalance your answer by too much focus on one or two issues – the question is looking for a balanced consideration of article 5 as a whole.

■ Spend too much time on English law (such as *habeas corpus*); the point is to consider the contribution of article 5.

■ Spend too much time on 'deprivation of liberty' – an important matter but not the focus of this question.

? Question 2

Able, Baker and Charlie are part of a large crowd of football supporters moving through the centre of a town.

Able is stopped and searched by the police, who suspect him of having stolen objects in his bag. Nothing is found. There are many people being searched and this results in Able being held for one hour. He misses the game.

Baker is shouting and threatening violence. He is detained by the police on the grounds of an anticipated breach of the peace. He is taken to the police station and held in the cells for four hours.

Charlie, who hates football, was caught up in the crowd. The crowd is becoming threatening. The police surround Charlie and another fifty or so fans and prevent them from going anywhere for three hours. Charlie misses an important job interview.

Advise Able, Baker and Charlie who believe that, in each case, the police have exercised their discretion in a way that breaches the right to liberty in article 5.

Answer plan

→ Show that the powers need to be exercised compatibly with Convention rights.

→ Note article 5 generally: deprivation of liberty, non-arbitrariness and the purpose in article 5(1)(a)–(c).

→ Able:
  – consider the compatibility of stop and search with article 5 and article 8;
  – discuss critically *R (Gillan)* v *Commissioner of Police of the Metropolis* [2006] UKHL 12 (House of Lords and Strasbourg);
  – consider whether *Gillan* controls the decision in Able's case?

→ Baker:
  – consider whether detention for an anticipated breach of the peace is compatible with article 5;
  – discuss *Steel* v *UK* (1999) 28 EHRR 603 and the concept of an 'offence';
  – apply to Baker's case.

→ Charlie:
  – consider whether article 5 applies in Charlie's case.
  – discuss the House of Lords' decision in *Austin* v *Commissioner of Police of the Metropolis* (2009) UKHL 5 and whether a purposive conception of deprivation of liberty is jurisprudentially sound;
  – apply to Charlie's case.

Diagram plan

Able	Baker	Charlie
• Stop and search – deprivation of liberty? • If yes: consider art 5(1)(b) • Consider art 8 (*Gillan* – UKHL or ECtHR?)	• Breach of the peace and art 5 • Consider *Steel* – general compatibility	• Police powers • *Austin* • Deprivation of liberty and purpose

A printable version of this diagram plan is available from www.pearsoned.co.uk/lawexpressqa

[1]Begin by showing why article 5 will be relevant to these issues as decided under English law.

Answer

Able, Baker and Charlie are dealt with by police acting under statutory powers (Police and Criminal Evidence Act 1984 (PACE)) reinforced by a Code of Practice. It can be inferred from the fact that the police are exercising discretion that it is 'possible' to interpret and apply these powers in a way that is compatible with Convention rights (s 3 HRA 1998).[1] The police also exercise common law powers and, as a public authority (s 6 HRA 1998), must ensure compatibility with Convention rights.

[2]This is not a civil liberties question so you are not expected to show specific knowledge of the statutes or principles, just that they have to be interpreted and applied in ways that are compatible with Convention rights. A basic knowledge of general police powers is helpful and is, anyway, found in the Convention rights case law.

Able is subject to the stop and search powers in Part 1 PACE.[2] These powers will only need to be compatible with article 5 if Able has been 'deprived of his liberty'. In **Guzzardi v Italy** (1981) 3 EHRR 333 (followed by the UK courts), a deprivation of liberty, compared with a restriction on movement, is a matter of degree and can be based on an accumulation of factors. UK courts also insist on a clear and significant element of prison-like containment (**Secretary of State for the Home Department v A** [2007] UKHL 45). **R (Gillan) v Commisioner of the Metropolitan Police** [2006] UKHL 12 dealt with powers of random stop and search under the Terrorism Act 2000.[3] It was thought that a stop and search without any aggravating aspects would be unlikely to be serious enough to deprive a person of his liberty. Aggravating factors, such as being taken to a police station, handcuffed or (as with Able) a long detention, may amount to a deprivation of liberty. If so, it would be likely to be compatible with article 5(1)(b), which allows detention to fulfil an 'obligation prescribed by law' (here the obligation of submitting to an otherwise lawful stop and search). The Law Lords also held that an ordinary stop and search was likely to be too trivial to be an interference with private life (article 8)[4] or, if the facts pointed to an interference, it would probably be justified under the terms of article 8(2). It was on this justification point that the ECtHR disagreed.[5] It found a violation of article 8 because there was insufficient legal control of police discretion. The ECtHR's judgment (**Gillan v UK** (2010) 50 EHRR 45) is focused on power of random search under the Terrorism Act 2000. Part 1 of PACE 1984 requires the police to have reasonable suspicion and this requirement is likely to meet many of the Strasbourg Court's concerns. Though the ECtHR did not decide on whether there had been a deprivation of liberty, it did not deny this as a possibility.

[3]Address this important case. Show your understanding that *Gillan* dealt with stop and search powers that did not need to be triggered by reasonable suspicion.

[4]Remember to discuss the article 8 issue (even though the question as a whole is mainly addressed to article 5). Stop and search is one of those issues which involve more than one Convention right and you should demonstrate to the examiners that you understand this.

[5]Move on to discuss the Strasbourg decision in *Gillan*. Specify the main point of disagreement; for Strasbourg the interference was not 'in accordance with the law' because of the lack of a sufficiently demanding legal framework as regards random stop and search.

[6]Try to draw a conclusion on Able's case – the question asks you to advise him. Though you cannot be certain, the examiner will expect you to have explored the main legal issues applied by a court to the facts.

Being held for an hour suggests that Able was deprived of liberty[6] but for a legitimate purpose found in article 5(1)(b); it may also be an interference with private life but, again, given reasonable suspicion, one capable of justification under article 8(2). If there is evidence of an abuse of power (e.g. bad faith, perhaps unnecessary delay) these justifications may not apply. Furthermore, the general principle in the first sentence of article 5 will not have been satisfied.

[7]Having pointed out clearly that Baker is deprived of his liberty, move on to discuss the main issue here – whether the detention is for one of the purposes listed in article 5(1).

[8]You will gain credit if you can flag up to the examiner that you know and can list (or at least summarise) the purposes for which deprivation of liberty may be legitimate.

Baker is held by police for four hours. There is clearly a sufficient element of containment for this to be a deprivation of liberty. Therefore the police action must meet the requirements of article 5. Depriving Baker of his liberty must have been for one of the purposes listed in article 5(1)(a)–(f).[7] But Baker is not being punished after conviction (article 5(1)(a)), nor is there his specific legal obligation his detention is supposed to secure (article 5(1)(b), nor is he a child, a drunk, vagrant, infectious or of unsound mind, nor is he in the process of being deported[8] (article 5(1)(d)–(f). Article 5(1)(c) allows deprivation of liberty of a person reasonably suspected of a criminal offence or where there are reasonable grounds to believe that detention will prevent his committing an offence. Breach of the peace, however, is not classified under domestic law as an offence. Nevertheless, in **Steel v UK** (1999) 28 EHRR 603 the ECtHR accepted that the initial detention of the applicant for many hours for breach of the peace could be compatible with article 5(1). First, the English case law was sufficiently developed and structured to ensure that the lawful exercise of police powers would not be arbitrary and so any deprivation followed a procedure prescribed by law. Secondly, it was not disputed, and was accepted by the ECtHR, that breach of the peace was, despite its English law classification, an 'offence'. Breach of the peace is linked to the threat of violence and the facts on which it is based may also constitute an offence (in **Brogan v UK** (1989) 11 EHRR 117 an arrest for 'terrorism' – not an offence – was nevertheless compatible with article 5(1)(c)). Thus Baker's detention, though a deprivation of his liberty, is likely to be compatible with article 5(1)(c).

As noted above, in **Steel**, detention to prevent an anticipated breach of the peace can be consistent with article 5(1). But Charlie is unwittingly caught up in the threatening behaviour of others. If he is deprived of his liberty it could be difficult to show that his treatment is compatible with article 5(1). The English courts, however, recognise the Police's dilemma in distinguishing, in a group, beween those acting lawfully and those who may be committing or threatening to commit offences or breaches of the peace.

[9]Now turn to *Austin* – this is an authoritative but controversial decision on when, if at all, there can be a deprivation of liberty in a public order context and you will be expected to discuss it.

[10]Although this is not the focus of the question, a brief reference to *Laporte* shows awareness of important developments and so impresses the examiners.

[11]You will get credit for showing your understanding of the differences in nuance between some of the judges.

In **Austin *v* Commissioner of Police of the Metropolis** (2009) UKHL 5[9] police had surrounded demonstrators and 'kettled' them in Oxford Circus for up to seven hours. The Court of Appeal had found that if members of the crowd were threatening immediate breaches of the peace **(R (Laporte)**[10] ***v* Chief Constable of Gloucestershire** [2006] UKHL 55), the police can contain the whole crowd if it is strictly necessary because it is not possible to discriminate between those whose actions are entirely lawful and the others. The House of Lords considered whether this could be compatible with article 5. The issue turned on whether such containment involved a 'deprivation of liberty'. The Law Lords held (though Lord Walker was more circumspect than Lord Hope)[11] that Strasbourg case law was consistent with the idea that the existence of a deprivation of liberty could be determined by reference to the purpose with which the authorities acted. Thus good faith and proportionate actions by the police to deal with threats to public order will not, even though there is significant containment, be deprivations of liberty engaging article 5. If police actions are taken in bad faith or are disproportionate they will not be in accordance with 'law' and then article 5 would cut in. Fenwick (2009) and others have criticised **Austin** for failing to protect the rights of political demonstrators.

In the absence of bad faith or lack of proportion, Charlie may find that the police actions were compatible with his right to liberty.

✓ Make your answer stand out

- Discuss more of the case law on article 5(1)(b) and stop and search, such as *Brogan* and *McVeigh* v *UK* (1993) 5 EHRR 71.

- Critics see the House of Lords' decision in *Gillan* as being too executive friendly and, in particular, not giving adequate protection to legitimate political protest. You could explore some of these points (see Edwards (2008)).

- Consider some of the criticism of the way *Austin* restricts rights of protest, e.g by Fenwick (2009). For further discussion of the case, focused on the definition of 'deprivation of liberty', see Mead (2009).

▶

■ Place emphasis on the general principle of a right to liberty in the first sentence of article 5; in other words, remember that the main point is to avoid arbitrary detention and you should not treat the article in too mechanical, tick-box a fashion.

! Don't be tempted to ...

■ Spend time and space on going though all the categories in article 5(1)(a)–(f). The question is focused on article 5(1)(a), (b) and (c).

■ Article 8 is relevant, especially to Able's case, but, again, you simply don't have space for a long general elaboration of the article. Your basic knowledge of it should be inferred from how you discuss the issues.

■ The answer requires some knowledge of breach of the peace (as is available from *Steel* and other human rights cases); but you do not have the space for a long exposition of the principles as developed under domestic law.

Question 3

Discuss the extent to which article 5 and other Convention rights have affected the way control orders (under the Prevention of Terrorism Act 2005) have been put into effect.

Answer plan

→ Distinguish between derogating and non-derogating control orders.

→ Discuss the significance of 'deprivation of liberty' and the European and the UK case law which defines the term.

→ Discuss the application of other Convention rights in relation to control orders.

→ Consider the application of article 6 to the control order procedure.

→ Conclude with a critical discussion of compatibility and the rule of law.

Diagram plan

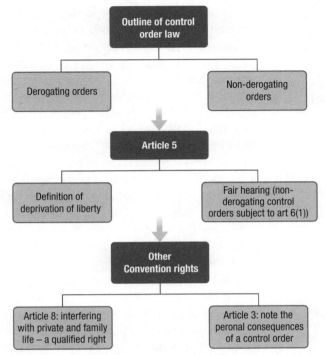

A printable version of this diagram is available from www.pearsoned.co.uk/lawexpressqa

Answer

[1]Begin with a brief introduction to control orders, which gets your answer going. You will get the basics of it from the control order cases; it is not necessary to go into great detail.

[2]Show your understanding of the significance of derogating/non-derogating control orders; if they involve a deprivation of liberty, that would probably violate Article 5.

The Prevention of Terrorism Act 2005[1] (PTA 2005) allows the Secretary of State to impose an unlimited, though exemplified, range of 'obligations' on terrorist suspects. An obligation which deprives the controllee of his or her liberty is unlikely to be compatible with article 5(1), a scheduled Convention right. Article 5(1) lists the exclusive purposes for which a person can lawfully be deprived of their physicial liberty.[2] Control orders are imposed on people suspected of 'terrorism-related activity'. Controllees are not being punished following conviction for an offence, there is no specific legal obligation whose performance can be achieved by detention and they have not been arrested on reasonable suspicion of an offence (see article 5(1)(a)–(c), etc). The Act therefore authorises two types of order. One is an order whose obligations amount to a

[3]Expressing yourself by showing that it is PTA 2005 that makes this type of order unlawful, demonstrates your understanding of the HRA, 1998.

[4]Mention article 2, because it helps to explain *Guzzardi* – but remember the UK has not ratified it, so don't spend too much time on it.

[5]These cases need to be discussed since they deal with the definition of 'deprivation of liberty' on which turns the issue of whether article 5 is engaged or not.

[6]It is worth mentioning the broad facts of *JJ* in order to measure the severity of control orders, a point you can come back to at the end.

[7]Note the point by reference to post-*JJ* cases. Lord Brown's original position was always likely to be too mechanical for pragmatic-minded judges. Nevertheless, some element of confinement seems to still be necessary.

[8]Now move on to discuss the impact of other articles, as invited by the question. Remember to show your understanding of the structure of article 8 as a qualified right.

'deprivation of liberty'. These are only lawful, under PTA 2005, if the government has derogated, under article 15 ECHR, from article 5.[3] The second type are orders whose obligations do not deprive the controllee of his or her liberty. Only the second type is lawful since no derogation has been made. Article 2 of the Fourth Protocol[4] guarantees a (qualified) right to liberty of movement and choice of residence; but the UK has not ratified it, nor is it a scheduled right in the HRA 1998. Thus lawfulness will depend on whether there is a 'deprivation of liberty'. The House of Lords adopted **Guzzardi v Italy** (1981) 3 EHRR 333 into UK law in **Secretary of State for the Home Department v JJ** [2007] UKHL **45**.[5] The central point is that distinguishing a deprivation of liberty from a restriction on movement is a matter of fact and degree. Imprisonment may be the typical case but there can be a deprivation of liberty, without imprisonment, given the cumulative effect of a range of factors. In **Guzzardi** a mafia suspect was required to live in a small village on a small island. Though not imprisoned, he was subject to a range of other requirements, such as reporting to the police. The European Court of Human Rights (ECtHR) held that, taking everything into account, he had been deprived of his liberty, not merely restricted in his movements. In JJ a controllee was required to reside for 18 hours, between 4.00 pm and 10.00 am,[6] in a one-room flat and was also subject to other restraints. The majority of the House of Lords held there was a deprivation of liberty. Some UK judges interpreted the Strasbourg case law as being consistent with requiring a significant core element of confinement (e.g. a curfew). Lord Brown, in **JJ**, held that confinements for less than 14–16 hours a day would not, whatever the other circumstances might be, amount to a deprivation of liberty. But this view has not been followed by the Supreme Court.[7] Thus other restraints can, cumulatively, amount to a deprivation of liberty but these will have to be unusually destructive of normal life if the confinement is less than 14–16 hours (**Secretary of State for the Home Department v AP** [2010] UKSC 24).

Control orders can also engage article 8[8] if there are restrictions on private and family life. Disproportionate provisions could be struck down by the courts as being unjustifiable under article 8(2) (**BX v Secretary of State for the Home Department** [2010] EWCA Civ 481); the same effect can be found through ordinary statutory inter-pretation, as in **Secretary of State for the Home Department** *v* **GG** [2009] EWCA Civ 786). Furthermore, the Supreme Court has held that interferences with private and family life, even if proprotionate and justifiable under article 8(2), may, nevertheless, if sufficiently serious, be weighed in the decision and could tip the balance towards a finding that there has been a deprivation of liberty (**AP**).

[9]Article 3 is worth mentioning – show you understand it acts as a backstop provision which should prevent conditions that leave a controllee in desperate straits.

Control orders must also be compatible with article 3,[9] the prohibition on degrading and inhuman treatment. Article 3 does not allow for justification of treatment above the threshold of severity. That threshold is determined by reference to facts and circumstances. There is evidence that the effect of orders on controllees can be very severe in terms of their physical and mental well-being. Where there is real risk that, if a controllee is identified, he might be the victim of attacks, the court may, on article 3 grounds, impose anonymity on proceedings (**Secretary of State for the Home Department *v* AP (2)** [2010] UKSC 26).

[10]Finish the discussion by reference to the procedural points – whether controllees get a fair hearing.

PTA 2005 allows control orders to be challenged in the courts on the grounds that the application is flawed.[10] The Act, in some circumstances, purports to require judges to keep the evidence against the controllee secret. 'Special advocates' can try to represent controllees but cannot discuss the case or take instructions from them. Nor do controllees (who are not deprived of their liberty) have the procedural protections in article 5(4), though article 6(1) applies to these proceedings. That is, controllees have the right to a fair hearing before an unbiased tribunal but not the additional rights enjoyed by criminal defendants. In **Secretary of State for the Home Department *v* MB** [2007] UKHL 46 the House of Lords held that, nevertheless, the authorities were put to a high standard of proof indistinguishable in effect from the criminal standard. It was also held that, depending on the facts of a case, it was not impossible to satisfy the 'equality of arms' requirement of article 6(1) by the use of special counsel. Following **A *v* UK** (2009) 49 EHRR 29, however,[11] the House of Lords accepted that a hearing on which the fate of the controllee was 'solely or decisively' based on closed evidence could not survive an article 6 challenge. The procedural provisions in PTA 2005 could be 'read down' under s 3 HRA 1998 to this effect.

[11]Showing awareness of recent cases in which UK courts reconsider their position following ECtHR rulings will gain you credit.

Control orders can be draconian in their effects. The legislation must be read, so far as possible, for compatibility with Convention

[12]Referring to the controversial nature not only of control orders themselves (which some see as little better than the imprisonment they replaced) but also of the response of the courts (which some see as weaker than it needed to be), shows you are aware of the strong academic and political criticisms made of control orders.

rights. Also, orders are put into effect by public officials bound by s 6 HRA 1998. UK courts have generally found it possible to interpret the legislation in ways that accommodate Convention rights. But, in doing so, the restraining effect of Convention rights on governments is taken near to breaking point. Critics, such as Ewing and Tham, argue that the courts have gone too far[12] and surrendered some of the protection of the rule of law at a time when, for the controllees, it is most needed. Rather than legal endorsement, critics argue, it would have been better to uphold the traditions of the rule of law by using s 4 and the declaration of incompatibility.[13]

[13]This is a good point to end on because it shows you understand the basic structure of the Human Rights Act, the balance it creates between courts and Parliament and the opportunities it gives the judiciary to uphold the rule of law.

✓ Make your answer stand out

- Place your answer in its specific context: control orders were the government's response to *A* v *Secretary of State for the Home Department* [2004] UKHL 56, where the House of Lords had declared that the detention without trial of foreign terrorist suspects who could not be deported (under Part IV of the Anti-terrorism, Crime and Security Act 2001) was incompatible with article 5.

- Note government proposals (January 2011) to replace control orders with Terrorist Prevention and Investigation Measures (T-PIMS).

- Refer to some of the careful and critical analysis of control orders. For example, Ewing and Tham (2008) is responded to by Kavanagh (2009). Tomkins (2010) analyses the law in terms of the broader context of national security law. Control orders specifically are discussed in Walker (2010).

! Don't be tempted to …

- Write in general terms about counter-terrorism law, such as under the Terrorism Act. Apart from (possibly) the briefest contextual reference, it is not relevant to this question which is focused on article 5 (mainly) and control orders.

■ Be too introductory in respect of the articles you are discussing. Try to balance your approach to article 5 and the other articles – you need to show, on the one hand, that you understand their basic structure and purpose but, on the other hand, you must avoid simply saying all you know about them. Keep focused on the question.

? Question 4

Julia is found sobbing uncontrollably in the city centre. She is unable to give coherent answers to any questions. Police, advised by social workers, take her to a mental hospital. After 72 hours statutory procedures are used and she is detained for treatment for three months. The only available place is in the high security wing of the hospital. She is then transferred to a residential hostel where there is no treatment available. This transfer to the hostel went ahead despite her belief that she is now recovered and should be allowed to go home. She is detained in a hostel for three months.

The English courts find that the authorities acted lawfully in regard to both common law and statutory principles.

Julia claims that her right to liberty and security under article 5 ECHR was violated.

Advise Julia on the general principles relevant to the assessment of this claim. You are not expected to show detailed knowledge of mental health law in England.

Answer plan

➡ Point out that Julia is deprived of her liberty so article 5 imposes certain requirements (the question says little of detail).

➡ Has Julia been detained on the basis of a legal procedure, as that term is understood?

➡ To what extent, if at all, does the institution in which Julia is detained and the nature of the treatment she receives therein need to be appropriate to her condition?

➡ Does Julia's transfer to a hostel suggest she is unlawfully detained, at least from the moment of transfer?

➡ Did Julia have access to a court able to order her release if she was being unlawfully detained?

Diagram plan

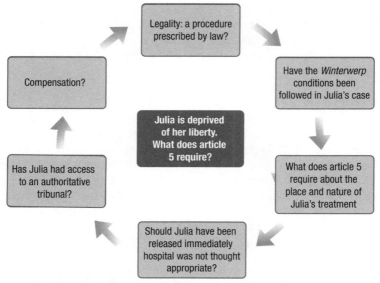

A printable version of this diagram is available from www.pearsoned.co.uk/lawexpressqa

Answer

[1]Begin by showing article 5 applies because of the deprivation of liberty.

Julia has suffered six months' confinement and so has been deprived of her liberty.[1] The fact that she may have wide freedom of movement within it makes no difference; she is there compulsorily (**JE v DE** [2006] EWHC 3459, regarding a care home). Article 5 imposes obligations on the authorities in these circumstances.

[2]The question does not give much detail. What you are expected to do is to point out the demands of article 5 which will govern whether, on the facts, whatever they turn out to be, the authorities have acted lawfully.

The question does not indicate[2] the powers under which Julia was arrested by the police and detained in hospital. Article 5 guarantees the right not to be arbitrarily deprived of liberty. Deprivation must be based on a 'procedure prescribed by law'.[3] This means that the legal authority for the initial detention and, later, under the statute, must be accessible (identifiable) and accessible (reasonably predictable in the way it is likely to be applied). Where the authorities act on the basis of wide common law powers or statutory rules which give them wide discretion[4] and where neither gives much by way of procedural protections (e.g. setting out specific grounds for detention), there may be a violation. What is an over-wide discretion will depend on circumstances. Where personal liberty is at stake, the need for a

[3]Show you understand the rule of law is important and pervasive in the Convention.

[4]Don't forget this point – the rules of law must not be so wide as to allow arbitrary action and what is appropriate depends on context, such as what right is involved.

clear legal basis and safeguards is likely to be high. Thus in **HL v UK** (2005) 40 EHRR 32 the applicant was detained using informal procedures, found in common law and based on social workers' judgments of a person's best interests rather than on the more specific requirements found in the Mental Health Act 1983. The European Court of Human Rights (ECtHR) held there had been a violation of article 5.

Again, structure your answer around the questions the question raises – by pointing these out you display your knowledge of the law.

The question does not identify the severity or nature of Julia's condition.[5] The hospital authorities must be able to show that depriving Julia of her liberty was not only prescribed by law but was also compatible with one of the purposes in article 5(1). Article 5(1)(e) permits otherwise lawful deprivations of persons of 'unsound mind'.[6] Three conditions were laid down in **Winterwerp v The Netherlands** (1979) 2 EHRR 387. The authorities must be able to show that Julia is suffering from a mental disorder objectively identified by medical practitioners. There is a margin of appreciation on the matter but there must be some kind of medical condition; using mental health laws to deal with merely deviant behaviour is incompatible with article 5. Secondly, it will be necessary for the authorities to prove an important additional point: that Julia's detention was 'warranted'.[7] In later cases this has come to mean 'necessary' – based on an assessment of non-custodial alternatives (**Varbanov v Bulgaria**, app 31365/96, judgment of 5 October 2000). The need to keep Julia's circumstances under review is the third condition (discussed below).

Now move on to analyse article 5(1)(e) (try to get the numbering right). Show your knowledge of some of the case law here by discussing the concept of persons of 'unsound mind' and the need to show a proper illness, not merely deviant behaviour.

Ensure you make this point – merely being ill is not enough; it must be warranted or necessary to detain – e.g. for the person's own good or the good of others.

The issue of the appropriateness of Julia's treatment is clearly raised in the question and so you should discuss it; again, in doing so you demonstrate your knowledge of this area of article 5.

The question does not indicate what would be appropriate treatment for Julia. A general principle in article 5 is the need for some link between the purpose for the deprivation of liberty and the nature of the institution and the conditions in and under which they are held.[8] Article 5 does not insist that a mental health detention can be justified only if the mental illness is treatable. People with untreatable conditions but with symptoms that can be controlled can also be detained (**Hutchison Reid v UK** (2003) 37 EHRR 9). Nevertheless, a person detained under article 5(1)(e) needs to be held in a therapeutic, not merely punitive or protective environment. Julia is first held in a high security hospital. It is clearly therapeutic but may be more intensive than appropriate for her condition. But, so long as treatment is broadly therapeutic, the ECtHR has resisted the idea that article 5 requires the conditions and types of treatment

[9]Again, the question does not indicate the reasons the authorities had for their actions; your job is to note the points about conditional and immediate release which indicate what those reasons need to be for compatibility.

to be appropriate to his or her particular illness (**Ashingdane v UK** (1987) 7 EHRR 528, followed by English courts in **R (B) v Ashworth Hospital Authority** [2005] UKHL 20). Julia is then held in a closed hostel which has no therapeutic facilities.[9] It is possible to detain someone under article 5(1)(e) if detention is not warranted on condition that alternative care in the community is provided and, for justifiable reasons, that care cannot be provided (e.g. the English case **R (IH) v Secretary of State for Health** [2003] UKHL 59). Likewise, the authorities can have a cautious release policy; they are not required to release immediately a person who seems not to be of unsound mind and may take rehabilitative steps such as moving someone to a hostel (**Johnson v UK** (1999) 27 EHRR 296). But if these conditions do not apply, detaining Julia on the basis of article 5(1)(e) when there is no therapeutic necessity is likely to be a violation.

[10]Now move on to judicial scrutiny. This is an essential part of article 5 and needs to be focused on and given proper attention.

There is no evidence in the question that Julia was, during the time she was detained, able to obtain judicial scrutiny[10] of the lawfulness (including, under the HRA 1998, compatibility with Article 5(1)) of her detention. Article 5(4) requires that detained persons are able to have the lawfulness of their detention decided speedily by a 'court'. To be a 'court' the body must be independent of the executive and impartial. It must decide, without unreasonable delay, on the basis of a fair judicial procedure (equality of arms, an oral hearing, etc). In particular, it must have the authority to order the release of a person unlawfully detained. In England, First Tier Tribunals (Mental Health), with appeal to the Upper Tribunal, have that authority as did Mental Health Review Tribunals which they replace (originally Mental Health Tribunals were merely advisory and this was held to violate the Convention in **X v UK** (1982) 4 EHRR 188). In **R (H) v Secretary of State for Health** [2005] UKHL 60 provisions in the Mental Health Act 1983 prevented someone in the applicant's situation from having access to a tribunal. However, the House of Lords refused a declaration of incompatibility.[11] A duty on the Secretary of State to bring such a case on behalf of such an applicant could be read into the statute using s 3 of the HRA 1998.

[11]Always remember that, when referring to English cases, the HRA 1998 itself will be in issue and you get credit for showing you understand how it works.

[12]The question is seeking compatibility of Julia's situation with article 5, so don't forget article 5(5).

If Julia's right to liberty and security was violated, she has a right to compensation[12] (article 5(5)). Under HRA 1998, domestic remedies will be adapted to meet Convention requirements. Compensation in the mental health context has been broadly based on tort principles

[13]This is not an easy point since the law is not well settled and is very fact dependent; nevertheless, *Greenfield* does give some useful guidance.

(**R (KB)** *v* **Mental Health Review Tribunal** [2003] EWHC 193). Following an article 6 prisoners case (**R (Greenfield)** *v* **Secretary of State for the Home Office** [2005] UKHL 14), however, English judges accept the distinctive nature of human rights law[13] when deciding *quantum* and give what may be lower damages than those available in tort; or, depending on circumstances, hold that a finding of a violation is sufficient.

 Make your answer stand out

■ In showing your awareness of article 5(4) and the need for judicial supervision and a fair hearing, note the link to article 6; the ECtHR seems to be relating these two provisions more closely together (see also questions and answers in Chapter 7).

■ Reflect in your answer some of the complexity (including about English mental health law) of the cases. A good example is the issue of informal admissions in *HL*. See, for example, Pedain (2005). Indeed, although you must be careful not to spend a lot of time on outlining English mental health law, showing awareness of the domestic legal issues can be helpful (e.g. on the issue of the 'next friend' in *H*; or on the question of whether there needs to be a treatable condition – note, though, the situation as discussed in *Hutchison Reid* has been changed, for England, by amendments to the Mental Health Act 1983 by the Mental Health Act 2007).

! Don't be tempted to ...

■ Discuss issues which are given in the question, such as the fact that Julia is deprived of her liberty. There is certainly interesting case law on this matter but it is not relevant to the answer.

■ Spend a great deal of space on English mental health legislation. It is clearly in the background but is very complicated and not the focus of the question – which is the human rights standards the legislation needs to be compatible with.

■ Indulge in too much speculation on the facts, on Julia's possible medical condition, on the motives of the hospital or the state of mental health services in Britain today, etc. What you are required to do is point out the legal standards which will apply, whatever the particular facts might be.

📝 Question 5

Discuss, with illustrations from both Strasbourg and English case law, the requirements of article 5, and other Convention rights where relevant, for ensuring that prisoners are deprived of their liberty in a lawful manner.

Answer plan

➡️ Discuss 'deprivation of liberty' and the application of article 5 to prisoners generally.

➡️ Consider the position of remand prisoners.

➡️ Discuss convicted prisoners and the lawfulness of their imprisonment.

➡️ Discuss article 5(4) and the need for judicial supervision.

➡️ Mention article 5(5) compensation.

➡️ Discuss other rights which may have a bearing on prisoners' right to liberty.

Diagram plan

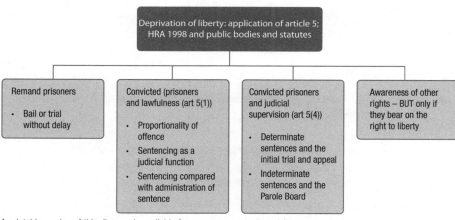

A printable version of this diagram is available from www.pearsoned.co.uk/lawexpressqa

[1]Thus a 'deprivation of liberty' is obvious and the definition of the term and comparison with restriction on movement does not need to be discussed.

Answer

Confinement in prison is the core instance of a 'deprivation of liberty'.[1] Thus prisoners should enjoy the right to liberty in article 5.

[2] You then should go on to show why article 5 applies to UK prison law via the HRA 1998 (this question includes references to English cases).

[3] You will get credit for this since you will demonstrate understanding of a pervasive theme of the ECtHR – the need for rights to be effective.

[4] The question refers to 'prisoners'; you demonstrate your understanding by including remand prisoners.

[5] Having discussed remand prisoners you now need to move on to discuss convicted prisoners, which is the main focus.

[6] A great deal is loaded into the requirement that a conviction should be by a procedure prescribed by law and you need to show your understanding of that.

[7] By making this point you show you understand the relevance and interrelationship of different articles.

[8] Again – get credit for demonstrating the interrelationship of different articles.

[9] Move on to discuss the need for the sentence to be proportionate; it is needed for an effective answer and shows your awareness of an important, general, human rights issue.

[10] Moving on to this issue shows you are aware of an area where article 5 has had major impact on UK law and so would be expected in an answer.

Prisons in the UK are administered by public authorities[2] or by private bodies exercising 'functions of a public nature'. Their authority comes from legislation such as the Prisons Act 1952. Thus the HRA 1998 applies. Prisoners enjoy Convention rights and, at common law, all fundamental rights not expressly or by necessary implication taken away. Of particular importance is the right of access to the court[3] by which prisoners must be free to pursue their legal rights and seek remedies from courts (e.g. **Golder v UK** (1979–80) 1 EHRR 524).

Unconvicted prisoners (who are on remand)[4] must have been arrested on 'reasonable suspicion of having committed an offence' (article 5(1)(c)). They are entitled, under article 5(3), to have their situation 'promptly' considered by a judicial officer (such as a magistrate). There is a presumption in favour of bail. This can be outweighed by other considerations (such as a risk of absconding: see **Wemhoff v Germany** (1979–80) 1 EHRR 1). If remanded, a prisoner is entitled to 'trial within a reasonable time'. The European Court of Human Rights (ECtHR) does not lay down guidance of what is reasonable in abstract; reasonableness depends on circumstances.

Convicted prisoners enjoy the guarantees of article 5(1)(a)[5] as well as benefiting from the core point of article 5, to protect against arbitrary deprivations of liberty. In particular, their conviction must be 'lawful'.[6] This means lawful under domestic law, but, also, that the domestic law is foreseeable (people are able to work out the likely consequences of their actions). The offence must also be compatible with article 7,[7] which prohibits retrospective or uncertain crimes and penalties. The conviction must also be based on a fair procedure (implicit in article 5(1) 'procedure prescribed by law'). Issues about the fairness of the original trial are most likely to relate to article 6,[8] which provides a general right to a fair hearing, the presumption of innocence and, in article 6(3), a range of specific rights for defendants.

A lawful sentence must be proportionate. This means the punishment must be appropriate (causally linked to) the offence.[9] This causal link was broken in **Stafford v UK** (2002) 35 EHRR 32, for instance, when an additional sentence, imposed on a murderer recalled on licence, aimed at preventing non-violent crimes.

Lawfulness also means that sentencing is a judicial function[10] and must be separated from the executive. One of the important changes,

[11]Show you understand what has happened; there is not space to go into too much detail but a mention will gain marks.

originally under the Convention and latterly under the HRA 1998, is the gradual and almost complete removal of the executive[11] (Home Secretary, now Justice Secretary) from the process of determining the overall length of indeterminate sentences (e.g. **Stafford** and **R (Anderson) v Home Secretary** [2002] UKHL 46). Indeterminate sentences include mandatory and discretionary life sentences and sentences for public protection. Their basic form is a minimum term set by the trial judge for punishment followed by release only when it is safe to do so. The decisive voice in the safety decision is the Parole Board (which has a judicial character) and not the Justice Secretary (a member of the executive). The decisions of the Parole Board are subject to judicial review on the grounds of a violation of article 5.

[12]This is a general distinction but one that is not easy to make in practice. Nevertheless, it is made in the cases and raising it indicates your understanding of these.

A distinction can be made between the determination of a sentence (a judicial matter) and the administration of the sentence and the prisons.[12] The latter is unlikely to engage article 5(1) except in extreme circumstances. The failure by the Justice Secretary to provide education courses, completion of which, the Parole Board had said, was necessary before a prisoner's case could be considered, was acknowledged to breach of the Justice Secretary's public law duty. But, although it meant that prisoners were staying longer in gaol because they had not taken a course, the House of Lords held that there was no breach of the causal link between the offence and the punishment. Such a link would only be broken if access to the Parole Board was delayed for years (**R (James) v Parole Board** [2009] UKHL 22).

[13]Now move on to discuss the impact of article 5(4) – the judicial supervision point is sometimes lost in an over-focus on article 5(1).

[14]This is a significant point which improves the overall structure of your answer by relating to the distinction between administrative matters and matters affecting the right to liberty made in the previous paragraph.

[15]Again, as with articles 7 and 6, above, you demonstrate sensitivity to the application of other rights.

Article 5(4) gives prisoners the right to a speedy review by a 'court' of the lawfulness of their detention.[13] This has little impact on those convicted of determinate sentences since adequate judicial supervision is found in the original trial and appeal process. Issues such as early release and 'home curfew' relate to the administration of the sentence rather than its lawfulness.[14] Such decisons can be taken by the executive, subject to ordinary public law principles (**Mason v Ministry of Justice** [2008] EWHC 1787) and the ECtHR has often said that there is no right to parole in article 5. Such decisions are, though, likely to be within the 'ambit' of article 5 and, if based on discrimination (such as between different classes of prisoner), can breach article 14[15] read with article 5 (**Clift v UK**, application 7205/07, judgment of 13 July 2010).

Article 5(4) is, therefore, of particular importance regarding indeterminate sentences and decisions to release on licence or to recall for breach of the licence. These decisions are taken by the Parole Board. There must be no procedural barriers to a prisoner having access to the Board. However, there is no positive duty to assist prisoners to be successful (thus failing to provide the necessary courses in **James** was not a breach of article 5(4)).

[16]Show you understand that these fair procedure rights are not absolute and are subject to restrictions (which in *Roberts* were very controversial).

Compatibility with article 5(4) means that the Parole Board must have the judicial qualities of a court. The procedure must be fair, done without unreasonable delay and embody 'equality of arms'; usually this means an oral hearing. Fair hearing rights are subject to restriction where necessary[16] – as in **Roberts v Parole Board** [2005] UKHL 45, where the House of Lords held, by a majority, that to preserve a source's safety, the Parole Board could take a decision on evidence only disclosed to a special advocate.

Compatibility with article 5(4) also means that the 'court' must be fully independent of the executive. Reforms were needed when the Parole Board was found to lack sufficient independence appropriate to its enhanced judicial role (which followed the removal of the Justice Secretary's sentencing role) because of its institutional links with the Justice Ministry (**R (Brooke) v Secretary of State for Justice** [2008] EWCA Civ 29).

[17]End by reference to compensation under article 5(5), which rounds off your answer.

Prisoners detained in contravention of article 5 have an enforceable right to compensation (article 5(5)).[17] This provision complements article 41 which empowers the ECtHR to award 'just satisfaction' for any breach, a provision which is recognised in s 8 HRA 1998.

✓ Make your answer stand out

- Regarding remand prisoners, you could develop the law on bail a little (principles are summarised in *Smirnova* v *Russia* (2004) 39 EHRR: see paras 56–64).

- A fuller discussion of article 7 and the principle of *nullum crimen, nulla poena sine lege* could include reference to the House of Lords' discussion in *R* v *Remington* [2005] UKHL 63.

- Although you need to avoid too detailed and lengthy a discussion on the removal of the executive from sentencing decisions (see below), it is an important point so try to be concise and informed. Further discussion is found, for instance, in Foster (2002).

■ Issues involving prisoner conditions are dealt with under other rights (e.g. articles 2, 3 and 8) and will usually not have a bearing on the right to liberty and so are not relevant. However, you could point out that a really serious failure to provide appropriate conditions for a particular prisoner could render continued detention unlawful – this would engage article 5.

! Don't be tempted to ...

■ Use up a lot of space in showing the gradual removal of the executive from sentencing. It is a long and complex story which involves dealing with a lot of case law and explaining the differences between different types of sentence, such as mandatory and discretionary life sentences. Exam room discipline is necessary here.

■ Say too much on general matters (e.g. aspects of article 5 which are unlikely to apply to prisoners or in introducing other articles such as articles 7, 6 and 14 which are clearly relevant); keep focused on prisoners.

■ Go on too much about prisoners' rights based on matters other than those which bear on the right to liberty (e.g. prison conditions are normally dealt with under articles 2, 3 and 8; there are interesting discussions about prisoners' rights under article 10 (but see the point in 'Make your answer stand out', above)).

Article 6 and fair hearings

How this topic may come up in exams

There can be questions, problem or essay, which focus either on whether the type of hearing is one to which article 6 applies or on the content of a 'fair hearing'. But, these two are linked – if a matter is 'criminal' fuller rights apply. Questions may also expect you to understand the importance of implied or inherent rights and, generally, the flexibility of article 6. Remember article 6 can relate to highly controversial areas, like counter-terrorism, which may be chosen as the scenario of a problem question. Don't forget that fair procedures are also an express provision of article 5(3) and (4).

■ Attack the question

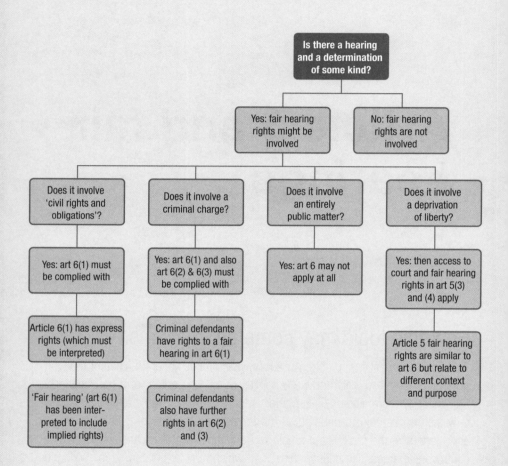

A printable version of this diagram is available from www.pearsoned.co.uk/lawexpressqa

🔍 Question 1

Identify and evaluate the main provisions of the Convention by which people have rights of access to courts and to fair hearings.

Answer plan

→ Summarise the importance of rights to a fair hearing.

→ Note article 13 (right to a remedy).

→ Discuss the civil and criminal applications of article 6.

→ Consider article 6(1), the express and implied rights, including access to court and equality of arms.

→ Explore additional guarantees for criminal defendants in article 6(2) and (3).

→ Note fair hearing rights in other articles (e.g. article 5(4)).

→ Conclude by considering context-based qualifications.

Diagram plan

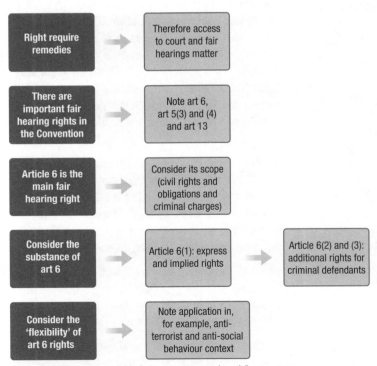

A printable version of this diagram is available from www.pearsoned.co.uk/lawexpressqa

Answer

[1]Articles 6 and 5(4) are
obviously of principal concern,
but you will get credit for
referring to article 13 which
is often overlooked (perhaps
because it is not scheduled in
the HRA 1998.

[2]You will get credit for a
formulation such as this since
it shows you understand that
the impact of the Convention
is on the overall fairness of
the procedures and not on the
generic name of the institution
as 'court' or 'tribunal', etc.

[3]Move on to article 6, which
is key to the question.

[4]It impresses if you can
remember the exact text, so try
to learn it during revision.

[5]Now move on to show
awareness of the complexity
of the concept of 'civil rights
and obligations'.

[6]This is the phrase used by
the Court and you will get
credit for using it.

[7]By using the ASBO
example, you gain credit for
demonstrating awareness of
current controversies.

[8]Again, show awareness of
the autonomous concept of a
criminal charge.

[9]This point will gain credit – it
is often ignored.

[10]Move on to discuss the
content of the right to a fair
hearing. Remember this
applies to both civil and
criminal hearings.

Express Convention rights of access to courts and fair hearings are found in article 5(4) (liberty) and can be inferred from substantive rights such as peaceful enjoyment of possessions (article 1 of the First Protocol (**Sporrong v Sweden** (1983) 5 EHRR 35)). Article 13[1] requires fair judicial procedures[2] to deal with allegations of breaches of human rights and, even though not a scheduled Convention right in the HRA 1998, is still binding in the UK as international law (e.g. **Peck v UK** (2003) 36 EHRR 41).

The main right is article 6.[3] This is a right to a 'fair and public hearing' within a 'reasonable time' before an 'independent' and 'impartial' tribunal 'established by law'.[4]

It applies, first, to hearings which determine 'civil rights and obligations'.[5] The meaning is 'autonomous'[6] (not dependent on national law categories). It includes hearings for determining private rights (contract or tort, etc) and some Convention rights, such as article 5 (liberty) (see **Reinprecht v Austria** (2007) 44 EHRR 390). Hearings dealing with methods of public protection rather than punishment (e.g. in the UK, anti-social behaviour orders) are generally held to determine civil obligations (see **R (McCann) v Manchester Crown Court** [2002] UKHL 39).[7] Administrative decisions (e.g. by planning officers) can involve civil rights but there need not be a breach of article 6 so long as there is a right of appeal to an article 6 compliant court.

Second, article 6 applies to trials which determine a 'criminal charge'.[8] At the heart of the Strasbourg test is whether the purpose of the hearing is punishment (**Engel v The Netherlands** (1979–80) 1 EHRR 647). In **Ezeh v UK** (2004) 39 EHRR 1 prison disciplinary proceedings, which could result in a prisoner being released later than otherwise, were held to be determining a criminal charge.

Decisions which are solely concerned with public law are outside the scope of article 6 altogether (e.g. disputes about taxation (**Ferrazzini v Italy** (2002) 34 EHRR 45) and immigration (**Maaouia v France** (2001) 33 EHRR 42)).[9]

Both civil and criminal hearings must guarantee the basic right to a fair hearing in article 6(1).[10] This includes express rights that the judges be independent and impartial, that there should not be undue delay and that hearings should normally be in public and (subject to exceptions) judgment pronounced publicly. The ECtHR has also identified some general rights inherent[11] in the idea of a fair hearing (e.g. an 'adversarial' process).

[11]Alternatively you could say 'implied'.

The role of the ECtHR is not to rule on the specifics of national legal processes (like whether there should be juries) but to decide whether the overall process is fair. Furthermore, the specific content of the right can be dependent on context[12] and in some situations, e.g. national security, may reduce to the 'essence' or absolute minimum. Departures from normal procedures, especially in respect of the inherent rights, are evaluated against tests of proportionality and necessity.

[12]Move on to discuss the way the specific requirements of article 6 can be context dependent.

Access to courts[13] is an important inherent right. This is a principle grounded in both the Convention (**Golder v UK** (1979–80) 1 EHRR 524) and also English common law (**Seal v Chief Constable of South Wales** [2007] UKHL 31). Legal aid is not a requirement of article 6(1) unless necessary for effective access to the court (**Airey v Ireland (1979–80) 2 EHRR 305**). Like all the implied rights, access to court can be subject to reasonable restrictions[14] such as those placed on children. Some normal procedural restrictions, such as limitation statutes or the principle of state immunity in civil actions (**Al-Adsani v UK** (2002) 34 EHRR 11), are likely to be compatible with the Convention. Restrictions on disclosure of evidence in national security cases can be harder to make compatible (as in **Tinnelly v UK** (1999) 27 EHRR 249).

[13]Move on to access to courts – required by the question.

[14]Demonstrating the 'flexible' nature of article 6 rights is important.

A complex issue is to distinguish between a procedural barrier which prevents access to the courts and a rule of law which defines what substantive rights[15] an individual enjoys. The ECtHR has moved away from its former view, in **Osman v UK** (2000) 29 EHRR 245, that the right of access to courts was violated by holding that police did not owe a duty of care to victims of crime. It now accepts that rulings about tortuous duties of care by public bodies are properly seen as defining substantive rights (**Z v UK** (2002) 34 EHRR 3).

[15]The procedure – substance distinction should be mentioned. It strengthens your answer by demonstrating understanding of the complexity of an apparently simple idea like access to courts.

'Equality of arms'[16] is another inherent right. The parties should be treated equally over matters like access to evidence and the right of cross-examination (**Dombo Beheer BV v The Netherlands** (1994) 18 EHRR 213). The principle matters in the context of trials involving

[16]The answer should address an example of an inherent right dealing with fair hearings. The equality of arms principle is a good one to choose because of its importance in counter-terrorism law, discussed later.

[17]The restraint on traditional fair trial procedures in the counter-terrorism context is so great that a reference in your answer will strengthen it.

evidence the government wants to keep secret from the parties.[17] Where article 6(1) is engaged, the courts accept that restrictions must be counter-balanced by adequate protections for the defence (especially security cleared 'special advocates' who can represent, but not contact, the claimant). But there is likely to be a breach of article 6(1) if the sole or decisive evidence is secret (**Secretary of State for the Home Department v AF** [2009] UKHL 28, a control order case).

As well as the rights in article 6(1), criminal defendants have additional protection found in article 6(2) (the presumption of innocence) and (3) (a range of additional defence rights). The right to examine witnesses (article 6(3)(d) is an example which has proved controversial.[18] A conviction based 'solely or decisively' on hearsay would, according to the ECtHR, violate article 6 (**Al-Khawaja v UK** (2009) 49 EHRR 1). English statute law allows hearsay under certain conditions and the Supreme Court, in **R v Horncastle** [2009] UKSC 14, has insisted that a combination of these conditions, with judicial discretion to exclude evidence, should mean that a conviction so based may, nevertheless, be fair and compatible. The view of the Grand Chamber on the point is awaited.

[18]There is not space to examine all the rights of the defence, so select as your example one which has raised problems that can be discussed.

Express rights to a fair hearing are found in respect of the right to liberty. Under article 5(3) and (4) arrested persons and those otherwise detained must have access to a judicial authority in order to test effectively the legal basis of the deprivation of their liberty. Although the context is different, the requirements for access to a judicial authority and for a fair, adversarial procedure based upon equality of arms, is similar to article 6.

Though article 6 and the other rights mentioned above aim to guarantee fair hearings, their limits need to be recognised. Some types of hearing are excluded altogether, the rights to a fair hearing are very flexible and in some of the most difficult of circumstances, such as special powers under counter-terrorism law, seem reduced almost to vanishing point.

 Make your answer stand out

- Make sure you not only identify the major themes (on what is a wide-ranging question) but also identify the difficult and controversial aspects attached to each issue.

- Refer to both cases decided by the Strasbourg Court and the English/UK courts. Remember, though, that English courts are bound to follow only the higher English courts (CA and SC) and, where the House of Lords/Supreme Court has given full analysis to a range of Strasbourg cases, it is the HL/SC analysis that should be followed.

- Demonstrating awareness of the different situations and contexts to which article 6 applies is, in a question like this, important. It enables you to discuss the flexible nature of article 6 rights.

- Make fuller reference to the role of articles 6 and 5(4) in respect of counter-terrorism law (though this can also be the particular focus of a question – see below in this chapter).

! Don't be tempted to ...

- Spend too much time on any one issue. The question is broad ranging and is expecting you to identify themes and particular issues.

- Use up too much space on facts of cases. Article 6 cases can be very complex (and often involve other articles, too). In revision, practise distilling the point of a case down to its absolute essentials.

? Question 2

Albert has applied for local authority funded accommodation in a care home. Under the Act of Parliament governing the matter, Albert is entitled to such accommodation if he is 'in need'. His request is turned down by Ms South, who is an official in the relevant department of the local authority. The statute also entitles him to a 'review' of Ms South's decision. This review is undertaken by Ms North, a more senior official in the same department as Ms South. Ms North confirms Ms South's decision.

Albert is aggrieved because he feels he has not had a fair hearing. He feels, in particular, that Ms North lacked independence since she is employed by the same local authority and is in the same department as Ms South. He also thinks she is biased because she has recently written an article in *Care Homes Today* (a weekly magazine) suggesting that a much tougher approach to funding care for the elderly should be taken.

Advise Albert on the extent to which the Human Rights Act 1998 may be able to assist his case as regards the procedural fairness of the handling of his case.

Answer plan

→ Explain how the Human Rights Act 1998 might apply in this situation.

→ Identify article 6 as the relevant right and discuss it in general terms.

→ Consider the application of article 6 to the decision of Ms South as confirmed by Ms North. This requires consideration of the concept of 'civil rights'.

→ Assuming the application of article 6, discuss whether Ms North was an 'independent' tribunal.

→ Likewise, consider whether Ms North was 'impartial'.

→ Discuss whether the fact of Ms North not being independent and impartial necessarily means there has been a breach of article 6. This involves a consideration of an appeal to a court that complies with article 6 and can deal with all the issues relating to article 6.

Diagram plan

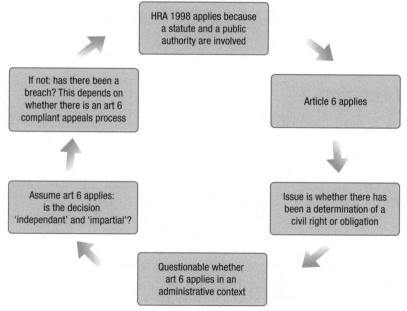

A printable version of this diagram is available from www.pearsoned.co.uk/lawexpressqa

Answer

¹Show why, because of the HRA 1998, Convention rights may be relevant.

This question concerns whether the right to a fair hearing can apply to an administrative decision under the Human Rights Act 1998 (HRA 1998). The legislation, under which Ms North and Ms South act, must be read, if possible, in a way that is compatible with Convention rights; likewise the local authority is a 'public authority' and so, unless compelled otherwise, it must act compatibly with Convention rights.[1]

²Show how you understand the main point of the question: article 6 – whether it applies and what it requires.

³It helps you answer if you can quote important phrases, but don't waste time quoting parts of article 6 that are not necessary.

Albert's complaint is that he has not had a fair hearing.[2] Article 6 gives a right to a 'fair ... hearing ... before an independent and impartial tribunal established by law'.[3] It applies to criminal trials (not relevant here)[4] and to the 'determination' of a person's 'civil rights and obligations'. The initial question, therefore, is whether Albert's 'civil rights and obligations' were being determined by the decisions made by Ms South and Ms North. A core meaning of 'civil rights and obligations'[5] involves the determination of private rights (e.g. tort, contract or property) and includes determinations of at least some Convention rights. Determinations of exclusively public law issues (e.g voting, immigration status, taxation) are excluded and, it seems, the initial idea was to exclude administrative decisions from article 6 and introduce, at a later date, an independent right to a fair administrative process (**R (Alconbury) v Secretary of State for Environment, Transport and the Regions** [2001] UKHL 23). However, the European Court of Human Rights (ECtHR) has extended article 6 to administrative decisions which are decisive of private law, particularly financial, entitlement. In **Ringeisen v Austria** (1979-80) 1 EHRR 455, the process of the authorities approving a land sale, where the sale was void without approval, was made subject to article 6(1).[6] The principle has been extended to include disputes about statutory welfare rights. Originally confined to those with a strong 'insurance' character (**Feldbrugge v The Netherlands** (1986) 8 EHRR 425) but now extended to welfare entitlements whether contributory or not (e.g. **Salesi v Italy** (1998) 26 EHRR 187). In **Tsfayo v UK** (2009) 48 EHRR 18 it was held that a dispute over the amount of housing benefit owed was covered by article 6(1).

⁴It is vital not to use up time and space on matters which are not relevant to the question.

⁵Now move on to introduce and discuss the issue of the application of civil rights and obligations.

⁶It shows a more specific and detailed understanding of Convention rights if you can refer to the relevant paragraph when citing a Convention right – thus article 6(1) rather than just article 6. This earns marks. It is a general point, though of particular importance in article 6(1) because article 6(2) and (3) do not apply to civil hearings.

⁷Now move on to discuss some of the UK case law. It is important to do this because the issue of fair hearings and administrative practices has led to a number of important decisions.

UK courts must deal with this jurisprudence because of s 2 HRA 1998.[7] In **Begum v Tower Hamlets LBC** [2003] UKHL 5 the

House of Lords simply assumed, without deciding, that article 6 was engaged in respect of the suitability of an offer of accommodation made to a homeless person. But the matter is complex. The more a welfare claim relates to a discretionary judgment, made by officials (who are responsible to Parliament or the council chamber) and based upon general, value laden, statutory criteria (like whether a matter is 'reasonable' or not), then the less it may engage article 6. The need for discretionary, policy-based judgments, indicates a decision not sufficiently like a private law right to engage article 6. Thus, in **R (A) v Croydon LBC** [2009] UKSC 8[8] the Supreme Court held that a dispute over whether a child was 'in need' (thereby entitled to accommodation) involved discretion and so was not the determination of a civil right.

[8]Reference to and awareness of recent cases is always helpful and impresses the examiner; you could also refer to **Ali v Birmingham CC** [2010] UKSC 8.

It is hard to assess whether Albert has article 6 rights so, following **Begum**, this essay will proceed on the basis of an assumption that article 6(1) is involved.

[9]Such a judgement can also be made in your answer here, particularly because of *Begum*. Often it is not possible to be so definite and what the examiner is looking for is your understanding of the legal issues that would determine the answer.

Under article 6, Ms North needs to be 'independent'. Independence is an individual criterion: a process can be fair but still lack independence. Factors such as freedom from executive pressure and control, guarantees against outside interference, the manner of appointment, social links with the parties, and so on, are important. In **Bryan v UK** (1996) 21 EHRR 342, for example, the degree of control the Secretary of State had over the planning process meant that planning inspectors, appointed by the Secretary, were not independent. In **Begum** the House of Lords held that a housing officer who was reviewing the decision made by another officer in the same council, was manifestly not independent. It can be said with confidence,[9] therefore, that Ms North was not independent.

[10]Awareness of the difference between 'impartiality' and 'independence' indicates that you understand the need to pay careful attention to the text of a legal source and to be able to define the terms found there.

Impartiality has both a subjective aspect (relating to the personal convictions of the judge or deciding official) and an objective aspect (relating to factors which might raise a legitimate doubt as to the fairness of the process). It is possible (as in **Begum**) for an official to be impartial without being independent.[10] The common law test for bias[11] (reformulated to make it consistent with article 6) is that a 'fair-minded and informed observer'[12] would come to the conclusion that there was a 'real possibility' of bias (**Porter v Magill** [2001] UKHL 67). Such a possibility has been found in respect of apparent pre-judgment based on previous writings on the subject that is directly before the court (**Locabail v Bayfield** [2000] QB 451 and

[11]Remember the importance in 'fair hearing' cases of dealing *both* with article 6 and natural justice (common law).

[12]It strengthens your answer if you can state the key terms of a legal test; try to learn phrases like this during revision.

Hoekstra v HM Advocate [2001] 1 AC 216) and so it is possible that Ms North might also be found to be lacking in impartiality.

[13]This is the vital point to make at the end. You would lose credit if you did not make it.

However, the fact that an administrative decision has been taken without proper independence or impartiality is not sufficient to establish a breach of article 6.[13] The ECtHR, followed by the UK courts, accepts that administrative failings can be remedied if the victim has a legal right to challenge the decision before a reviewing or appellate court or tribunal which, itself, complies with article 6 and which is able to deal with the issues raised by an article 6 challenge. In **Begum**, for example, there was a statutory right of appeal to the county court which satisfied article 6; in **Bryan** the right of judicial review in the High Court was sufficient. But the reviewing court must have 'full jurisdiction'[14] to deal with the main areas of dispute. There have been cases where judicial review has been held to be insufficient because it is not, normally, a procedure by which factual disputes can be fully dealt with (e.g. **Tsfayo** – though this was a case decided before the HRA 1998 had been brought into effect). The question does not say whether Albert has a statutory right of appeal; he is, though, likely to be able to challenge Ms North's decision by way of judicial review and so, under the HRA 1998, the Administrative Court will be able to deal with the issues of independence and impartiality that have arisen in the case.

[14]This is an important point, not to be missed, which shows that you have understood the issue in its complexity.

[15]It helps to conclude with an assessment of the likely outcome given the points made above.

Albert is unlikely to be able to show that Ms South's decision was incompatible with article 6.[15] This is either because article 6 does not apply to such an administrative decision or because, assuming article 6 does apply, any failings at the administrative stage can be remedied by access to a court of full jurisdiction.

✓ Make your answer stand out

- On this topic there are some important judicial contributions (such as Lord Hoffmann in *R (Alconbury)* v *Secretary of State for Environment Transport and the Regions* [2001] UKHL 23 on the scope of article 6) which might be referred to more extensively.

- Show some awareness of the social consequences of the issues discussed. You might remind us that human rights should protect the interests of the most vulnerable; it is not clear that this occurs on the basis of the law discussed in the question.

■ On issues like impartiality and independence, remember and demonstrate the way in which article 6 rights and common law natural justice can complement each other.

■ Try to give authority, in case law or statute, for the claims you make.

! Don't be tempted to ...

■ Spend too much time on general introduction – which is easy to do on an article 6 question.

■ Similarly, avoid spending too much time on the full range of issues that can arise in respect of article 6. This question, for instance, does not involve a 'criminal charge' and so a long discussion of the criminal side, including article 6(2) and (3) should be avoided. Concentrate on the particular issue of the question: the application of article 6 rights in the administrative and welfare contexts.

■ Note that although the question refers to a 'care home' this does not mean that you should deal with the question about whether 'care homes' are bound by human rights (this can be an important topic in relation to s 6 HRA 1998 and the definition of a public authority, but it is not the question here). The question involves the obligations of a local authority, clearly a public authority bound by the HRA 1998.

🔖 Question 3

A fair hearing requires that the court or tribunal should be 'independent' and 'impartial'. Explain these two terms and evaluate their impact on the development of law and administration in the United Kingdom.

Answer plan

→ Briefly indicate the importance of independence and impartiality and article 6.

→ Note that independence and impartiality are distinct concepts.

→ Discuss independence and its particular features.

→ Discuss impartiality and its particular features.

→ Refer to 'natural justice' (English law) and 'bias'.

→ Consider the impact of independence and impartiality on both judicial institutions and also administrative bodies in the United Kingdom.

Diagram plan

Introduction	The concepts of independence and impartiality	Impact
• Importance of the rule of law • Need for an independent and impartial judiciary	• Independence and impartiality are separate requirements of a fair hearing • The idea of independence as interpreted by the European Court of Human Rights • The idea of impartiality as interpreted by the European Court of Human Rights • The link with the rule of natural justice in English administrative law	• The aligning of English administrative law on bias with the Strasbourg conception of impartiality • The impact of (in particular) 'independence' on various judicial bodies in the United Kingdom • The (lesser) impact of 'independence' on administrative bodies because of 'curative appeal'

A printable version of this diagram is available from www.pearsoned.co.uk/lawexpressqa

Answer

[1] Begin by pointing out the importance of the issue dealt with by the question.

[2] Though not the focus of the question, at least recall the types of hearing to which article 6 applies.

[3] It gets credit to show, without needing to elaborate, that you know there is more to a fair hearing than independence and impartiality.

[4] It strengthens your answer if you are able to quote the important phrases.

[5] The point about the importance of appearance of bias, etc, not fact, must be clear throughout your answer.

The rule of law, a core value underlying human rights, requires that individuals should have access to a judiciary with the authority to determine and enforce legal rights. The legitimacy of the judiciary depends on its being independent, especially of the executive, and impartial as between the parties.[1]

Article 6 requires civil rights and obligations and criminal charges[2] to be determined, *inter alia*,[3] by an 'independent and impartial tribunal established by law'.[4] Though often linked, these are treated as two distinct concepts (thus a hearing can be impartial but not independent and vice versa) and as free-standing requirements of a fair hearing (a hearing can be fair overall but still breach article 6 for want of independence or impartiality, as in **Bryan *v* UK** (1996) 21 EHRR 342). Both concepts are concerned with reasonable perceptions about the process rather than the quality of the decision that results.[5]

[6]You will get credit for demonstrating your understanding that article 6 applies to any body determining civil rights, etc, not just 'courts'.

[7]Use cautious and qualified language. The question of independence is usually a matter of judgement on the facts and you will strengthen your answer if you make that clear.

[8]Article 6 is case rich. Avoid being swamped. *Le Compte* is worth referring to because it is an early leading case that continues to be referred to today.

[9]The question refers to the UK, to which you should now move.

[10]As with article 6, it is helpful to demonstrate some sensitivity to the scope of the right to a fair hearing.

The concept of 'independence' invokes the idea that the court, tribunal or other body determining a civil or criminal matter[6] should be, and should appear to be, free to form its own judgment on the matter and not to be or appear to be under another's control. Independence of the court, etc, from the executive is of particular importance. There is no single litmus test. A great deal depends on the nature of the body concerned – a body which is clearly part of the judicial system, fully independent of the executive, may be subject to more rigorous standards when compared to a body which is more closely allied to the administration. Issues such as the system for appointment or the basis for confirmation or renewal of office can be decisive factors.[7] Article 6 can be breached if these matters are controlled too closely by the executive (see, for example, **Le Compte v Belgium** (1982) 4 EHRR 1)[8] and if the guarantees against outside pressures are inadequate (**Piersack v Belgium** (1983) 5 EHRR 169). Bodies that are required to follow executive guidelines may lack independence unless the guidelines can be departed from if warranted by individual circumstances (**Campbell & Fell v UK** (1985) 7 EHRR 165). Independence can also be in issue where a body both administers policies and resolves disputes (though prison visitors who had both administrative and disciplinary functions were found to be sufficiently independent in **Campbell & Fell**).

Impartiality connotes the idea that a judge, etc, does not have a predisposition towards one party or another. Again, the focus is on appearance. The perspective is that of an objective, informed, reasonable observer rather than that of the claimant. The ECtHR distinguishes between objective and subjective factors (**Piersack**). Objective factors, for example, relate to institutional and structural matters which might, reasonably, lead to concerns about possible bias. This can include a judge's previous involvement in the trial (such as where magistrates who have dealt with a bail hearing go on to try the case). Subjective factors are those that relate to the person of the judge. A breach of article 6 can arise only if the personal factors pointing to bias are sufficiently strong to outweigh the presumption that a judge is not biased.

English administrative law[9] provides a right to 'a fair hearing before an unbiased tribunal'. The rules of 'natural justice' apply to a wide range of decisions[10] taken not only by inferior courts but also by administrative bodies if they concern the rights and legitimate expectations of individuals. Such decisions can be set aside by the High Court if there is the appearance of bias. There are two kinds of bias: first, where the judge has an interest in the outcome (which could be political as well as financial (**R v Bow Street Magistrates ex p Pinochet 2** [2000] 1 AC 119)) – here the judge is under a duty to recuse[11] him or herself; and, secondly, cases in which various factors might give rise to an appearance of a bias. English law has been re-formulated for consistency with article 6: 'whether the fair-minded and informed observer, having considered the facts, would conclude there was a real possibility that the tribunal was biased'.[12]

There is extensive case law.[13] For example, inactive involvement in a related political organisation or questions of religious affiliation are unlikely in themselves to give rise to a real danger of apparent bias (e.g. **Helow v Advocate General for Scotland** [2008] UKHL 62); but where a judge has expressed in public views about significant issues in the case then apparent bias may be a real danger (e.g. **Hoekstra v HM Lord Advocate** [2001] 1 AC 216).

Adverse findings by the Strasbourg Court, particularly regarding independence, have led to some major changes in the UK,[14] especially in respect of various bodies and offices that have a judicial character.[15] The Courts Martial system was changed following **Findlay v UK** (1997) 24 EHRR 221 because[16] the role and rank of the Convening Officer created doubts about the independence of the court from the prosecution. In **Starrs v Ruxton** 2000 JC 208, Scottish courts held that the system of temporary sheriffs was incompatible with article 6 because the Lord Advocate, the chief prosecutor, confirmed the sheriffs in their posts. In **McGonnell v UK** (2000) 30 EHRR 289 the ECtHR found against the combined legislative and judicial role of the Bailiff of Guernsey.

The issue of independence has also arisen in respect of administrative decisions[17] that arguably affected the 'civil rights and obligations' of individuals: for example, planning decisions (**R (Alconbury) v Secretary of State for Environment, Transport and the Regions** [2001] UKHL 23) and decisions by local authorities on housing allocations (**Begum v Tower Hamlets LBC** [2003] UKHL 5). Had these challenges succeeded, there would have been major, expensive consequences for public administration in Britain. But the challenges have generally failed. Though there may be a lack of independence, based, for example, on the influence of

---

Margin notes:

[11] It will impress the examiner if you use 'recuse'. It is the term used in the cases and so should be used here.

[12] This is one of the phrases that should be remembered if possible, though stating the crucial terms ('real possibility' of bias from the viewpoint of a 'fair-minded and informed observer') is sufficient.

[13] This question is about the effect of article 6, so one or two references to recent cases is sufficient.

[14] Move on to discuss impact. Stressing the potential seriousness of this will strengthen your answer.

[15] You show some depth of analysis by recognising the distinction between judicial bodies as distinct from administrative bodies.

[16] Showing awareness of the complicated facts of cases gets you credit.

[17] Now move on to discuss impact on administrative bodies.

the Secretary of State over planning applications or the in-house system for dealing with housing appeals, such defects can usually be adequately dealt with through judicial review in the High Court (**Alconbury**) or appeal to the county court (**Begum**). The review or appeal court in question must have full jurisdiction and be article 6 compliant in terms of its procedure.[18]

Independence and impartiality are important concepts which are central to the idea of a fair hearing and, therefore, to the rule of law. Independence in article 6 has had a significant impact on UK law and has been responsible for some important institutional changes. The possibility of curative appeal means that the impact has been less in respect of administrative decisions.

✓ Make your answer stand out

- From the beginning, show awareness of the potential impact of the need for independence on long-established institutions and systems – article 6 is no respecter of tradition.

- Make the distinction between independence and impartiality as clear as you can.

- This is a case-rich topic and awareness of a range of cases will help – but beware of spending too much time and space on facts and of merely adding cases which make the same point.

- Always think carefully about whether you are dealing with Strasbourg cases or with English administrative law – it is important that the different contexts are recognised.

- The 'curative appeal' point, which applies, in particular, to independence in the administrative context, needs to be carefully handled – the court dealing with the review or appeal must be of 'full jurisdiction' and this has not always been the case, especially when the core of the appeal is an alleged mistake of fact.

! Don't be tempted to ...

- Spend too much time introducing article 6 – it is a long article with many points to it; remember to keep the focus on independence.

- Overwhelm your answer with too many cases which do not advance the argument – it is better to spend time carefully analysing a number of key cases rather than merely naming a larger number.

- To explore English administrative law in general – it is important that bias cases be discussed but do not then continue to discuss wider issues about fair hearings, etc.

❓ Question 4

Under relevant English legislation mental patients are prevented from taking legal action against hospital staff without first obtaining leave from the court. After a disturbance at a hospital, a number of people complain that they were badly treated by staff and they now wish to take legal action for compensation.

(a) Albert (a patient) is denied leave to take legal action. He is then arrested for wasting police time. At the police station he is denied access to a solicitor and refuses to answer any questions. At his trial, the jury are directed that they may take into account his refusal to answer questions.

(b) Beatrice was a visitor at the hospital. Her claim in negligence is thrown out on the grounds that staff do not owe a duty of care to visitors. Her claim in trespass is lost. She and her legal advisers were not allowed to see a confidential report which the court relied on.

(c) Claude, the director of the hospital, is questioned by government inspectors and is required by statute to answer their questions. On the basis of the answers he gave, Claude is then prosecuted for criminal negligence.

Advise Albert, Beatrice and Claude, all of whom allege that their article 6 rights have been violated.[1]

[1]Long questions need to be carefully read before commencing an answer. It might be useful to make brief notes, as you read through, about the salient points.

Answer plan

→ Introduce article 6 in both its civil and criminal parts and note it applies to civil and criminal trials in the UK by virtue of HRA 1998.

→ Indicate the importance of implied or inherent rights derived from the general right to a 'fair hearing' in article 6(1).

→ Consider Albert's case: has he been denied the right of 'access to court' and the right to silence?

→ Consider Beatrice's case: has she been denied access to court and her right to 'equality of arms'?

→ Consider Claude's case: has he been denied the right against self-incrimination?

needed for definite answers ignoring answer given in jam

Diagram plan

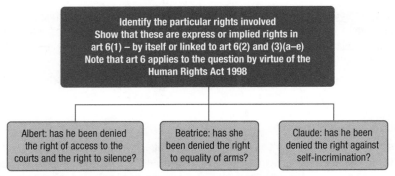

Identify the particular rights involved
Show that these are express or implied rights in
art 6(1) – by itself or linked to art 6(2) and (3)(a–e)
Note that art 6 applies to the question by virtue of the
Human Rights Act 1998

| Albert: has he been denied the right of access to the courts and the right to silence? | Beatrice: has she been denied the right to equality of arms? | Claude: has he been denied the right against self-incrimination? |

A printable version of this diagram is available from www.pearsoned.co.uk/lawexpressqa

[2]Begin by identifying article 6 and showing how it affects English law through the terms of the HRA 1998.

[3]Again, a sentence such as this not only sets up some of the points you will be making later in the answer but also demonstrates your general understanding of how article 6 works.

[4]Now move on to consider Albert's case.

[5]A brief reference to the probable causes of action indicates you are aware of the legal context and this strengthens your answer.

[6]The right of access to court is an important right inherent in article 6(1) and you will be expected to discuss it.

[7]*Golder* is one of the leading article 6 cases in which, in an early judgment, the Court laid down some important principles which are relevant to the answer.

Answer

Albert, Beatrice and Claude seek to rely on rights to a fair hearing found in article 6 which is a Convention right[2] and so must be followed, unless compelled otherwise by statute, by the civil and criminal courts in England and the UK. Article 6 contains both the expressed rights in the text but also implied rights which are inherent in the idea of a fair hearing. The application of both express and implied rights may vary according to context. The European Court of Human Rights (ECtHR) has always said[3] that its concern is with the overall fairness of a hearing rather than the specific institutions and practices adopted by signatory states.

Albert[4] is denied the right of access to court in respect of his allegations of bad treatment which appear to engage his 'civil rights' (he is alleging he is the victim of a serious tort, trespass, or, perhaps, misfeasance in public office,[5] which, if proved, entitles him to a remedy). The ECtHR has been very clear that implicit in article 6(1),[6] is a right of access to courts to have allegations tested and, if proven, remedies ordered. Legal and administrative barriers to this right are violations of article 6. In **Golder v UK**[7] (1979–80) 1 EHRR 524, a prisoner was prevented by the Prison Governor from contacting a solicitor with a view to suing a prison officer for libel. The ECtHR strongly asserted that the right of access to court was essential for the rule of law, and had been violated.

[8]You will gain credit by making this point and showing you understand the context-dependent nature of the rights inherent in article 6(1) and the concept of a fair hearing.

[9]You will impress by making a point like this. You indicate you understand the complex interaction, the often complementary relationship, of common law and Convention rights under the HRA 1998.

[10]This is not a tort exam but some basic knowledge, necessary to understand the human rights point, can be presumed. It is found in the case law, anyway.

However, the right of access to the court, being implied from the general right to a fair hearing, can be restricted by proportionate restrictions[8] that pursue a legitimate aim such as, for example, upholding the principle of Parliamentary privilege (**A v UK** (2003) 36 EHRR 51) and which do not undermine the essence of the right. In **Ashingdane v UK (1985) 7 EHRR 528** the ECtHR accepted that statutory restrictions on mental patients' access to court served the legitimate aim of protecting the nurses from harassment, but the case did not involve allegations of bad faith or negligence. By implication, an absolute statutory bar, in respect of such allegations, might breach article 6. Here, though, the court has discretion to allow the case. A strong right of access to court exists at common law[9] (**Pyx Granite v Ministry of Housing and Local Government** [1960] AC 260) but it, too, is subject to restrictions. In **Seal v South Wales Police** [2007] UKHL 31 the House of Lords (without reference to article 6) found (by a majority) that a statutory requirement for mental patients to obtain leave did not violate the principle. Albert's right of access to court has not been violated.

Albert's next concern is with his right to silence. This is an important right but is not absolute and can be subject to proportionate restrictions so long as the essence of a fair trial is not denied (**Murray v UK** (1996) 22 EHRR 29). It is important to take into account the plausibility of the reasons for silence (**Condron v UK** (2001) 31 EHRR 1) and a conviction based entirely on an inference from silence, with no other supporting evidence, would be likely to violate article 6. So provisions such as s 34 Criminal Justice and Public Order Act 1994 need to be interpreted with these principles in mind. The right to legal advice is another right of great importance. It is inherent in article 6(1) and implied from (3)(c). Again, it is subject to proportionate restrictions (**Brennan v UK** (2002) 34 EHRR 18). In **Murray**, an important reason for finding a violation was the fact that adverse inferences from silence could be drawn even where there had not been access to legal advice. As that is the case here, Albert's rights may have been violated.

Beatrice is unable to sue for negligence because of the absence of a legal duty of care.[10] A similar inability to sue the police was taken to be a procedural barrier preventing access to court in **Osman v UK** (2000) 29 EHRR 245. However, the alternative perspective is that the non-existence of a duty of care is a matter of substantive law

[11]The question clearly seeks a comment on the issue whether the absence of legal duty of care amounts to a restriction on the right of access to court or just a definition of a substantive right. It is a bit complex so you will strengthen your answer if you mention it.

[12]This is an important inherent right, which you should be aware of and able to discuss.

[13]It can be useful, in context, briefly to summarise the facts and outcome of a case. The danger of spending too much time on this, though, is obvious.

[14]Remember that important rights can be both inherent in the idea of a 'fair hearing' and also be an aspect of the guarantees for criminal defendants in article 6(2)–(3).

[15]By demonstrating your understanding of the flexibility of article 6 rights you will give the examiner confidence in your overall appreciation of the significance of article 6.

(the legal rights enjoyed), not a procedural barrier to enforcing such rights, and this perspective has been accepted by the ECtHR (**Z v UK** (2002) 34 EHRR 3).[11] So Beatrice is not denied her article 6(1) right of access to court.

Inherent in article 6(1) is the principle of 'equality of arms' – the equal treatment of the parties in an adversarial process.[12] Denying one party access to important documents seen by the other side and relied on by the court is a prima facie breach of this principle (**Ruiz Mateos v Spain** (1993) 16 EHRR 505). Implied rights are subject to proportionate restrictions which do not undermine the essence of a right. Public interest withholding of documents, for example, can be compatible with article 6 if there are adequate safeguards for the defence and restriction is no more than necessary (**Rowe & Davis v UK** (2000) 30 EHRR 1, adopted in **R v H** [2004] UKHL 3). Allowing the withholding of the confidential report in Beatrice's case is likely, in the absence of overwhelming reasons of public interest, to violate article 6(1) (see, for example, **McMichael v UK** (1995) 20 EHRR 205 – denying parents access to social work reports in care proceedings breached article 6(1)).[13]

The principle against self-incrimination is inherent in the idea of a fair hearing in article 6(1) and is closely linked with the presumption of innocence in article 6(2).[14] In **Saunders v UK** (1997) 23 EHRR 313, article 6(1) was violated when a company director was compelled by law to answer questions asked by company inspectors investigating allegations about a takeover; his answers were then accepted as evidence in a later, separate criminal prosecution for fraud. However, the right is not absolute and its application can depend upon context.[15] For instance, penal requirements that people disclose whether they were the driver of a car where the disclosure can then lead to prosecution for speeding or drink drive offences, serve an important social purpose and if not otherwise oppressive are likely to be compatible with article 6 (**O'Halloran & Francis v UK** (2008) 46 EHRR 21 and (Scots law) **Brown v Stott** [2003] 1 AC 681).

Claude's position is unlikely to be distinguishable from **Saunders** and so a breach of article 6(1) is likely.

Make your answer stand out

- Refer to academic debates: e.g. Sedley (2002) has questioned whether people filling roles which provide regulated privileges and responsibilities (e.g. company directors) should benefit from the principle against self-incrimination.

- Note the way English law has responded to adverse decisions. The Youth Justice and Criminal Evidence Act 1995 (s 58 and Sch 3, for example) makes the kind of compelled evidence in *Saunders* inadmissible in other criminal proceedings.

- Deal with cases decided under the Human Rights Act 1998 as well as those decided by Strasbourg.

! Don't be tempted to ...

- Spend any time on mental health law. It is not the subject of the question.

- Spend too much time on general discussion of article 6. This would not only cause you to write about irrelevant material but might (given the nature of article 6) unintentionally become dangerously long and leave you short of time.

- Spend much time on speculating about facts that are not given in the question – a number of aspects to this question involve the issue whether a restricted application of a general principle is proportionate and justified. This might involve weighing the significance of information you are not given in the question.

- Spend too much time reproducing the facts of the question.

Question 5

Assess the impact of article 6 on general principles governing criminal trials in the United Kingdom.

Answer plan

→ Relevance of article 6 through HRA 1998.

→ Application not only of article 6(1) but also article 6(2) and (3).

→ Article 6(1) and criminal trials.

→ Examples of impact of article 6(1) such as independence, equality of arms and unlawfully obtained evidence.

→ Presumption of innocence: article 6(2).

→ Example of impact of article 6(2): reverse onus defences.

→ Rights of the defence: article 6(3).

→ Example of impact of article 6(3): hearsay and anonymous witnesses.

Diagram plan

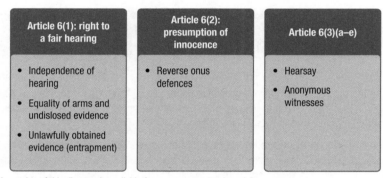

Article 6(1): right to a fair hearing	Article 6(2): presumption of innocence	Article 6(3)(a–e)
• Independence of hearing • Equality of arms and undislosed evidence • Unlawfully obtained evidence (entrapment)	• Reverse onus defences	• Hearsay • Anonymous witnesses

A printable version of this diagram is available from www.pearsoned.co.uk/lawexpressqa

Answer

[1]Begin by showing briefly why article 6 is relevant to the conduct of criminal trials in England.

Under the Human Rights Act 1998[1] criminal trials should accord with article 6 unless prevented by statute: courts are public authorities and there is a good deal of criminal procedural law which is found in Acts of Parliament.

[2]If possible, quote the exact words of article 6.

Article 6 applies to the 'determination of … any criminal charge'.[2]

[3]Use this term, 'autonomous' – it shows you are aware of the language used by the ECtHR. It should not need further definition so long as you make your understanding clear from usage.

The identification of a matter as criminal relates to an autonomous Convention definition[3] and so is not merely dependent on how a matter is categorised in national laws. At the heart of the definition is that a hearing is likely to be criminal if its purpose is punishment (**Engel v The Netherlands** (1979–80) 1 EHRR 647). This idea is fully adopted into English law. Thus domestic measures which are preventative and protective rather than punitive do not involve criminal charges (e.g **R (McCann) v Manchester Crown Court** [2002] UKHL 39 referring to ASBOS).

[4]Move on to discuss the importance of determining whether or not a matter is criminal.

Whether an issue is criminal or civil is important because article 6(2) and (3) only apply to criminal defendants.[4] Thus, in **Ezeh v UK** (2004) 39 EHRR 1 the Court of Human Rights (ECtHR) held that prison disciplinary proceedings involved determining a criminal charge and so the applicant should have had a right to be represented under article 6(3)(c). The practical impact may be lessened by the insistence of English courts on a high, criminal, standard of proof on non-criminal matters, such as ASBOSs or control orders which nevertheless involve restrictions on freedom of movement (**McCann**).

[5]Continue by making the point that criminal defendants enjoy the general right to a fair hearing.

[6]It is not necessary, in terms of keeping to the issue in the question, to explore the meaning of 'civil rights and obligations'.

Criminal defendants enjoy the general right to a fair hearing found in article 6(1)[5] which is shared with civil litigants.[6] This is a grouping of the rights expressed in the text and also a range of rights inherent in a 'fair hearing',[7] such as the right of equal access to the evidence ('equality of arms'[8]). For criminal trials the specific content of any such right will be appropriate to criminal proceedings reflecting the fact, in particular, that they can result in punishment. Independence and impartiality were in issue in **Findlay v UK** (1997) 24 EHRR 221,[9] where the ECtHR held that Courts Martial were not independent – this triggered a reform to the system. Equality of arms has been in issue in respect of the use of public interest immunity. Adopting Strasbourg principles, the House of Lords in **R v H** [2004] UKHL 3 emphasised the need for proper measures to safeguard the interests of the defence (such as the use of special counsel) where there is a compelling public interest reason against disclosure of evidence to the defence.

[7]Again, it always reads better and communicates the sense of a proper concern with the law if you can quote the terms of the article (if you can remember them or have access to a statute book); i.e. fair hearing rather than fair trial.

[8]Use of the phrase indicates an understanding of the law, but it is not necessary to explore the concept.

[9]Giving an example of the application of article 6(1) to criminal trials will strengthen your answer and show you are aware of the kinds of situation to which the criminal aspect of article 6 applies.

Although there is no absolute prohibition of admitting unlawfully or improperly obtained evidence, the way evidence has been obtained may undermine the overall fairness of the trial (**Ludi v Switzerland** (1993) 15 EHRR 173). The general principles in the leading Strasbourg case on entrapment, for example (**Teixeira de Castro v Portugal** (1999) 28 EHRR 101), have been adopted by the House of Lords into English law in **R v Looseley** [2001] UKHL 53.[10] Whilst it is acceptable for undercover police to give criminals an opportunity to commit a crime they would be likely to commit, the police must not instigate crimes which would not otherwise have occurred. In

[10]You should note the main authorities in which the Strasbourg principles have been restated and adopted by UK courts – these are now the main direct authority in UK cases.

[11]Section 78 Police and Criminal Evidence Act 1984 gives a trial judge in criminal proceedings discretion to exclude otherwise admissible evidence. It is an important general provision which should be known by students.

[12]Discuss the additional rights enjoyed by criminal defendants but note their frequent overlap with article 6(1).

such circumstances the English trial judge, exercising his or her discretion under s 78 PACE[11] and compatibly with article 6, should refuse to admit the evidence.

Those charged with criminal offences enjoy additional rights[12] in article 6(2) and (3) which are not available to and may not be appropriate for parties to civil proceedings. Often the rights in article 6(1) and in article 6(2) or (3) overlap. Sometimes the ECtHR deals with the case under article 6(1) alone, and at other times in conjunction with article 6(2) (or (3). For example, where statute requires a person to disclose information which can then be used against the person in separate criminal proceedings, the right against self-incrimination is engaged. This has been treated not as involving the presumption of innocence but as an aspect of the general right to a fair hearing. In **Saunders v UK** (1997) 23 EHRR 313 a company director convicted of fraud on the basis of compelled evidence was held to have suffered a breach of article 6, whilst speeding motorists, caught on speed cameras and compelled to disclose their identities to prosecutors, suffered no such breach – in particular because of the context of road safety legislation (**O'Halloran and Francis v UK** (2008) 46 EHRR 21).

[13]Discuss article 6(2) and give a few examples of its significance in a criminal context.

[14]Get the main point of this complex matter.

Article 6(2) provides for the presumption of innocence.[13] Although this principle is fully recognised by the common law, the Convention right has been in issue respecting English law where, for example, statute has created defences to a criminal charge that require a defendant to prove something (e.g. that, though drunk and in possession of a motor car, he did not intend to drive). This is a complex matter[14] but, so long as the overall burden stays with the prosecution and the defendant need only raise an issue, leaving it to the prosecution to prove that the defence has not been made out, article 6(2) is likely to have been complied with (**Sheldrake v DPP** [2004] UKHL 43).

[15]There is no point in listing the article 6(3) rights. Consider 'impact' by reference to examples.

[16]Issues of compatibility with article 6 are most likely to occur in respect of statute law which amends conventional fair trial procedures. Have one or two examples ready (e.g. hearsay or the right to silence or legal advice).

Article 6(3)(a)–(e)[15] establishes a range of further rights of the defence. Mostly these rights (such as the right to be informed promptly of the nature of the charge) are embedded in English law. But, again, there are examples of statute law[16] which raise issues about compatibility.

An important example is whether hearsay evidence or the use of anonymous witnesses can be compatible with article 6(1), which requires an adversarial procedure, in conjunction with article 6(3)(d), which gives defendants a right to 'examine witnesses' (s 116 Criminal Justice Act 2003, for instance, allows the use of hearsay evidence in certain circumstances). The ECtHR recognises that allowing hearsay, etc, can serve important and legitimate purposes, such as enabling a trial to go ahead in the face of witness intimidation. But there have to be adequate safeguards (usually some process, such as a pre-trial hearing, at which the evidence can be tested by the defendant – see **Doorson v The Netherlands (1996) 22 EHRR 330).**[17] Furthermore, the Court has ruled that a conviction will not be compatible with article 6 if it is based 'solely or decisively' on unchallengeable evidence, even if there is a range of other safeguards for the defence available (**Al-Khawaja v UK** (2009) 49 EHRR 1). The UK Supreme Court has strongly disagreed with this 'sole or decisive' approach and said that, for English law, the detailed requirements found in the legislation which permits hearsay or anonymity, along with the judge's discretion not to admit under s 78 PACE, meet the needs for overall fairness in article 6 (**R v Horncastle** [2009] UKSC 14).

[17]Choose one or two cases, but no more, as examples.

✓ Make your answer stand out

- On the concept of a criminal offence you could refer to cases such as *Secretary of State for the Home Department* v *MB* [2007] UKHL 46 in which counter-terrorism control order hearings are held to be determining civil rights and not criminal charges and yet the authorities are held to a high, in effect criminal, standard of proof.

- Where there is space, introduce other elements of a right to a fair hearing, such as the right of access to a court.

- Compare the position at common law as indicated by *R* v *Davis* [2008] UKHL 36. The House of Lords refused to depart from the general common law principle against allowing witnesses to be anonymous. Such changes require statutory authorisation (*Horncastle* relates to statutory rules of evidence).

- Discuss a little more the potential role of special counsel (the main issue in *R* v *H*). Special counsel are security cleared counsel who represent the defendant but are not allowed to take instructions from the defendant or the details of the case with him or her. The issue for the courts, in each case, is whether they amount to adequate safeguards and counter-balance the defendant's disadvantages.

> ## ! Don't be tempted to ...
>
> ■ Spend too much time on a general discussion of article 6, including its scope (the definition of 'civil rights and obligations' and 'criminal charge'). These important matters are not the focus of the question.
>
> ■ Focus your answer on article 6(2) and (3) – you must give at least as much attention to the importance of article 6(1) in respect of fair hearings.

? Question 6

The Home Secretary receives evidence against A and B that convinces her that they may have been involved in terrorism. A is a British citizen and B is an asylum applicant. Much of the evidence against A and B was disclosed to the British government by a foreign secret service on the basis of strict confidentiality.

The Home Secretary decides to exercise her statutory powers. She places A under continual supervision and a range of other restrictions (which do not deprive anyone of their liberty). She also decides to deport B, which she has the statutory power to do.

A is entitled to challenge the Home Secretary's decision in the High Court and B can challenge the deportation decision before a special court. Both courts are required to exclude the applicant and his representatives from their hearings if disclosure of relevant evidence would not be in the public interest as this is determined by the Home Secretary.

Advise the Home Secretary on the difficulties, based on the Human Rights Act, she is likely to encounter in trying to persuade the High Court and the special court to uphold her decisions without disclosing the evidence to the applicants directly.

Answer plan

➡ Introduce the use, in the context of counter-terrorism law, of special powers and procedures including special courts.

➡ Introduce the right to a fair hearing as a Convention right in the HRA 1998.

➡ Outline the general principle of equality of arms but note that restrictions are allowed if adequate, compensating protective measures are available.

➡ Discuss special counsel and whether they can provide adequate protection.

➡ Comment on the 'sole or decisive' rule and its acceptance into UK law.

➡ Discuss the position under the HRA 1998: reading down under s 3 and the problem this poses for the Home Secretary.

Diagram plan

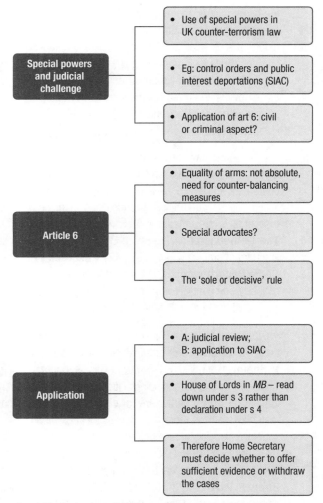

Special powers and judicial challenge

- Use of special powers in UK counter-terrorism law
- Eg: control orders and public interest deportations (SIAC)
- Application of art 6: civil or criminal aspect?

Article 6

- Equality of arms: not absolute, need for counter-balancing measures
- Special advocates?
- The 'sole or decisive' rule

Application

- A: judicial review; B: application to SIAC
- House of Lords in *MB* – read down under s 3 rather than declaration under s 4
- Therefore Home Secretary must decide whether to offer sufficient evidence or withdraw the cases

A printable version of this diagram is available from www.pearsoned.co.uk/lawexpressqa

Answer

Counter-terrorism law in the United Kingdom allows the government to exercise special powers, including empowering the Home Secretary to impose restrictions on ordinary life through control orders and deportation on public interest and national security grounds. These

[1]Show you have a broad understanding of UK counter-terrorism law.

[2]Show you are aware of this important 'special court' whose procedures are in issue in this question.

[3]The question clearly looks for an understanding of the authorities under the HRA 1998.

[4]In any brief summary of the HRA 1998 you will confirm the examiner's confidence if you remember the 'so far as is possible' proviso.

[5]Make the point that article 6(1) (but not article 6(2) and (3)) is in issue.

[6]The point is mentioned in the question and so should be briefly addressed.

[7]An alternative approach is to attribute the principle to the UK case and say 'based upon Strasbourg case law such as …'.

[8]Move on to the difficult area – whether special counsel are a sufficient counter-balancing measure.

[9]If fair hearing rights in a counter-terrorism context are likely to come up in an exam, be prepared to summarise the role of special counsel.

restrictions have the authority of statute law and can be challenged in courts. Thus control orders can be challenged in the High Court on the basis, initially, that the grounds are 'flawed' or, at a later stage, 'obviously flawed'.[1] Public interest deportations can be challenged before the Special Immigration Appeals Commission[2] (SIAC) on grounds which include the illegality of deporting to a country where there is a real risk of torture or death. Given the statutory basis of these powers and given that they are exercised by courts which are 'public authorities' they must, under the HRA 1998,[3] be exercised compatibly with Convention rights unless this is not possible.[4]

The UK courts have held that such special powers will involve 'civil rights and obligations' and thus engage article 6(1).[5] A criminal charge (which would have engaged article 6(2) and (3) as well) is not being determined because the purpose of the special measures is preventative rather than punitive (following **Engel v The Netherlands** (1979–80) 1 EHRR 647). Nevertheless, a high standard of proof is required (**R (MB) v Secretary of State for the Home Department** [2007] UKHL 46). Since there is no deprivation of liberty, compatibility with article 5(4) (a right to a fair hearing in the context of the right to liberty) is not in issue.[6]

An important principle inherent in a 'fair hearing' is 'equality of arms' in the context of an adversarial principle (e.g. **Ruiz Mateos v Spain** (1993) 16 EHRR 505). This is not an absolute right. Competing interests, including national security, can justify limiting equality of arms (particularly disclosure of evidence) so long as restrictions are no more than necessary and, importantly, there are counter-balancing protections for the defendant (**Rowe & Davis v UK** (2000) 30 EHRR 1). These might be, for example, disclosure of a summary to the defence with a right to make submissions (as in **Botmeh v UK** (2008) 46 EHRR 31). These general principles are adopted into English law[7] in **R v H** [2004] UKHL 3.

If, in this case, even a summary would break the agreement,[8] the Home Secretary might accept disclosure to 'special counsel' as a counter-balancing measure. Special counsel[9] are security cleared barristers who see the closed evidence and can seek to represent the defendant's interests before a court. However, they cannot consult with or take instructions from the defendant once they have seen the closed evidence. In **Chahal v UK** (1997) 23 EHRR

[10]This is important authority on fair hearings in the context of counter-terrorist special powers and you will get credit for demonstrating that you have absorbed it. Remember, though, its effects are limited by AF, to be discussed later.

[11]The Strasbourg decision in the 'Belmarsh case' is important in respect of fair hearing rights and you will be expected to mention it.

[12]You will get credit for demonstrating your understanding that fair hearing rights are also found in respect of deprivations of liberty and that article 5(4) and article 6(1) are increasingly seen as raising similar issues on the nature of a fair adversarial hearing.

[13]It is important that you note when Strasbourg decisions are made by a Grand Chamber – this is the ultimate authority and should be based on a careful and deliberate conclusion on a controversial issue of interpretation.

[14]It is worth learning the phrase, given its importance.

[15]Although this is a problem question, you will get credit for noting the controversial nature of these matters.

413 the ECtHR gave credence to the idea of special counsel being effective as a counter-balancing measure. They have been widely used in the United Kingdom in contexts including control orders and public interest deportations. The judiciary are aware of the limits to the remedial function of special counsel and the unfairness of the defendant's position that remains (as in **R v H**). In **MB**,[10] a control order case, UKHL held that special counsel could be a sufficient means of counter-balancing the unfairness of closed evidence but, a majority held, this might not always be the case. Under article 6 the overriding responsibility of the courts is to ensure that, in all the circumstances, there has been a fair trial. This would depend on detailed examination of the particular facts and cannot be presumed just because there are special counsel.

In **A v UK**[11] (2009) 49 EHRR 29 the ECtHR held that there had been a violation of article 5(4)[12] in respect of foreign terrorist suspects who had been deprived of their liberty and whose claims had been rejected by SIAC. The Grand Chamber[13] accepted that, in SIAC hearings, a special advocate could play an important role but went on to rule that a hearing would not be fair, notwithstanding such counter-balancing measures, if an order depriving someone of their liberty was upheld, 'solely or to a decisive degree',[14] on the basis of closed evidence. The Grand Chamber expressly aligns article 5(4) with article 6(1) (though in its 'criminal aspect'). In relation to article 6, the 'sole or decisive' principle was accepted (by some judges reluctantly) in respect of UK law on control orders by UKHL in **Secretary of State for the Home Department v AF** [2009] UKHL 28. The decision removed any residual discretion, left to a domestic court by **MB**, which would have allowed it to uphold an order based solely or decisively on closed material if there were adequate counter-balancing measures.

Such a move can be justified[15] in terms of making a clear statement of the absolute minimum entitlement to a fair hearing required by the rule of law and in doing so it strengthens the positions of vulnerable people such as A and B. It means, though, that, when the sole or decisive evidence is closed, the Home Secretary's reasons for seeking orders or deportations are not subject to judicial scrutiny. The open material is likely to be too general to justify an order and so a person believed by the Home Secretary to be dangerous is not controlled (see judicial comment in **BM v Secretary of State for the Home Department** [2009] EWHC 1572).

[16]Make sure you discuss the consequences of these legal principles in terms of the HRA 1998. There is not, though, time to give an exposition of the main terms of the Act. The examiner should be able to appreciate your understanding from the discussion.

[17]In your conclusion, return to the point of the question – giving advice to the Home Secretary.

In **MB** the House of Lords was dealing with a statutory provision which seemingly required a court to hear evidence in secret. They refused a declaration of incompatibility,[16] under s 4 HRA 1998, preferring instead to read down the provisions under s 3 so that it would always be applied compatibly with the requirements of article 6 by domestic courts.

The Home Secretary, therefore, has to decide.[17] A's case involves judicial review of the Home Secretary's decision to seek an order. The Home Secretary must release sufficient evidence so that, whilst full equality of arms is not necessary, there is enough open evidence to satisfy the minimum standard laid down in **AF** (a control order case). The alternative is to withdraw the case. B's case involves a special tribunal. In themselves, tribunals such as SIAC do not violate article 6. But they, too, are subject to the sole or decisive rule (at least when dealing with refusals of bail in deportation cases (**R (U) v Special Immigration Appeals Commission** [2009] EWHC 3052)). So, again, the Home Secretary will have to decide about the amount of information she is prepared to release and whether this is sufficient to meet the sole and decisive test notwithstanding her use of special counsel or other methods of compensating for departures from the basic principle of open justice and equality of arms.

 Make your answer stand out

- Awareness of the basic provisions of UK counter-terrorism law is clearly needed for this answer. Thus you can be expected (if counter-terrorism is on the syllabus) to have a general (not detailed) knowledge of control orders and deportation.

- When referring to counter-terrorist measures, try to be as specific as you can by (following the examples in the first sentence) giving references to the Prevention of Terrorism Act 2005 and s 3(5) Immigration Act 1971.

- Although this is a problem question it relates to law which causes both judges and commentators great difficulty. There is no harm in referring to this debate. For example: Ewing and Tham (2008).

- On special advocates, read Ip (2008).

- On *A* v *UK* and the 'sole or decisive rule' see Elliott (2009).

! **Don't be tempted to ...**

■ Spend too much time on showing general knowledge of counter-terrorism law. There is not space to discuss areas other than control orders and deportation (such as proscription or pre-charge detention) even though they raise similar fair hearing issues to those in the question.

■ Spend too much time on other aspects of deportation and control order law – these are both important issues but are not the focus of the question. In particular there is no need to spend a lot of time on the issue of the legality of deportation to a country in which Convention rights will be violated.

Political and religious expression and action

8

How this topic may come up in exams

Both problem or essay questions are likely and will probably engage your understanding of articles 10 and 11(possibly article 3 Protocol 1, in Chapter 9); also article 9, if belief is the theme. Questions are likely to involve justification for an interference with expression, association or religious manifestation. Two issues are most likely: whether the interference is based on the Convention concept of 'law' and/or whether the interference is proportionate. The latter requires a sense of detail and awareness of prominent cases. Be aware of the different issues that can arise depending on whether the focus is on Strasbourg or UK cases involving the HRA, or both.

■ Attack the question

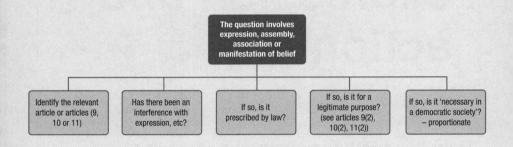

📝 Question 1

In what ways does article 10 provide protection for the media and for journalists?

Answer plan

→ Discuss the importance of a free media to the Convention system.

→ Note that article 10 is a qualified right.

→ Note the importance, in this context, of the 'duties and responsibilities' clause.

→ Discuss examples where media freedom may push on the limits to freedom of expression.

→ Discuss the need to protect journalist's sources.

Diagram plan

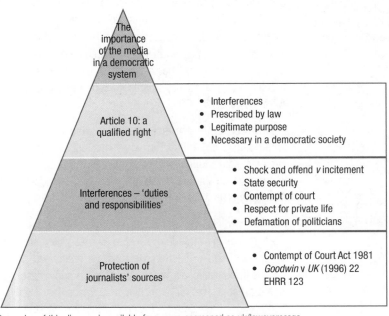

A printable version of this diagram is available from www.pearsoned.co.uk/lawexpressqa

[1]Get credit by focusing on the most relevant terms regarding the media. Merely quoting the whole article will count for little, especially if you are allowed a statute book in the exam.

[2]It is a good idea to choose, in your revision, one of many cases in which general principles underlying article 10 and the media are summarised – it gives your introductory remarks authority.

[3]Demonstrate the recognition of the importance of the media – it sets you up to consider more specific points later.

[4]Mentioning the licensing provision demonstrates your understanding of article 10 and that the provision has a potential side effect on content.

[5]This, of course, is the central point which you must address.

Answer

Article 10 protects the right to 'receive' information as well as to 'impart' it[1] and it is in respect of the former that the importance for the media arises.

In many cases such as **Fressoz v France** (2001) 31 EHRR 2[2] the European Court of Human Rights (ECtHR) has recognised the importance of the media.[3] It is seen as a 'watchdog' whose 'essential' role is to convey information and ideas on matters of public interest and to be part of the process by which government is held to account. The Court refers to a media 'duty', something more than a right which can be exercised or not. It is an imperfect duty: there is no obligation on states to compel media organisations to report stories.

Nevertheless, the importance of the media means that states can be under positive duties to protect a free press, to take reasonable steps to prevent the violent closure of a newspaper (for instance (**Özgür Gündem v Turkey** (2001) 31 EHRR 49). Article 10 allows states to license broadcasting, television and cinema (not the press).[4] This can involve limiting the range of broadcast outlets, which could have an effect on content and be in tension with the population's right to receive information. A state monopoly of broadcasting might also be incompatible. So long as there is reasonable pluralism, there is no right of access to the media though, where there is public access to the media, potential applicants must be treated fairly (**R (ProLife Alliance) v BBC** [2003] UKHL 23).

Freedom of expression in article 10(1) protects public affairs in a broad sense: any matter on which the public can have genuine interests, not just party politics. It includes, for example, commercial information on the availability of goods and services (**Barthold v Germany** (1985) 7 EHRR 383).

However, article 10 is not an absolute but a qualified right.[5] Interferences with freedom of expression can be justified in terms of article 10(2). An interference must be prescribed by law (have a basis in domestic law which is accessible and whose application is foreseeable), be for a legitimate purpose (as listed in article 10(2)) and be 'necessary in a democratic society' (representing a proportionate way of meeting a pressing social need). The ECtHR

[6]You will get credit for
the right terminology and
showing your understanding
of ECtHR's approach to
proportionality in the media
context.

allows little margin of appreciation on the need for restrictions on political speech,[6] though the extent to which UK courts will 'defer' to administrative bodies is not clear. In **ProLife** the Court of Appeal held there was censorship but the House of Lords accepted the BBC's judgement on whether an election broadcast was offensive.

Where information that the media wishes to publish is, for example, bound by alleged confidentiality or privacy, the courts may issue an injunction. This is 'prior restraint', which is particularly serious because it prevents information getting into the public domain. The ECtHR does not bar prior restraints but subjects them to careful scrutiny. In particular, 'temporary' injunctions (which may be granted on a balance of convenience rather than following full argument on rights) may destroy the freshness and currency of a news story[7] (**Association Ekin v France** (2002) 35 EHRR 35). Section 12 Human Rights Act 1998 (HRA 1998) requires UK courts to take into account the likely outcome of a full hearing when deciding whether to issue such an injunction.

[7]Discussing the prior restraint point shows your understanding of the effects the law can have. Reference to s 12 HRA 1998 will show that you know more of the Act than just its key provisions on statutory interpretation and public authorities – this gives examiners confidence.

Article 10(2) expressly acknowledges that freedom of expression involves 'duties and responsibilities'.[8] These have been applied to the media. One particular tension is the border line between expression which 'disturbs, shocks and offends'[9] and expression which is an incitement to violence. The former enjoys the protection of article 10 (**Handyside v UK** (1979–80) 1 EHRR 737) and should be permitted unless supression is to protect the rights of others, etc, under article 10(2). The latter falls outside the protection of article 10(1) altogether. Much depends upon context and the journalistic intention (e.g. **Sener v Turkey** (2003) 37 EHRR 34).

[8]This is the only reference to 'duties' in the Convention and you should ensure you discuss it in relation to the ECtHR's approach to the media.

[9]This is one of the phrases you will get credit for remembering (try to learn it whilst revising).

Other areas where media freedom is curtailed include, for instance, contempt of court (**Worm v Austria** (1998) 25 EHRR 454) and protecting information, including state secrets, obtained in confidence, whilst confidentiality remains (**Observer v UK** (1992) 14 EHRR 153).

[10]You could say more about the matters in the previous paragraph but the media freedom versus privacy issue is so prominent and problematic that it is wise to focus on it.

In modern media there can be a clash between the media interest and an individual's right to respect for private life founded on article 8.[10] The issue turns on the relative weight to be given to freedom of expression and privacy. UK courts, consistent with ECtHR, are clear that the rights are of equal status and the issue of 'weight' must be determined on the facts. A strong privacy claim will outweigh a weak

[11]You can impress with your analysis of this point and the distinction made between the public's interests and what they may be merely interested in.

[12]Though referring to UK law under the HRA 1998, you will get credit for your understanding of the 'indirect horizontal effect' (its effect on private law and the relations between private parties) of the Act.

[13]Again, by quoting the words (like 'chilling') that are used you show you have read some of the primary materials.

[14]You will get credit for this – you are not confusing the ECHR with UK law but showing how developments in the latter illustrate the requirements of the former.

[15]Having discussed the media in general, now move on to discuss provisions in the Convention that refer to journalists specifically; it is required by the question.

expression claim. An expression can be weak in this sense when, in the view of the ECtHR, it makes little contribution to debate on public issues[11] but focuses on an individual's private life. Article 10 offers little protection to expression which merely feeds public curiosity (**Von Hannover v Germany** (2005) 40 EHRR 1). This issue continues to be problematic in UK courts over the extent to which the media can intrude on a celebrity's reasonable expectation of privacy. Although, since newspapers and commercial broadcasters are not public authorities,[12] this is a common law matter, the courts deal with it by weighing articles 8 and 10 (**Campbell v MGN** [2005] UKHL 61).

Performing its watchdog role can lead the media to publish statements critical of politicians. Politicians may sue to protect their reputation and the courts need to apply the law compatibly with article 10. Under article 10, politicians do not surrender their rights to reputation or private life, but may have to accept deeper, more hurtful, criticism than others because they have voluntarily entered public life. There would be a 'chilling' effect on freedom of expression and effective media criticism if the threshold of a successful action for a politician was placed too low.[13] UK courts allow a form of qualified privilege to the media[14] (which requires the claimant to prove malice) in respect of such defamation actions, conditional upon the journalism being 'responsible' (**Reynolds v Times Newspapers** [1999] 4 All ER 609).

The most important protection article 10 provides for journalists is the requirement that journalists be able to protect their sources.[15] This is seen as essential if journalists are to obtain information and perform their watchdog role. In the UK, s 10 Contempt of Court Act 1981 supports the general principle but is subject to exceptions. In **Goodwin v UK** (1996) 22 EHRR 123 the ECtHR found a violation on the grounds that the House of Lords in domestic proceedings had given insufficient weight to the principle.

✓ **Make your answer stand out**

■ Discuss whether public bodies (as distinct from individual politicians and officials) ought to be able to sue to protect their reputations. The English courts have prevented this in order to limit the chilling effect of legal action (*Derbyshire County Council* v *Times*

Newspapers [1993] AC 534). The ECtHR does not have a hard and fast rule and will deal with the issue as a matter of proportionality. In *Jameel* v *Wall Street Journal* [2006] UKHL 44 the idea of extending the ban to corporations (because of their considerable economic and social power) was canvassed but dismissed for England, and has not found approval in Strasbourg: *Steel and Morris* v *UK* (2005) 41 EHRR 22.

■ Further comment on *Von Hannover* would be interesting because it involves the ECtHR evaluating the worth of speech in terms of an objective account of the public interest – does this speech (and, in the case, do these photographs) contribute to debate on public affairs? A brief linkage to other areas (e.g. the idea of morally worthless speech such as holocaust denial) might help to make the point, but don't get carried too far away from the focus of the question.

■ Academic writing and case law on the protection of journalists sources could be referred to (for instance, *Ashworth Security Hospital* v *MGN Ltd* [2002] UKHL 29; and, following, *Mersey Care NHS Trust* v *Ackroyd* [2007] EWCA Civ 101). On academic writing see Costigan (2007).

! Don't be tempted to ...

■ Be too long-winded and descriptive in general about article 10(2). Although article 10(2) is important, a general discussion of proportionality, necessity, legality, etc, will take you away from the media focus.

■ Trawl through all the various areas in which restrictions on media freedom might occur. Your answer should cite one or two and give a fuller discussion of one or two but answers which become lists can be tedious and, also, become, in reality, a discussion of freedom of expression generally.

? Question 2

Bond is a member of the UK Secret Services and, without authority, he disclosed security information to a national newspaper, *The Daily Globe*. The government immediately sought and obtained a temporary injunction from the High Court to prevent *The Daily Globe* from publishing any of the disclosed material. In the same week the information is published on the internet. Later, Bond was prosecuted and convicted under the Official Secrets Act 1989.

(1) *The Daily Globe* appeals against the injunction on the grounds that it is a violation of its right to freedom of expression under article 10 of Sch 1 to the Human Rights Act 1998 (HRA 1998).

(2) Bond appeals against his conviction on the grounds that, under the terms of the Official Secrets Act, he was not able to argue that his disclosure was in the public interest and that compatibility of the offence with article 10 required this.

Explain the general principles that will be applied by the courts hearing these appeals.

Answer plan

→ *The Globe* and the civil injunction: introduce the issuing of temporary injunctions in English law and demonstrate why, because of the Human Rights Act, article 10 is relevant if they interfere with freedom of expression.

→ Identify and explain the grounds, found in article 10(2), on which an interference by an injunction might be justified; discuss, in particular, the matter of proportionality (and consider the specific arguments in *The Observer* v *UK* (1992) 14 EHRR 153).

→ Bond's criminal conviction: discuss the implications of the Human Rights Act as regards Bond's claim that there should be a public interest test.

→ Discuss and analyse article 10 and consider, in particular, whether 'proportionality' requires a public interest defence.

→ Consider the House of Lord's argument in *R* v *Shayler* [2002] UKHL 1 and apply to the question.

Diagram plan

The Globe – temporary injunction	Bond – criminal appeal
• Relevance of article 10 via HRA 1998	• Relevance of article 10 via HRA 1998
• Justification for injunction under article 10(2)	• Justification for convictions under article 10(2)
• Prescribed by law	• Prescribed by law
• Purpose	• Purpose
• Necessary in a democratic society (proportionality)	• Necessary in a democratic society (proportionality)
• Apply *Spycatcher* case on proportionality issue	• Apply *Shayler* case on proportionality issue

A printable version of this diagram is available from www.pearsoned.co.uk/lawexpressqa

Answer

[1]Begin by pointing out
why article 10 will be the
underlying principle in *The
Daily Globe*'s case, which is to
be decided under English law.
You need to do this, otherwise
it implies that the Convention
(ECHR) is directly effective in
UK law.

The Daily Globe can argue its case in terms of the right to freedom of expression under article 10 because, first, the injunction will be issued by the courts which are public authorities by virtue of s 6(3)(a) HRA 1998.[1] Furthermore, states are responsible, under the ECHR, to ensure freedom of expression and, in this regard, state responsibility is on the courts. The government applying for the injunction is a public authority and must act compatibly with article 10.

Injunctions restricting freedom of expression can be obtained from the English courts to prevent the disclosure of confidential information. This protects information which is personal or commercially sensitive but has been extended to include political information (e.g. **Attorney General v Jonathan Cape** [1976] QB 752) and security secrets (**Attorney General v Guardian Newspapers Ltd** [1987] 3 All ER 316).[2] A full injunction deals with the issue in full as a matter of right; a temporary injunction maintains confidentiality until the full injunction can be heard.

[2]As this question concerns
English law under the HRA
1998, you will get credit for
showing you understand the
availability of injunctions and
that you make the distinction
between full and temporary.
This information is found in
the human rights case law.

In **Attorney General v Punch** [2002] UKHL 50 the issue was whether an editor had breached the terms of a temporary injunction obtained against a former member of the Security Service. The House of Lords accepted the relevance of Convention rights[3] and that an injunction is clearly an interference with freedom of expression and so the editor enjoyed the protection of article 10(1). The question for the court, therefore, is whether the interference is justified within the terms of article 10(2).

[3]Again, you will get credit for
dealing with the question as a
matter of English law.

The injunction must be prescribed by law. Its legal basis must be accessible and likely application be foreseeable.[4] The European Court of Human Rights (ECtHR) accepts that temporary injunctions are based on sufficiently clear principles developed by judges to meet this test (**The Observer v UK** (1992) 14 EHRR 153). Accessibility can also be based on s 12 HRA 1998 which lays down rules governing the issuing of injunctions that impinge on freedom of expression and media freedom.

[4]Remember to use these
terms and give confidence by
showing you understand their
meaning.

The injunction must be for a legitimate purpose. The point of a temporary injunction is to maintain the 'authority of the judiciary' (listed in article 10(2))[5] so that confidentiality is maintained pending

[5]You will get credit for
this – the purpose behind
a temporary injunction is
different from a permanent
one.

the full trial. At the full trial the purpose will be the protection of national security, which is also listed.

The injunction must be necessary in a democratic society; it must be proportionate. Following **R (Daly) v Secretary of State for the Home Department** [2001] UKHL 26, there must be an objective which justifies limiting a right (here the threat to national security); the proposed measure must serve the purpose (here to keep confidentiality until the trial) and the injunction should be no greater a restriction than necessary. Overall there must be a 'fair balance' of interests in the context of article 10 (**Huang v Secretary of State for the Home Department** [2007] UKHL 11).[6]

Guidance on proportionality will come from the leading Strasbourg case, **The Observer v UK** (1992) 14 EHRR 153,[7] where a temporary injunction was found not to violate article 10. The case concerned the long-running attempt by the UK government to prevent serialisation by British newspapers of *Spycatcher*, a book written by a retired security agent and which allegedly breached his personal duty of lifelong confidentiality. The interlocutory injunction originally obtained from the UK courts was held not to be a violation of article 10. The central finding was that it was proportionate to the needs of preparing for a full trial. However, article 10 was breached when the temporary injunctions were renewed after publication in the USA meant there was no longer any confidentiality left.[8] The government's argument that the injunctions were still necessary to protect the efficiency and reputation of the security services[9] was not considered sufficient to outweigh the right and duty of the press to impart information on a matter of public interest.

In *The Daily Globe*'s case the appeal court will have to decide whether the publication on the internet so weakens confidentiality as to make an otherwise justified injunction pointless.[10] An argument that the injunction should, nevertheless, be granted on the distinct ground of upholding the authority and morale of the security service will probably fail. Under s 12 HRA 1998 the court will need to consider the likely outcome of the full trial and, most importantly, the extent to which matters are effectively confidential and whether the public interest requires publication.[11]

Bond has imparted information to the *Globe* and so his right to freedom of expression is in issue. He has to show that article 10

[6]Again, keep the focus on English law by expressing the general proportionality as articulated by the House of Lords.

[7]You will be expected to mention this case as laying down principles to be followed by the courts on the basis of s 2 HRA 1998.

[8]This is an important point. It shows you have understood what was decided and you will get credit.

[9]You will impress the examiner if you make this point. You will show you understand the different arguments being made.

[10]Following the *Spycatcher* case, you can try to draw a conclusion on *The Daily Globe*'s injunction.

[11]You will get credit for knowing the substance of s 12, not just (see above) that it lays down some legal rules.

[12]Now move on to Bond's case. Remember it is dealing with a criminal prosecution, not a civil injunction.

[13]You get credit for showing your understanding of the HRA 1998 and how it would apply in the given circumstances.

[14]There are obvious similarities, so the case needs to be discussed. It is, speaking generally, important regarding the UK's reception of article 10.

[15]By referring to the need for individual circumstances to be testable and for the public interest to be considered by the courts, you indicate your understanding of proportionality and will thereby impress the examiner.

[16]You will get credit for this point: it shows you have read and understood the House of Lords' approach.

is legally relevant.[12] He needs to show, first, that article 10 requires a public interest defence and, second, that, under s 3 HRA 1998, it is 'possible' to give effect to the Official Secrets Act 1989 (OSA 1989) in a way that is compatible with this requirement. If he is correct on the first but not the second point, his conviction would still stand but a UK court could issue a declaration of incompatibility.[13] In **R v Shayler** [2002] UKHL 1, on facts similar to the question,[14] the House of Lords held that the OSA 1998 could not be read as permitting a public interest defence, but it held there was no incompatibility with article 10 nevertheless.

There has clearly been an interference with Bond's freedom of expression, so the issue is justification under article 10(2). The offence, being statutory, is likely to be prescribed by law and in the interests of national security, which is one of the legitimate purposes listed in article 10(2).

Bond's argument is that the need for the offence in a democratic society (proportionality) requires a public interest test. This is necessary so that the circumstances and motives of individual defendants can be analysed by the court.[15] In particular, it is necessary to allow consideration of the possibility that disclosure was overwhelmingly in the public interest (because it disclosed serious wrongdoing, for instance). In **Shayler** the House of Lords found that proportionality, regarding article 10, was satisfied because of the availability of internal processes by which security officers could have legitimate grievances dealt with, without going to the media. Lawful disclosures could then be made if authorised. The House of Lords dealt with scepticism about the credibility and robustness of internal processes. They suggested that issues of unreasonable refusals to sanction disclosure or bias and lack of independence (which might engage article 6) could be dealt with by judicial review.[16] Of course, any judicial review would require the same issue of balancing the national security reasons to prevent disclosure against the public interest in disclosing wrongdoing.

Following **Shayler**, and assuming that Bond has internal opportunities to air his concerns, his appeal is likely to fail.

✓ Make your answer stand out

- Explore a little more the legal basis on which a temporary injunction can be issued. Following *American Cyanamid* v *Ethicon* [1975] 2 WLR 316, the broad test is a balance of convenience (who would suffer more if prevented from doing what, at the full hearing, it turns out they have a right to do). The problem that an injunction stops things in their tracks can be noted. So in some situations the court must take into account its view of the likely outcome of the full hearing – s 12 HRA 1998 requires this when free speech is in issue.

- Discuss breach of confidence injunctions and their application in the political realm more fully; note that, following *Spycatcher*, the lifelong duty of confidentiality has become explicit and contractual (e.g. *Ministry of Defence* v *Griffin* [2008] EWHC 1542).

- Don't shy away from critical discussion of the implications of the law; e.g. should the courts be more demanding in testing government claims about risk to national security; should there be a stricter rule aimed at ensuring that well-grounded allegations of wrongdoing cannot be suppressed (scepticism about *Shayler*, for instance)?

! Don't be tempted to ...

- Discuss the specific terms of the Official Secrets Act 1989, etc. Your knowledge of the Act is not being tested. The question tells you that Bond was convicted under the Act – the issue is whether this can be compatible with the requirements of article 10.

- Discuss in detail the history of the *Spycatcher* saga. It was a huge series of cases both in the UK and in other jurisdictions. The point is to get to the central issues which come from the ECtHR cases (*Sunday Times* v *UK* (1992) 14 EHRR 229 is broadly the same as *The Observer* case). You do not have time for more and it is not clear what would be gained.

❓ Question 3

A protest against university fees is planned. There will be a march and meeting in the centre of town. The senior police officer, Superintendent Bannem, fears, on good evidence, that the protest may get violent, due to the actions of a minority, and lead to damage to property. He knows that, under the Public Order Act 1986 (POA 1986) and under common law powers to take action to maintain the peace, he can expect to have notice of the march and that he can impose conditions on marches and assemblies and even detain people. Advise him on the human rights standards, derived from the Human Rights Act 1998 (HRA 1998) that he must meet when making his decisions on how to police this march.

Answer plan

→ Show how, through the terms of the Human Rights Act 1998 (HRA 1998), Convention rights will be relevant to the nature and standards of policing applied.

→ Note the application of various Convention rights in a public order context but focus, in particular, on article 11.

→ Discuss the fact that article 11 is a qualified right and so interferences with the right can be justified under the terms of article 11(2).

→ State the requirements for legitimate interferences and discuss relevant European case law, particularly on the issue of interferences being 'prescribed by law' and proportionality.

→ Expand your discussion, especially of issues pertaining to proportionality, by reference to important UK cases in a public order context.

→ Briefly discuss the relevance (or lack of relevance) of article 5 in a public order context.

Diagram plan

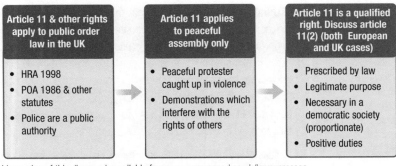

Article 11 & other rights apply to public order law in the UK	Article 11 applies to peaceful assembly only	Article 11 is a qualified right. Discuss article 11(2) (both European and UK cases)
• HRA 1998 • POA 1986 & other statutes • Police are a public authority	• Peaceful protester caught up in violence • Demonstrations which interfere with the rights of others	• Prescribed by law • Legitimate purpose • Necessary in a democratic society (proportionate) • Positive duties

A printable version of this diagram is available from www.pearsoned.co.uk/lawexpressqa

Answer

[1]Begin by demonstrating, briefly, your understanding of why it is that, because of the HRA 1998, Convention rights will set a basic standard.

[2]You will get credit for this point since it is all too easy just to focus on articles 10 or 11 in a public order context.

The police are a public authority and must exercise their powers compatibly with scheduled Convention rights (s 6 Human Rights Act 1998 (HRA 1998)) and their statutory powers must be interpreted, so far as possible, only to authorise actions which are thus compatible (s 3 HRA 1998).[1]

A number of Convention rights are relevant to the policing of public demonstrations.[2] Article 3 means that police tactics and actions must not be 'inhuman' or 'degrading' as these terms are defined by the courts. 'Treatment' by the authorities must also overcome a threshold of severity which will be set by reference to context. Likewise, any arrests or other deprivations of liberty must be compatible with article 5.

Rights of protest are likely to engage article 11 or article 10. Where the focus is on meetings and marches the ECtHR is likely to treat article 11 as the *lex specialis* and only considers article 10 if additional matters, usually individual expressive actions, arise (e.g. **Ezelin v France** (1992) 14 EHRR 362).[3] The broad definition of 'expression' in article 10 extends to political acts, as in **Steel v UK** (1999) 28 EHRR 603. Inspector Bannem will need to focus on article 11.

[3]You will impress with this point, again by avoiding a headlong rush to article 11. The Latin term is used by the ECtHR and so is appropriate.

Article 11(1) guarantees the right to 'peaceful' assembly.[4] Superintendent Bannem will have to bear in mind that organisers and participants who intend violent disorder do not enjoy the protection of article 11(1). Peaceful participants who get caught up in a demonstration that has turned violent, however, still enjoy its protection (**Ezelin**). Methods of policing that fail to separate the violent from the non-violent can be controversial. The right to assemble is an important necessity of a properly functioning democracy. Because of this a demonstration can still be 'peaceful' even if it involves interferences with the rights and freedoms of others, such as by obstruction of the highway (e.g. **MC v Germany**, app 13079/87, admissibility decision of 6 March 1989). The policing of such demonstrations then falls to be examined in terms of article 11(2).[5]

[4]Having identified article 11 as the principal Convention right in issue, you should now explore some of its terms. First consider the border between peaceful and non-peaceful demonstrations.

[5]You will get credit for this point, which is easily missed.

Article 11 is a qualified right. Interferences by police and others need to be justified under the terms of article 11(2).[6]

[6]Now move on to discuss the impact of article 11. There is no objection to considering the terms of article 11(2) in order since this is how the courts often approach the matter.

Interferences must be 'prescribed by law' which means, in particular, that the likely application of the rules must be foreseeable.[7] This depends on context and the ECtHR has accepted considerable discretion in the context of public order policing, though the laws should be expressed to ensure that their application is not based entirely on subjective opinion (e.g. **Chorherr v Austria** (1994) 17 EHRR 289; *cf* **Hashman v UK** (2000) 30 EHRR 241).[8] Superintendent Bannem's powers are based on statutory rules or on common law which, in the case of detaining to prevent an anticipated breach of the peace, has been subject to refinement through

[7]Use this term to show the examiner that you understand the requirements of 'law' under the Convention.

[8]You will get credit for stressing the contextual nature of the 'law' requirement but you will indicate you have read and understood the case law if you also make the objective basis point.

[9]Although you are not being tested on the detail of breach of the peace, it will give the examiner confidence if you show knowledge of the issues insisted upon by the UK courts – these matters helped to persuade the ECtHR that breach of the peace did not confer arbitrary powers on the police.

[10]In this context linking purpose and proportionality is perfectly OK – purpose is usually obvious.

[11]Although not necessarily part of a human rights course, if you can give outline information about the statutory provisions involved you will get credit. Sufficient information is available in the human rights case law.

[12]This is an important English case and you will get credit for showing your awareness of it both here and later in the answer.

[13]Take care with this point and explain that the duty is only to take reasonable steps and would be hard to enforce.

case law (**Steel**). In particular, English case law on breach of the peace requires the police to take the right of assembly into account.[9] Issues such as where responsibility lies for threats to order and whether people are acting legitimately and exercising a right, have to be considered when making their decisions. Police cannot merely adopt what seems, in the circumstances, the most convenient way to ensure public order. (See, for example, **Redmond-Bate v DPP** [2000] HRLR 249.)

Article 11(2) requires interferences to be for a legitimate purpose and proportionate. Actions in good faith by the police, which take into account the right of assembly and which are, in the circumstances, proportionate to the need to protect 'public order' and the 'rights of others'[10] (both listed in article 11(2)) are likely to be compatible with article 11. In domestic terms, it can be difficult for a court not to give great weight to the police's assessment of the need for the actions they have taken.

But proportionality is, ultimately, for the court to determine. A court must be satisfied that the interferences reflect a fair balance between the individual and public interests involved.

The notice requirement is based on s 11 Public Order Act 1986 (POA 1986).[11] Police are entitled to notice of a march from its organisers. It is not incompatible with article 11 for there to be provisions such as this, even when backed up by a penal sanction, because they enable the police to organise appropriate policing (**Ziliberberg v Moldova**, app 61821/00, judgment of 1 February 2005). This has been accepted regarding s 11 POA 1986 by the House of Lords in **R (Laporte) v Chief Constable of Gloucester** [2006] UKHL 55.[12]

Both POA 1986 and breach of the peace empower the police, in certain circumstances, to impose conditions on marchers. These must be applied proportionally and not in ways which undermine the right to peaceful assembly. Police need to take into account a positive duty to facilitate the right of peaceful assembly.[13] This is a duty to take reasonable steps. They should try, within what is reasonable, to ensure that a peaceful demonstration can go ahead. It should not be stopped, for example, simply because that is the easiest way of dealing with threats from a counter-demonstration (**Plattform Ärzte für das Leben v Austria** (1988) 13 EHRR 204). Furthermore, where a demonstration is peaceful, the police need to show some tolerance in their methods to ensure that they are not the cause of violence (**Nurettin v Turkey**, app 32124/02, judgment of 18 December 2007).

English courts have tended to emphasise that a proportionate approach is one in which restrictions are no more than necessary to achieve the purpose (**R (Daly) v Secretary of State for the Home Department** [2001] UKHL 26). Proportionality is fact-dependent and applied by the domestic courts. In **Laporte**, police acted to prevent an anticipated breach of the peace by stopping demonstrators reaching a military base. The House of Lords took article 11 into account and held that it was not enough for the police to act in this way just because they had reasonable grounds for believing violence might break out; the likely outbreak of violence had to be immediate. A proportionate approach is also likely to require the police to give adequate reasons for restrictions they impose on an assembly (**R (Brehony) v Chief Constable of Greater Manchester Police** [2005] EWHC 640).

In the course of controlling the policing, Superintendent Bannem may consider steps that involve restricting the movements of demonstrators by containing them in a particlar area of town. Such a policy was considered in **Austin v Commissioner of Police of the Metropolis** [2009] UKHL 5. The House of Lords held that good faith and proportionate actions taken to preserve public order did not involve a 'deprivation of liberty' and, therefore, did not breach article 5.[14]

[14]You will get credit for discussing this controversial case.

✓ Make your answer stand out

- Discuss in greater detail *Austin* and note Lord Hope's controversial approach to the effect that the application of any Convention right can depend upon purpose – thus whether there has been a deprivation of liberty was a matter of purpose rather than based on an assessment of circumstances. Not all the judges went all the way with Lord Hope on this point. For a comparison with *Laporte* in relation to the right of assembly in the context of political protest, see Fenwick (2009).

- Consider more exactly the way in which English courts have refined the common law on detention for anticipated breaches of the peace. As well as *Redmond-Bate*, consider *Laporte* (which has a full discussion of the law); *Percy* v *DPP* [1995] 3 All ER 124, QBD; *Nicol* and *Selvanayagam* v *DPP* (1996) 160 JP 155; and *Bibby* v *Chief Constable of Essex* (2000) 164 JP 297.

■ Mention briefly general police powers in the Police and Criminal Evidence Act 1984 and other statutes. The power of arrest and to stop and search can be exercised in a public order context. Indeed, the controversial random stop and search (under the Terrorism Act 2000) upheld in *Gillan* was in the context of a political demonstration.

! Don't be tempted to ...

■ Explore the Public Order Act 1986 in too much detail. The basic powers are given in the question and the issue is not what they are but the human rights principles with which the application of the powers must comply.

■ Discuss other areas of public order law which are not strictly relevant to police powers. There are important issues about, for example, land use and the right to use the highway for political meetings, but these are not relevant to the question and would not gain you credit.

? Question 4

The Secretary of State for the Home Department (Home Secretary) wishes to proscribe (ban) a militant Islamist political party, with offices in London, which she believes is fomenting violence in Iraq. Her lawyers correctly advise her that she has the power to do this under Part Two of the Terrorism Act 2000, which, again correctly, they say can be read and given effect in a way which is compatible with Convention rights. The organisation claims that it is simply trying to promote a radical form of Sharia law in Iraq and should not be blamed for the violence perpetrated by others.

The Secretary of State seeks your advice on the human rights principles which must guide the way in which she exercises her powers.

Advise her.

Answer plan

→ Introduce article 11 as the determinant right but note, in particular, its links with article 10.

→ Consider restrictions: are Home Secretary's actions prescribed by law?

→ Discuss proportionality, especially the concept of democracy inherent in the Convention and the importance of political parties and organisations.

> → Focus on the promotion of constitutional change against a background of violence and the border between mere offence, etc, and incitement to violence.
>
> → Discuss the justifications of proscribing an organisation because the ideas and policies it stands would, if implemented, violate human rights.

Diagram plan

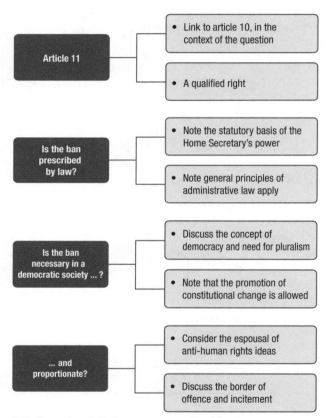

A printable version of this diagram is available from www.pearsoned.co.uk/lawexpressqa

Answer

The Home Secretary must exercise her powers compatibly with article 11. This guarantees a 'right to freedom of association'.

¹Having begun by identifying the Convention rights which will be the main focus of the question, you will get credit for pointing out the significance of other rights, especially article 10 which, in this context, governs the way article 11 is applied.

²A point such as this should win a mark or two because it shows you are aware of general ideas which underlie the Convention as a whole.

³This is a good phrase to learn and shows the examiner you have read some cases.

⁴This point will impress because it shows your awareness of common law principles relating to the exercise of executive power (you probably studied administrative law in your Constitutional and Administrative Law unit, which is a normal part of a law degree).

⁵You will get credit for showing knowledge of the terms of the Act in this regard.

Though not expressly mentioned, this includes the right to form, join and participate in political parties. Banning a political party also restricts freedom of expression guranteed under article 10 and can also interfere with the right to free elections in article 3 of the First Protocol.¹ Articles 10 and 11 aim at ensuring the plurality of public ideas and proper opportunities for debate which are essential for democracy; and democracy is the only political model that can sustain human rights.² Article 11 is, therefore, to be interpreted in the light of the requirements of article 10 (see, for example, **United Communist Party of Turkey v Turkey** (1998) 26 EHRR 121).

The fact that a party's policies, manifestos, actions, etc, may 'offend, shock or disturb'³ established or majority opinion is not enough to justify proscription. From earliest cases the ECtHR has insisted that articles 11(1) and 10(1) still offer protection in these circumstances. Justification for an interence requires futher effects on the rights of others, etc, or the needs of a democratic society.

Article 11, the main focus, is a qualified right and so justification for any interference with freedom of association must be consistent with the terms in article 11(2).

An interference must be 'prescribed by law'. The application of the power must be, given the context, foreseeable. In other words, the circumstances in which the power will be applied can, within appropriate limits, be foreseen by a person or his or her adviser. Here the power to proscribe is found in an Act of Parliament with detailed provisions. Furthermore, the proscription is an administrative act which, under general principles of administrative law, must be exercised lawfully – on relevant and not on irrelevant grounds, for example.⁴ The criterion of 'law' also means that the organisation must have access to an independent judicial body to test the lawfulness of the ban (a requirement reinforced if the matter involves the party's 'civil rights' and hence engages article 6). Under the Terrorism Act 2000 a special tribunal (the Proscribed Organisations Appeal Commission) hears such cases⁵ (**R (Kurdistan Workers Party) v Secretary of State for the Home Department** [2002] EWHC 644). The right of access to a court will be satisfied so long as any use of closed material can be adequately compensated for by countervailing measures.

[6]Even if you are allowed the Convention text with you in the exam, it is worthwhile remembering all or some of the purposes in the second paragraphs of articles 8–11 (though they are all slightly different). If all else fails, at least remember 'rights and freedoms of others', which is virtually common (article 10 does not say 'freedoms of others') and nearly always relevant.

[7]Proportionality is pervasive and it is always difficult to deal in general terms with a concept that places attention on the particular. Nevertheless, you will show your understanding of the topic if you can introduce and discuss some general principles that emerge from the cases.

[8]Using the phrase gives confidence in your familiarity with the Convention.

[9]Now move on to the issue of the protection available to radical political parties seeking major constitutional changes – this is clearly the focus of the question.

[10]Make sure you discuss this point – try to identify some general themes which indicate whether or not the border with incitement to violence has been crossed.

The ban must be for a purpose in article 11(2). These include 'national security', 'public safety' and the 'rights and freedoms of others',[6] so there is unlikely to be an issue on this ground.

The main focus of human rights law concern is on the proportionality of the ban. Restrictions on freedom of association must be 'necessary in a democratic society'. As always, this involves a consideration of the specific issues and context in the case. There are some general points that can be made.[7]

Proscription of other interference must be consistent with the conception of 'democracy' inherent in the Convention. There is no express theory of democracy found in the Convention but the ECtHR identifies 'pluralism, tolerance and broadmindedness'[8] as hallmarks (e.g. **Leyla Sahin v Turkey** (2007) 44 EHRR 5). Political parties have an essential role to play in ensuring the pluralism necessary for an effective democracy (e.g. **United Communist Party**). There is a presumption in favour of democracy, therefore restrictions on freedom of association need convincing and compelling reasons.

Proportionality requires a consideration of the actions, not just the words, of a political party. Thus, in the **United Communist Party** case the party was banned largely on its words rather than its actions and this was partly the basis of the breach of article 11.

Political parties must be free to promote constitutional change, including separatism.[9] The only conditions that a state can insist upon are that the party act lawfully and consistently with democracy. Thus, in **Tsonev v Bulgaria** (2008) 46 EHRR 8, the refusal to register a party, which campaigned within the law but expressed its aims as revolutionary, was a breach of article 11.

The promotion of constitutional change can be done lawfully even in the context of political violence by others (as in **United Communist Party**). What political parties cannot do is promote or incite violence. Whether there is an incitement or not depends on the circumstances and not just the words used.[10] Furthermore, the focus of concern must be on words or actions attributable to the party itself and not just to individual members or others. Above all, a court scrutinising party policies, etc, will need to be concerned with the likely impact on others – whether the threat is sufficiently severe to be dealt with by proscription (see, for example, **Partidul Comunistilor v Romania** (2007) 44 EHRR 17).

Radical parties should not be seeking to impose laws and policies which would create a society that would undermine democracy and human rights. Where proscription is proportionate to such a threat it will be compatible with article 11. Thus, in **Refah Partisi v Turkey** (2003) 37 EHRR 1 a Grand Chamber upheld Turkey's ban on an Islamicist party which, if in power, would seek to impose Sharia law. The Chamber found that significant elements of Sharia law were incompatible with human rights. Success in an election meant that the party was capable of being part of a coalition government and states, under article 11(2), are entitled to take pre-emptive action in order to preserve a state's democratic and rights-respecting character.[11]

[11]*Refah Partisi* is a very controversial case, which you will get credit for discussing.

In such circumstances, article 17 would allow a court to hold that the party was seeking to assert its rights in order to abuse the rights of others.[12] But this involves refusing to deal with the issues and the ECtHR usually prefers to apply article 11 (or 10) in the ways indicated above.

[12]Examiners are impressed if you show you have the Convention as a whole in mind and can spot the relevance of articles even though they are not the main focus of the question.

Thus the Home Secretary can use her proscription powers if she can satisfy a court that the organisation is inciting violence and a ban is proportionate to the threat.[13] If the facts disclose merely that the organisation is pursuing policies offensive to the majority, then the ban is likely to violate article 11. The Home Secretary could argue that she is taking pre-emptive action to prevent the imposition of Sharia law in Iraq. If so, this is clearly an issue of proportionality. Sharia law would not be imposed in the UK. Also, unlike in **Refah Partisi**, the organisation is not in power in Iraq. Lack of support is a relevant factor which weighs against a claim that proscription is proportionate (e.g. **Stankov v Bulgaria** app 29221/95, judgment of 2 October 2001).

[13]Conclude your answer by applying the general principles identified earlier to the issues in the question.

✓ Make your answer stand out

■ Discuss more fully the concept of democracy that the ECtHR has found in the Convention. Academic writings include Marks (1995), Mowbray (1999) and Gearty (2000). But be careful, the critics are mainly concerned with the lack of principles aimed at promoting and enabling political participation rather than how to deal with anti-democratic organisations and expressions.

■ Say more on the border of incitement and simply offensive words and actions. The matter is dealt with largely through proportionality and is very fact and context

▶

dependent. The ECtHR has not really worked out a broad doctrine on the matter. Whether it could is doubtful (compare the US Supreme Court's 'clear and present danger' test, which has needed to be profoundly revised if not rejected). A number of free speech cases involving Turkey provide insight into how the ECtHR judges whether the border has been crossed (see Davis, 2005).

■ Explore *Refah Partisi* a bit more. This is a profoundly controversial case because it involved the ECtHR upholding a ban on a party which had triumphed in an election. Its attitude towards Sharia law is also interesting. A case comment is given by Olbourne (2003). The case involves 'militant democracy' – see Harvey (2004).

! Don't be tempted to ...

■ Write a lot on the HRA 1998. The fact that the proscription power in the Terrorism Act 2000 is capable of being read and given effect compatibly with article 11 is given in the question.

■ Write much on the Terrorism Act 2000 and, in particular, the proscription power generally. You are told in the question that it is possible to exercise it compatibly with Convention rights.

■ Confuse 'proscription', which means prohibiting or banning with 'prescription', which means requiring something. The question is about proscribing a party which can only be done if it is prescribed by law.

📷 Question 5

Discuss the extent to which article 9 ECHR guarantees a right to manifest beliefs in ways that involve seeking exemption from what would otherwise be a requirement or legal obligation.

Answer plan

→ Introduce article 9, as a qualified right, in general terms.

→ Discuss general features of article 9 such as the way important terms are defined.

→ Consider some important Strasbourg cases in which these principles have been applied.

→ Apply to UK cases, noting that relevant regulations have to be interpreted compatibly with article 9.

→ Discuss issues relevant to justification, especially proportionality.

Diagram plan

Introduce article 9	General features	Apply to conscientious exemption cases
• Freedom of belief, etc. • Manifestation as a qualified right • Importance in a democracy	• Definitions • Minimal need to respect human dignity • Distinguish manifestation from motivation	• ECtHR cases • UK cases (standards to be met by EU and other regulations) • Note issues on which proportionality may turn

A printable version of this diagram is available from www.pearsoned.co.uk/lawexpressqa

Answer

[1] Since the question expressly refers to article 9, it is useful to begin with a general outline and discussion of the article. Quote crucial phrases and ensure you show it covers more than just religion.

Claims of conscientious exemption from general obligations on grounds of belief will engage article 9. Article 9 guarantees a right to freedom of 'thought, conscience and religion' which includes a right to change a religious or other belief and also a right to 'manifest' religion or belief in 'worship, teaching, practice and observance'.[1]

[2] You should get credit for this point because it shows you are alive to the range and significance of other rights – in this case the generally applicable ancillary rights.

The rights to hold and change beliefs are absolute, in the sense that they cannot be limited to protect the rights of others or pressing social needs (though they can be derogated from under article 15 and cannot be used to abuse the rights of others under article 17).[2] The right to manifest religion or belief, by contrast, is qualified. It

[3] You demonstrate your understanding of the general issues by not only listing the conditions for limitation but also indicating you understand what those conditions, broadly speaking, imply.

is not a breach of article 9 for a state to impose or allow limitations on belief which are prescribed by law (including that they are foreseeable in their application and non-arbitrary in effect), for a legitimate purpose (these are listed in article 9(2) and include the protection of the rights and freedoms of others) and 'necessary in a democratic society' (the limitation meets a pressing social need in a proportionate way which reflects a fair balance of interests).[3]

[4] Having introduced article 9 generally, move on to 'manifestations' of belief, which are the point of the question.

Belief-based claims for exception are likely to relate to manifestations of belief.[4] In other words, the law or practice complained of or the refusal to allow exception will normally be seen as an interference which requires justification.[5]

[5] Make sure you express this point – there is no breach of article 9 unless there is an interference.

The ECtHR recognises that respecting people's beliefs is of vital importance in an effective democracy. It indicates the genuine

[6]You will get credit for noticing the two broad justifications: one relating to the general nature of society and the other to the subjective needs of individuals.

pluralism which should characterise such a society, and so links article 9 to article 11, freedom of association (**Metropolitan Church of Bessarabia v Moldova** (2002) 35 EHRR 13). Beliefs, religious or otherwise, are also of subjective importance to the individual and to his or her sense of identity (**Sahin v Turkey** (2007) 44 EHRR 5).[6] It follows that any limitations will need careful scutiny by a court (in English law terms, limitations must be proportionate and not merely within a range of reasonable restrictions). These general principles are adopted into UK law in, for example, **R (Williamson) v Secretary of State for Education and Employment** [2005] UKHL 15.

Religion or belief is widely defined. As well as the principal world religions, the religious nature of other beliefs, such as Druidism and Rastafarianism, are accepted. Non-religious beliefs include pacifism (**Arrowsmith v UK** (1981) 3 EHRR 218) and could include vegetarianism and temperance (**Williamson**). In a UK case (**Grainger v Nicholson** [2010] ICR 360) views on climate change were accepted as a 'philosophical belief' (although this was in the context of the Employment Equality (Religion or Belief) Regulations 2002, the article 9 jurisprudence was taken into account).[7]

[7]It is important that you show you understand that protection for beliefs arises in other contexts, especially employment regulations; in fact, these may be more commonly used than article 9 directly.

[8]You will get credit for making this point but also for pointing out the difficulty it raises regarding the neutrality of the state.

[9]The overlap with article 9, although not the main point of the question, is nevertheless a point worth making – it shows you do not over-compartmentalise your understanding of human rights law.

There is some evidence that the beliefs manifested must reach some minimum requirement of seriousness and they need to be consistent with basic human dignity which is upheld by the Convention overall.[8]

The ECtHR has suggested this when considering a state's duty to take parents' religious and philosophical convictions into account when providing education (article 2 of the First Protocol).[9] The approach is followed in English courts (e.g. **Grainger**, following **Williamson**). This approach must be treated with great care: indeed, in **Williamson** Lord Walker found it alarming. It is at most a minimum standard to prevent the abuse of rights. Otherwise, any assessment by a court of the reasonableness of a belief would come into tension with the duty of states to be neutral and protective of pluralism (**Sahin**).

Manifestation of belief involves an outward and visible sign which is intimately connected with the belief. It is distinguished from actions which are merely motivated by belief. Thus, in **Arrowsmith**, the distribution of leaflets urging soldiers not to serve in Northern Ireland did not manifest a belief, and neither did a claim, based on Quaker

[10]This is an important point
which illustrates the limits
to claims to be manifesting
beliefs and if you can
illustrate from both European
and English case law you will
get credit.

[11]This is the leading ECtHR
case and should be
discussed.

[12]Having established the
general principles under
article 9 and some basic
Strasbourg case law, now
move on to discuss the
developing case law in
England and the UK.

[13]This is a leading case under
the HRA 1998 and should be
discussed. You will get credit
for discussing some of the
important points on which the
decision turned.

[14]You will earn marks for
seeing the distinction between
employees and officials who
(though they may be treated
as employees) also have
public duties to perform on
which others rely.

belief, to pay a portion of income tax into a fund which could not
be used for weaponry (**R (Broughton) v Her Majesty's Treasury**
[2005] EWHC 1914).[10]

These general principles have been applied to claims for religious
and belief-based exceptions. In **Sahin** the ECtHR upheld Turkey's
ban on university students wearing headscarves. Important matters
of proportionality were Turkey's principle of secularism and the care
taken over deciding the policy. This meant it was not arbitrary or an
expression of bigotry.[11]

Under the Human Rights Act 1998 (HRA 1998),[12] the House of Lords
upheld a school rule allowing Muslim girls to wear the shalwar
kameez but not, as the claimant wished, the jilbab (**R (Begum) v
Denbigh High School Governors** [2006] UKHL 15).[13] The ban was
prescribed by law – the rules had been carefully considered and
confirmed with religious leaders. Also it was for a legitimate purpose,
including preventing harassment. Finally the ban was proportionate
in the claimant's case; there were, for example, other schools
available to her which would accept the jilbab. In **R (Watkins-
Singh) v Aberdare School** [2008] EWHC 1865, on the other hand
(a case brought under the Race Relations Act 1976), the banning
by a school of wearing a Kara (a plain bangle with significance for
Hindus) was, on the facts, disproportionate. In particular, it was a
much less visible manifestation than in **Begum**.

Issues of conscientious exemption also arise at work where, for
example, employers require employees to work on a sabbath. Here,
article 9 may not directly apply since there is no express right to work
in the Convention. Strasbourg cases embody the rather unrealistic
assumption that employment is voluntary and so employees are free
to leave and avoid onerous requirements (**Stedman v UK** (1997)
23 EHRR CD 168). Issues in the UK are most likely to arise under
employment regulations (as in **Grainger**, above). These need to be
interpreted compatibly with Convention rights (s 3 HRA 1998) even
when dealing with private employer–employee relations.

Officials may seek exemption from public duties which they believe
are inconsistent with their beliefs.[14] Where the relevant equality
legislation allows the imposition complained of, UK courts must
ensure that it is, nevertheless, consistent with article 9. In **Ladele v
Islington LBC** [2009] EWCA Civ 1357, a registrar was disciplined

and threatened with dismissal for refusing to register civil partnerships. The Court of Appeal considered the relevant regulations in the light of the qualified nature of article 9. Issues going to proportionality included that the claimant's views on marriage were not core to her beliefs and they could not outweigh the fact that she was a public official and that Islington had a proper desire to ensure its public services were provided without discrimination.

[15]Now conclude your answer by trying to embody the general effect of the ideas and cases you have discussed.

Though article 9 protects religious manifestation, its qualified nature means that restrictions imposed carefully, which aim to protect the rights of others and which are not expressions of bigotry, are likely to be upheld.[15]

 Make your answer stand out

■ Consider a wider range of cases on religious and other forms of belief. Recent cases in 2010 are surveyed in Leach and Fallon (2010). Remember, though, that these often tend to arise in the context of regulations (such as the Employment Equality (Religion or Belief) and (Sexual Orientation) Regulations 2003. They have to be related to the anti-discrimination provisions in the Equality Act 2010 (see McColgan, 2009).

■ Say a bit more about the operation of article 2 of the First Protocol. It has given rise to some important cases on belief-based exceptions claims, in particular *Campbell and Cosans* v *UK* (1982) 4 EHRR 293.

■ Be more explicit on the issues in the *Williamson* case. It involved a claim by Christian parents and schools to be exempt from the ban on the use of corporal punishment in all schools in the UK. Following *Campbell and Cosans* a majority of the House of Lords accepted that this was a manifestation of belief.

! Don't be tempted to ...

■ Write too much on the ethical or philosophical issues. These are important and interesting but you need to ensure you focus on the legal points the question asks you to address.

■ Spend much time, if any, discussing theological points on, for example, whether the best account of Islam requires women to wear a certain sort of dress. Article 9 guarantees respect for people to manifest their belief in ways they see as appropriate, not in ways that are in some sense objectively true.

■ Write too much about other legal rights to religious freedom and non-discrimination. This is an area where there has been a lot of change.

First Protocol rights

How this topic may come up in exams

Any of the three areas in the First Protocol could generate essay or problem questions. Article 1 questions are likely to focus on the structural approach of the European Court of Human Rights (the three 'rules') and the issues of proportionality and compensation. Property cases can involve fair hearing issues under article 6. Article 2 questions are likely to focus on parental rights, which is an issue that can overlap with article 9. Article 3 relates to issues about elections. There is plenty of UK case law, so expect HRA 1998 questions as well as ones based on Strasbourg case law.

■ Attack the question

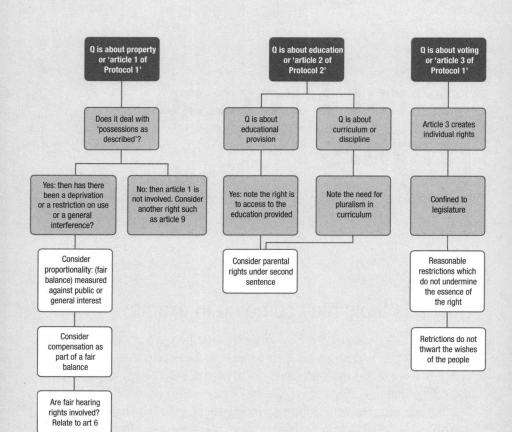

Question 1

Explain the way the European Court of Human Rights (ECtHR) has interpreted the right to peaceful enjoyment of possessions (article 1 of the First Protocol) and discuss the extent to which, if at all, the article prevents states pursuing social and economic policies from taking over ownership, or restricting the use, of private property.

Answer plan

→ Introduce article 1 and describe the three 'rules'.

→ Discuss the definition of possessions.

→ Discuss the Court's approach to interferences: lawfulness and legitimate purpose.

→ Focus on proportionality in relation to the text of article 1.

→ Discuss the application of proportionality to interferences done in pursuit of social policy.

Diagram plan

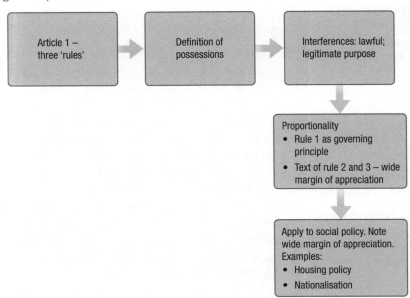

Article 1 – three 'rules' → Definition of possessions → Interferences: lawful; legitimate purpose

Proportionality
- Rule 1 as governing principle
- Text of rule 2 and 3 – wide margin of appreciation

Apply to social policy. Note wide margin of appreciation. Examples:
- Housing policy
- Nationalisation

A printable version of this diagram is available from www.pearsoned.co.uk/lawexpressqa

Answer

[1]Start by indicating the different perspectives on property as a right – it indicates why protection of property is in Protocol 1 but also prepares the ground for discussing the social policy part of the question.

[2]This basic approach of the Court needs to be noticed; it also enables you to structure your answer.

[3]Try to remember the important phrases from the text of article 1. It enables you to introduce significant concepts (like 'possessions').

[4]Try to give examples of 'deprivation' and also, later, 'control' – it shows you are familiar with the case law.

Article 1 of the First Protocol (article 1) is a right to the 'protection of property'. Delays in agreeing the text (which caused it to be in the First Protocol) reflected a basic tension between the idea of property as an expression of personality and as an expression of economic power[1] (nationalisation was a policy of the UK government at the time).

ECtHR has applied article 1 of the First Protocol on the basis of three related rules.[2] Rule 1 expresses the basic principle of a person's entitlement to the 'peaceful enjoyment of his possessions'.[3] Rule 2 refers to deprivation of property. This can refer to a full transfer of ownership rights and includes, for example, nationalisation, or where a sale of property is required by tax authorities (**Hentrich v France** (1994) 18 EHRR 440) or the law compels the sale of freehold from one private owner to another (**James v UK** (1986) 8 EHRR 123).[4] Rule 3 relates to laws and actions which 'control the use of property'. These include planning and development control as well as direct control over use, as in **Chassagnou v France** (2000) 29 EHRR 615. Seizure and forfeiture of property (e.g. by Customs) is normally considered as a control of use because it does not involve a full transfer of rights; likewise, obtaining title through adverse possession under English land law (**Pye v UK** (2008) 46 EHRR 45).

'Possessions' is given a wide definition. It includes money and rights over land and goods; also rights over other things of value such as licences, intellectual property rights or a right to practise a profession. There is no right to acquire possessions in the future (e.g. inheritance of property: **Marckx v Belgium** (1979–80) 2 EHRR 330). However, article 1 does protect a legitimate expectation to possessions such as a right to bring a tort action for damages which was retrospectively removed by legislation (**Pressos Compania**

[5]You need to give examples of the meaning of 'possessions' and reference to the recent case law on welfare payments shows you are up to date. But make sure you refer to a clear existing right and do not suggest there is a right to a benefit which a state has not chosen to provide.

Naviera SA v Belgium (1996) 4 EHRR 301). Pensions and welfare payments are accepted as 'possessions'. A distinction between contributory benefits (which have similarities with contract-based commercial insurance) and non-contributory benefits (based on statute) no longer applies; a clear, existing, statutory right to a benefit is a possession (**Stec v UK** (2005) 41 EHRR SE18).[5]

Interferences with the enjoyment of possessions (engaging any of the three rules) must be justified on the basis not only of the

[6]Show you understand that 'law' is an autonomous concept and that it requires non-arbitrary, accessible and foreseeable rules and principles. You do not need to embark on a long discussion but can illustrate your knowledge through your example.

[7]Now move on to discuss legitimate purpose. It is here that you can best discuss the broad terminology found in respect at least of rule 2 and rule 3.

[8]Sensitivity to the different standards regarding judicial tests for compatibility with Convention rights will get you credit. Of particular importance is to communicate the idea that the nature of the test controls the degree of supervision allowed to the Court.

[9]Make sure you use the term. It is not necessary to explain its meaning – which is obvious from the context.

[10]It is vital to make this point and, also, to refer to *Sporrong* since it is the seminal case on article 1.

text of article 1 but also the general principles which pervade the Convention. This includes rule 3, despite its 'nothing shall prevent' formulation.

In particular, interferences must be lawful, under the autonomous conception of law. They must not permit arbitrary actions. In **Hentrich**, for instance, the application of the power of the authorities to force a sale of property was too discretionary and so not foreseeable.[6]

Likewise, any interference must also be for a legitimate purpose.[7] Rule 2 expressly allows interferences which are 'in the public interest', and, rule 3, interferences which a state deems necessary for the 'general interest'. These are clearly broad terms which do not impose an objective necessity test for the court to determine, as with 'necessary in a democratic society' regarding articles 8–11.[8] The ECtHR, therefore, allows a wide margin of appreciation[9] to states over the policies needed to give effect to their public or general interests.

At the heart of interpretation is proportionality. Despite their different wording, the ECtHR requires rule 2 and rule 3 to be applied in the light of the general principle, peaceful enjoyment, in rule 1 (e.g. **Broniowski v Poland** (2005) 40 EHRR 21). Rule 1 of itself is in issue where there is an interference but not a deprivation or restriction of use. It follows from the pervasive character of rule 1 that any interference with possessions is only justified if proportionate. In **Sporrong v Sweden** (1982) 5 EHRR 35 the ECtHR defined this as the court satisfying itself that a 'fair balance' had been reached between an individual's rights and the public or general good pursued.[10] But proportionality involves a fair balance measured against the public and general interest standard and so the wide margin of appreciation on these matters will inform the approach. This is likely to transpose into a significant degree of deference by a domestic court in the UK for the judgements of the authorities (e.g. **R (Alconbury) v Secretary of State for the Environment, Transport and the Regions** [2001] UKHL 23).

Proportionality is fact dependent. Examples of interferences which, despite the wide margin of appreciation, have been found to be disproportionate are damaging delays in planning procedures (**Sporrong**), retrospective interferences by the legislature with a

[11]There are many cases but you will get credit for illustrations. So prepare one or two examples of breaches under all three rules when revising.

[12]You will get credit for demonstrating the need for procedures and showing a non-compartmentalised view of the Convention by referring to article 6.

court judgment (**Pressos***)* and controlling use by giving rights to others to use the land in a way that the owner finds unconscionable (**Chassagnou**).[11]

People are entitled to fair judicial procedures relating to interferences with their property. Procedural failures, such as lack of effective access to a court, can contribute to the proportionality issue but are as likely to be dealt with under article 6(1), as in **Sporrong**.[12]

Article 1 has not been used to supress policies which interfere with property in order to pursue economic and social policies. Thus, for example, housing policy, which may cause loss of value to landowners, is likely to survive an article 1 challenge. In **Mellacher v Austria** (1990) 12 EHRR 391 the ECtHR held that, given the wide margin of appreciation regarding rule 3, it would only find a breach if the policy was 'manifestly without reasonable foundation'. This still leaves the Court assessing the reasons for social policy albeit against a low threshold of compatibility. Specifically it was accepted that interference with contracts could be compatible with article 1 if justified by reasonable social objectives. In **James** the Court allowed leasehold reform laws on similar grounds.

Nationalisation (involving deprivation of possessions) is also likely to be compatible with the Convention so long as the grounds are not wholly without foundation. Article 1 is mostly engaged in respect of compensation. This must be reasonably related to the value of the assets but compensation at less than market value may be acceptable (**Lithgow**). Similar principles were followed in the UK case: **SRM Global Master Fund LP v Commissioners of Her Majesty's Treasury** [2009] EWCA Civ 788 where the Court of Appeal upheld the government's system for determining compensation for 'nationalising' Northern Rock, even though it foreseeably left shareholders with nothing.

A government's social and economic policies are likely to survive an article 1 challenge if they pursue purposes which are not wholly unreasonable. Proportionality is likely to be satisfied because of the wide margin of appreciation allowed given the references to the public and general interest in the text.

✓ **Make your answer stand out**

■ Discuss international law a little – it is expressly referred to in the text. Its main impact has been in respect of compensation.

■ Refer to corporate rights. You could note that article 1 contains the only express reference to 'legal', in contrast to 'natural', persons.

■ Refer to some of the other purposes, accepted by the ECtHR as being in the public or general interest, which can justify interferences with possession. The prevention of crime is a good example. There are a number of cases often involving confiscation and forfeiture and thus engaging rule 3.

■ Say more on compensation. Note that compensation reasonably related to value is normally (other than exceptionally) essential if a deprivation of property is to be a proportionate interference under rule 2 (deprivations). There is much more discretion available for a state under rule 3 (interference with use).

! **Don't be tempted to ...**

■ Write too much on the broad question, rooted in political theory, on whether there is or ought to be a human right to property or whether the arguments in favour of positive rights to property are essentially utilitarian arguments based on economic efficiency. Likewise, don't explore the rights and wrongs of the social policy arguments. The only relevance of such discussion would be to show that such policies are without rational foundation – a more radical criticism than merely pointing out that the policies may be politically or economically controversial. These are interesting topics but you have to stay with the question.

■ Fail to distinguish the proportionality test under article 1 with proportionality under other articles. Of course there are links but the text of article 1 (referring to the government's view of public and general interest and the negative formulation of rule 3) creates a different standard from 'necessary in a democratic society'.

? Question 2

(a) Billy is a pupil at Blue School, a UK school. A fellow pupil makes an allegation of serious bullying against Billy. The headteacher follows statutory procedures and excludes him. Billy is offered part-time teaching at home for three hours each week. He rejects this and, instead, brings a case under the Human Rights Act 1998 (HRA 1998) alleging a breach of article 2 of the First Protocol.

(b) Sally, also a pupil at Blue School, is required to take lessons on protecting the environment. Teaching is based on the assumption that man-made global warming is true. Sally's parents are climate change sceptics and wish to withdraw her from the classes. The headteacher refuses. Sally's parents make a challenge under the HRA 1998, alleging their rights under article 2 of the First Protocol have been violated.

Discuss the general principles which will govern the way the High Court will apply article 2 when dealing with these two cases.

Answer plan

→ In Billy's case, introduce the first sentence of article 2 of the First Protocol (article 2).

→ Discuss the point that it is a right of access to the education that is provided by the state.

→ Consider whether article 2 protects against exclusion from school and apply to the facts in Billy's case.

→ In Sally's case introduce and discuss the second sentence of article 2 and identify the nature of the right it introduces.

→ Continue with Sally's case by considering whether parental views on the environment and, specifically, climate change denial, are likely to be appropriate for protection under article 2.

Diagram plan

Billy

Article 2 – applies via HRA 1998

First sentence: right to education

Just a right to education system that exists

No right not to be excluded in article 2

UK case law – general principles and leading cases

Sally

Article 2 – applies via HRA 1998

Second sentence: parental rights

What is meant by philosophical convictions?

Relate to curriculum issues and need for impartiality in education

Apply to environmental views and climate change denial, specifically

A printable version of this diagram is available from www.pearsoned.co.uk/lawexpressqa

Answer

The powers of a headteacher, in the UK, will be found in statutes which must be interpreted (if possible) for compatibility with Convention rights (s 3 HRA 1998). The headteacher and others in authority will be a public authority (**A v Head Teacher and Governors of Lord Grey School** [2006] UKHL 14), and so must act compatibly (unless statute requires otherwise) with Convention rights (s 6 HRA 1998).[1]

[1]This question is expressly dealing with Convention rights in UK law, so begin by showing how they apply under the terms of the HRA 1998.

Article 2 of the First Protocol says that 'no person shall be denied the right to education'. The basic analysis in **Belgian Linguistics** (1979–80) 1 EHRR 252, however, makes it clear that, despite the negative fomulation, article 2 protects individual rights.[2] These are only rights of access to the education that the state is willing to provide, not rights to education where, otherwise, none has been provided. It is now clear that it extends to all levels of education including university (**Sahin v Turkey** (2007) 44 EHRR 5). A complete absence of any educational provision might be a breach. States may choose the education system appropriate to their needs and regulate it accordingly.[3] These regulations must, however, be compatible with other Convention rights (such as article 9, freedom of belief) and the education system must not discriminate under article 14.

[2]Because of s 2 HRA 1998, you will be expected to show knowledge of the basic principles in the Strasbourg case law; make sure you refer to *Belgian Linguistics* since it is the leading case.

[3]It is important to stress the limited role of article 2 in mandating any particular level of educational provision; this point also, of course, assists you in the second part of the question.

Exclusion from school is not in itself a violation of article 2. This has been said by the House of Lords in **A**, citing **Eren v Turkey** (2006) 44 EHRR 619. The only exception could be where no alternative educational provision is made available.

The general principles, above, were adopted in **A**.[4] Here a pupil was excluded, alternative provision was made available and it was his own actions that delayed his return to education. There was no breach of article 2. If the authorities have behaved reasonably, there is unlikely to be a breach of article 2 (**A v Essex CC** [2008] EWCA Civ 364). In **Re Application of JR17** [2010] UKSC 27, the Supreme Court, following **A**, held that an alleged bully was unlawfully excluded because the relevant regulations had not been properly applied, but there was not a breach of article 2. There is no right to be allowed to stay in school, there was not a total denial of education since eight hours per week of alternative provision had been made available, and the question of the standard of this education, above a minimum, was not a relevant issue under article 2.[5]

[4]Make sure you mention *A* – it is the leading case on school exclusion and article 2 and you would be expected to refer to it.

[5]You will impress the examiner by reference to recent cases which build on *A*, especially where they have Supreme Court authority.

[6]Try to draw a conclusion, based on what you have written, to the first part.

[7]Now move on to the second part of the question. It will help your cause if you can briefly summarise what the second sentence of article 2 says. Quotation would just take up space and not get credit (especially if you are allowed a statute book).

[8]You will get credit for emphasising this word. It shows that you are aware of the significance of the text of the Convention in setting the standard of human rights protection.

[9]The question clearly wants you to consider the nature of parental 'beliefs' that can be accommodated by article 2, so move on to discuss the pluralistic notion of education presumed by the Convention.

[10]Given the focus on the curriculum in the question, it is important that you mention this, the leading case.

[11]But you will also get credit for more recent cases.

In Billy's case, therefore, there is unlikely to be a violation of article 2.[6] It is, however, possible that the provision of only three hours a week of alternative tuition was below the minimum required as a reasonable response by the education authority. In **JR17** Baroness Hale was sceptical that eight hours was sufficient.

The second sentence of article 2 requires states to take necessary steps to 'respect' the 'religious and philosophical beliefs' of parents when providing education.[7] 'Respect' implies something more than merely being taken into account.[8]

These parental rights, however, can be restricted in proportionate ways in order to ensure they are exercised only in ways that are compatible with the right to education. Such education must be more than indoctrination into orthodoxy.[9] In a democratic society education needs to recognise pluralism and diversity, although the Convention does not require any particular syllabus. Respect for parental convictions cannot mean that a child can be denied education of this character (**Campbell v UK** (1982) 4 EHRR 293). Likewise, it is only convictions that are worthy of respect in a democratic society, reach a sufficient standard of coherence and reasonableness, and are not incompatible with human dignity, that need to be considered. So some degree of judicial evaluation of beliefs is inherent in the application of this provision (a view of the judicial role that Lord Walker found 'alarming' in **R (Williamson) v Secretary of State for Education and Employment** [2005] UKHL 15). An inclusive approach is taken to the idea of religious or philosophical 'convictions'. It includes, for example, parental beliefs about punishment.

Sally's parents are concerned with the curriculum. The concept of education means that they are not able to insist upon a curriculum that is not reasonably diverse and pluralist in its scope. Nor can parents object to controversial and sensitive subjects being taught, so long as the approach is balanced and ethically neutral or at least not merely doctrinaire. In **Kjeldsen v Denmark** (1976) 1 EHRR 711 a group of parents objected to compulsory sex education. The European Court of Human Rights (ECtHR) found that there was no violation of article 2 because the pedagogic approach was aimed at giving information and was neutral on ethical matters.[10] In **Folgero v Norway** (2008) 46 EHRR 47,[11] on the other hand, the ECtHR found a breach of article 2 in the case of humanist parents who objected to the Christian ethos of a compulsory course on Christianity, Religion and Philosophy in Norwegian schools. By a 9–8 majority, a Grand Chamber held that the course failed the tests of appropriate neutrality in a pluralist environment. Furthermore, the provision in the law, allowing parents to exempt their children, itself raised issues under the Convention since it required parents to disclose too much about their own beliefs to officials.

[12]Now apply your discussion of the law to the question.

In Sally's parents' case, a court must be satisfied that climate change scepticism is a belief for the purpose of article 2.[12] Beliefs about the environment are likely to be included (in **Grainger v Nicholson** [2010] ICR 360 such views were accepted as beliefs for the purpose of discrimination in employment). Liikewise, a judge might find it a challenge to his or her own judicial impartiality to say that climate change scepticism was sufficiently incoherent and irrational to fall outside the protection of article 2. However, there will only be a breach if these views are not adequately respected. Sally's parents will not benefit from article 2 if the course and its delivery are sufficiently impartial and pluralist and, if necessary, give space to the sceptic position in some way. UK education law requires a non-partisan approach[13] and in **R (Dimmock) v Secretary of State for Education and Science** [2007] EWHC 2288 it was held that this had been fulfilled when *An Inconvenient Truth* (a film which warns against man-made climate change) was distributed. This case was not decided directly under the HRA 1998.[14]

[13]You will do well if you can relate these matters to UK or at least English education law and the general principle of impartiality found therein.

[14]Even so, the case is so relevant to the facts of the question that you will impress if you mention it.

[15]You will get credit for mentioning the Reservation and relating to the HRA 1998; but don't overstate the point since its impact is not clear.

The government's case may be strengthened by the Reservation to the parental convictions provision.[15] This limits UK liability to parental wishes which are compatible with 'efficient instruction and training and the avoidance of unreasonable public expenditure'. Section 1(2) HRA 1998 makes it clear that UK Reservations limit the application of Convention rights in domestic law, too.

 Make your answer stand out

■ Discuss the scope of 'convictions' for the purpose of article 2. The 'corporal punishment' cases can be useful. In *Campbell*, it was accepted that deeply held views on corporal punishment were protected by article 2. Failure to exempt the applicant's children was a breach. This view was adopted, under the HRA 1998, in *Williamson*, where the facts were the other way around. The case was brought by Christian parents and schools, for whom corporal punishment was seen as a necessary element of proper discipline. Here, though, the House of Lords held that there was no violation since the statutory ban was a proportionate limit on parental rights.

■ Discuss the Reservation more critically. Reservations can be adopted under article 57. However, their validity depends upon their being sufficiently certain and precise on what they do and on what provision of domestic law they protect from Convention scrutiny (see, for example, *Belilos* v *Switzerland* (1988) 10 EHRR 466). In *SP* v *UK* (1997) 23 EHRR CD 139 the Commission (which until 1998, dealt with admissibility) questioned whether the UK's Reservation concerning article 2 might not have these qualities).

■ Draw some parallels with article 9, freedom of thought, conscience and religion. The link with parental beliefs in the second sentence of article 2 is commonly made. On a strictly educational matter, article 2 is likely to be the *lex specialis*.

! Don't be tempted to ...

■ Write solely in terms of Convention rights and cases. Try to ensure you show knowledge of English/UK cases as well, such as *Williamson, A* and *JR17*.

■ Express your own views on religious and ethical education, interesting though they may be. The question is exploring your knowledge of Convention case law on article 2 and some of the UK cases which have received it into UK law under the HRA 1998.

📰 Question 3

Explain the origins, nature and extent of a right to vote found in the European Convention of Human Rights. Include in your answer a discussion of the application of this right to prisoners.

Answer plan

→ Introduce article 3 of the First Protocol and the implied rights.

→ Discuss the limits to the application of article 3.

→ Discuss the acceptable limits to individual rights.

→ Explain why convicted serving prisoners are denied the vote in the UK.

→ Discuss the different approach to this issue by the UK Courts and European Court of Human Rights, and consider the consequences for the UK government.

Diagram plan

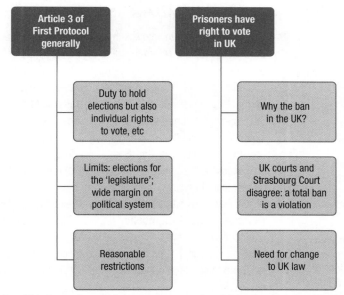

A printable version of this diagram is available from www.pearsoned.co.uk/lawexpressqa

Answer

[1]Having made the point that article 3 does not expressly grant a right to vote, you will get credit for explaining this in terms of the context of Protocol 1; in particular it will help explain the flexible nature of the individual rights which are implied into article 3.

[2]Make sure you mention this key case.

[3]This individual right is not mentioned in *Mathieu-Mohin* but expressed in later cases – you will get credit for demonstrating your wider reading.

Article 3 of the First Protocol (Article 3) places an obligation on the states to hold elections. This is the only direct reference to representative political processes in the Convention. It needed to be added as part of the First Protocol because the wide variety of political systems of the High Contracting Parties meant that agreement on anything specific regarding institutional forms and processes was impossible.[1]

Expressly, article 3 merely places obligations on states. However, the European Court of Human Rights (ECtHR) has derived an individual right to vote from the text (**Mathieu-Mohin and Clerfayt v Belgium** (1987) 10 EHRR 1),[2] as well as a right to stand in an election and, if elected, to sit in the legislature[3] (**Salim Sadak v Turkey** (2003) 36 EHRR 23). Implying individual rights into article 3 is a necessary consequence of the importance of democracy as the only political system compatible with human rights (confirmed in

4You will impress if you
stress the emphasis on the
importance of democracy by
ECtHR.

4You will impress if you
stress the emphasis on the
importance of democracy by
ECtHR.

5Give a full discussion of this
point as it can allow you to
develop some critical points
about the rather narrow reach
of the rights dependent on
article 3.

6This is an important point
that suggests you are aware
of the fact of the wide range
of political systems in Europe
and the consequence found in
the vague wording of article 3.

7This will gain you credit
because it shows you are
relating your understanding
of article 3 to the wider
conception of democracy
found in the case law and in
the founding principles of the
Council of Europe.

8This can gain you marks by
showing the limits to article 3.

9Try to use this phrase
('thwart' is found in some
case law, 'free expression …'
is in the text of article 3). It
always helps to show you are
aware of the text the judges
are interpreting and analysing.

Yumak v Turkey (2009) 48 EHRR 4). That there is a human right to vote, no longer a privilege, was stressed by the Grand Chamber in **Hirst v UK** (2006) 42 EHRR 41.[4]

The individual right to vote is subject to important limits. In particular, the text of article 3 refers to voting for the 'legislature'.[5] There is an autonomous definition of the term (i.e. it is not dependent on how countries describe their institutions). Furthermore, the identification of the legislature relates to the general constitutional system of the country.[6] Countries have a very wide margin of appreciation over their constitutional arrangements. In the UK, for instance, one part of the legislature (the House of Lords) is not elected. Limits are expressed in general terms: states must have elections at 'reasonable intervals', be pluralist (allowing political parties and political associations to act freely) and respect the rule of law.[7] **R (Barclay) v Lord Chancellor** [2009] UKSC 9 concerned the new constitutional system in Sark. It authorised an elected legislature but retained important roles for unelected officers. The House of Lords, following the general principles of the ECtHR, held that article 3 was not violated.

The 'legislature' is defined in terms of function – the institution or group of institutions that have a decisive role in and responsibility for primary legislation within the constitution of a state. The legislature may, therefore, be made up of more than one institution. For member states of the European Union, their 'legislature' is likely to include the European Parliament (see **Matthews v UK** (1999) 28 EHRR 361). Local councils are not part of the legislature; neither does article 3 apply to other kinds of vote such as in a referendum or, indeed, for a President who does not have a significant role in legislation.[8]

The individual right to vote is not absolute and is subject to reasonable limits and restrictions. States, with their different systems, enjoy a margin of appreciation over voting rights. Restrictions must have a legitimate aim and be proportionate in relation to that aim. In particular, restrictions must not thwart the 'free expression of the opinion of the people'.[9]

Commonly found requirements for voters, like residency, nationality or age, are, if normal in Europe, likely to be compatible with article 3. The prohibition of EU nationals resident in the UK voting in UK general elections has not raised an issue under article 3. Registration procedures that make it hard for those with mental disabilities to vote, if applied in a blanket way without justified differentiation, are likely to breach article 3 (**Kiss v Hungary**, app 38832/06, judgment of 20 May 2010).

A number of countries have prohibited people felt to have forfeited their civic rights, such as Nazi sympathisers after World War II or Mafia suspects in Italy, and these have been considered under article 3. The UK is one of a number of European countries that deny the vote to serving, convicted (not remand) prisoners (s 3 Representation of the People Act 1983 (RPA 1983)).

The reasons are that prisoners have shown lack of respect for the law and that denial of the franchise for the period of imprisonment is both a proportionate part of punishment and symbolic assertion of social responsibility.

[10]You will get credit for linking the judgment in this case with the idea of deference. This enables you to note, later, the Grand Chamber's view that, in fact, Parliament had not expressly considered the impact of the ban on different categories of prisoners.

UK courts upheld the ban in **R (Pearson) v Secretary of State for the Home Department** [2001] EWHC Admin 239. It was noted that the right to vote is subject to reasonable restrictions, and, in particular, that Parliament had recently considered the issue and its view should be deferred to.[10] The ban was not incompatible with article 3.

However, the Grand Chamber of the ECtHR held, in **Hirst**, that the UK had violated article 3. The importance of the matter means there is a presumption that an individual is entitled to vote, which needs compelling reasons to be set aside. Prisoners do not lose their Convention rights (their imprisonment must be compatible with article 5) though the application of Convention rights can be moderated to reflect the requirements of imprisonment. Disenfranchisement is not an expressed part of the sentence. Moreover, the penalty is arbitrary. Its effect applies only if a convict is incarcerated during an election. It is also arbitrary because not all prisoners are equally morally blameworthy.

[11]Make sure you establish this point. It is not that no prisoner can ever be denied the vote; it is that if the vote is to be denied to prisoners it must be for weighty reasons which are likely to apply to some but not all prisoners.

The Grand Chamber's finding was that the total nature of the ban did not enable relevant differences between prisoners to be reflected in law,[11] and so it could not be said to be proportionate to the stated purpose. In contrast with the High Court, the Grand Chamber did not give much weight to the fact that Parliament had recently re-enacted the ban. Parliament did not appear to have seriously considered the competing arguments.

[12]You will give confidence to the examiner if you show your understanding of this point and your ability to distinguish international from domestic law on the issue. Make sure you use the word 'directly' to show you know that the Convention continues to have influence over the development of UK law.

A decision of the ECtHR does not directly affect UK law;[12] indeed the 2010 general election was conducted without prisoners having the vote. Subsequent challenges in the UK courts have met with a declaration of incompatibility (*Scott* v *Smith* 2007 SC 345) and a refusal to read down s 3 RPA 1983 (and s 8 on European elections) to allow some prisoners to vote using s 3 HRA 1998 (**R (Chester) *v* Secretary of State for Justice** [2009] EWHC 2923).

The Grand Chamber's decision places a duty, based on article 1 ECHR, on the UK to give effect to the judgment. In 2010 a consultation process had not generated a clear option. The Council of Europe, through the Committee on Legal Affairs and Human Rights, said that the UK needed to put the **Hirst** ruling into effect. For a ban to serve a legitimate purpose in a non-arbitrary way, differentiation between different classes of prisoner will be necessary.

 Make your answer stand out

- Discuss some of the academic commentary on prisoners and voting; see in particular Lardy (2002), Foster (2009).

- Consider some of the alternatives for the UK given the obligation to put the *Hirst* ruling into effect. The government's response was a consultation exercise which, in 2009, entered a second stage (see Ministry of Justice, 2009).

- In discussing article 3 you could briefly consider whether article 3 is fit for purpose in a modern democracy. In the UK, there is political pressure for appropriate decisions to be taken more locally; also there is greater use in the UK of referendums on constitutional issues (perhaps a constitutional convention); yet article 3 does not apply.

- Briefly refer to other political claims made by prisoners: e.g. *R (Hirst)* v *Secretary of State for the Home Department* [2002] EWHC 602 held that article 10 meant a blanket ban on discussing prison conditions in the media was unlawful.

- In discussing article 3 you could refer to devolution. The Scottish Parliament and Northern Ireland Assembly both have clear authority over primary legislation. The Welsh Assembly has mainly given content to powers delegated by primary legislation. Legislative changes are now increasing its powers over primary legislation.

! Don't be tempted to ...

■ Confuse the ECHR and UK law under the HRA 1998, especially when discussing *Hirst* in comparison with *Pearson*.

■ Spend much time, if any, discussing the other implied individual rights in article 3 – the right to stand and, if elected, to sit in the legislature. There is lots of interesting Strasbourg case law on the matter but it is not relevant to the question, which is focused on the right to vote. It would be unlikely to enhance your answer.

■ Use up time and space on prisoners' rights generally.

Bibliography

Allan, TRS (2001) *Constitutional Justice* Oxford: OUP.

Allan, TRS (2006) 'Human rights and judicial review: a critique of 'due deference' *Cambridge Law Journal* 65(3), 671–695.

Amos, Merris (2007) 'The Impact of the Human Rights Act on the United Kingdom's Performance before the European Court of Human Rights' *Public Law* 655.

Beattie, K. (2009) 'S and Marper v UK: Privacy, DNA and Crime Prevention' EHRLR 2, 229–238.

Billings and Edwards (2004) 'Safeguarding asylum seekers' dignity: clarifying the interface beween Convention rights and asylum law' *Journal of Social Security Law* 11(2), 83–111.

Buxton, The Rt Hon Sir Richard (2000) 'The Human Rights Act and Private Law' *L.Q.R.* 116, January, 48–65.

Cook, Kate (2002) 'Environmental rights as human rights' EHRLR 2, 196–215.

Costigan, Ruth (2007) 'Protection of journalist's sources' *Public Law* Autumn, 464–487.

Craig, Paul (2002) 'Contracting out, the Human Rights Act and the scope of judicial review' *L.Q.R.* 118 (Oct) 551–568.

Davis, Howard, (2005) 'Lessons from Turkey: Anti-terrorism Legislation and the Protection of Free Speech', in: *European Human Rights Law Review*, 1 (2005), pp. 75–85.

Department for Constitutional Affairs (2006) *Review of the Implementation of the Human Rights Act.*

Dupre, Catherine (2006) 'Human Dignity and the withdrawal of medical treatment: a missed opportunity' EHRLR 6, 678–694.

Dworkin, Ronald 1977 *Taking Rights Seriously* London: Duckworth.

Edwards, Richard (2008) 'Stop and search, terrorism and the human rights deficit' *Common Law World Review* 37(3), 211–256.

Elliott, Mark (2009) 'Kafkaesque procedures are unfair' C.L.J. 68(3), 495–498.

Ewing, K.D and Tham, Jee-Cheong (2008) 'The Continuing Futility of the Human Rights Act' *Public Law* Winter, 668–693.

Fenwick, Helen, (2009) 'Marginalising human rights: breach of the peace, 'kettling', the Human Rights Act and public protest' *Public Law* October, 737–765.

Finnis, John (1980) *Natural Law and Natural Rights* Oxford: Clarendon Press.

Fisher, Jonathan. (2006) *A British Bill of Rights and Obligations* London: Conservative Liberty Forum.

Foster, Steve (2002) 'Prisoners' rights: mandatory lifers, the Home Secretary and the Euroepan Court of Human Rights' *Coventry Law Journal* 7(1), 53–56.

Foster, Steve (2005a) 'Prison authorities, the duty of care and the protection of prisoners' rights' *Coventry Law Journal* 10(1), 1–17.

Foster, Steve (2005b) 'Prison Conditions, human rights and Article 3 ECHR' *Public Law* Spring, 35–44.

Foster, Steve (2009) 'Reluctantly restoring rights: responding to the prisoner's right to vote' *Human Rights Law Review* 9(3) 489–507.

Fredman, Sandra (2010) 'New horizons: incorporating socio-economic rights into a new British Bill of Rights' *Public Law* April, 297–320.

Gearty, Connor (2000) 'Democracy and Human Rights in the European Court of Human Rights: A Critical Appraisal' 51 *NILQ* 381.

Gearty, Connor (2005) *Principles of Human Rights Adjudication* Oxford: OUP.

Geddis, A, (2010) 'What we cannot talk about we must pass over in silence: judicial orders and the reporting of Parliamentary speech' *Public Law* July, 443–451.

Gentili, G. (2010) 'European Court of Human Rights: an absolute ban on deportation of foreign citizens to countries where torture or ill-treatment is a genuine risk' *International Journal of Constitutional Law* 8(2), 311–322,

Greasley, Kate (2010) '*R (Purdy)* and the case for wilful blindness' O.J.L.S. 30(2), 301–326.

Greer, Steven (2005) 'Protocol 14 and the future of the European Court of Human Rights' *Public Law* Spring, 83–106.

Griffin, James (2001) 'First Steps in an Account of Human Rights' *European Journal of Philosophy* 9, 3, 306–327.

Griffith, JAG (1979) 'The Political Constitution' *Modern Law Review,* 42, 1.

Harvey, P. (2004) 'Militant Democracy and the European Convention on Human Rights' *European Law Review* 29(3), 407–420.

Hickman, Tom (2005) 'Constitutional Dialogue, Constitutional Theories and the Human Rights Act 1998' *Public Law* Summer, 306–335.

Hickman, Tom (2008) 'The Courts and Politics after the Human Rights Act: a comment' *Public Law* Spring, 84–100.

Hickman, Tom (2010) *Public Law and Human Rights* Oxford: Hart Publishing.

Hunt, Murray (1998) 'The 'horizontal effect' of the Human Rights Act' *Public Law* Autumn, 423–443.

Ip, John (2008) 'The Rise and Spread of the Special Advocate' *Public Law* Winter, 717–741.

Johnson, Paul (2010) ''An essentially private manifestation of human personality': constructions of homosexuality in the European Court of Human Rights' *Human Rights Law Review* 10(1), 67–97.

Joint Committee (2003) House of Lords House of Commons Joint Committee on Human Rights Seventh Report of the session 2003–2004 *The Meaning of a Public Authority under the Human Rights Act.*

Joseph, Sarah *et al* (2004) *The International Covenant on Civil and Political Rights* Oxford: OUP.

Judge, Lord, the Rt Hon (Lord Chief Justice) (2010) *Judicial Studies Board Lecture 2010* Inner Temple 17 March 2010.

Kavanagh, Aileen 2010 'Defending deference in public law and constitutional theory' L.Q.R. 2010, 126(Apr), 222–250.

Kavanagh, Alison (2009) 'Judging the judges under the Human Rights Act: deference, disillusionment and the 'war on terror'' *Public Law* April, 287–304.

Kavanagh, Alison (2009) *Constitutional Review under the UK Human Rights Act* Cambridge: CUP.

King, Hugh (2009) 'The Extraterritorial Human Rights Obligations of States' H.R.L. Rev. 9(4), 521–556.

Lardy, Heather (2002) 'Prisoner Disenfranchisement: Constitutional Rights and Wrongs' *Public Law* Autumn, 524–546.

Leach, Joanne and Fallon, Caroline (2010) 'Employment Law: religion and belief discrimination – a round-up of recent developments' *Corporate Briefing* June, 3–6.

Lewis, Jonathan. (2007) 'The European Ceiling on Human Rights' *Public Law* Winter, 720–747.

Loftus, Bethan, Goold, Benjamin, MacGiollabhui, Shane (2010) 'Covert policing and the Regulation of Investigatory Powers Act 2000 *Archbold Review* 8, 5–9.

Loucaides, Loukis G. (2006) 'Determining the extra-territorial effect of the European Convention: facts, jurisprudence and the Bankovic case' EHRLR 4, 391–407.

Loveland, Ian. (2009) 'A tale of two trespassers: reconsidering the impact of the Human Rights Act on rights of residence in rented housing' Part 1: EHRLR 2, 148–169; Part 2: EHRLR., 4, 495–511.

Marks, S. (1995) 'The European Convention on Human Rights and its 'Democratic Society' *British Yearbook of International Law*, 209.

McColgan, Aileen (2009) 'Class wars? Religion and (in)equality in the workplace' I.L.J. 38(1), 1–29.

McIvor, Claire (2010) 'Getting defensive about police negligence: the Hill principle, the Human Rights Act 1998 and the House of Lords'. C.L.J. 69(1), 133–150.

Mead, David (2009) 'Of kettles, cordons and crowd control – Austin *v* Commisioner of Police for the Metropolis and the meaning of 'deprivation of liberty' EHRLR 3, 376–394.

Ministry of Justice (2009) *Voting Rights of Convicted Prisoners Detained within the United Kingdom, second stage consultation* CP6/09 (April 2009).

Moreham, N.A. (2006) 'Privacy in public places' *Cambridge Law Journal* 65, 3, 606–635.

Moreham, N.A.(2008) 'The right to respect for private life in the European Convention on Human Rights: a re-exmination' EHRLR 2008 1, 44–79

Morris, Anne and Nott, Sue (2009) 'Rights and responsibilities: contested parenthood' *Journal of Social Welfare and Family Law* 31,(1), 3–16.

Morrow, K.L. (2005) 'The Rights Question: the initial impact of the Human Rights Act on Domestic Law relating to the environment' *Journal of Planning and Environment Law* August, 1010–1021.

Mowbray, A.(1999) 'The Role of the European Court of Human Rights in the Promotion of Democracy' *Public Law* (Winter) 703–725.

Mowbray, Alastair (2006) 'Beyond Protocol 14' *Human Rights Law Review*, 6(3), 578–584.

Nicol, Danny (2005) 'Original Intent and the European Convention on Human Rights' *Public Law* Spring, 152–172.

Nicol, Danny (2006) 'Law and Politics after the Human Rights Act' *Public Law* Winter, 722–751.

Nowak, Manfred (2005) *UN Covenant on Civil and Political Rights* Kehl, Germany: N.P. Engel.

O'Beirne, Brian (2009) 'The European Court of Human Rights' recent expansion of the right of privacy: a positive development? *Coventry Law Journal* 14, 2, 14–22.

O'Cinneide, Colm (2008) 'A Modest Proposal: destitution, state responsibility and the European Convention on Human Rights' EHRLR 5, 583–605.

Oldbourne, Ben (2003) *Refah Partisi (The Welfare Party)* v *Turkey* EHRLR 4, 437–444.

Oliver, Dawn (2000) 'The Frontiers of the State: Public Authorities and Public Functions under the Human Rights Act' *Public Law* 476.

Oliver, Dawn (2004) 'Functions of a Public Nature under the Human Rights Act' *Public Law* Summer, 329.

Palmer, Ellie (2007) *Judicial Review, Socio-Economic Rights and the Human Rights Act* Oxford: Hart Publishing.

Pedain, Antje (2003) 'The human rights dimension of the Diane Pretty case' C.L.J. 62(1), 181–206.

Pedain, Antje (2005) 'Requiem for a fairy tale' C.L.J. 64(1), 11–14.

Pitt-Payne, Timothy (2003) 'Privacy versus freedom of information: is there a conflict?' EHRLR (special issue: privacy), 109–119.

Postiglione, Amedeo (2010) 'Human Rights and the Environment' *International Journal of Human Rights* 14(4), 524–541.

Rasiah, Nathan (2009) 'The Court-Martial of Corporal Payne and Others and the Future Landscape of International Criminal Justice' *Journal of International Criminal Justice*, 7(1), 177–199.

Requa, Marny (2009) 'Defence rights in the shadow of RIPA: covert surveillance of privileged consultations after *Re McE Archbold News* 4, 6–9.

Rivers, Julian (2006) 'Proportionality and variable intensity of review' *C.L.J.* 65(1), 174.

Sedley, Sir Stephen (2002) 'On Self-Incrimination' *London Review of Books* 24, 27.

Smith, Rhona (2010) *Textbook on International Human Rights* Oxford: OUP.

Steyn, Lord (2005) 'Deference: a tangled story' *Public Law* Summer, 346–359.

Tomkins, Adam (2005) *Our Republican Constitution* Oxford: Hart Publishing.

Tomkins, Adam (2010) 'National Security and the role of the court: a changed landscape' L.Q.R. 126 (October), 543–567.

Tooze, J. (2010) 'Deportations with Assurances: the Approach of the UK Courts' *Public Law* Summer, 362.

Wade, Sir William (2000) 'Horizons of Horizontality' *L.Q.R.* (2000) 116, April 217–224.

Walker, Clive (2010) 'The threat of terrorism and the fate of control orders' *Public Law* January, 4–17.

Wright, Jane (2009) 'Interpreting Section 2 of the Human Rights Act 1998: Towards an Indigenous Jurisprudence of Human Rights' *Public Law* July, 595–616.

Young, Rachel and Leech, Stewart (2001) 'Marriage, divorce and ancillary relief under the Human Rights Act 1998: an introduction' EHRLR 3, 300–311.

Zuckerman, A, (2010) 'Super-injunctions – curiosity-suppressant orders undermine the rule of law' *Civil Justice Quarterly* 29(2), 131–138.

Index

A (Children) Conjoined Twins Medical Treatment (2000) 116
A (FC) v Secretary of State for the Home Department (2004) 80
A v B plc (2002) 127
A v Essex (2007) 54–5, 249
A v Head Teacher and Governor of Lord Grey School (2006) 249
A v Secretary of State for the Home Department (2004) 50, 172
A v Secretary of State for the Home Department (2005) 88
A v UK (2009) 36, 66, 79, 171, 201, 211–2
Abdulaziz v UK (1985) 75, 130
absolute necessity 86, 91
absolute rights 64
abuse 98
access to courts 185–9
accessibility 60, 68–70, 125, 130, 134
accordance with the law 111
accordance with law 167
actio popularis 25, 53, 56
actions of political/religious nature 215–40
actions undermining democracy 77–82
'acts' of public authorities 41
AD v UK (2010) 130
admissibility criteria 22
adoption 129
A.D.T. v UK (2001) 19
adverse Strasbourg judgments 17
African Charter on Human and People's Rights 3, 6
Ahmed v Austria (1997) 154
Airey v Ireland (1979-80) 187

Aksoy v Turkey (1997) 80
Al-Adsani v UK (2002) 5–6, 187
Al-Khawaja v UK (2009) 36, 188, 207
Al-Saadoon v UK (2010) 5
Ali v Birmingham CC (2010) 146
Ali v Croydon LBC (2009) 192
aliens 153
alleged breaches 53
ambiguity 39
American Cynanamid v Ethicon (1975) 226
ancillary rights 57–82
anti-discrimination provision 74
anti-terrorism 79
Anti-Terrorism, Crime and Security Act 2001 172
AnufrijevaSouthwark LBC (2003) 145–6
applications to ECtHR 12–6
arbitrary deprivation of liberty 50
'Argentoratum loutum, iudicium finitum' 36
arming the police 89–94
Arrowsmith v UK (1981) 238–9
article 2 83–106
article 3 83–156
article 5 157–82
article 6 183–212
article 8 107–56
Ashingdane v UK (1987) 163, 176, 201
Ashley v Chief Constable of Sussex Police (2008) 91
Ashworth Hospital Authority v MGN Ltd (2002) 221
assisted suicide 114
Association Ekin v France (2002) 219
Aston Cantlow … PCC v Wallbank (2003) 43–4, 148

asylum seeking 142–7
Attorney General v *Guardian Newspapers Ltd* (1987) 223
Attorney General v *Jonathan Cape* (1976) 223
Attorney General v *Punch* (2002) 223
Austin v *Commissioner of Police of the Metropolis* (2009) 164, 167, 230
authority force 83–106
authority of judiciary 223
autocracy 9
autonomy 9, 58, 60, 68–9, 110, 114, 117
awareness 55

balance of interests 67
Bankovic v *Belgium* (2007) 84, 103–6
Barthold v *Germany* (1985) 218
Begum v *Tower Hamlets LBC* (2003) 191–3, 197–8
being of unsound mind 166
Belgian Linguistics Case (1979-80) 74, 249
Belilos v *Switzerland* (1988) 252
Bellinger v *Bellinger* (2003) 40
Bensaid v *UK* (2001) 155
Bentham, Jeremy 9
bias 194, 197
Bibby v *Chief Constable of Essex* (2000) 230
BM v *SSHD* (2009) 211
Botmeh v *UK* (2008) 210
breach of the peace 230
breaking resistance 87, 144
British bill of rights 33–7
British forces overseas 102–6
broadmindedness 234
Brogan v *UK* (1989) 162, 166–7
Broniowski v *Poland* (2006) 120, 245
Brown v *Stott* (2003) 202
Bryan v *UK* (1996) 192–3, 195
Bubbins v *UK* (2005) 92
Buckley v *UK* (1997) 138
bullying 247–52
Burden & Burden v *UK* (2008) 23–4, 31, 34, 128
Burton v *UK* (1996) 138

BX v *Secretary of State for the Home Department* (2010) 170

Campbell & Fell v *UK* (1985) 196, 220
Campbell and Cosans v *UK* (1982) 140
Campbell v *MGN* (2004) 124, 126
Campbell v *UK* (1982) 250–1
capital punishment 154
Chahal v *UK* (1997) 88, 153, 210–1
Chassagnou v *France* (2000) 244, 246
chemotherapy 96
child molestation 98–102
child protection 129, 144
Chorherr v *Austria* (1994) 228
circumstances of death 87–8
'civil liberties' 10
civil partnerships 128–9
civil rights 186, 190–1, 208
clean environment 118–22
Clift v *UK* (2010) 35, 75, 77, 180
coercion 83–5
coherence of principles 7
collective interests 65
common law principles 100
compatibility 30, 74
compensation 51, 55, 159, 199–203
compulsory purchase 51
concept of 'home' 138
concept of 'law' in ECHR 59–63
concept of 'private life' 109–13
Condron v *UK* (2001) 201
confidentiality 70, 122
confinement in prison 178
confiscation of indecent material 68
Conka v *Belgium* (2002) 61, 161
constitutional balance 29
Contempt of Court Act 1981 220
contextual themes of human rights 1–26
   applications to ECtHR 12–6
   impact of ECHR 16–21
   influence of international law 2–7
   interferences with majority will 7–12
   procedural obstacles 21–6

continual supervision 208–13
control orders 168–73, 212
controversies of environmental science 122
Convention rights 57–82
  application of rights in actions undermining
    democracy 77–82
  differences between three types of Convention
    right 63–8
  eligibility for release on licence 73–7
  significance of ECHR 'law' for UK law 59–63
  statutory power to confiscate 68–72
convicted prisoners 178
core entitlement 66
core/hybrid distinction 44
Council of Europe 14–5
counter-balancing measures 210
counter-terrorism 66, 208–9, 212
courts martial 35–6
Criminal Court Act 2001 106
Criminal Justice Act 1988 95
Criminal Justice and Immigration Act 200APp8
  91
Criminal Justice and Public Order Act 1994
  201
Criminal Law Act 1967 91
criminal trials 203–8
cross-examination 187
cruel suffering 95
see also torture
curative appeal 198

D v UK (1997) 144, 154
Danderryds Kommun v Sweden (2001) 24
Data Protection Act 1998 133
De Freitas v Permanent Secretary of Ministry of
    Agriculture, Lands and Housing (1999) 67
de Menezes, Jean Charles 92
decision in banking disputes 37–8
Declaration of Human Rights 1948 3–4, 74
declaration of incompatibility 30–1
declaration of incompatibility 225
deference see judicial deference
degrading treatment 52, 84–7, 94–5, 144, 228

degree of deference 41
degree of divergence 35
deliberate infliction of harm 144
Dennis v Ministry of Defence (2003) 121
denying prisoners the vote 252
deportation 88, 144, 152–6, 208
deprivation of liberty 157–82, 230
Derbyshire County Council v Times Newspapers
    (1993) 20, 220–1
derogation 66, 79–80, 85
deterrents 90
dialogue with Parliament 11
dictatorship 9, 79
differences between types of Convention right
    63–8
dilemma of liberal theory and liberal practice
    79
diplomatic assurances 156
Director of Public Prosecutions 115
disability 88, 94, 96–7, 138
disclosure of security information 221–6
discretion 68, 164, 204
discretionary remedy 55
disproportionate provision 170
divergence 35
divorce 51, 129
Dobson v Thames Water (2009) 121
Doherty v Birmingham City Council (2008) 20–1,
    139
Dombo Beheer v The Netherlands (1994) 187
domestic law 17, 60, 69, 86, 89–90, 118
Doorson v The Netherlands (1996) 205
Douglas v Hello! (2001) 125–6
DPP see Director of Public Prosecutions
dualism 17
due process 163
Dunn v Parole Board, (2008) 54
duties and responsibilities clause 217
duty of care 201
Dworkin, Ronald 11

Eastern bloc 14
ECHR see European Convention on Human Rights

ECHR rights and actions undermining democracy 77–82

Eckle v *Germany* (1983) 23, 53

economic well-being 132, 135, 146

Editions Plon v *France* (2006) 124–5

Edwards v *UK* (2002) 100

ejusdem generis 75

eligibility for release on licence 73–7

EM (Lebanon) v *Secretary of State for the Home Department* (2008) 155

Employment Equality (Religion or Belief) and (Sexual Orientation) Regulations 2003 240

enforceable right to compensation 55

engagement 111, 115

Engel v *The Netherlands* (1979-80) 172, 186, 204, 210

entering into contracts 45

Equality Act 2010 240

equality of arms 187, 199, 208

equitability 52, 54

Eren v *Turkey* (2006) 249

'espace juridique' 104

European Committee for the Prevention of Torture and Inhuman or Degrading Treatment or Punishment 98

European Communities Act 1972 35

European Convention on Human Rights 17, 79

European Convention for the Prevention of Torture 96

European Court of Human Rights 12–3, 17–8, 22, 95, 223

euthanasia 115, 117

Evans v *Amicus Healthcare Ltd* (2004) 129

Evans v *UK* (2008) 110, 129

exceptional powers 80

exemption from legal obligation 236–40

expectation of privacy 124

extradition 153

extremism 77

Ezeh v *UK* (2004) 186, 203

Ezelin 6 *France* (1992) 228

F v *Berkshire* (1989) 116

Fadeyeva v *Russia* (2005) 120

fair balance 48, 54, 58, 102, 120–1, 125, 129, 245

fair hearings 66, 183–212
  access to courts 185–9
  compensation 199–203
  continual supervision 208–13
  criminal trials 203–8
  independent, impartial court 194–8
  local authority funded accommodation 189–94

fair-mindedness 192, 197

Feldbrugge v *The Netherlands* (1986) 191

Ferrazzini v *Italy* (2002) 186

Findlay v *UK* (1997) 197, 203

First Protocol rights 76, 142, 145, 241–56
  bullying 247–52
  peaceful enjoyment of possessions 243–7
  right to vote 252–7

Folgero v *Norway* (2008) 250–1

foreseeability 50, 60, 68, 70, 125, 130, 134

Fourth Protocol 170

freedom of association 232

freedom of expression 69

freedom of information 136

Freedom of Information Act 2000 137

freestanding rights 73–4

Fressoz v *France* (2001) 81, 218

Friedl v *Austria* (1996) 149

Gaskin v *UK* (1989) 134

gays in the military 48

general interest 245

Geneva Convention 3, 6

Ghaidan v *Ghodin-Mendoza* (2004) 30, 39–40, 138

Giacomelli v *Italy* (2007) 138

Gillan v *UK* (2010) 161, 165, 231

Gillow v *UK* (1989) 138

Glass v *UK* (2004) 116

Glimmerveen and Hagenbeek v *The Netherlands* (2005) 81

global warming 122, 248

Godin 139
Golder v *UK* (1979-80) 20, 179, 187, 200
Goodwin v *UK* (2002) 71, 129, 220
Gorgulu v *Germany* (2004) 130
Grainger v *Nicholson* (2010) 238–9, 251
Grand Chamber 23, 36, 70, 86, 211, 255
Guzzardi v *Italy* (1981) 165, 170

Halford v *UK* (1997) 60
Handyside v *UK* (1979-80) 65, 71–2, 219
Hashman & Harrap 62
Hashman v *UK* (2000) 228
Hatton v *UK* (2003) 121
Health and Safety legislation 92
Hentrich v *France* (1994) 244–5
Helow v *Advocate General for Scotland* (2008) 197
Herczegfalvy v *Austria* (1992) 97, 116
Hirst v *Secretary of State for the Home Department* (2002) 256
Hirst v *UK* (2006) 254, 256
HL v *UK* (2005) 67, 161, 175, 177
HM Treasury v *Ahmed & Others* (2010) 6, 106
Hoekstra v *HM Advocate* (2001) 193, 197
holocaust denial 58, 81, 221
homelessness 42, 138
homosexual marriage 128
homosexuality 54
honest mistake 84
honesty of belief 91
HRA 1998 *see* Human Rights Act 1998
Huang v *Secretary of State for the Home Department* (2001) 48–9, 129–30, 224
Human Rights Act 1998 27–56, 99, 103–4, 124, 139, 188–91
    British bill of rights 33–7
    judicial deference 47–51
    power of random search 37–42
    'public authority', 'public function' 42–7
    relationship of courts and Parliament 29–33
    rights of fathers 51–6
humiliation 87, 96, 116, 144
Hutchison Reid v *UK* (2003) 163, 175, 177

'hybrid' authorities 43

ICESCR *see* International Covenant on Economic, Social and Cultural Rights
idea of democracy 7
idea of law 59–62
illness and human rights 113–7
Immigration Act 1971 212
immigration control 127, 129–30
impact of ECHR 16–21
impartiality 190, 194–8
implementation of ECHR 2–7
implied rights 252
incompatibility 225
incompetence 114, 116
An Inconvenient Truth 251
indecent material 68
independence 194–6
independent courts 194–8
independent investigation 89
independent tribunal 190, 194–8
indirect horizontal effect 46
influence of international law 2–7
informed observation 192, 197
inhuman treatment 52, 94–5, 228
injunctions 223–4
intentional killing 84–6, 89–90, 99
Interception of Communications Act 1987 63
interference with privacy 126
interferences with majority will 7–12
interlocutory injunction 224
International Covenant on Civil and Political Rights 13, 16, 131
International Covenant on Economic, Social and Cultural Rights 5
International Criminal Court 7
interpretation of concept of 'private life' 109–13
interpretative duty 38
intolerance 77
Ionescu v *Romania* (2010) 25
Ireland v *UK* (1978) 87, 95–6
issue of 'weight' 219

Jameel v *Wall Street Journal* (2006) 221
James v *UK* (1986) 244, 246
JE v *DE* (2006) 174
Jersild v *Denmark* (1995) 79
Johnson v *UK* (1999) 176
Joint Committee 45
Jordan v *UK* (2003) 87, 93, 101
judicial deference 41, 47–51, 72, 112
judicial review 53
judicial supervision 159
jurisdiction 103–4
jurisprudence 164
jus cogens 87, 95
'just and appropriate' remedies 55
'just satisfaction' 55, 163
justification 58, 74–5, 91, 134, 148

Kadi v *Council of European Union* (2009) 6
Kay v *Lambeth* (2006) 139, 141
Keenan v *UK* (2001) 88, 95, 97, 100
Kennedy v *UK* (2010) 62
'kiss and tell' stories 122–7
Kiss v *Hungary* (2010) 255
Kjeldsen v *Denmark* (1979-80) 75, 250
Klass v *Germany* (1979-80) 24, 150
known risk 97
Kroon v *The Netherlands* (1995) 129

Ladele v *Islington LBC* (2009) 239–40
Laskey, Jaggard and Brown v *UK* (1997) 72
last resort 42
law as pervasive 59
lawful acts of war 86, 90
lawful imprisonment 96
lawful interference 121
lawfulness 179–80
Lawless v *Ireland No 3* (1979-80) 80
LCB v *UK* (1999) 119
Le Comte v *Belgium* (1982) 196
Leander v *Sweden* (1987) 110, 134
leases 45
'legal persons' 24
legal persons 247

legal powers to deport 152–6
legality 50, 62
legality of British forces' activities 102–6
lethal force 91, 94
Leyla Sahin v *Turkey* (2007) 234, 238–9, 249
liberal theory 79
liberty 65, 157–82
life imprisonment 73
Limitation Act 1980 54
Lithgow 246
Locabail v *Bayfield* (2000) 193
local authority funded accommodation 189–94
López Ostra v *Spain* (1995) 119
Lord Chief Justice 36
Lorse v *The Netherlands* (2003) 98
Ludi v *Switzerland* (1993) 203

M v *Secretary of State for Work and Pensions*
      (2006) 76
Maaouia v *France* (2001) 186
McCann v *UK* (1995) 86, 89, 91–2, 101, 139
McGonnell v *UK* (2000) 197
McMichael v *UK* (1995) 202
McVeigh v *UK* (1993) 167
maintaining the peace 226–31
majority will 7–8
Makaratazisv *Greece* (2005) 92
malice 220
Malone v *Commissioner* (XXXX) 63
Malone v *UK* (1985) 18, 63, 112
Manchester City Council v *Pinnock* (2010)
      140–1
marches 226–31
Marcic v *Thames Water* (2003) 121
Marckx v *Belgium* (1979-80) 14, 244
margin of appreciation 11, 68, 71, 75, 138–9
Marper v *UK* (2009) 61–2, 132, 134–6, 150
marriage 128–9
Mason v *Ministry of Justice* (2008) 180
Mathieu-Mohin and Clerfayt v *Belgium* (1987)
      253
Matthews v *UK* (1999) 254
Mayzit v *Russia* (2006) 98

MC v *Germany* (1989) 28
Mellacher v *Austria* (1990) 246
mental health 173–7, 199–203
Mental Health Act 2007! 177
Mersey Care NHS Trust v *Ackroyd* (2007) 221
Metropolitan Church of Bessarabia v *Moldova* (2002) 238
Metropolitan Police Service 92
Ministry of Defence v *Griffin* (2008) 226
'mirror Strasbourg' principle 33, 53, 55, 103
mistake of fact 91
modern administrative state 44
Monnat v *Switzerland* (2010) 54
monopoly of legitimate force 85
Mosley v *News Group Newspapers* (2008) 149
Murray v *Express Newspapers* (2008) 125, 201
Murray v *UK*(1995) 135
mutual reinforcement 8

N v *UK* (2008) 154
Napier v *Scottish Ministers* (2005) 88, 96
national laws 127, 129
national securit 234
nationalisation 246
natural justice 194, 196
natural persons 247
necessity for coherence 7
need 189
Neulinger v *Switzerland* (2010) 5–6
NGOs *see* non-governmental organisations
NHS Trust v *A* (2001) 116
Nicol and Selvanayagamn v *DPP* (1996) 230
Niemetz v *Germany* (1993) 110, 138
noise nuisance 121
non-arbitrariness 63
non-contributory benefits 145–6
non-derogable status 85
non-discrimination 240
non-governmental organisations 43–4
non-life-saving treatment 113, 116
Norris v *Ireland* (1986) 54
Norris v *US* (2010) 155
Northern Ireland Assembly 256

Northern Rock 246
'nothing shall prevent' formulation 245
nullem crimen, nulla poena sine lege 181
Nurettin v *Turkey* (2007) 230

objectivity 75
obligations prescribed by law 160, 169, 186, 190–1, 208
Observer v *UK* (1992) 219, 222–4
obtaining leave 199
Öcalan v *Turkey* (2005) 23
Official Secrets Act 1989 221–2, 226
O'Halloran & Francis v *UK* (2008) 202, 204
Öneryildiz v *Turkey* (2005) 100, 119
Open Door Counselling v *Ireland* (1993) 25
'ordinary' judicial review 56
O'Reilly v *Mackman* (1983) 56
Osman v *UK* (2000) 86, 99–102, 105, 119, 187, 201
'other status' prisoners 73–4
Othman v *Secretary of State for the Home Department* (2009) 88, 154–5
overcrowding, 96ü
Özgür Gündem v *Turkey* (2001) 218

P v *South Gloucestershire Council* (2007) 131
PACE 1984 *see* Police and Criminal Evidence Act 1984
parental rights 116
Partidul Comunistilor v *Romania* (2007) 234
peaceful assembly 228
peaceful enjoyment of possessions 51, 66, 243–7
Peck v *UK* (2003) 148–9, 151, 186
Peers v *Greece* (2001) 96
Percy v *DPP* (1995) 230
permanent injunctions 221–6
persistent vegetative state 116
pervasive rights 57–82
PG & JH v *UK* (2008) 150
phone tapping 60, 63
physical liberty 160, 169
Piersack v *Belgium* (1983) 196

Plattform Ärtze für das Leben v *Austria* (1988)
229–30
pluralism 10, 234
POA 1986 *see* Public Order Act 1986
Police Complaints Authority 93
Police and Criminal Evidence Act 1984 88, 151,
165
political constitution 10, 31–2
political expression 215–40
disclosure of security information 221–6
proscription of political view 231–6
protection of media 217–21
protests and marches 226–31
seeking exemption from legal obligation
236–40
political tensions 71
Poplar HRCA v *Donoghue* (2001) 44
Porter v *Magill* (2001) 192
positive duties 99, 102, 118
power of random search 37–42
preference 79
prescription by law 60
Press Complaints Commission 125–6
pressing social need 70, 218, 237
Pressos Compania Naviera SA v *Belgium* (1996)
244, 246
Pretty v *UK* (2002) 87, 96, 109–10, 113–5, 117,
144–5
Prevention of Terrorism Act 2005 168–9, 212
Price v *UK* (2002) 97
primary legislation 42, 256
principles governing criminal trials 203–8
prior restraint 123–4
prisoners 52, 88, 96, 178–82
rights of 102, 178
privacy 107–56
asylum seeking 142–7
clean and safe environment 118–22
human rights and illness 113–7
interpretation of concept of 'private life'
109–13
'kiss and tell' stories 122–7
legal powers to deportation 152–6

rights to marriage and family 127–31
storing personal information 132–7
unqualified right to evict 137–41
violation of right to private life 147–52
private acts 42
procedural fairness 189
procedural obstacles 21–6
prohibition on torture 66, 84–8, 94–5
promulgation 69–70
proportionality 47–51, 58, 63–4, 67, 71, 109,
120, 125–6, 130, 135
Proscribed Organisations Appeal Commission
233
proscription of political view 231–6
protection of liberty 159–63
protection of the media 217–21
protection of morals 68, 72
protests 226–31
Protocol 11 12–3, 15, 18
Protocol 14 12
'public authority', 'public function' 42–7, 115,
191
public curiosity 220
public emergency 66, 81–2, 86, 88, 90
public funding 44
public interest 125, 208, 245
Public Order Act 1986 226, 231
public safety 234
Purdy v *Director of Public Prosecutions* (2009)
60–1, 113–4, 117
PVS *see* persistent vegetative state
Pye v *UK* (2008) 244
Pyx Granite v *Ministry of Housing and Local
Government* (1960) 201

Qazi v *Harrow LBC* (2003) 139
qualified rights 65, 115, 124

R (A) v *Bloody Sunday Inquiry* (2001) 102
R (Al-Jedda) v *Secretary of State for Defence*
(2007) 5, 106
R (Al-Saadoon) v *Secretary of State for Defence*
(2009) 105–6

R (Al-Skeini) v Secretary of State for Defence (2007) 104

R (Alconbury) v Secretary of State for the Environment, Transport and the Regions (2001) 191, 193, 197–8, 245

R (Amin) v Secretary of State for the Home Department (2003) 87, 92–3, 101–2

R (Anderson) v Home Secretary (2002) 179

R (Anderson) v Secretary of State for the Home Department (2002) 30, 40

R (Animal Defenders International) v Secretary of State for Culture, Media and Sport (2008) 35, 49

R (B) v Ashworth Hospital Authority (2005) 176

R (Baiai) v Secretary of State for the Home Department (2008) 129

R (Barclay) v Lord Chancellor (2009) 254

R (Begum) v Denbigh High School Governors (2006) 239

R (Bloggs 61) v Secretary of State for the Home Department (2003) 100–1

R (Brehony) v Chief Constable of Greater Manchester (2005) 230

R (Brooke) v Secretary of State for Justice (2008) 162, 181

R (Broughton) v Her Majesty's Treasury (2005) 239

R (Burke) v General Medical Council (2005) 114, 117

R (Carson) v Secretary of State for Work and Pensions (2005) 76

R (Chester) v Secretary of State for Justice (2009) 256

R (Clift) v SSHD (2006) 75

R (Countryside Alliance) v AG (2007) 110, 112

R (Daly) v Secretary of State for the Home Department (2001) 31, 48–9, 224, 230

R (Dimmock) v Secretary of State for Education and Science (2007) 251

R (Faizovas) v Secretary of State for Justice (2009) 96

R (Gentle) v PM (2008) 87, 93, 101–2, 105

R (Gillan) v Commissioner of the Metropolitan Police (2006) 61, 70, 161, 164–5

R (Greenfield) v Secretary of State for the Home Office (2005) 55, 163, 177

R (H) v Secretary of State for Health (2005) 176

R (Heather) v Leonard Cheshire Homes (2003) 45

R (Howard League for Penal Reform) v Secretary of State for the Home Department (2002) 53

R (Hurst) v London Northern District Coroner (2007) 20, 35

R (IL) v Secretary of State for Health (2003) 176

R (Jackson) v Attorney General (2005) 32

R (James) v Parole Board (2009) 180–1

R (JF) v Secretary of State for the Home Department (2010) 41

R (JL) v Secretary of State for the Home Department (2008) 92, 101–2, 120

R (Johnson) v Havering LBC (2007) 46

R (JS) (Sri Lanka) v SSHD (2010) 156

R (KB) v Mental Health Review Tribunal (2003) 55, 177

R (Kurdistan Workers Party) v Secretary of State for the Home Department (2002) 233

R (L) v Commissioner of Police for the Metropolis (2009) 134, 136

R (Laporte) v Chief Constable of Gloucestershire (2006) 167, 230

R (Limbuela) v Secretary of State for the Home Department (2005) 142, 146

R (M) v Secretary of State for Work and Pensions (2008) 145–6

R (McCann) v Manchester Crown Court (2002) 186, 205

R (Marper) v Chief Constable of South Yorkshire (2004) 36, 134

R (MB) v Secretary of State for the Home Department (2007) 210–2

R (Middleton) v West Somerset Coroner (2004) 87, 93

R (N) v Secretary of State for the Home Department 154

R (Pearson) v *Secretary of State for the Home Department* (2001) 255

R (ProLife Alliance) v *BBC* (2003) 31, 50, 218–9

R (Razgar) v *Secretary of State for the Home Department* (2004) 65, 67, 110, 112, 155

R (SB) v *Governors of Denbigh High School* (2006) 44

R (Smith) v *Oxfordshire Coroner* (2010) 105

R (Spinks) v *Secretary of State for the Home Department* (2005) 88, 97

R (U) v *Special Immigration Appeals Commission* (2009) 212

R (Ullah) v *Special Adjudicator* (2004) 35–6, 39, 154–5

R v *A* (2001) 30, 39, 41

R v *Bieber* (2008) 154

R v *Bow Street Magistrates ex p Pinochet* (2000) 197

R v *Davis* (2008) 207

R v *DPP ex parte Kebeline* (2000) 49

R v *H* (2004) 150–1, 203, 211

R v *Hammond* (2005) 40

R v *Horncastle* (2009) 36, 188, 207

R v *Loosely* (2001) 203–4

R v *Lord Chancellor ex p Witham* (1998) 19

R v *Lyons* (2002) 19, 29

R v *Mason* (2002) 151

R v *N & E Devon HA ex p Coughlan* (2001) 138

R v *Remington* (2005) 181

R v *Secretary of State for the Home Department ex p Daly* (2001) 67

R v *Secretary of State for the Home Office ex p Simms* (2000) 19

R v *Shayler* (2001) 60, 62, 222, 225–6

R v *Somerset CC ex p Fewings* (1995) 46

R v *Spear* (2002) 36, 39

R (Watkins-Singh) v *Aberdare School* (2008) 239

R (Weaver) v *LQHT* (2009) 44–6, 140

R (Wilkinson) v *Broadmoor Hospital* (2001) 97, 116

R (Williamson) v *Secretary of State for Education and Employment* (2005) 238, 240, 250–2

racism 79

radicalism 82

Ramsahai v *The Netherlands* (XXXX) 93

random search 37–42

rape trials 39

Re Application of JR17 249–50, 252

Re F (a Child) (Northern Ireland) (2008) 95

Re McE 148, 151

Re Officer L (2007) 86, 100–1

Re S (2002) 131

Re V (a Child) (care proceedings: human rights claim) (2004) 131

real and immediate risk 97, 100–1, 105

reasonable force 91

reasonable justification 74

reasonable restrictions 187

recuse 197

Redmond-Bate v *DPP* (2000) 229–30

Refah Partisi v *Turkey* (2003) 81, 235–6

reform of penal laws 54

Regulation of Investigatory Powers Act 2000 63, 150, 152

Reinpecht v *Austria* (2007) 186

relationship of courts and Parliament 29–33

relevant substantive rights 76

religious expression 215–40

remedial orders 31, 38, 41–2

reporting to the police 170

reputation 79

respect 114–5, 129, 138

responsible journalism 220

restraint of powers 152–6

retrospective crimes 66

retrospective interferences 245–6

reunification of Europe 14

Reynolds v *Times Newspapers* (1999) 220

right to clean and safe environment 118–22

right to evict 137–41

right to a home 137–41

right to marriage and family 127–31

right to receive information 218

right to vote 252–7

rights of fathers 51–6

rights and freedoms of others 234, 236
rights of others 79
rights to fair hearing 185
rights-based constitution 31
Ringeisen v *Austria* (1979-80) 191
Roberts v *Parole Board* (2005) 181
Rome Statute 7
Rowe & Davis v *UK* (2000) 202, 210
Royal Prerogative 18, 63
Ruiz Matoes v *Spain* (1993) 202, 210
'rule of law' 63, 69

Saadi v *Italy* (2009) 154, 156
safe environment 118–22
Sahin v *Turkey* (2005) 70
Salim Sadak v *Turkey* (2003) 253–4
same-sex relationships 39, 127–8, 131
Saunders v *UK* (1997) 202–4
Schalk & Kopf v *Austria* (2010) 128
Scordino v *Italy* 25
Scottish Parliament 256
Seal v *Chief Constable of South Wales* (2007)
    187, 201
Second World War 3, 79
secret evidence 188
Secretary of State for the Home Department v *A*
    (2007) 165
Secretary of State for the Home Department v *AF*
    (2009) 36, 188, 211–2
Secretary of State for the Home Department v *AP*
    (2010) 170–1
Secretary of State for the Home Department v
    GG (2009) 170–1
Secretary of State for the Home Department v *JJ*
    (2007) 170
Secretary of State for the Home Department v
    MB (2007) 171, 207
Secretary of State for the Home Department v
    Rehman (2001) 49
security 157–82
    control orders 168–73
    mental health 172–7
    prisoners 178–82

protection of liberty 159–63
stop and search policy 163–8
Security Service 18, 63, 223
Security Services Act 1989 63
seeking exemption from legal obligation 236–40
self-incrimination 199, 203
self-rule 9
Selmouni v *France* (2000) 5, 87, 95–6
Sener v *Turkey* (2003) 219
Senior Courts Act 1982 56
sexual history 39
Sharia law 81, 231
Sheldrake v *DPP* 204
Sidabras and Dziautus v *Lithuania* (2006) 76,
    110
significance of ECHR 'law' for UK law 59–63
significant disadvantage 22
Silih v *Slovenia* 86
Simms v *Secretary of State for the Home
    Department* (2000) 62
slavery 66
slopping out 88
Smirnova v *Russia* (2004) 181
Smith v *UK* (2000) 19–20
social need 218
social reality 129
social rights 76
socio-economic rights 146
Soering v *UK* (1989) 105, 153
soft measures 117
sole rule 208, 212
Somerville v *Scottish Ministers* (2007) 21, 54
South Ossetia 15
special advocates 188, 208, 210, 212
Sporrong and Lonnroth v *Sweden* (1983) 48,
    64–5, 71, 186, 245–6
Spycatcher 224–6
SRM Global Master Fund LP v *Commissioners of
    Her Majesty's Treasury* (2009) 246
Stafford v *UK* (2002) 179–80
standards concerning state use of force 85–9
Stankov v *Bulgaria* (2001) 235
Starrs v *Ruxton* (2000) 197

state detention 94–8
state institutions 110
statutory power to confiscate 68–72
Stec v *UK* (2006) 76, 145–6, 244
Stedman v *UK* (1997) 239
Steel v *Morris* (2005) 221
Steel v *UK* (1999) 61, 70, 164, 166, 228–9
sterilisation 113–4, 116
stop and search policy 70, 163–8
storing personal details 132–7
strip search 96
substantive rights 76
'sufficient interest' 56
suicide 87
Sunday Times v *UK* (1979-80) 60, 62, 69, 117, 134
super-Wednesbury judicial scrutiny 20
supervision of discretion 68
surveillance 147–51

Taylor v *UK* (1994) 102
Teixeira de Castro v *Portugal* (1999) 203
temporary injunctions 221–6
Terrorism Act 2000 165, 231
terrorism-related activity 169
therapeutic necessity 116
threat to life of nation 88
threshold of severity 71, 95, 228
thwarting 254
tick box identification 49, 61
Tinnelly v *UK* (1999) 187
tolerance 234
torture 66, 84–8, 94–5
totalitarianism 79
Trafigura 126
Tsfayo v *UK* (2009) 146, 191, 193
Tsonev v *Bulgaria* (2008) 234
Turkish invasion of Cyprus 15
TV v *Finland* (1994) 134
types of Convention right 63–8

UN bill of rights 3
UN Convention against Torture 95

UN Convention relating to the Status of Refugees 1954 156
UNCAT *see* UN Convention against Torture
UNDHR *see* Declaration of Human Rights 1948
Uner v *The Netherlands* (2007) 155
United Communist Party of Turkey v *Turkey* (1998) 233–4
unlawful violence 91
unpacking proportionality 67
unqualified right to evict 137–41
urgency 38, 58
use of force 83–106
    arming the police 89–94
    child molestation 98–102
    general standards concerning force 85–9
    legality of British forces' activities 102–6
    state detainees 94–8

Valenzuela Contreras v *Spain* (1999) 150
validity of the law 31
Van Colle v *Chief Constable of Hertfordshire* (2008) 101
Van der Leer v *The Netherlands* (1990) 161
Varbanov v *Bulgaria* (2000) 175
'victim rule' 52
victims 22, 53, 74
Vienna Convention 3
vigilance 97
violation of right life 21
violation of right to private life 147–52
Von Hannover v *Germany* (2005) 124–6, 149–50, 212
vulnerability 42, 96–7, 115

war 66, 82, 86, 88
war crimes tribunals 7, 156
Webster v *Norfolk County Council* (2009) 131
Weeks v *UK* (1988) 20
welfare 107–56
welfare gap 45
welfare rights 145
Welsh Assembly 256

Wemhoff v *Germany* (1979-80) 179
Whiteside v *UK* (1994) 138–9
Wieser v *Austria* (2007) 96
Winder v *Wandsworth LBC* (1985) 141
Winterwerp v *The Netherlands* (1979) 160–1,
 175
Wood v *Commissioner of Police for the
 Metropolis* (2009) 149
Worm v *Austria* (1998) 219

X & Y v *The Netherlands* (1986) 111
X v *UK* (1982) 176

Yasa v *Turkey* (1999) 23, 99
YL v *Birmingham City Council* (2007)
 44–5
Yumak v *Turkey* (2009) 23, 254

Z v *Finland* (1994) 134
Z v *UK* (2002) 130, 144, 202
Zdanoka v *Latvia* (2007) 81
Zentralrat DSRR v *Germany* (1997)
 24
Ziliberberg v *Moldova* (2005) 229